The New Power Politics

The New Power Politics

Networks and Transnational Security Governance

EDITED BY DEBORAH AVANT
and
OLIVER WESTERWINTER

OXFORD
UNIVERSITY PRESS

OXFORD
UNIVERSITY PRESS

Oxford University Press is a department of the University of Oxford. It furthers
the University's objective of excellence in research, scholarship, and education
by publishing worldwide. Oxford is a registered trade mark of Oxford University
Press in the UK and certain other countries.

Published in the United States of America by Oxford University Press
198 Madison Avenue, New York, NY 10016, United States of America.

Library of Congress Cataloging-in-Publication Data
Names: Avant, Deborah D. (Deborah Denise), 1958– editor. | Westerwinter, Oliver, 1983– editor.
Title: The new power politics : networks and transnational security governance /
Deborah Avant and Oliver Westerwinter, editors.
Description: New York, NY: Oxford University Press, 2016. | Includes bibliographical references.
Identifiers: LCCN 2015044615 (print) | LCCN 2016005458 (ebook) |
ISBN 978-0-19-060449-3 (hardcover: alk. paper) | ISBN 978-0-19-060450-9 (pbk.: alk. paper) |
ISBN 978-0-19-060451-6 (E-book) | ISBN 978-0-19-060452-3 (E-book) |
ISBN 978-0-19-060453-0 (Online Component)
Subjects: LCSH: Security, International—International cooperation. | International organization.
Classification: LCC JZ5588 .N494 2016 (print) | LCC JZ5588 (ebook) | DDC 355/.031—dc23
LC record available at http://lccn.loc.gov/2015044615

1 3 5 7 9 8 6 4 2
Printed by Webcom, Inc., Canada

CONTENTS

PART II   NETWORKS AND GOVERNANCE OUTCOMES

ACKNOWLEDGMENTS

This project began with an International Studies Association (ISA) Venture Grant so we would like to begin by thanking the ISA and this program for its generous support. The first workshop meeting at the 2012 ISA Annual Convention in San Diego resulted in the outlines of a framework and involved many of our final contributors. We could not have stretched the ISA funding as far as we did without the support of the Sié Chéou-Kang Center for International Security and Diplomacy at the University of Denver's Josef Korbel School and the Denver-based NGO and Think Tank, One Earth Future (OEF). The Sié Center and OEF jointly funded a second author's workshop at the Josef Korbel School of International Studies at the University of Denver during which we developed the project's framework.

We were fortunate to engage during these two workshops (as well as at an ISA panel) with a large number of colleagues, all of whom shared valuable insights and advice. We are grateful to Stacie Goddard, Annelies Kamran, Amanda Murdie, Michael Lipson, David Kinsella, Michael Kinney, Amy Grubb, Seth Masket, Ronald Krebs, Eamon Aloyo, Conor Seyle, Tim Sisk, Anja Jakobi, Lindsay Heger, Sarah Parkinson, Erica Chenoweth, and Katherine Sikkink. We also thank our contributors for their influence on the overall shape of the project. Alex Montgomery deserves special thanks for his detailed comments on the first draft of the framing chapter (though he was rewarded quite nicely in the process). Others gave us much appreciated comments on all or parts of the manuscript along the way. Thanks to Tom Biersteker, Fritz Kratochwil, Miles Kahler, Klaus Dingwerth, and Patrick Emmenegger. We appreciate the students and staff at the University of Denver (Jill Hereau, Liz McKinney, Kara Kingma, and Sarah Bakhtiari) and the University of St. Gallen (Ruslan Aybazov) who contributed in important ways to the workshops and/or the final manuscript.

Finally, as is often the case, the manuscript is better as a result of the review process. We are indebted to Dave McBride and two anonymous reviewers for

Oxford University Press for their useful comments on the volume's content and shape. And our contributors get one last nod for their cheerful and (mostly) timely response to reviews and edits. We also thank Dave McBride, Katie Weaver, and the Oxford University Press for their efficient editorial and production support.

ACRONYMS

ACDA	Arms Control and Disarmament Agency (United States)
AG	Australia Group
AIC	Akaike Information Criteria
ANSI	American National Standards Institute
AP	Antipersonnel
APII	Amended Protocol II (Convention on Certain Conventional Weapons)
ATT	Arms Trade Treaty
BMP	Best Management Practices
BTC	Baku-Tbilisi-Ceyhan Pipeline
C3IC	Coalition Coordination, Communication, and Integration Center
CBP	Customs and Border Protection (United States)
CFGS	Conflict-Free Gold Standard
CGPCS	Contact Group on Piracy off the Somali Coast
CGS	Center for Global Solutions
CIS	Commonwealth of Independent States
CIVIC	Campaign for Innocent Victims in Conflict
CMF	Combined Military Forces
CSR	Corporate Social Responsibility
CSTO	Collective Security Treaty Organization (Russia)
CWC	Chemical Weapons Convention
DoD	Department of Defense (United States)
DoS	Department of State (United States)
EITI	Extractive Industries Transparency Initiative
EU	European Union
EUNAFOR	European Union Naval Force
FCO	Foreign & Commonwealth Office (United Kingdom)

GAO	Government Accountability Office (United States)
GeSI	Global eSustainability Initiative
HRD	Hoge Raad voor Diamant (Diamond High Council)
IAEA	International Atomic Energy Agency
IANSA	International Action Network on Small Arms
ICBL	International Campaign to Ban Landmines
ICGLR	International Conference on the Great Lakes Region
ICFL	International Conference on Firearms Legislation
ICMM	International Council on Mining and Metals
ICoC	International Code of Conduct for Private Security Providers
ICoCA	International Code of Conduct for Private Security Providers Association
ICRC	International Commission for the Red Cross
IDP	Internally Displaced Person
IGO	Inter-Governmental Organization
IHL	International Humanitarian Law
IMO	International Maritime Organization
IO	International Organization
IR	International Relations
IRTC	Internationally Recognized Transit Corridor
ISAF	International Security Assistance Force (Afghanistan)
ISO	International Organization for Standardization
ISU	Implementation Support Unit (Mine Ban Treaty)
ITO	Indium Tin Oxide
ITRI	Industrial Technology Research Institute
iTSCI	ITRI Tin Supply Chain Initiative
JA	Jewelers of America
JVC	Jewelers Vigilance Committee
KP	Kimberley Process
KPCS	Kimberley Process Certification Scheme
MAC	Making Amends Campaign
MAP	Member Action Plan (NATO)
MBT	Mine Ban Treaty
MMSD	Mining, Minerals and Sustainable Development
MOU	Memorandum of Understanding
MSCHOA	Maritime Security Centre Horn of Africa
MTCR	Missile Technology Control Regime
NATO	North Atlantic Treaty Organization
NDN	Northern Distribution Network (Afghanistan)
NGO	Non-Governmental Organization
NPT	Non-Proliferation Treaty

NRA	National Rifle Association
NSC	National Security Council
OCHA	United Nations Office for the Coordination of Humanitarian Affairs
OECD	Organization for Economic Co-operation and Development
OEG	Operational Experts Group
ONT	Organizational Network Theory
OSCE	Organization for Security and Cooperation in Europe
PMSC	Private Military and Security Company
POA	Program of Action
PoC	Protection of Civilians
PSI	Proliferation Security Initiative
R2P	Responsibility to Protect
SNA	Social Network Analysis
TAN	Transnational Advocacy Network
TGN	Trans-Governmental Network
UN	United Nations
UNCLOS	United Nations Convention on the Law of the Sea
UNDP	United Nations Development Programme
UNGA	United Nations General Assembly
UNGC	United Nations Global Compact
UNHCHR	United Nations High Commission for Human Rights
UNHCR	United Nations High Commission for Refugees
UNIDIR	United Nations Institute for Disarmament Research
UNM	United National Movement (Georgia)
UNODC	United Nations Office for Drugs and Crime
UNSC	United Nations Security Council
USAID	United States Agency for International Development
WBCSD	World Business Council for Sustainable Development
WDC	World Diamond Council
WFSA	World Forum on Sports Shooting Activities
WMD	Weapons of Mass Destruction

CONTRIBUTORS

Deborah Avant, University of Denver

Adam Bower, University of St. Andrews

Charli Carpenter, University of Massachusetts–Amherst

Alexander Cooley, Barnard College

Mette Eilstrup-Sangiovanni, Cambridge University

Virginia Haufler, University of Maryland–College Park

Alexander H. Montgomery, Reed College

Daniel Nexon, Georgetown University

Sarah Percy, University of Queensland

Oliver Westerwinter, University of St. Gallen

The New Power Politics

Introduction

Networks and Transnational Security Governance

DEBORAH AVANT AND OLIVER WESTERWINTER

How is it that the United States could work together with China and Iran (among others) to combat piracy at a moment when US tensions with China were on the rise and many US politicians were unwilling to even negotiate over nuclear issues with Iran? How do we account for instances when the United States acts in ways that threaten global stability rather than working to generate it the way theories of hegemony would expect? How can we explain the clearly consequential involvement of commercial and human rights groups in security arrangements that affect sovereign concerns? Why are many issues to do with weapons of mass destruction governed through informal transgovernmental arrangements rather than institutions that involve the highest levels of government? Traditional analyses of global security politics do not ask on these questions. Assuming the benefits of US hegemony, they focus on its stability, the rise of new powers, and the intransigence of various rogue states. Nor can traditional theories answer them. They cannot explain why there is "governance" (or not) of important security issues—from combatting piracy to curtailing nuclear proliferation to reducing the contributions of extractive industries to violence and conflict. They often miss collective efforts resulting from non-state action or taking less traditional forms. And they cannot explain why governance sometimes serves broad concerns (as liberal theories expect) and other times narrow ones (as realist theories expect). This volume uses network theory to develop a framework within which to answer these questions that puzzle traditional security analysts.

In the last fifteen years, there has been a surge of writing about new forms of governance constituted by various mixtures—often termed networks—of state and non-state actors (Keck and Sikkink 1998; Reinicke 1998; Reinicke and Deng 2000; Slaughter 2004; Kahler 2009). In these new modes of regulation, authority to govern does not reside exclusively with states but is wielded by a

variety of actors at different levels, including national bureaucrats, intergovernmental organizations (IGOs), nongovernmental organizations (NGOs), transnational corporations, and business associations (Abbot and Snidal 2009; Mattli
and Woods 2009; Avant et al. 2010; Lake 2010). Building on the insights of
these studies and network theory's foundational logic, we propose a framework
for the study of a power politics that goes beyond states alone— what we call
the new power politics. We examine networking—or building relationships—
as a dynamic force through which agents can shape their future fates and governance outcomes. We also look at the relations surrounding particular issues
as "networks" and explore how the positions of actors in these networks, the
distribution of ties, and the quality of ties can offer insights into (1) why governance arises around some security issues and not others and (2) the concerns
governance serves.

Our approach engenders a fresh look at power and how it works in global politics. Unlike some global governance analyses, we see power as integral to governance (see also Barnett and Duval 2005). Rather than conceptualizing power as
a commodity that actors own, as traditional analyses often do, we see power as
emerging from, and depending on, relationships. This view of power is dynamic.
While an actor's relational position shapes her power, it is also something she
can take action to shape strategically. Charli Carpenter's analysis in this volume
ties agenda setting and policy change related to the compensation of civilians in
wartime to just this kind of action. The new power politics is thus about maintaining, developing, and shaping relationships as well as about working through
these relationships to affect governance outcomes.

By and large, we agree with the claims of traditional security studies scholars that the governance of transnational issues is the product of power politics rather than its transformation into "powerless" cooperation. We maintain,
though, that traditional conceptions of both power and politics are too narrow. The new power politics we analyze is the management of relationships that
allow agents (whether states, state agencies, companies, NGOs, or individuals)
to affect their fates and inclinations through collective mobilization (see also
Goddard and Nexon 2016). Useful analyses of when and why power politics
leads to more or less effective governance and governance that serves many or
few in the contemporary world requires attention to relationships among these
varied actors.

Transnational Security Governance Puzzles

What is transnational security governance, how does it vary, and why is
this surprising to traditional international relations theory? We accept the

common definition of governance as the ability to steer or manage a collective (Commission on Global Governance 1995; Keohane and Nye 2000). Governance has been used to describe processes in governments, within or among corporations (Gourevitch and Shinn 2007), NGOs, and, increasingly, in the transnational or global spaces that we focus on in this volume (Rosenau 1992; Held et al. 1999; Duffield 2002). Central elements to transnational governance include: creating issues, setting and managing agendas, negotiating rules or standards, implementing policy, and monitoring, enforcing, and adjudicating outcomes (Abbott and Snidal 2009; Avant et al. 2010a). Leadership to create a collective and management to maintain it are important parts of transnational governance (Young 1991; Tallberg 2010), as are shaping expectations, generating collective action (including the provision of "public goods"[1]), and otherwise "ordering" a shared enterprise.

At the global level, arguments about governance have taken at least two different forms. Analyses of regimes, defined as "principles, norms, rules and decision making procedures around which actor expectations converge in a given issue area" (Krasner 1983, 2), examined the conditions under which a thin veneer of governance developed among states (Stein 1982; Krasner 1983; Keohane 1984; Snidal 1985). In the early 1990s, though, James Rosenau and others noted an increasing likelihood that one could see steering in the transnational arena outside the participation of states. To paraphrase his seminal work with Ernst-Otto Czempiel, it was increasingly common to have "governance without government" (Rosenau and Czempiel 1992). Transnational steering could be generated by a wide variety of actors, including but not limited to states. This spawned a large literature looking at the nature and extent of both global order and order in particular transnational issue areas.

We see security issues as those that actors identify as relevant to their security and mobilize collective resources around (Buzan 1991). Our contributors are attentive to contemporary security challenges. Many of these focus on the management of violence as is familiar within traditional definitions of security (Walt 1991). Other papers extend to human security or broader efforts to shape security outcomes in ways that avoid the use of violence. Affecting the degree of order around a security issue, then, is security governance.

---

[1] In economic terms, public goods are defined as goods that are non-excludable and non-rivalrous in consumption. Although there are difficulties with using this term that have been explored elsewhere (Avant et al. 2010b, 365–367), it is widely used in the global governance literature and so we use it here. We do not assume that a public good is "good" or distinguish public "goods" from public "bads"—both are simply non-excludable and non-rival in consumption.

How Transnational Security Governance Varies

This volume focuses on two ways in which this collective ordering of security may vary. First, and most fundamental, is the degree or effectiveness of governance (Young 1994, 30; 1999, 11–15). In principle, governance can be present or absent (Young 1980). A situation of true anarchy, confused and inchoate could be characterized by an absence of governance. More commonly, governance is more or less effective. Effectiveness refers to the degree to which collective steering or management—or what looks this way in retrospect—is present, either generally in a system of governance, or specifically in a given issue area. Unlike a situation that is entirely ungoverned, in some situations rules or standards may exist but not be acted on and lead to confused expectations and little collective order. These would be situations of weak governance. As expectations grow clearer, processes for resolving distributional conflicts are known, and some level of collective order is apparent, the effectiveness or functionality of the governance situation grows. Most effective are situations in which expectations are clear and the capacity for collective action is widespread.

The ability to take action and "solve" global or transnational problems—or alternatively, the degree to which governance is ineffective or dysfunctional—has been a core point of debate among scholars of global governance. Traditionally, the mostly realist scholars focused on security have been pessimistic about the potential for effective governance of the issues they study. As Robert Jervis (1982, 358) explained, security regimes are both especially valuable and especially difficult to achieve. Our survey of the world, however, reflects more governance than realists expect on a variety of security issues. Some of this takes the familiar form of agreements among states (Montgomery, this volume) or hegemonic leadership by the United States (Cooley and Nexon, this volume). More, however, is the result of forms of governance that the realist literature has left unexamined; from the transgovernmental linkages among state bureaucrats that govern weapons of mass destruction (Eilstrup-Sangiovanni, this volume) to the multi-stakeholder initiatives that govern private military and security services and conflict diamonds (Avant, Westerwinter, this volume) to informal arrangements to counter piracy or generate state responsibility for civilians harmed in their military actions (Carpenter, Percy, this volume). The effectiveness of governance on security issues as well as its form is puzzling to realist analysis.

But extrapolating from liberal analyses (more prominent in other issue areas) does little better. As often as not, governance is not led by the United States or other major powers, as liberal theories of hegemony expect, but by much smaller states or even non-state actors. Governance does sometimes result from the shared interests that liberals expect to generate cooperation, as in the case of antipiracy (Percy, this volume). In many issues, though, shared interests are the result of the process itself. This is particularly the case in the governance of private military and security services (Avant, forthcoming).

To the extent that they expect governance at all, traditional realist analyses should expect that the processes reflect and serve the concerns of dominant states. This is the second dimension of variation we focus on: who governance serves. We examine who governance serves in two different ways. First, it can serve some ideas and/or interests rather than others. Much of the literature on global governance, for instance, focuses on the way it reflects liberal ideas and/ or the interests of dominant powers, such as the United States or the United States and the European Union (Drezner 2007). Second, it can serve many or only a few. Mattli and Woods (2009, 12) differentiate between common interest regulation (where processes for inclusion and accounting for the interests of those governed are in place and there is broad demand for these processes) and captured regulation (where processes for inclusion are not present and demand for inclusion is absent). The more potential for participation and mechanisms for the weak to check the powerful, the more inclusive the process is; processes characterized by capture are exclusive. Those focused on the accountability of governance (Kahler and Lake 2003; Grant and Keohane 2005) or the ability of the weak to check the powerful (Burris et al. 2005) also look generally at who governance serves.

Realists generally assume any governance process is likely to be captured by the major powers—the United States and Europe (Drezner 2007), perhaps China. Only to the degree that what serves the concerns of dominant powers is also valued by others—something implicitly assumed in hegemonic stability theory—should more general concerns be served (Drezner 2007; Brooks and Wohlforth 2008). Liberals and rationalists have often looked to states for mechanisms through which weaker players or more general interests might be served. Some thus look to state-dominated international treaties or "hard" law for the best results (Abbot and Snidal 1998). Others expect international agreements to remove power from governments and thus suffer from democratic deficit (Grant and Keohane 2005). Our analyses show that governance processes do not line up so neatly. Sometimes we observe governance processes in which even the hegemon can be captured by narrowly interested clients (Avant, Cooley and Nexon, this volume). Furthermore, as Cooley and Nexon show, these interests need not be within the United States at all. Interpersonal connections between Georgian elites and the George W. Bush administration led the United States to take action that risked stability in Eastern Europe (Cooley and Nexon, this volume). Informal processes can be tools for generating capture for hegemonic states (Eilstrup-Sangiovanni, this volume) but also for seemingly weaker non-state actors (Westerwinter, this volume). Informal processes can yield results that serve broad (Eilstrup-Sangiovanni, Avant, Percy, this volume) or narrow (Cooley and Nexon, Westerwinter, this volume) concerns.

In sum, there is broad variation in the effectiveness of security governance across issues. When there is governance there is also variation in who it serves. Neither traditional realists nor liberal and rationalist approaches can explain the pattern of variation we see. We thus turn to the logic behind social network theory for a framework through which we might begin to solve these puzzles of transnational security governance.

Networks

We define a network as a set of nodes and a set of ties representing the presence or absence of relationships between nodes.[2] Nodes are individuals, though they may be aggregated into corporate entities, such as states or NGOs. Ties are relationships. They signify interactions and can allow for the flow of material and nonmaterial resources, such as money, weapons, information, or advice. Network structures are "persistent patterns of relations among agents that can define, enable, or constrain those agents" (Hafner-Burton, Kahler, and Montgomery 2009, 561). Rather than reified dots and lines, the contributions to this volume consider social networks as the substrate of past social interactions, as "the congealed residues of history" (Padgett and Powell 2012, 3).

Given our broad understanding of networks, any organizational form can be represented and examined as a network. As will be familiar to many, transnational advocacy networks and global policy networks can be analyzed in terms of the patterns of relationships that exist among the actors involved and how these patterns affect outcomes, such as advocacy success or the provision of public goods (Keck and Sikkink 1998; Reinicke 1998). But markets and hierarchies can also be represented in terms of their structural network features (Podolny and Page 1998). A spot market, for example, can be conceived of as an assemblage of isolated nodes with solely transitory ties; an oligopolistic market as a network with several hubs; and a monopoly as a star-shaped network where the majority of nodes are connected asymmetrically to one highly central unit.

This perspective is analytically distinct from approaches that understand networks as a particular form of organization different from markets and hierarchies (Powell 1990). It flows from a relational ontology that sees actors as constituted by, rather than independent of, relations. As put by Harrison White, "*without persons being presupposed as actors, attention necessarily shifts to confluences of*

---

[2] For general overviews of network theory, see Wasserman and Faust 1994 and Scott 2000.

observable processes-in-relations. Out of these emerge actors and locations of social action" (White 1997, 59–60, italics in original). The analytical wager of this approach is that "significant aspects of causation in social and political life inhere in transactions themselves" (Nexon 2009, 27). From this approach we look at how the structure and/or quality of network relations affect the dynamics of collective action—and thus governance—rather than claiming that a "network" is a particular form of governance.

Studies focused on networks as a particular organizational form tend to bundle together various relational features. They assume that "networked" organizations are structurally flat, benign, power free, and characterized by informality and high levels of trust (Powell 1990; Sørensen and Torfing 2007). We concur that flat relations, informality, and trust can be important features of networks. Rather than assuming that these features are inherent to particular groupings, though, we investigate the actual features of particular networks as likely to affect governance dynamics and outcomes. As many have demonstrated, informal networks can nonetheless be quite centralized (Carpenter 2011; Westerwinter 2013). An informal centralized network should lead to different expectations than an informal flat one. To understand the way these variables should matter, we turn to the literature on networks for insights into which variations might be important for understanding variation in transnational security governance.

How Networks Vary

There are many ways that networks can vary. We focus on three broad variations likely to be important in transnational security governance. First is the position of actors within the network. In sociopolitical life, most networks reflect unevenly distributed ties among nodes. This creates differences in their positions. Actors with a large number of direct connections to others occupy central network positions (Freeman 1978; Bonacich 1987). Centrality is a key mechanism through which nodes garner influence in network theory and thus one prominent source of power in the analyses in this volume. Actors can also vary in the degree to which they connect otherwise unconnected others. Such brokers are located at critical junctures and bridge "structural holes" that separate different actors or regions of a network (Granovetter 1973; Burt 1992). Brokers can also connect different types of networks. When one actor simultaneously participates in more than one network, that actor is a *multiplex node*. Multiplex nodes can link interpersonal to interorganizational or interstate networks, or link networks in different issue areas. Multiplexity is implicit in arguments about regime complexes where some actors are part of several institutions that govern a policy problem and thereby connect these institutions to each other (Raustiala and Victor 2004; Orsini et al. 2013). Centrality and broker positions have been key to a variety of arguments about international relations outcomes (Nexon and Wright 2007; Nexon 2009; Goddard 2009, 2012; Carpenter 2011; Murdie 2014). Multiplexity has not received as much attention in analyses of global politics but we demonstrate that the degree to which nodes overlap and whether they introduce competitive or complementary dynamics is a key concept for understanding the security governance issues we address in this volume. It is likely to have increasingly important effects on contemporary global politics and is worthy of much more study.

Our second variable is the distribution of ties within the network. A primary distinction between networks is whether they are decentralized or centralized. In a decentralized network, nodes are similar to each other in terms of their pattern of connectedness with the majority of nodes having roughly the same number of links (Barabási 2003; Butts 2009). A decentralized network resembles the "flat" structure that analyses of networks as distinct types of organization often assume (Powell 1990). One might imagine a spontaneous online community to resemble a flat network. Studies of Anonymous, for instance, suggest that it is highly connected with no particularly central nodes (Kushner 2014). Centralized networks, by contrast, are dominated by one or a small number of highly central nodes (hubs) while the majority of actors have few relations. The coexistence of a few hubs with a large number of sparsely connected nodes establishes a hierarchy among nodes (Barabási 2003, 70). Flat networks can be good for spreading information but are unpredictable in generating sustained action. Centralized networks can be efficient for generating collective action by establishing, and reinforcing a focal point. They can be less suitable for the fast dissemination of information particularly in situations in which the network hubs are unable or unwilling to operate effectively.

The third broad category of variation across networks that we highlight is the quality of ties. This can refer to a range of phenomena. Some actors may be linked by friendship, others by enmity with obviously different consequences for interaction. Ties can interact to promote brokerage (enhancing additional connections) or closure (tighten existing connections) (Burt 2005; Obstfeld et al. 2014). Both brokerage and closure are forms of social capital but activate different social dynamics among network actors. Closure leads to strong ties, indicating high frequency and strong coupling, while brokerage is frequently among weaker ties, indicating lower frequency and more fragile coupling. Both brokerage and closure have a dark side. Closure can generate rigidity and "echo" (echo blocks new information and builds "us" versus "them" categories) that makes networks fragile; brokerage can yield instability. Finally, relations can be formal or informal. Formal ties can, for example, be constituted by contractual relationships among actors as defined in international agreements. Informal ties include connections grounded in actors' memberships in the same international or transnational institutions and exchanges of information and advice. Although formal ties have traditionally been seen as more effective in enabling political actors to overcome collective action problems and shaping behavior (Abbot and Snidal 1998), many of the contributors to this project focus on the importance of informal ties for governance.

To summarize, network theory places relationships among actors and the properties of these relationships at the center of studying political processes. We focus on variation in the position of actors, the distribution of ties, and the quality of ties to better understand variation in transnational security governance across a broad range of empirically relevant policy problems.

Networks and Power

Our network approach broadens conventional analyses of power in several ways. To begin, a network perspective places a premium on relational understandings of power; power that derives from and is exercised through actual or potential relationships rather than residing only in a node. Also, since it is agnostic with respect to what entities constitute the nodes in a network, network analysis allows for a multiplicity of actor configurations ranging from states to IGOs, companies, NGOs, and even individuals to be seen as power wielders. Finally, it makes no stipulation that the use of power be detrimental to those it affects.

Many have argued that power is intrinsically relational (Simon 1953; Dahl 1957; Nagel 1968; Baldwin 1979; Barnett and Duval 2005). Robert Dahl's "intuitive idea" that "A has power over B to the extent that he can get B to do something that B would not otherwise do" is, for example, firmly based on the idea that "power is a relation" (Dahl 1957, 202–203). As Baldwin (2013, 274) notes, the change in actor B's behavior "may be understood broadly to include beliefs, attitudes, preferences, opinions, expectations, emotions or predispositions to act." Barnett and Duval (2005, 8) define power as "the production, in and through social relations, of effects that shape the capacities of actors to determine their own circumstances and fate."

Relational perspectives on power stand in contrast with conventional international relations scholars who often conceive of power as an attribute, something an individual actor can have (or not) and which can be used to affect others' behavior and accomplish ends. Often, power resources are treated as if they were power itself (Baldwin 2002, 180). This "power-as-resource" conception figures prominently in Waltz's (1979, 98) structural realism where military and economic capabilities are defined as "attributes of units" (i.e., states) and has since then exerted sustained influence on the thinking and theorizing about power and influence in the discipline of international relations.[3]

Moving away from a commitment to states as the only relevant nodes allows network frameworks to fit more easily with analyses of power that see many different sources and dimensions of power. Moving away from the fixation on national power as the key to global governance leads to a more open examination of why it is that any particular actor A can generate different behavior from actor B than we would otherwise expect. This acknowledges a greater variety of potential political spaces (Berenskoetter 2007, 17). There are various sources of power and different types of actors have more access to some than others. Multinational corporations have greater access to money, states to military force, NGOs to principles, but each of these can be important for generating changes in others' behavior.

Finally, network analysis is open to the idea that power may be "power to" rather than "power over." This notion of power to generate something new, connected to collective action is downplayed in traditional security studies, which has been more attentive to zero sum notions of power. As Berenskoetter (2007, 4) points out, though, it is fundamental in Hannah Arendt's analysis, which focused on power as something creative and productive, and also present in Talcott Parsons' work. The "power to" is agnostic about the zero sum (or not) qualities that generate capacities but is focused on their potential for generating creativity and collective action (Baldwin 2013, 278–279).

Thinking of power as relational, attached to different nodes with various bases, and with a broad range of effects pulls our analysts away from general statements about generic power and toward a more nuanced analysis of how different manifestations of power work in particular issue areas. This is consistent with those who have broken power down by its relational specificity and mode of operation (Barnett and Duvall 2005) or with those who emphasize the way different bases of power (or "capital") operation in various fields (Bourdieu 1986). Most important, it is open to understanding power in its many and various forms (Berenskoetter and Williams 2007).

This volume's contributors highlight several particular insights. First, an actor's relative position in a group of governors can be seen as an independent basis of power in international relations (Kahler 2009). This network power resides in the persistent patterns of relations among the actors involved in governing an issue (Hafner-Burton, Kahler, and Montgomery 2009). Relational structures

---

[3] A recent example which continues this theoretical lineage is Drezner's (2007) notion of state power as the size of its national economy measured in gross domestic product. Note, however, that Drezner complements the size of the national economy with a state's level of vulnerability, which introduces a relational dimension in his understanding of power.

are a source of power because they provide actors in specific positions with social capital, information, coalitional opportunities, and other resources which can be exploited to pursue collective action (Knoke 1990; Burt 1992; Lin 2001). In the anti–land-mines network, for example, NGOs in central positions used the informational and coalitional advantages emanating from their positions to shape the agenda of negotiations over an intergovernmental land mine treaty and influence both the contents of the treaty as well as the development of the institutional regime created to implement it (Bower, this volume). Similarly, multinational corporations that participate in several regimes to govern different conflict minerals used their multiplex positions to disseminate governance structures across regimes (Haufler, this volume).

Power often works through diffuse mechanisms. The structural and productive power that Barnett and Duvall (2005) highlight are two important ways in which diffuse power works. Montgomery (this volume) demonstrates that diffuse power can have greater impact than direct power in many situations. And Avant (this volume) shows that diffuse power can even affect the preferences of the United States and its support for transnational governance processes.

How an actor behaves in a relational setting depends on how that actor sees the relationships it is involved in. An actor may think that she has more friends— or enemies—than others do. There may be more or less agreement about the configuration of power among the actors in a network. These perceptions may shift with issue areas or recent interactions. Thus, while Kahler (2009) usefully describes network power vis-à-vis its bargaining leverage, social power, and exit capacities, we must bear in mind that network relations are, in part, a function of different actors' perceptions. For instance, as Carpenter explains in this volume, advocates for the making amends campaign were not successful in making this a global campaign to change global norms of war until the organizers were able to change the perception of the Campaign for Innocent Victims in Conflict (CIVIC). Reconstituting its perceived relationships with both actors (at the UN) and issues (protecting civilians) in the global human security network was critical to CIVIC's success in global agenda setting.

If power emerges from and depends on the formation and continuation of relationships, it implies that as relationships build, power can grow; and if they change or break down, power can shift and dissipate. This dynamic view of power implicitly sits behind the notion of networking, or strategically creating relationships to help one reach her goal (Lake and Wong 2009). Its implications for thinking about power in global politics are significant. The actions an agent takes not only affect the task at hand but also affect that agent's relationships and thus future possibilities to shape governance processes. Different actions, drawing on different sources of power can thus have consequences for future possibilities. Using coercion, for instance, may undermine some relationships in ways that diminish an actor's network position and thus power. Using persuasion or appealing to social norms, may enhance an actor's institutional authority or network position (though may constrain the conditions under which she can use coercion). This approach thus emphasizes that wielding one form of power may have consequences for an actor's ability to wield another form of power, enhancing or diminishing overall power. It also highlights the agency of those who relate to a powerful actor for that actor's continued power.

Networks, Power, and Governance

Many of the recent analyses of networks in global governance take networks as they find them (Kahler 2009). While this is useful for explaining whether governance is effective or not and who it serves, it ignores the degree to which agents actively shape their network position and the overall qualities of the networks they participate in. We are interested in both the dynamic elements of networking and the network qualities at any particular moment. Both affect governance. The power of network logic can generate new tools for evaluating, and elaborating on, existing arguments in the field of security analysis. Network logic also offers new insights into strategic networking and the way in which network structure affects governance outcomes. Table 1.1 describes the way these conceptions structure this volume.

To begin, Alexander Montgomery offers novel insights on the value of centrality. Using network techniques, he demonstrates new insights into how centrality matters for both governance effectiveness and whom it serves. First, with regard to the literature on conflict management, network techniques uncover a new mechanism—diffuse socialization—that is more important than dispute resolution in efforts to govern conflict. Second, with regard to the literature on international hierarchy, he shows that its core insights might apply more broadly. Although the United States' centrality allows it to exercise domination through its alliance system, so does the centrality of other players in other alliance systems.

The next three chapters look explicitly at strategic networking and its impact on who governance serves. Charli Carpenter analyzes the way norm entrepreneurs constructed relationships within the context of particular structural constraints. Constructing connections with central actors and central issues gave these entrepreneurs greater agenda-setting effectiveness. Activists wanting to generate a norm that militaries should make amends to civilians harmed by (even lawful) military operations constructed relational ties first with central actors in the United States and then with central issues in the human security network in order to attract the support of powerful gatekeeping hubs.

Alexander Cooley and Daniel Nexon analyze how multiplex nodes—particularly those that sit simultaneously in personal and high-level governmental networks—can shape government perceptions in perverse ways. In the case they examine, the strategic construction of personal relationships between Tbilisi and members of the Bush administration nearly hijacked US foreign policy. Interpersonal connections between Georgian elite and US administration officials led the United States to support the aims of a narrow set of Georgian elite in a way that exacerbated the potential for conflict between Georgia and Russia, something the United States did not want.

Deborah Avant examines how multiplex nodes and the logic through which they connect can affect US preferences. Connecting with the United States or "netting the empire" was key to both frustrating (small arms) and achieving (private military and security companies, PMSCs) effective governance and to serving narrow (small arms) or broad (PMSCs) aims. She finds that brokerage strategies are more supportive of effective transnational governance and closure strategies more easily used to halt governance efforts. Forming connections to affect US preferences and authority claims is an important avenue for both domestic and transnational actors to influence the direction of transnational security governance.

The final five chapters focus on how network variables affect governance outcomes in particular issues. Mette Eilstrup-Sangiovanni argues that informal transgovernmental networks (TGNs) to control the proliferation of weapons of mass destruction (WMD) rather than formal IGOs are most likely to arise when powerful central actors face domestic veto players and expect enforcement to be rare. TGNs are more likely to be effective when the participating numbers are small. In their execution, though, she argues that TGNs generate more benefits to central (and powerful) actors and thus may be associated with narrower interests. She uses the Proliferation Security Initiative and Missile Technology Control Regime to illustrate her claims.

Adam Bower argues that the ban on antipersonnel mines codified in the 1997 Mine Ban Treaty is not reducible to the properties of the actors involved or the quality of particular ideas, but is rather the product of the relationships among the actors involved. Specifically, key actors with central positions had disproportionate influence in reshaping the policy agenda concerning antipersonnel mines. His account explains how the goal of a complete prohibition won-out in the face of sustained opposition, and why global military powers led by the United States were unable to generate support for an alternative framing that retained antipersonnel mines as legitimate weapons of war. His analysis suggests that central positions can generate effective governance even in the face of traditionally powerful resistance.

Oliver Westerwinter examines how the informal communication networks among states, the diamond industry, and NGOs affected the development of a more rigorous formal monitoring system in the Kimberley Process (KP) that governs conflict diamonds. Particularly, those with central and broker positions were able to use these to push for monitoring that increased the effectiveness and broadened the interests served by the agreement despite resistance from materially powerful but structurally poorly positioned actors. Like Bower, his analysis suggests that centrality, even informal centrality, can lead even weaker players to generate effective governance that serves broader interests.

Virginia Haufler compares the governance of conflict diamonds in the Kimberly Process to the governance of other conflict minerals. While the push to regulate rough diamonds occurred quickly, was negotiated in a multi-stakeholder forum that included almost the entire diamond market, and resulted in a single comprehensive public-private regulatory institution leading to relatively effective governance, pressure to regulate other conflict minerals (tin, tantalum, tungsten, gold) has meandered through in a stop-and-start manner, has not always involved multi-stakeholder processes, and has not resulted in the creation of a single global regime. She explains this puzzle by looking at the way in which associational networks (such as membership in business policy organizations) and contractual networks (relationships within an industry value chain) interact. The KPs resulted from associational relationships embracing corporate social responsibility (CSR) and a dominant central player (De Beers) who reinforced that orientation. Without value chain support, work on other conflict minerals has not been as effective despite a model for action in the KPs. The relationships among networks can be important for reinforcing or undermining effective governance.

Finally Sarah Percy explains why effective multinational military cooperation against piracy has been possible—even among states that are at times hostile toward one another. An informal but centralized system, she argues, has allowed brokers to mediate timely communication and coordination among navies of states that share a goal but lack positive relationships. Cooperation has also been facilitated by the shared values and discourses among navies and a relatively clear international legal framework for surrounding piracy. In contrast to cases examined by other contributions (Avant, Cooley and Nexon, Carpenter, Westerwinter, this volume) the actors that occupy central and broker positions in the counter-piracy network have not used their position to strategically manipulate governance processes and outcomes in their favor. Percy ties this to agreement on the goal (countering piracy) and beliefs that any strategic use of network positions would jeopardize achieving this goal.

Table 1.1 **Overview of Variables and Cases**

Network Variables	Governance Outcomes	
	Effective or Ineffective	*Benefits Broad or Narrow Concerns*
Position of actors Central Broker Multiplex	Montgomery—central position, **conflict reduction** Carpenter—construction of relationships with central actors, **making amends** Bower—central position, **land mines** Westerwinter—central and broker positions, **governance of conflict diamonds** Haufler—multiplex nodes, **conflict diamonds versus conflict minerals**	Montgomery—central position, **alliance concerns** Cooley and Nexon— multiplexity, US preferences, **Georgia** Avant—multiplexity, US preferences, **small arms versus PMSCs** Bower—central position, **land mines** **Westerwinter**—central and broker positions, **governance of conflict diamonds**
Distribution of ties Decentralized/flat Centralized/ hierarchical	Haufler—multiplex nodes, **conflict diamonds versus conflict minerals** Percy—informal centralized, **antipiracy**	Percy—informal centralized, **antipiracy**
Quality of ties Brokerage versus closure Formal versus informal	Avant—brokerage versus closure, **small arms versus PMSCs** Eilstrup-Sangiovanni— informal, **WMD** Percy—informal centralized, **antipiracy**	Eilstrup-Sangiovanni— informal, **WMD** Westerwinter—informal, **governance of conflict diamonds**

Conclusion

Much of what we see in security governance is puzzling to traditional analyses. We see more and different governance than realists expect and different routes to governance than liberals anticipate. Collective ordering is not free of power but the new power politics involves more types of actors with various bases of power, and works through forms that are left out of many theories. Focusing on the nodes and ties present in different issue areas and using some basic theoretical tools from network logic, we were able to generate explanations for a wide range of security governance behavior and outcomes. Network theory can yield new insights even in well-studied areas of global governance such as how international organizations affect conflict management and whose interests shape alliance concerns (Montgomery, this volume). Beyond that, the volume's analyses yield important new insights relevant to our understanding of transnational security governance.

First, relations are dynamic. Actors can improve their network position by constructing new linkages. While this is implied in the logic of "networking," our contributors explicitly attend to the strategic construction of network position. Constructing perceived associations with key hubs and gatekeepers can build actual ties and lead to agenda-setting effectiveness (Carpenter, this volume). And constructing interpersonal linkages with key nodes in powerful networks can be an important way through which otherwise less powerful players can attempt to generate governance outcomes that serve their interests (Cooley and Nexon, this volume). Although many of the contributions focus on network dynamics over time, the chapters in the networking section look most explicitly at the strategic qualities of these dynamics.

Second, multiplexity—a situation where one node sits simultaneously in more than one network—can be a key strategic resource affecting power politics and transnational governance. Network theorists have long held that multiplexity can lead to the spread of ideas from one network to another and the emergence of new institutional forms (Padgett and Powell 2012). This idea implicitly animates the logic of interdependence theory (Keohane and Nye 1977). Fewer analyses, however, have examined the power implications of the mechanisms through which this occurs. Our contributors examine several mechanisms through which multiplex nodes can strategically affect the identity and inclinations of the networks of which they are a part. Interpersonal ties can be used to affect organizational inclinations (Cooley and Nexon, this volume); transnational as well as domestic ties can affect national inclinations (Avant, this volume); and informal ties can affect formal institutional structures (Westerwinter, this volume).

The power agents deploy has consequences for future power. Power rooted in violence or economic capacity and used alone to bribe or punish others may be useful for forestalling action and for producing short-run effects, but this use of power often erodes relationships in ways that hinder future collective action. Generating collective action is more likely when prospective governors root their action in expertise, principles and relations, and leverage military and/or economic capacity in their service. Leveraging various power sources in combined strategies can generate greater influence over governance processes through layered relational ties. Thus, using power as traditionally envisioned can be degenerative, eroding future capacity, while "softer" forms of power often hold a generative quality leading to greater future capacities (Avant, Eilstrup-Sangiovanni, this volume).

Also relations can be power tools for both the weak and the strong. Networks have often been portrayed as a means to empower otherwise weak actors, such as NGOs or small states, to voice their interests and influence governance outcomes (Keck and Sikkink 1998; Reinicke and Deng 2000). As the chapters of this volume show, the picture is more complex. Central positions in formal and informal networks enabled NGOs to shape the contents and development of the international regime to ban land mines (Bower, this volume) and successfully bargain for a formal monitoring system in the KP that went beyond what many states and diamond industry representatives were initially willing to agree to. However, often networks are just another way for already powerful players, such as major powers and multinational companies, to achieve their goals. The United States, for example, used its privileged network position in order to shape the form and content of the transnational regulation of private security companies (Avant, this volume) and large multinational corporations exploit the leverage that emanates from their multiplex positions at the intersection of economic and political networks to shape the evolution of the institutional complex that governs conflict minerals (Haufler, this volume). In short, relations are not always the power tool of the otherwise weak but can be used by both weak and strong players. The question of who uses networks to exert influence is more fruitfully treated as a matter for careful empirical investigation rather than theoretical assumption.

We may have been too quick to toss out the importance of functional explanations for security concerns. While it is clearly the case that many obvious problems are not solved and there are roles for entrepreneurs in constructing problems, the perceived need for governance can be important for generating it. While this point is most clearly made in Percy's chapter on antipiracy, it is also important for the story Avant tells about governing private military and security services and Bower tells about governing land mines. Establishing a problem and gathering stakeholders around it can shift relational dynamics in ways that can engender greater collaboration.

Finally, our analyses have significant implications for how to understand the role of the United States and other central players in the contemporary global system. Traditional realist and liberal analyses have assumed that hegemons use their power (military or financial) to lead others to governance outcomes through force or encouragement. While no doubt true at times, the relational ontology that informs our project leads us to imagine other possibilities. Hegemons like the United States are also networks of individuals and agencies. The increased connections noted by globalization theorists have generated more and more multiplex nodes in these networks. Thinking of the United States as a central and powerful network means the United States can work through multiplex nodes to shape the inclinations and actions of others (Eilstrup-Sangiovanni, this volume) and the reverse (Avant, Cooley and Nexon, this volume).

2

Centrality in Transnational Governance

How Networks of International Institutions Shape Power Processes

ALEXANDER H. MONTGOMERY

A traditional view of power in international politics holds that it resides in the possession of important resources. Actors with significant stocks of military hardware, economic wealth, and other high-value assets, the argument goes, enjoy advantages when it comes to influencing others. But a great deal of research suggests that power also resides in ties (patterns of association) that link together actors in networks (Avant and Westerwinter, this volume). Some of these ties are material, such as trade and capital flows, while others are symbolic, such as friendship. Whether material or symbolic, however, these ties determine actors' relative positions in networks. These positions, in turn, profoundly structure agents' abilities to determine their circumstances and fates.

The power-political consequences of network position have received increasing attention in the field of international relations. Much of that attention focuses on centrality—a measure of actors' importance in a network. Recent work calls attention to network centrality as a direct source of power for states, individuals, and movements. It consequently neglects how occupying a central position in a network can also powerfully constrain actors; it also emphasizes direct dyadic effects of power while slighting diffuse, network-wide implications. In this chapter, I argue that network centrality can be used to understand these broader power processes in international relations in ways that enhance existing scholarly analyses.

I illustrate my point by replicating and extending two important papers in the field that engage with power processes around socialization dynamics and international order. Jon Pevehouse and Bruce Russett's (2006) paper sits at the conjunction of three foundational literatures on international organizations (IOs), the democratic peace, and dispute resolution. They posit that as the density of ties between states through democratic IOs increases, conflicts will abate. I build upon their research by demonstrating that this is caused by diffuse socialization through all democratic IOs rather than direct socialization by states or dispute resolution mechanisms. David Lake's (2007) paper challenges dominant understandings of anarchy in international relations. It posits that countries that lack alliance network ties to countries other than the United States are in subordinate positions within a hierarchical relationship. I extend his research by demonstrating that the same power dynamics have diffuse structural effects that order the entire international alliance system. Through these examples, I demonstrate that employing network analysis allows for better connections between theory and empirics, more precise hypothesis testing, broadened scope, and improved models.

Network Analysis as an Approach

Networks create social structures that can influence agents' identities, the options they enjoy, the pressures they face, and how they make decisions. Network analysis offers practical tools to measure these potential sources of influence and constraint and their distributions in any system of actors. It concerns relationships defined by ties among nodes (or actors). Nodes can be individuals such as people or corporate actors such as organizations and states. Ties can be conduits for the exchange of material resources (e.g., weapons, money, drugs, or disease) or nonmaterial resources (e.g., information, beliefs, symbols, and norms). Network analysis examines the associations among nodes in addition to the attributes of particular nodes: relationships are not properties of actors but of systems of actors. While this study is necessarily limited in scope to the effects of network positions, network analysis can also analyze the creation and growth of networks through processes including selection and contagion. I make no assumptions here about which processes dominate network creation.

Like rational choice approaches, network analysis is not a unified set of theories about behavior but rather a framework for analysis based on a set of assumptions and tools that can be applied to an assortment of processes, from conflict to norm diffusion. It is grounded in three principles: nodes and their behaviors are mutually dependent, not autonomous; ties between nodes are channels for transmission and co-constitution; and persistent patterns of association among nodes create structures that can define, enable, or restrict the behavior of nodes. The underlying difference between network analysis and standard ways of analyzing processes is accordingly the use of concepts and indicators that identify associations among units rather than solely focusing on the attributes of the units. Networks are defined as any set or sets of ties between any set or sets of nodes; no assumptions are made about the homogeneity or other characteristics of the nodes or ties. Consequently, network analysis can be used to analyze any kind of ties, including market or hierarchical transactions. Beyond these basic principles, network analysis enables calculation of structural properties, such as centrality of nodes, groups, or the entire network.[1]

Networks, International Relations, and Centrality

As the methodology of network analysis continues to advance, so too do applications to the study of international relations.[2] However, current network centrality approaches in international relations remain wedded to a "capabilities" model of political power. Network ties, in this approach, amount to an additional resource that—like military hardware and hard currency stocks—actors may accumulate to enhance their influence. For example, a number of scholars have focused on how the centrality of NGOs enables some organizations to be much more important or effective than others. This is due to their ability to receive or spread information more quickly, their possession of exclusive ties to important actors, or the sheer number of ties to other organizations (Moore, Eng, and Daniel 2003; Lake and Wong 2009; Carpenter 2011; Murdie and Davis 2012; Böhmelt, Koubi, and Bernauer 2014; Carpenter 2014; Carpenter et al. 2014; Murdie 2014; Carpenter, this volume). Other scholars have adopted a social network approach to analyzing patterns of conflict and cooperation between states. These approaches focus on centrality as an asset that can be used to coerce or convince other states due to a relative or absolute advantage in mobilization of support, a general indicator of status or prestige, or a conduit for important information on relative capabilities (Hafner-Burton and Montgomery 2006, 2008, 2012; Maoz et al. 2006; Ward 2006; Dorussen and Ward 2008; Kim 2010; Maoz 2010, ch. 7; Murdie, Wilson, and Davis 2016).[3]

---

[1] For a good overview of network analysis, see Scott 2013. The most comprehensive, if slightly dated, technical overview is Wasserman and Faust 1994. For recent additions to Wasserman and Faust, see Carrington, Scott, and Wasserman 2005. For a much more concise and up-to-date reference, see Knoke and Yang 2008; also see Carrington and Scott 2011. A useful online textbook is Hanneman and Riddle 2005. For a historical overview of the development of the field, see Freeman 2004.

[2] Notable recent work in international relations using network analysis principles and techniques other than centrality includes Ward, Siverson, and Cao 2007; Elkins 2009; Corbetta 2010; Maoz 2010; Cranmer, Desmarais, and Menninga 2012; Manger, Pickup, and Snijders 2012; Kinne 2013, 2014; Oatley et al. 2013; Ward, Ahlquist, and Rozenas 2013; Cranmer, Heinrich, and Desmarais 2014.

[3] But see Kinne 2012 for a conception of centrality as a constraint on action.

Such work provides important insights, but it downplays the structural character of networks and consequently misses important power processes. Indeed, one of the key purposes of network analysis is to measure social structure. If social structure is shorthand for relatively durable patterns of interaction, then network analysis provides a rigorous means of measuring structural variation.[4] Yet a significant proportion of international-relations applications of network analysis use relational data but conjoin it to an agent-centric understanding of power. Once a more relational ontology is adopted—one consistent with standard sociological interpretations of network analysis—we gain a fuller appreciation of the connection between power and networks. This allows us to use network analysis to talk about a variety of different dimensions of power, including how positions constrain as well as enable and how power can act in diffuse as well as direct ways (Avant and Westerwinter, this volume).

Indeed, there exists very little consensus about what particular network positions provide actors with the greatest advantages or influence. This lack of consensus resides in the fact that network position, such as the centrality of a given actor, does not automatically translate into the possession of greater influence. Rather, the relative agency constituted by the positions of actors in networks—combined with the capacity to exercise that agency—determines whether power is possessed by those agents and whether they can successfully use that power.

To complicate matters, network analysis includes a panoply of different measures of centrality. Many of these were created to analyze specific networks or particular types of ties—and therefore often involve theoretical foundations that do not translate to other domains.[5] The communications-network origins of classic centrality measures (i.e., degree, betweenness, and closeness) means that while the behavior of these metrics are well understood, they must be re-theorized when used in other domains. More recent measures often suffer from a lack of theoretical underpinnings or systematic testing of properties, making it hazardous to apply them across domains. These difficulties make it problematic to articulate clear connections between centrality and various phenomena.

[4] Neorealist approaches to the structure of the international system focus on the distribution of material properties, creating a structure that can be measured by the number and capabilities of great powers (Waltz 1979; Mearsheimer 2001). However, these accounts do not exclude and are generally complementary to network conceptions of social structure; see Goddard and Nexon 2005; Hafner-Burton and Montgomery 2006; Hafner-Burton, Kahler, and Montgomery 2009.

[5] Attempts to provide theoretical foundations are often based on specific processes (e.g., Friedkin 1991). These often end up articulating additional measures whose properties are not well understood.

Power and Centrality

These difficulties are particularly acute with respect to power, due to the relatively narrow conception of power in networks expressed by "power centrality" (Bonacich 1987). This measure covers situations where being connected to other powerful individuals is most useful as well as situations where being connected to relatively isolated individuals is advantageous. It does not cover brokerage between two powerful, but not directly connected individuals or groups, nor does it evaluate the efficiency of propagation through a network. It is also intimately connected to the idea of power as a resource held by individuals rather than as a constraining force across entire networks. Calculation of power centrality also requires specification of parameters for which little clear theoretical or empirical guidance exists. Consequently, parameters are often chosen without any grounding in theory or practice, and so it is difficult to interpret the results in meaningful ways. It is a potentially useful measure of a particular conception of power, but does not exhaust the possibilities for power in centrality measures.

Although the nature and source of power in networks has been discussed by many others across disciplines, these discussions have primarily to do with either the power of specific individuals or exchange relations.[6] Similarly, since centrality scores were originally based on communications networks, these metrics are commonly understood in the networks literature as prestige or status indicators of individuals rather than as indicators of underlying social structures.[7] Centrality measures cannot be assumed to mean the same thing when applied to networks of states as networks of overlapping executive boards or schoolchildren on the playground. Moreover, these notions of power are focused on individual agents and ignore wider processes that involve power that operates through structural constraints and pressures.

Consequently, I follow Duvall and Barnett in broadly defining power as "the production, in and through social relations, of effects that shape the capacities of actors to determine their circumstances and fate" (Barnett and Duvall

---

[6] For an early discussion of power exerted through networks in world politics, see Ward and House 1988; Stoll and Ward 1989. For a general political science treatment of power in political networks, see Knoke 1990. For a general discussion of power dependence in exchange networks in sociology, see Emerson 1962; Cook and Yamagishi 1992. On social capital and network power, see Borgatti, Jones, and Everett 1998; Lin, Cook, and Burt 2001; Borgatti 2006.

[7] Freeman's classic articulation of the definitions of degree, closeness, and betweenness centrality were based on notions of network communication and consequently although the measures are useful, these conceptions are not directly applicable to most international relations networks. See Freeman 1979. For such accounts in international relations, see Hafner-Burton and Montgomery 2006, 2008, 2012; Maoz et al. 2006; Kim 2010; Maoz 2010, ch. 7.

2005, 42).[8] This is a notion of power that bridges across the four faces of power, which were formulated historically rather than designed as a deliberate typology.[9] They divide power into two categories: the specificity of social relations of power (direct/diffuse) and how power is expressed (interaction/constitution). The first distinction very closely aligns with the problem faced by most centrality approaches: they treat power and centrality as "mechanistic, flush with contact, direct, or logically necessary." By contrast, diffuse approaches "allow for the possibility of power even if the connections are detached and mediated, or operate at a physical, temporal, or social distance" (Barnett and Duvall 2005, 47–48). By including not only direct and intentional effects but also diffuse and unintentional ones, this definition is a broad notion of power that, I argue, can be operationalized through centrality measures.

Centrality measures cannot be directly mapped onto the direct/diffuse distinction. However, it is possible to tease out some basic guidelines for conceptualizing and measuring power processes through centrality. In general, direct relations may involve political effects that can be captured by a centrality metric that weighs proximate ties more heavily than more distant ones, while analyzing power processes due to diffuse relations might call for a metric that takes into account more indirect ties. For example, degree centrality is a sum of the strength of the ties immediately connected to a given individual and so is direct.[10] Eigenvector and power centrality also focus on immediate ties but are somewhat more diffuse, since they also take into account the centrality of those actors as well.[11] Betweenness measures the importance of an actor by determining the number of geodesics (shortest paths) that actor is on between all pairs of actors in a network. It is consequently more diffuse than degree, eigenvector, and power measures. But it still favors some paths over others; flow betweenness corrects this by taking into account all possible paths (even those that are not the shortest) between every pair and therefore is even more diffuse. Actors with high closeness centrality have short paths between them and all other actors, and information central actors have short paths over strong ties, and so both

[8] Barnett and Duvall follow Scott's network-based definition of social power, "an agent's intentional use of causal powers to affect the conduct of other agents" (Scott 2008, 29). For Scott's complete formulation, see Scott 2001.

[9] Barnett and Duvall 2005, 43n13. For a discussion of the faces of power and networks, see Hafner-Burton and Montgomery 2009.

[10] This assumes a one-mode network (i.e., all of the nodes are of one type). In an n-mode network ($n > 1$), nodes of one type must go through at least one other type in order to produce effects, making degree centrality potentially indirect. See my analysis below of Pevehouse and Russett.

[11] In a sense, these could be seen as very diffuse, since ultimately the centrality of actors throughout an entire network component is affected by the addition or subtraction of a single tie. However, the effects of doing so drop off significantly with increased distance.

depend on the structure of an entire network component. As a result, these are very diffuse measures, although they emphasize slightly different types of diffusion.[12] The choice of which metric to use will depend on the particular type of power process—whether it is through access to other important actors (e.g., degree, eigenvector, and power), brokerage between unconnected groups (e.g., betweenness and flow betweenness), or speed of diffusion through a network (e.g., closeness and information).[13]

Power works through the ties studied in this article (international organizations) through both direct and diffuse relations. To begin with the simplest concept, mutual membership in a given organization allows for direct interaction between states that belong to the organization. This measure is typically interpreted as the tie strength among these states. These ties enable power processes through, for example, dispute resolution mechanisms and direct, regularized interactions between states. Through frequent interactions, states can socialize each other to norms of behavior due to having more access to each other; the more organizations that both belong to, the greater the chance of socialization.

But looking at the effects of interactions over a large set of organizations adds a second component of socialization. In addition to direct interactions between states, diffuse power processes come into play. Organizations not only provide mechanisms and meeting places, they also socialize states through the teaching of appropriate behavior. Organizational membership both provides identities for states through membership and teaches regulatory norms (Powell and DiMaggio 1991; Finnemore 1996b; Meyer et al. 1997; Gheciu 2005; Lewis 2005). Overall organizational membership of an individual state thus provides a measure of the diffuse structural pressures placed on that state to conform to the rules and norms of those organizations. These rules, norms, and ideas of appropriate behavior then act as an aggregate structural constraint on the actions of those states. While socialization is ultimately a process that involves the internalization of rules and norms even in the absence of structural constraints,[14] the effects of constraints in behavior should be observable even prior to internalization.

However, these are not the only mechanisms through which membership operates. Exclusion is often as important as inclusion, and so while membership produces effects, nonmembership also can produce effects, whether in a single

---

[12] See Kinne 2012 for a conceptualization of closeness centrality in trade networks as a constraint on disputes.

[13] For overviews of degree, betweenness, closeness, and information centrality, see Wasserman and Faust 1994, ch. 5. For eigenvector and power centrality, see Bonacich 1987.

[14] Successful socialization depends on the internalization of these diffuse, external constraints (Schimmelfennig 2000, 2005) and can best be observed in the absence of those constraints.

organization or across multiple organizations. To take an extreme example, exclusion of certain states from international organizations—whether by their choice or not—can make certain states structurally weak, placing them in the categorical roles of being pariahs, rogues, and outlaws. This constrains behavior of both the included and the excluded through (among other mechanisms) role expectations. The role of a given state likely depends on the density of ties in multiple, intersecting networks, rather than just in organizations, but the latter are often a crucial determinant; the most obvious example is that UN membership is usually taken as an indication of stateness itself.

It does not necessarily require a large number of organizational ties for a state to be structurally powerful nor do states have to be entirely excluded from all international organizations to be positioned in roguish categorical roles. For example, being a member of two organizations with otherwise disjoint membership makes a state a structurally powerful broker between those organizations or the states within them. Brokerage thus creates hierarchies of influence, with dominant and subordinate roles.[15] Yet highly central network positions are not only a source of influence for the central actors but also create constraining effects for each actor depending on their positions over the entire network. For example, with divide-and-conquer rule comes the expectation of the provision of collective goods by the most central actor (Nexon and Wright 2007; MacDonald 2014). Subordinate positions may face varying degrees of pressures to contribute as well, while those outside the entire network face an entirely different set of pressures due to exclusion. Brokers may experience role strain if they cannot act in consistent ways across multiple sets of role expectations; such positions are tricky to navigate and may prove disastrous if multivocal strategies come apart.[16] Selective inclusion and exclusion from some organizations but not others thus also creates important brokerage effects.

The distribution of organizational ties thus helps to order international relations by placing states in particular roles. These roles are often overlooked by approaches that examine membership in individual organizations or sum up the total number of organizations a state or pair of states belongs to. These approaches ignore the emergent effects of nominally symmetrical international organization membership. In aggregate, patterns of organizational ties constitute

---

[15] Brokerage power is not limited to inter-state relationships. As the contributions of Avant and Westerwinter in this volume illustrate, brokers also emerge and exert influence on governance in situations where state and non-state actors in various configurations collaborate to govern an issue area.

[16] On multivocality and the manipulation of identity and interests in networks by brokers, the classic study is Padgett and Ansell 1993. On an international scale, and particularly for contrasts between successful and unsuccessful attempts, see Goddard 2009. For recent work that incorporates multivocality into wider frameworks, see Padgett and Powell 2012.

a dominance ordering over the entire system. This ordering constrains not only the ostensibly isolated and weak but also the apparently powerful by exerting pressure on both to fulfill particular roles associated with those positions.

Applications to International Relations

International relations scholars can—and should—use measures of network centrality to test theories about power processes. In this section, I highlight two examples where a network centrality approach informs existing exemplary research by offering new insights into power politics. In each of these applications, I use the original methodology and add or substitute the appropriate network measure(s) that can extend the research. Ideally, network models include the dynamics of the network itself, treating the evolution of the network as endogenous.[17] However, in order to produce results that are as directly comparable as possible to the original results, I limit the scope here to direct replication and extension. Finally, while my analyses here use binary connections (whether an alliance exists or not, and whether a state belongs to an international organization), many of these measures can be generalized to valued flows as well.

Democratic Socialization through International Organizations

It is a long-standing controversy whether or not joint memberships in IOs reduce violence between states. On one side of the controversy are scholars who argue that IOs stave off wars between members. They allow states to communicate information and facilitate bargaining, provide states with mechanisms to make credible commitments and resolve disputes, and expand states' understandings of identity and self-interest (Keohane and Martin 1995; Martin and Simmons 1998; Russett, Oneal, and Davis 1998; Oneal and Russett 1999; Russett and Oneal 2001; Oneal, Russett, and Berbaum 2003; Dorussen and Ward 2008). On the other side of the controversy are scholars that see IOs either as epiphenomenal or as exacerbating conflicts between members by increasing competition over resources and aggravating long-standing differences (Mearsheimer 1994;

---

[17] Recent models are able to model cross-sectional network dynamics; see, in particular, the ergm and latentnet packages in statnet: Handcock et al. 2008. There are two general classes of models that currently simulate full longitudinal network dynamics along with behavior: Stochastic Actor-Oriented Models (SAOMs, see Snijders, van de Bunt, and Steglich 2010) and Temporal Exponential Random Graph Models (TERGMs, see Cranmer and Desmarais 2011).

Boehmer, Gartzke, and Nordstrom 2004; Hafner-Burton and Montgomery 2006; Ward, Siverson, and Cao 2007).

In a seminal article, Jon Pevehouse and Bruce Russett propose a theory about IOs composed mainly of democracies (Pevehouse and Russett 2006). They argue that densely democratic IOs are far more likely to bring about peaceful relations between members than are IOs with a smaller proportion of democracies. To test their theory, Pevehouse and Russett measure IOs from 1885 to 2000, counting joint dyadic membership in IOs whose members' average level of democracy is equal to or greater than 7 on the Polity scale. Their statistical results show that for a given dyad, the more joint memberships in IOs composed of democracies they possess, the less likely it is that the states in the dyad will engage in fatal militarized international disputes. From these results, the authors conclude that densely democratic IOs help quell violent conflict between member states in ways that other IOs do not. Pevehouse and Russett acknowledge that their statistical results cannot explain how democratic IOs help keep the peace. This metric measures multiple different aspects of intergovernmental relations at the same time: indicators of trust, shared interests, willingness to cooperate, and so forth. Consequently, it is a noisy indicator, and as with all indicators, must be carefully unpacked.[18]

Their theory is that democratic IOs (1) monitor members' behavior and prevent autocratic backsliding; (2) provide dispute settlement and mediation mechanisms; and (3) socialize members to trust each other and find peaceful alternatives to deal with potential conflicts. The first two mechanisms are straightforward, direct applications of power, and are properly measured through joint democratic IOs; the third, however, not only requires a different measure, but could either be direct (states socializing each other) or diffuse (organizations socializing the states) applications of power. A centrality approach can help to differentiate this third mechanism.

It is difficult to measure socialization directly, but it is possible to measure the totality of the structural pressures that any particular state (or other actor) is subject to due to a network. In the IO literature, socialization is defined as a "process by which actors acquire different identities, leading to new interests through regular and sustained interactions within broader social contexts and structures" (Bearce and Bondanella 2007, 706). I create two measures to reflect diffuse (by democratic IOs) and direct (by democratic states in IOs) socialization. To gauge the diffuse socialization pressures on states by democratic IOs, I set the variable *Democratic IO Socialization* to the indegree centrality of states in the two-mode state-democratic IO network. Although one-mode indegree

---

[18] I thank Deborah Avant and Oliver Westerwinter for pointing this out.

centrality is a direct measure, here two-mode indegree centrality is an indirect and diffuse measure, since it is the institutions rather than the states that created those institutions who are the agents of socialization. Two-mode indegree centrality is the total number of incoming ties from democratic IOs for each state (i.e., the number of democratic IOs they belong to). If x_{ij} is the strength of the tie between actors i and j, then the indegree centrality of actor i is:[19]

$$C_D(n_i) = \sum_{j}^{g} x_{ij}$$

States may also socialize each other directly through interactions in IOs. In this conceptualization, IOs are simply venues for socialization and so the effect is direct rather than diffuse. I measure this democratic socialization effect for a given target state by summing up the number of democratic states (polity score equal to or greater than 7) in each IO the target state belongs to. This results in the variable *Democratic State Socialization*. For both variables, I hypothesize that a weak-link mechanism operates: the extent to which either socialization mechanism could dampen down conflict depends on the less pressured member of a dyad.

Figure 2.1 illustrates the distribution of the values of these two variables relating socialization, IOs, and conflict. The number of incoming ties for each state indicates *Democratic IO Socialization*, that is, the number of democratic IOs each state belonged to in 1950 (e.g., Switzerland has 3, while Turkey has 2). The node size is proportional to *Democratic State Socialization* the same year. Some states are potentially open to socialization by multiple democratic IOs, but not *Democratic State Socialization* (such as Pakistan and Sri Lanka); whereas, others are likely to be socialized by democratic states but possess few ties to democratic IOs (e.g., Norway). Centrality measures can thus be used to determine whether it is simply democratic IOs themselves, ties from democratic states in IOs, or both that dampen conflict.

Table 2.1 shows my findings. Model 1 of table 2.1 replicates Pevehouse and Russett (2006) (their Model 1 on page 984); the dependent variable is the onset of a militarized dispute between two states in which at least one fatality occurs.[20] Model 2 substitutes *Democratic IO Socialization* for *Joint Democratic IOs*, demonstrating that states that are subject to more structural pressure from these IOs are less likely to engage in militarized disputes. Model 3 substitutes *Democratic State Socialization*; while states subject to socialization pressures from other

---

[19] Wasserman and Faust 1994, 178.
[20] Following them, I use a logit model and lag the dependent variable by one year.

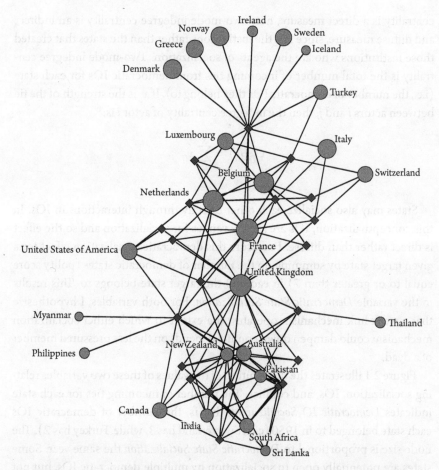

Figure 2.1 Democratic IO Network, 1950. Round nodes are states, diamond nodes are democratic IOs. *Note*: Node size indicates the potential for Democratic State Socialization, while the number of incoming ties from IOs indicates potential for Democratic IO Socialization. Only states that belong to at least one democratic IO are pictured. Graphs plotted using the sna package in R (Butts 2013). Defaults were used (e.g., Fruchterman-Reingold was used for vertex placement) except for employing two-mode plotting.

democratic states are slightly less likely to engage in disputes, the results are not statistically significant. Model 4 is a simultaneous test of Pevehouse and Russett's *Joint Democratic IOs* and *Democratic State Socialization*, while Model 5 tests both socialization pathways simultaneously. Due to the high correlation between *Joint Democratic IOs* and *Democratic IO Socialization* (0.8172), a direct test of which of these two causal pathways dominates is not possible. However, Akaike Information Criterion (AIC) tests indicate that overall Model 1.2 (*Democratic IO Socialization*) is preferred.

Only two out of the three effects—both *Joint Democratic IOs* and *Democratic IO Socialization*, but not *Democratic State Socialization*—are statistically

Table 2.1 **Fatal Militarized Disputes and Centrality, 1885–2000**

	Model				
	1.1	*1.2*	*1.3*	*1.4*	*1.5*
Joint Democratic IOs	−0.0791*			−0.0779*	
	(0.0366)			(0.0369)	
Democratic IO Socialization$_s$		−0.0963*			−0.0942*
		(0.0392)			(0.0397)
Democratic State Socialization$_s$			−0.0001	−0.0001	−0.0001
			(0.0002)	(0.0002)	(0.0002)
Democracy$_s$	−0.0627***	−0.0635***	−0.0731***	−0.0624***	−0.0635***
	(0.0141)	(0.0148)	(0.0155)	(0.0142)	(0.0147)
Dependence$_s$	−52.0107**	−62.3092**	−59.9219**	−53.3720**	−63.7466*
	(18.2724)	(24.1725)	(19.0724)	(18.9104)	(25.0648)
Contiguity	1.6353***	1.6298***	1.6275***	1.6225***	1.6206***
	(0.2635)	(0.2624)	(0.2587)	(0.2593)	(0.2586)
Distance	−0.6933***	−0.7067***	−0.6910***	−0.6898***	−0.7043***
	(0.1036)	(0.1078)	(0.1027)	(0.1045)	(0.1087)
Major Power	1.3484***	1.4919***	1.3183***	1.3442***	1.4891***
	(0.1903)	(0.1922)	(0.1906)	(0.1907)	(0.1926)
Cumulative MIDs	0.1175***	0.1132***	0.1189***	0.1182***	0.1136***
	(0.0145)	(0.0145)	(0.0143)	(0.0144)	(0.0143)
Joint IOs	−0.0013	−0.0004	−0.0023	0.0018	0.0019
	(0.0068)	(0.0067)	(0.0101)	(0.0103)	(0.0104)
N	454,380	448,087	454,380	454,380	448,087
AIC	5,709	5,486	5,709	5,703	5,488

Note: * = p < .05; ** = p < .01; *** = p < .001. I use robust standard errors with clustering on dyads.

significant. Since the first two cannot be run together in a single model, I used the models where each was tested separately to determine substantive significance. In each case, I compared the base rate of fatal militarized disputes (MIDs) to the rate when the variable of concern was raised from the median to the 95% level.[21] *Joint Democratic IOs* decreased the probability of a fatal militarized dispute by 14% in Model 1, while *Democratic IO Socialization* decreased it by 24% in Model 2.

[21] I chose the 95% level due to the asymmetrical distribution of democratic IOs. At median, the number is 0; at 95%, 3 (e.g., Switzerland in figure 2.1); at maximum, 47.

Degree centrality measures thus shed new light on Pevehouse and Russett's theoretical model, providing a better connection between theory and empirics and more precise hypothesis testing: it allows a way to measure two different variants of the socialization mechanism as distinct from the credible commitment or dispute settlement mechanisms. The authors' original results hold up: the general relationship between democratic IOs and conflict is negative and statistically significant. The additional results show that the relationship between conflict and *Democratic IO Socialization* is not only in the same direction, but is more substantively significant and an improved model as well. It is clearly the organizations themselves and not simply exposure to individual states in the organizations that is causing the socialization effect. In other words, democratic IOs are shaping the identities and interests of other states in the network through socialization: the diffuse effects of power matter more than the direct effects.

International Order through Alliance Hierarchies

The diffuse effects of power are not limited to enabling or constraining disputes; the distribution of ties across international institutions can also order international relations and create hierarchies. Many important historical and contemporary international actors, such as empires, dependencies, and protectorates interact with each under hierarchical, rather than anarchical, relationships.[22] In these relationships, one state subordinates some or all of its sovereignty to a dominant state in exchange for social order. David Lake (2007, 2009) develops a groundbreaking theoretical framework for identifying and understanding hierarchies. His theory is that the legitimate authority of the dominant state in a hierarchy relationship rests on the provision of a stable international social order for the subordinate, lessening their need to spend on defense. To test his theory, Lake measures alliance hierarchies from 1950 to 2000 by counting up the number of alliance partners that each subordinate has that are not also partners of the dominant state—in this case, the United States. He divides 1 by this number to produce a measure of hierarchy vis-à-vis the United States, where higher values represent fewer independent (or politically autonomous) alliances and thus greater hierarchy. He uses this measure to show that states subordinate to the United States in international alliance hierarchies are likely to spend less on defense.

Lake's analysis derives hierarchies from states' network positions. His measure of alliance hierarchies is closely related to a network concept (structural

---

[22] The current US basing network is one; see Cooley and Nexon 2013.

similarity) that is better used to determine whether two actors hold similar network positions rather than whether one actor is dominant over the other (Nexon and Wright 2007; MacDonald 2014). Network centrality, and in particular flow betweenness, offers an alternative that provides for generalization of Lake's theory to the entire international system. In Lake's theory, hierarchy is present when the subordinate state has either weak or no independent ties to other states (i.e., when the dominant state acts as a broker between the subordinate state and other states). What makes an empire or colonial dominance successful is the creation of strong ties with subordinate units, while fragmenting or minimizing ties between the subordinates. Yet this powerfully affects both units: the subordinate can decrease its defense efforts and extract concessions from the dominant, while as the broker, the dominant must compensate for this by increasing its efforts.[23] The extent of this brokerage role can be measured through betweenness.

In this case, the most appropriate measure to test this theory is flow betweenness centrality, since it considers all possible paths for brokerage instead of simply the most direct (shortest) ones. Flow betweenness is derived from the capacity of every pathway that connects each actor to every other actor. The maximum flow m_{jk} between two actors j and k is the minimum of (1) the direct flow out of j and into k and (2) the capacity of each path between the intermediate actors, where the capacity of a series of ties is equal to the strength of the weakest tie. If $m_{jk}(n_i)$ is the maximum flow between j and k that passes through node i, then where $j < k$ and $i \neq j \neq k$, then the flow betweenness of node i in a graph of g nodes is:[24]

$$C_F(n_i) = \sum_{j}^{g} \sum_{k}^{g} m_{jk}(n_i)$$

This is standardized to the range $(0, 1)$ by dividing it by the total flow between all actors where actor i is neither a origin nor a destination:

$$C'_F(n_i) = \frac{\sum_{j}^{g} \sum_{k}^{g} m_{jk}(n_i)}{\sum_{jk}^{g} \sum_{k}^{g} m_{jk}}$$

---

[23] Cooley and Nexon 2013.
[24] Freeman, Borgatti, and White 1991, 148.

Figure 2.2 illustrates the advantages of using flow betweenness to measure hierarchy. In 1950, the United States was the sole broker between European and Latin American countries. While structural similarity captures some useful aspects of the alliance network, flow betweenness allows us to distinguish between a state that is only allied to one country (e.g., Mongolia to the USSR) and a state that is allied to many countries other than the United States, whether through the same alliance or not (e.g., Brazil is allied to nineteen other states as well as to the United States). Conventional betweenness centrality does not distinguish between these two cases, since it calculates only the shortest, most direct path. Moreover, it measures the diffuse effects of alliances, since changes in any part of the international alliance structure can potentially alter the flow betweenness of a given state, regardless of how distant.

This brokerage measure can be used to determine whether hierarchical relationships have a diffuse effect throughout the international system, or whether the effect is only direct for states that are specifically subordinate to the most central state in the network, the United States. Lake tests whether states subordinate to the United States will spend less on their defense effort; I extend this hypothesis with respect to all subordinate states, as well as all dominant states. I also test whether there is a separate, stronger effect specific to the lead state; that is, whether subordinate states that are allied to the United States will make even less of a defense effort than states that are in otherwise similar positions that are not allied to the United States. Finally, to distinguish between marginal states that are entirely dependent on one other state (such as Iraq in figure 2.2), which have a flow betweenness of zero, and states that are complete isolates with no alliances, which also have a flow betweenness of zero, I include a dummy variable for having no allies.

Table 2.2 illustrates the results. Model 1 of table 2.2 replicates Lake's (2007) analysis (his Model 3 on page 74), in which the dependent variable is defense spending as a percentage of GDP.[25] Following Lake, I test for a unique US effect in Model 2. These results provide additional support for Lake's findings. Simply being allied to the most powerful state (in this case the United States) decreases the defense effort by about the same as Lake's index of independent alliances. There is something special about being in a subordinate relationship to the United States that affects military spending. It is possible that US alliances are more voluntary than others; for example, the USSR's allies during the Cold War had to be kept in line through coercion. The relationship between the United States and its allies may involve more trust, which can reflect a qualitatively different role relationship that permits even less defense spending than usual.

---

[25] Following Lake, my model is a time-series cross-sectional regression with correction for

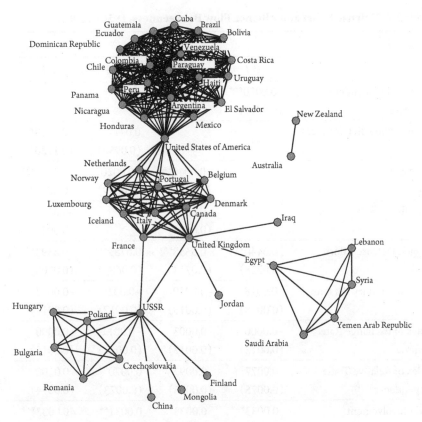

Figure 2.2 International Alliance Network, 1950. *Note:* Only states that have at least one alliance are pictured. Graphs plotted using the sna package in R (Butts 2013).

Alternatively, simply being allied to the most powerful state in the system may have an additional effect.

What about hierarchical relationships with states other than the United States? Model 3 replaces Lake's measure of US alliance hierarchies with the variable *Alliance Flow Betweenness*, measuring the effects of strong and weak brokerage positions throughout the entire network, while also including a dummy for states with no alliances (*No Allies*) at all. If the international alliance system had hierarchical effects but not a US-specific effect, we would expect the estimate for flow betweenness to be positive and significant. While it is indeed in the right direction, in this regression it lacks significance.

If there is a general effect of alliance hierarchy, it may be masked by the US-specific alliance effect seen in Model 2. In Model 4, I control for the US-specific alliance effect, including the variable *US Ally*. I find that flow betweenness is

first-order autoregression and panel corrected standard errors. All independent variables are lagged one year.

Table 2.2 **Defense Effort and Alliance Flow Betweenness, 1950–2000**

	Model			
	2.1	2.2	2.3	2.4
Index of Independent Alliances	−0.0090*** (0.0027)			
Alliance Flow Betweenness			0.0417 (0.0950)	0.2709* (0.1120)
No Allies		−0.0043*** (0.0012)	−0.0020* (0.0009)	−0.0039*** (0.0012)
US Ally		−0.0096*** (0.0027)		−0.0121*** (0.0031)
Lagged Defense Effort	0.6440*** (0.0728)	0.6558*** (0.0714)	0.6789*** (0.0689)	0.6593*** (0.0708)
Index of Military Personnel	−0.0018 (0.0018)	−0.0019 (0.0018)	−0.0029 (0.0017)	−0.0022 (0.0017)
Index of Exchange Rate Regime	−0.0000 (0.0012)	0.0003 (0.0012)	−0.0011 (0.0012)	0.0000 (0.0012)
Index of Relative Trade Dependence	0.0077 (0.0075)	0.0092 (0.0075)	0.0070 (0.0073)	0.0100 (0.0074)
MID Involvement	0.0033*** (0.0010)	0.0033*** (0.0010)	0.0031** (0.0010)	0.0033*** (0.0010)
Number of Other Allies	0.0003** (0.0001)	0.0001 (0.0001)	−0.0001 (0.0001)	0.0000 (0.0001)
Real GDP per Capita	0.0000* (0.0000)	0.0000* (0.0000)	0.0000 (0.0000)	0.0000 (0.0000)
Democracy (Polity2)	−0.0003* (0.0001)	−0.0003* (0.0001)	−0.0004** (0.0002)	−0.0003* (0.0001)
Constant	0.0026 (0.0017)	0.0057** (0.0021)	0.0039 (0.0020)	0.0054** (0.0020)
N	4,522	4,522	4,522	4,522
Pseudo-R^2	.4441	.4649	.4702	.4753

Note: $^* = p < .05$; $^{**} = p < .01$; $^{***} = p < .001$.

positive and significant. States with low centrality (flow betweenness) in the alliance network—those more dependent on others—are likely to spend less on their military than other states, just as Lake predicted. Conversely, states with high centrality (in figure 2.2, the United States, the USSR, the United Kingdom, France, and Egypt) are likely to spend more. States with no alliances at all, however, also make less of a defense effort in Models 2, 3, and 4—this may be an effect of being minor states that are less involved in the international system and are operating outside of the structural power dynamics that constrain both dominant and subordinate.

The magnitude of these effects is substantial. The average alliance flow betweenness centrality for states that possess at least one alliance is 0.0154 (about Libya in 1989). The maximum flow betweenness centrality by a state other than the United States is 0.188 (France in 1963), while for the United States the maximum is 0.476, reached in 1955. Moving from the mean to the minimum (zero) decreases a state's defense efforts by about a half a percent of GDP, while moving from the mean to the French level in 1963 increases it by about 4.7% of GDP; increasing it to the maximum US level leads to an increase of 12.5% of GDP. AIC tests are unavailable in Stata for the class of models used in this estimation, but pseudo-R^2 scores indicate an improved model fit across my three models.

These centrality measures thus build upon Lake's important findings by making better connections between theory and empirics, improving model fit, and broadening the scope of his theory by extending it to include diffuse effects across the entire international system as well as direct effects. States with higher flow betweenness centrality are likely to spend more on their military than other states, while states with low flow betweenness spend less. But there is something special about the US alliance hierarchy, which provides bigger incentives for subordinates to spend less on defense. This may be a hegemonic effect rather than a US-specific effect, but during the time period studied, these are indistinguishable.

Conclusion

A network approach to measuring the influence of institutions has much to offer the study of transnational governance and security. Theoretically, it allows for an expanded notion of power that takes into account the diffuse effects of institutional networks as well as the direct ones. Empirically, centrality measures can offer scholars a way to analyze power effects that come from both diffuse and direct structural constraints placed on agents by their network positions rather than their possession of resources. Network conceptualizations and measurements of these processes allow for better connections between theory and empirics, more precise hypothesis testing, broadened scope, and improved models.

As a small but growing number of scholars are beginning to realize, a centrality approach is fundamentally changing the way the core of political behavior in international relations can be conceptualized and analyzed, from conflict to markets to norm diffusion. I have demonstrated this through extensions of research on two different structural effects by international institutions: socialization to different interests and identities by democratic international organizations and ordering the international system through hierarchies of alliances. A centrality approach shows that socialization by democratic IOs is more important than dispute resolution mechanisms in preventing conflict and that ordering through hierarchical structures occurs throughout the entire international alliance system. Here, it is a complement rather than a wholesale replacement for existing theoretical notions and measures; centrality alone cannot account for the unique role of the United States in the international system.

Although my analysis here is limited to diffuse power and centrality measures, network analysis offers a wide array of theoretical concepts and complementary structural measures of positions within networks. The particular measure here, centrality, can inform debates not only on politics but also on any other issues that involve network ties. Moreover, network methodologies can account for structures of complex interdependence. The results here are inherently preliminary in that they only represent a partial inclusion of network methodologies; since even long-standing results like the democratic peace have already been demonstrated to be an artifact of network structures,[26] probably no dyadic result is safe until tested using the full range of network tools.

Network analysis remains underused and underappreciated, although a growing community of scholars is taking up network tools and applying them to the study of politics, particularly in International Relations. The potential for theoretical and empirical innovation for the field, however, is vast. Network analysis offers new insights into the nature of power politics as a set of relations among actors at all levels involved in relationships of all kinds, while network methodologies in general, and centrality concepts in particular, offer new ways to measure and test long-standing concepts and theories that have yet to be fully explored.

[26] Both latent network (Ward, Siverson, and Cao 2007) and TERGM (Cranmer and Desmarais 2011) approaches have found joint democracy to be insignificant.

PART I

NETWORKING STRATEGIES AND GOVERNANCE ATTEMPTS

3

Network Relations and Human Security Norm Development

Agenda-Setting and Agenda-Vetting around Collateral Damage Control

CHARLI CARPENTER

The crucial role of transnational advocacy networks in human security norm development has long been recognized.[1] But of all the new ideas out there, how do advocacy networks select which norms to promote? The standard answers to this question overemphasize factors exogenous to the structure of advocacy networks themselves: actors in advocacy networks presumably select issues either based on the organizational interests of specific agents or based on factors external to and beyond the control of the activist networks (the intrinsic nature of issues, of targets of influence, or of the broader political environment); or both. Much less attention has been paid to how the structural relations among organizations within these networks themselves enable or foreclose advocacy around specific issues, framed in specific ways, at specific points in history.

In this chapter, I first recast the case literature on advocacy campaigns to describe the ways in which network structure shapes the content and success of networking by advocates of new issues. Network structure matters in two ways: (1) it shapes the relative influence of organizations over the network agenda; (2) it shapes the preferences of advocacy elites in those organizations with the most power to decide. In short, network structure (through its impact on which organizations hold sway and the preferences of elites in those organizations) shapes the character of governance (whether an issue is taken up or not).

[1] I am grateful to Jim Vreeland, Rebecca Gibbons, Deborah Avant, Oliver Westerwinter, Alex Montgomery, and all the participants in the New Network Politics ISA Workshop for feedback on this chapter. All remaining errors are obviously mine alone.

I then illustrate how these dynamics work through a case study of a new norm campaign: the campaign to amend civilians harmed in lawful military operations.[2] The case of the Making Amends Campaign shows how the success of norm entrepreneurs hinges on their ability to attract allies from powerful network "hubs" in the issue area most closely associated with the concept they are advocating; and how "gatekeepers'" willingness to adopt new issues onto their agenda is also mediated by gatekeepers' perceptions of relational ties—between actors, between issues, and between issue areas.

Network Ties and Issue Selection within Advocacy Domains

Numerous studies of international norm creation credit the activities of transnational advocacy networks in identifying human security problems, providing information to states, and reconstituting their interests through persuasion and shaming to develop new normative standards (Price 1998; Tannenwald 2007). Yet the understanding of networks in this literature has led to an impoverished view of how norm creation within networks occurs and thus how to explain why advocates mobilize around some problems and not others.

As Hafner-Burton and her colleagues have argued, Transnational Advocacy Network (TAN) literature has long appropriated the metaphor of the "network" as a way to describe the non-state political sector, yet has rarely examined how structural relationships within networks shape political outcomes (Hafner-Burton, Kahler, and Montgomery 2009; Kahler 2009). For example, in their landmark study of transnational advocacy networks, Margaret Keck and Kathryn Sikkink defined them as "those relevant actors working internationally on an issue, bound together by shared values, a common discourse, and dense exchanges of information and services . . . networks are forms of organization characterized by voluntary, reciprocal, and horizontal patterns of communication and exchange . . . their goal is to change the behavior of states and of international organizations" (1998, 2, 8).

---

[2] The case study draws heavily on a chapter in my book *Lost Causes: Agenda-Setting and Agenda-Vetting in Global Issue Networks*. It is based on five years of archival research, iterated interviews, and informal conversations with staff persons associated with the key norm entrepreneur, the Campaign for Innocent Civilians in Conflict (CIVIC). It also draws on six focus groups in 2009 and thirty interviews with human security elites familiar with CIVIC's work over the same period. I also conducted a further set of dialogues with CIVIC staff persons regarding the findings to polish and fact-check the analysis.

Much of the earlier literature on advocacy networks uncritically adopted this view: early TAN literature often described networks as "actors" rather than incorporating a sociological understanding of networks as structures composed of nodes connected by social ties of different types and strengths. "Networking" was seen as a generic verb to describe the various activities of global civil society, and "networks" used as a metaphor to distinguish such activity from the hierarchical leadership associated with states, although hierarchical state and imperial structures are also networks in the sociological sense, and the modern state is disaggregating into transnational networks of its component parts.[3]

Such analyses fail to theorize how advocacy network structures impact outcomes and "mask power relations within networks." But this view has also caused scholars to under-theorize (or incompletely theorize) substantively important questions about the role of advocacy networks—such as the origins of normative ideas within them. Much of the advocacy networks literature has focused on explaining advocates' success vis-à-vis states; much less attention has been paid to the politics by which networks select or form around certain global policy problems and not others. Those studies that have looked at issue selection have tended to focus on factors exogenous to network structures themselves. For example, some scholars have focused on the importance of issue entrepreneurs in constructing social conditions as political problems and selling these new understandings to governments or NGO gatekeepers through strategic framing processes (Finnemore 1996b; Bob 2005). Others have focused on the nature of issues themselves, arguing that some are more or less amenable to advocacy and that activists choose issues where they believe they can succeed (Keck and Sikkink 1998; Carpenter 2005). Conversely, significant attention has been paid to the wider political opportunity structure in which activists operate: if the likelihood of success structures activists' efforts, then activist bets about the extant conditions for that success may influence issue selection as well as campaign strategy (Joachim 2007). All of these arguments, however, locate the source of variation in issue creation in the attributes of actors or issues, or the wider environment in which advocates operate. Little attention has been given to how relations among activist organizations themselves affect the creation and survival of issues.

Newer studies call for a closer examination of the effects that network structures have on the actors and issues themselves in transnational networks; and in this chapter I apply this perspective to an analysis of how networks select issues (Goddard 2009b; Carpenter 2010). In opening up the black box of networks,

---

[3] Keck and Sikkink's seminal work on advocacy networks fits this description. On empires as networks, see Nexon 2009b. On intergovernmental networks, see Slaughter 2004; and Eilstrup-Sangiovanni, this volume.

advocacy networks are not simply the loci of people power vis-à-vis hierarchical states (Hafner-Burton, Kahler, and Montgomery 2009, 561). Rather, as highlighted in the introduction to this volume, they are sociopolitical structures with their own kinds of hierarchies, power relations, and governing mechanisms (Avant and Westerwinter, this volume). And these network structures impact the nature of the political agendas they espouse.

I advance two explanatory claims regarding the effects of network structure on issue selection specifically—one causal, one constitutive. First, the structure of advocacy networks confers greater influence on some organizations than on others, and the advocacy network agenda in a given issue area reflects the organizational choices made by these advocacy "super-powers" due to contagion effects. Second, beliefs about intra-networks relationships help constitute these advocacy "superpowers'" understanding of their own preferences when it comes to selecting or rejecting specific candidate issues. I explain each of these briefly below, before illustrating them through the case of the Making Amends Campaign.

Causal Effects: "Network Hubs" as Veto Players in Issue Construction

Keck and Sikkink's landmark study of advocacy networks argued that network density was important to activist success, but asserted that density was a function of quality as well as quantity: "access to an ability to disseminate information, credibility with targets, ability to speak to and for other social networks" (Kech and Sikkink 1998, 29). In network analytical terms, this claim is imprecise, but the authors are alluding to an important insight: nodes in networks vary in these crucial attributes for advocacy success, and networks around specific issues vary in the extent to which they attract nodes with these attributes. Issue networks that include nodes with the characteristics listed above are likelier to become politically salient. Therefore, the readiness of certain organizations to join emerging issue networks—to "adopt" emerging issues—is an important reason why some concerns become politically salient in specific issue areas and others do not.

Indeed, several later studies have found that the organizational agenda of the most powerful actors in an actor network around an issue area have an important impact on the issue agenda for that issue area, suggesting that any new issue being "formatted" to that issue area requires the legitimation of the most powerful nodes. In the context of the human rights network, Clifford Bob posits that such organizations function as network "gatekeepers," legitimizing certain new ideas and not others. He defines human rights gatekeepers as "entities at the core of the human rights movement, whose support for a claim can boost it substantially . . . typically these are the organizations with the largest budgets, best staff, and greatest credibility in the human rights movement" (Bob 2008, 6). According to Bob, when such organizations "adopt" or embrace a new issue as an advocacy priority, "support for a claim is perceived by activists and governments to legitimize it substantially within that issue area" (Bob 2008, 6).[4] Although Bob stresses material resources, other studies show it is actually relational position within networks that confers this influence (Brewington, Murdie, and Davis 2009; Wong 2009; Carpenter 2011). In short, the more central organizations are to an advocacy network, the more influence they have over its agenda.

Two particular measures of centrality are crucial to the power of central organizations in advocacy networks. First, connectedness is a measure of how prominent an organization is within a network, measured in the number of organizations who establish or attempt to establish links with that node.[5] "A network node with a high in- degree centrality (strong links from many other nodes) may possess social power, easily accessing resources and information from other nodes because of its central position" (Hafner-Burton, Kahler, and Montgomery 2009, 19). This centrality translates into influence over the agenda because actors within and outside the network look to the organization agenda of these players as an indicator of the network agenda. As Wendy Wong writes, "centrality allow[s] for certain nodes to control the flow of information and distribute information within the network" (2008, 32).[6]

Organizations can also exercise disproportionate influence on issue emergence within the network as a function of their between-ness. A node's betweenness is high when it "possesses exclusive ties to otherwise marginalized or weakly connected nodes or groups of nodes . . . social capital can be turned into social power by a node that bridges structural holes in the network" (Hafner-Burton, Kahler, and Montgomery 2009, 21).[7] But since advocacy networks are networks

---

[4] This can include committing resources to advocacy on an issue, as when Amnesty International undertakes a fact-finding study; but it can also be as simple and symbolic as referencing the issue on its website or in its broader advocacy materials, or lending its name to a coalition around the issues.

[5] In network theory, a link can be anything: an interaction, a joint membership, a hyperlink, or a citation. In the human security network, I measured network centrality through hyperlinks and through citations in survey data. The organizations receiving the most hyperlinks on their websites from the members of the network, and those most often mentioned when survey respondents were asked to list "organizations that come to mind when you think of human security" correspond to the same central players in the human security network.

[6] In this volume, Bower and Westerwinter also emphasize the informational advantages central actors derive from their positions and how these lead to disproportionate influence over governance agendas and outcomes.

[7] For example, Dan Nexon's work on empires suggests that much of their power was derived by positioning themselves as exclusive access points between nodes on the periphery. Stacie Goddard

both of actors and of issues, the kind of between-ness centrality that matters in constituting network gatekeepers is of two varieties. First, some organizations possess *relatively greater ties to global policy stakeholders*, including governments or access to international forums. This makes these organizations themselves targets of influence for entrepreneurs who would like to access such stakeholders (Brewington, Murdie, and Davis 2009).[8] Second, organizations may occupy an ideational space at the *interstices of networks of meaning* (Avant, Cooley and Nexon, this volume).[9] Global civil society is composed of synergistic but distinct issue networks: human rights, development, conflict prevention, arms control, and the environment. But since the many effective campaigns often cut across these thematic divides, organizations whose work spans several issue clusters are valued resources for issue entrepreneurs aiming to frame their issue in such a way as to attract a broad coalition. Such organizations play a brokerage role in networks.[10]

In short, when it comes to agenda-setting, all nodes in advocacy networks are not equal: whether the most powerful nodes are governments, NGOs, UN agencies, or think tanks, their organizational agenda will carry disproportionate weight within the broader issue network or networks in which they are embedded. Once these advocacy "superpowers" have adopted an issue, it is not only likelier to result in policy interventions from states, but it is likelier to proliferate within advocacy networks, thereby creating the "classroom" environment for socializing states so crucial to new norm development (Price 1998). By extension, the choice by network "hubs" not to adopt new issues has an equally dampening effect on some advocacy claims (Bob 2008; Carpenter 2011).

postulates that nodes with a high degree of "between-ness" are able to serve as "brokers" by "maintaining ties with actors who would otherwise remain unconnected." See Goddard 2009b.

[8] In the human rights network, for example, Brewington, Davis, and Murdie found that more central organizations engage in the bulk of all international advocacy activities with governments; for players on the margins of the network, the dominant strategy is to attempt to get the attention of the network hubs in order to exploit their brokerage role vis-à-vis governments.

[9] Drawing on Tilly, Nexon argues that collective mobilization is easiest in networks characterized not only by high density (in Tilly's words, "netness") but also by high levels of categorical homogeneity ("catness"). Network hubs and brokers encourage the proliferation of issues through contagion, thus enhancing the "netness" of issues. But as brokers, they also help create issue frames that transcend multiple categorical identities within advocacy clusters, increasing an issue's "catness" as well. See Nexon 2009b.

[10] For example, Human Rights Watch's position at the intersection of the human rights and humanitarian law issue clusters has given it an influence over not only human rights agenda-setting but also arms control campaigns, and it has played an important role in reframing such issues from security to human rights, though its overall centrality is lower than either Amnesty International or the International Committee of the Red Cross in the human security network. Similarly, the World Food Program is closely connected to both the humanitarian affairs and development clusters in the human security area. See Carpenter et al. 2014.

Constitutive Effects: The Social Construction
of Gatekeeper Preferences

It therefore follows that to understand issue selection within networks, one must understand the dialectic between norm entrepreneurs and network hubs, and in particular how "hub" organizations choose among competing claims. I argue that *perceptions of network structures* by practitioners embedded in hubs are also crucial in this decision-making process: these perceptions of ties between actors and issues within the network exert constitutive effects on actor understandings of their interests in adopting or rejecting a new normative claim (Avant, this volume). Three kinds of ties matter: ties among issues, ties among actors, and ties among issue areas.

First, one set of questions practitioners ask themselves is about the nature of the relationship between the emerging issue and their existing issue agenda. As Bob's notion of "substantive matching" predicts, network actors think of issue attributes in relational terms. Advocacy space and advocacy resources are viewed as finite, and participants described a zero-sum relationship between new issues and existing issues. Sometimes issues are perceived as being in competition with one another; sometimes they are seen as conflicting entirely. A new issue must be different enough from the current issue agenda to merit inclusion but also similar enough not to conflict with or undermine an organization's existing issue pool.

Second, ties among organizations matter. First, practitioners often consider their organization's existing coalitions when determining whether or not to sign onto a new campaign, and they avoid adopting issues that would create controversies or compromise alliances with partner organizations. So the nature of those ties can be significant. Moreover, in making guesses about the relationship between a candidate issue and its suitability for advocacy within the network, hubs do not simply consider the overall "fit" of the issue in their eyes and the eyes of their partners but also the composition and density of organizational ties to that issue. It is not necessarily true that denser networks around an issue lead to greater likelihood of issue adoption by hubs: this effect hits a tipping point after a short initial bout of issue proliferation, as potential adopters try to gauge whether an issue is still at an early enough stage that they can be seen to be making a significant contribution rather than simply jumping on the bandwagon.

Finally, perceptions of ties between issue areas matter. The issue agenda within and across organizations itself has a network structure, with some issues closely related to one another and some barely connected at all. An issue's perceived relationship to the existing issue area helps shape adopters' judgments about whether it is a "fit" for them relative to some other organization (Carpenter 2011).[11] Categorical heterogeneity within networks also leads to

---

[11] Depleted uranium munitions, for example, have long been ignored by hubs in the weapons

buck-passing. The disaggregation of the human security network into subnet-works, and increasingly cross-cutting nature of issues allows some issues to fall between the cracks. This dynamic arises from the compartmentalization of issue turf within the network. In short there may be a sense of which organization, or which type of organization, an issue "belongs" to, and other organizations may not pick up an issue if they feel it has a better "home" elsewhere (Praelle 2003).[12]

In the rest of the chapter, I demonstrate how these dynamics played out in the gradual and tentative emergence of a new human security claim: that warring parties should provide recognition and compensation to collateral damage victims. I trace the origins of this idea and the networks of actors and issues out of which it emerged. I then document norm entrepreneurs' difficulty in pitching the idea to hubs in the human security network. Finally I show how they were able to shift gatekeepers' preferences through "network power-building": by reconstituting their own network ties, they changed gatekeepers' understandings of the issue.

Case Study: The Making Amends Campaign

War always weighs hard on civilians (Grimsley and Rogers 2008; Slim 2010) and most of the harms they experience are perfectly legal—so long as governments inflict them by accident, instead of deliberately; so long as the harms are incidental, rather than direct (Chuter 2003). Although governments are required under international humanitarian law not to target civilians as such, accidental harm to civilians is considered a legitimate and inevitable aspect of war (Byers 2005; Gross 2010). Therefore, while states are sometimes required to pay reparations for war crimes, no international law requires governments to recognize or compensate the families of civilians killed or maimed in legitimate combat operations: those unfortunate enough to suffer such calamities are not victims of war crimes, merely "collateral damage" (Carpenter 2010).

In 2003, an NGO based in Washington, DC, began advocating for states to recognize and compensate war's unintentional civilian victims.[13] Now a full-fledged movement, the Campaign for Innocent Victims in Conflict (CIVIC) presses all parties in conflict to "establish a new standard of behavior by providing recognition

and arms control area, primarily because the issue is strongly associated in their minds with the antinuclear and environmental lobby.

[12] An issue can also end up "belonging" to a particular venue as a result of norm entrepreneurs' preferences, foreclosing alternative frames later on.

[13] For a more detailed discussion of this case, see Carpenter 2014.

and help to civilians harmed by their bombs and bullets."[14] According to campaign director Golzar Kheiltash: "Civilian harm has long been dismissed as collateral damage: to some extent it's legally permissible and viewed by warring parties as an acceptable cost of war. The concept we pursue is that civilian victims deserve amends, even when warring parties haven't violated their legal obligations."[15]

The novelty of the issue as originally defined by CIVIC may at first not be obvious, as civilian war victims, whether or not intentionally targeted, already draw a significant amount of policy attention from the UN system, humanitarian NGOs, and governments (Chaulia 2011). Hundreds of NGOs and international organizations, funded by donations from individuals, foundations, or government aid agencies, flock to the world's conflict zones delivering shelter, food, and medicine to displaced and traumatized war victims (Cooley and Ron 2002). Others work in post-conflict reconstruction, rebuilding houses, reintegrating refugees, and training former combatants for civilian jobs (Weiss and Collins 2000). But since the system is based on voluntary donations, resources for humanitarian aid and peace-building work tends to be transitory, flowing to the countries most in the media spotlight at any given time, and moving on when the attention of donors shifts. And since needs often vastly outweigh funding, aid agencies often engage in "humanitarian triage," and spend much of their time and resources begging governments for funding (Minear and Smillie 2004).

The idea proposed by CIVIC represents a significant, if subtle, departure from this existing system.[16] By making compensation for deaths and maimings an expectation of warring parties, rather than a chance humanitarian act by donors and NGOs, they aimed to turn what was currently a charity act into a right owed to victims' families by governments. They also sought a linkage between belligerent militaries and the civilians affected by those militaries' operations—whereas previously the civilian humanitarian sector was a mechanism by which resources were transferred to besieged civilians.[17] Third, they

---

[14] Campaign for Innocent Victims in Conflict Website, http://www.civicworldwide.org/about-us/our-history. It should be noted that the Making Amends Campaign is only one component of CIVIC's work, which includes documenting civilian harm, policy advocacy, and military training.

[15] Phone interview, Golzar Kheiltash, February 17, 2012.

[16] Yael Ronen provides a detailed overview about how the concept of liability for incidental harms fits conceptually into existing legal regimes. See Ronen 2008.

[17] In other words, CIVIC's strategy was to reconstitute the nature of network ties between civilians, warring parties, and humanitarian organizations. Under the conventional humanitarian system, Government A might send Military A to carry out operations causing civilian harm in the territory of Government B. Government A might simultaneously provide funding to UN agencies and humanitarian organizations to carry out independent, impartial, and neutral civilian relief activities in the territory of Government B, though there is no obligation under international law for it to do so. What CIVIC proposed was that Government A feel socially obligated to have Military A directly make amends to civilians in Government B, irrespective of and in addition to the support Government A might also provide to the civilian humanitarian sector.

openly challenged what many commentators had already identified as a serious gap in the laws of war—the indifference to incidental harms inflicted on civilians.[18] By contrast, CIVIC emphasized the symbolic and moral significance of recognizing and responding to all civilian victims as an expression of human dignity and respect.

Many human security experts I interviewed as part of this project expressed an intuitive sense that this was a fantastic idea. And CIVIC was successful at lobbying both governments and military officials to make specific policy changes, including condolence payments. Yet the initial response to CIVIC's campaign for a new normative standard was far from uniformly positive within the human security network. While CIVIC enjoyed some vital early support from matchmaker NGOs, and a relatively privileged position of access within the human rights and humanitarian networks due to the renown of its founder, Marla Ruzicka, many human security gatekeepers were initially skeptical of the idea that the existing rules of war were inadequate or that norm development in this direction would have a positive effect on civilian populations. CIVIC was successful only after this changed, and those changes, I argue, were directly related to a reconstitution of CIVIC's structural position in networks of issues, issue clusters, and organizations.

In the next two sections I elaborate on these dynamics to illustrate the overall theoretical argument: (1) that recognition by network hubs exerts a powerful causal effect on the survival and emergence of new norms within networks; and (2) that perceptions of network structure shape the preferences of human security elites in hub organizations themselves.

Causal Effects: The Network Power of Global Advocacy Hubs

The first step in social change is always politicization of a previously accepted social condition, and literature on global norm development has often stressed the role of norm entrepreneurs. But political entrepreneurship alone is not enough to assure successful human security norm-building. While specific policy changes can result from the efforts of a single entrepreneur, the dissemination of wider intersubjective understandings about those policies through global network requires the engagement of network hubs. The case of CIVIC illustrates this distinction and the causal importance of gatekeeper adoption on the diffusion of normative understandings, as distinct from practices, through the human security network.

---

[18] This indifference is grounded in the just war notion of "double effect." See Walzer 2006.

The Limits of Political Entrepreneurship

The movement to increase state accountability for assisting civilians affected by legitimate military operations began with Marla Ruzicka, a 25-year-old grassroots activist from San Francisco originally working with Global Exchange. After the attacks of 9/11, Global Exchange geared up for a mission to monitor and evaluate the civilian costs of the quickly looming war in Afghanistan.

Young Ruzicka found herself on the ground in Peshawar interviewing refugees and connecting with the ex-patriate journalist and aid worker community. Humanitarian and human rights organizations were in the field to assist, monitor, and protect. But "protection" by these organizations consisted primarily of reminding belligerents of their obligations under the rules of war; "assistance" was doled out to needy civilians as a kind of charity, and demand was always greater than supply. Inspired by first-person testimonials of lost homes, limbs, and family members, Ruzicka began collecting data on civilian losses one family at a time and approaching the guards at the US Embassy, often with colorful demonstrations staged to be captured by foreign journalists, demanding restitution for civilian victims as a form of justice.[19] She also began building an informal network in Afghanistan with human rights and humanitarian organizations on the ground there, drawing the foreign aid community into her social circle through wild nightly parties in Kabul. Through these interactions, Ruzicka developed the idea of starting her own organization to lobby for war victims, an idea that came to fruition on a trip home in spring 2002 (Abrahamson 2006).

Ruzicka landed in Washington, DC, in July on her way back to Afghanistan from San Francisco, determined to secure a compensation fund from the US government. Although she possessed the charisma and passion characteristic of most successful political entrepreneurs, Ruzicka also lacked a few qualities necessary for global advocacy: a sense of professionalism, procedural skills, and access to funding. She compensated with her intuitive ability to attract well-connected allies.[20] Examples included Human Rights Watch's legal research director Sam Zia-Zarifi, who encouraged her to assume the best of military

---

[19] According to Abrahamson, "On February 13, Marla led a group of these victims in a demonstration outside the US Embassy. . . . Marla demanded that the United States create a twenty-million dollar fund to compensate civilian war victims. . . . She had recruited much of Kabul's international press corps to attend the show. [One] later said that was the moment when Marla's real fame began" (2006, 105–106). By April 2002, Ruzicka was referred to by *Newsweek* as "arguably the best-known foreign figure in Kabul" (Abrahamson 2006, 118).

[20] Later Peter Bergen described what he called "the Marla treatment": "Phase one: 'Everyone says you're great!' Phase two: 'You're great. In fact, you're the most amazing person on this Earth.' Phase three: 'Let me tell you about my work.' Phase four: 'How can you help?'" Quoted in Abrahamson 2006, 252.

personnel and learn to speak their language rather than scream at them; CNN
terrorism expert Peter Bergen, who helped her network throughout the belt-
way; and friendships in the US Congress cultivated through Senator Leahy's
office, where she had been directed to Tim Reiser by Bobby Mueller (a former
land-mine campaigner) for coaching in how to frame the issue. By 2003 when
she landed in Iraq, "everyone noticed the shift in her from radical activist to
human rights professional" (Abrahamson 2006, 176).

In addition to skill-building, Ruzicka was also able to convert these connec-
tions into funding. After filing 501(c) paperwork establishing the Campaign for
Innocent Victims of Conflict, the Open Society Institute and Ford Foundation,
as well as private donors, offered her new organization financial support
(Abrahamson 2006, 190, 198, 236). By 2005, Ruzicka had helped Global
Exchange complete the first testimonial account of civilian harm in Afghanistan.
Moreover, with Tim Reiser's help she had convinced the US Congress to
pass a law to provide assistance to civilians in Iraq harmed incidentally by US
weapons.[21] Working family by family in Iraq, Ruzicka identified individuals in
need of medical attention or solace, assisted them in completing the required
forms to benefit from this new law and existing condolence payment programs
(Abrahamson 2006, 202–203).

CIVIC's nonprofit status was still pending on April 16, 2005, when Marla
Ruzicka was killed alongside her country director Faiz Ali Salim in a suicide
attack. The tragedy galvanized her powerful network around her legacy. Members
of the CIVIC board determined that her dream would live on through her organization. The Board of Directors recruited a new executive directorship in early
fall 2005, hiring Sarah Holewinski and Marla Keenan to run the organization.
By late 2007, CIVIC had an office space in downtown Washington, DC, a new
website, a small staff, and a thriving internship program. It also had a reconsti-
tuted set of goals, targets of influence, and strategies—one which continued to
shift over time through interactions with government and advocacy gatekeepers.

From Policy to Norm Entrepreneurship: Network Hubs
as Advocacy Targets and Gatekeepers

While Ruzicka was an issue entrepreneur, she was not technically speaking a
global norm entrepreneur. Her objective was to name a problem and directly help
the suffering, not to create new international moral understandings. Her suc-
cessors had farther reaching goals, shaped by their personal convictions, their

[21] See "Backgrounder: The Marla Ruzicka Iraqi War Victims Fund." Available at http://www.civ-
icworldwide.org/storage/civicdev/marlafund_backgrounder.pdf.

professional trajectories, and their evolving perception of the constraints and political opportunities in which they operated.

Under Holewinski and Keenan, three significant changes took place in CIVIC's organizational behavior between 2007 and 2011. First, CIVIC's goals shifted during its early years. For all her revolutionary intensity, Ruzicka's aims had been modest in relative terms: to secure resources from a single warring government and get them into the hands of certain needy civilians. After her death, CIVIC's agenda quickly broadened as it became clear that this problem was bigger than the United States and bigger than any specific conflict. While CIVIC continued to catalogue victim testimonials and secure condolence payments for specific civilians through its connections with the military,[22] its work increasingly took on a third track as well. Between 2005 and 2007, the content on the website expanded from "service delivery" and "voice for victims" to include "change the rules."[23] By March 2008, the website highlighted the absence of responsibility for lawful civilian harms in the laws of war, calling for new international standards.[24] This new goal of "changing the rules" was also expressed through CIVIC's staff recruitment and outreach. The organization hired Jessi Schimmel straight out of University of Denver's Korbel School and put her to work researching global norm development and providing recommendations to the CIVIC leadership. As Holewinski put it at the time: "We believe this should be a global norm and value, but when you look at international law nothing there states 'collateral damage' victims should be recognized and helped. And that's when we started to say, this could be the next place for international law to go."[25]

The shift in goals entailed a series of shifts in CIVIC's *targets of influence*: from the US government to the global community of states and the structure of international law broadly. Ruzicka's target had consistently been the United States, and she had worked through US policy networks in both Washington and the expatriate communities in US zones of occupation. But in learning how to

---

[22] A significant portion of Holewinski and Keenan's time remained focused on traveling to war zones to collect video interviews with civilians; or to liaise with generals and lawyers in NATO countries about the concept of amends.

[23] The site read: "[We] believe that no warring party should walk away from the harm it has caused ordinary people caught up in fighting, no matter how unintentional." See http://www.civic-worldwide.org/index.php?option=com_content&task=view&id=162&Itemid=99.

[24] The new language read: "In the past century, we've seen marked improvements in how we treat each other . . . through the Geneva Conventions and treaties banning weapons like landmines, nations have promised to protect civilians when they go to war. But no treaty, custom or norm requires nations to help those they fail to protect. No matter how many civilians are killed in a war, no matter how many are left homeless, no matter how much property is destroyed, those who do the damage have no legal duty to help. It's time for a change." CIVIC web archive, on file with author.

[25] Personal interview, Sarah Holewinski, February 2008.

"message" the notion of "help where you've harmed" to the US government, Holewinski and Keenan began taking the message to other governments as well: "We began to question why, if the US is making the effort to help civilians it has harmed, other countries shouldn't be doing so as well?"[26] Indeed, CIVIC was documenting civilian harm in many conflicts, and in each case the absence of formal accountability by belligerents left needy civilians without recognition or assistance (Tracy 2007, 16–19).[27]

But a key early question was what "changing the rules" actually meant in practice: Should CIVIC call for updates to the laws of war, work toward a customary law standard, or adopt a soft law approach? Unlike land-mine campaigners and those who sought to end child soldiering, CIVIC decided early on not to propose a new treaty or formal amendment to existing humanitarian law, nor did they at first attempt to spread this sensibility through global civil society. Rather, they expected that a new standard of conduct would emerge organically as more and more states began to normalize condolence payments through their defense ministries. In 2007, CIVIC's key strategy was to change and improve state practice one warring party at a time.

The belief that changed practice could lead to normative change was grounded in the notion of customary international law: law that is based on state behavior rather than codified in treaties (Byers 1999). It also stemmed from the observation of CIVIC's staff that numerous "norms"—such as the Responsibility to Protect—get codified in UN resolutions but poorly implemented. By contrast: "We wanted our norm to be built from the ground up. We were trying to knit together instances of amends into a larger momentum."[28]

For a tiny NGO, CIVIC was wildly successful at convincing warring governments to establish condolence payments.[29] But over time it became clear that

---

[26] When I first spoke with Holewinski in spring 2008, she had just returned from a trip to Europe enthused by the Netherlands' success in convincing NATO countries to establish a Post-Operations Humanitarian Relief Fund: the US condolence payment program had not until then been replicated by other IS-AF countries, leaving the amends civilians could expect in Afghanistan contingent on which troops happened to shoot them: those countries with condolence programs would give payments, but some did not have any. "That's morally wrong. Compensation should be given uniformly; everyone deserves some sort of recognition and aid. So I said, 'you guys have to get on board with this, the US does it, you can do it.' The NATO Secretary General Chief of Staff has been a great supporter of this and now we're pitching it to every single NATO country."

[27] Similarly, in summer of that year CIVIC staff spent weeks in Israel and Lebanon creating videos of civilians harmed in the 2006 war.

[28] Holewinski, email correspondence, March 2012.

[29] CIVIC convinced NATO to adopt its first compensation policy for Afghan war victims, and numerous NATO countries in Afghanistan established programs as well; the US Congress created three aid programs to help civilians harmed by US combat operations in Iraq, Afghanistan, and Pakistan; the African Union adopted a civilian harm policy for Somalia that included the principle of

these programs alone did not necessarily change governments' perceptions about their moral responsibilities: changed practices did not necessarily change expectations unless the meanings of those practices were changed as well. The US condolence payment program was often held up by CIVIC as an example of this emerging practice when encouraging other governments to follow suit. But Holewinski told me in 2008, "I don't think any of these countries want to think of themselves as setting a precedent."

CIVIC staff continued to lobby governments for concrete policy shifts. But between 2008 and 2009, CIVIC expanded its repertoire of contention to include a concerted effort to change global discourse as well, or how transnational actors talk and think about the laws of war. They still were not hoping for a treaty. But they wanted to embed the language of "making amends" widely in human rights and humanitarian discourse, changing the normative environment in which government diplomats would think about civilians and keeping unintended victims on the advocacy agenda.

This involved another shift in the targets of influence to emphasize global civil society organizations and multilateral institutions: in short, CIVIC recognized the significance of obtaining symbolic support from global advocacy gatekeepers. Between 2008 and 2011, CIVIC actively targeted leading development, human rights, humanitarian law, and transitional justice NGOs, UN bodies, and government "champions" to join their coalition. A separate website was established to promote the concept of "making amends." CIVIC hired a new staff person in summer 2009 to garner support for the idea in UN circles.

Agenda-Vetting, Issue Adoption, and Norm Development: The Causal Role of Hubs

Early on, CIVIC had enjoyed support from several powerful allies, providing the organization several natural advantages as a political entrepreneur. The Open Society Institute had provided an infusion of funding early on. And CIVIC had the ear and sympathetic support of the Washington branch of one key human rights organization, Human Rights Watch. Holewinski told me unequivocally in 2008, "We couldn't have done this without Human Rights Watch."

But this support by these particular organizations fell short of the sort of global issue adoption described by Clifford Bob in certain important ways. First, because Ruzicka had been focused on US foreign policy her network focused on Washington. ConnectUS, Democracy in Action, Citizens for Global Solutions,

---

amends; the Pakistan Interior Minister pledge a new program for war victims. Yet few admitted this was a moral requirement; most saw it as a pragmatic move at their own discretion.

even the Washington chapter of Human Rights Watch were all focused on changing US foreign policy, not spreading thematic moral understandings at the global level. Second, the type of support given by these organizations is closer to what Bob describes as "match-making" rather than "issue adoption." Groups did not adopt the issue of "making amends" so much as they adopted CIVIC. In Ruzicka's day this meant providing office space, helping the organization stay afloat at key junctures, providing contacts and introductions, and training her in advocacy skills like op-ed and grant-writing. Under Holewinski and Kennan, support from human security groups included brainstorming on advocacy strategy and information-sharing on the history of specific conflict zones and data-gathering methods.

To spread a new normative expectation at the global level, CIVIC needed (and sought) to cultivate more formal alliances with organizations focused and networked thematically at the global level, in issue areas adjacent to the idea they were promoting. Such alliances were seen as valuable not simply in practical terms but for the boost in legitimacy that accompanies formal alliances with advocacy heavyweights in particular issue areas.[30] But although individuals within large organizations like OXFAM or the ICRC were supportive and sympathetic, organizations themselves were reluctant to sign on. Moreover CIVIC's early efforts to market the issue to broader thematic coalitions had resulted as often in significant pushback as in sympathy and support. In 2008 Holewinski described her surprise when pitching the condolence payments issue to progressive NGOs in Los Angeles:

> It was my first month on the job and I was going to talk to this large group of pacifists, humanitarians, you know and I thought, "this is going to be great! These are our people!"
> Not at all. I got blasted. It was really eye-opening.

In the winter of 2008–2009, CIVIC began taking stock of its strategy. It had already reached out to academic institutions for ideas, inviting strategy papers and briefings from University of Massachusetts' Center for Public Policy and Administration and from Harvard University's International Human Rights

---

[30] Bob 2008. For example, Jessi Schimmel emphasized the legitimating effect of formal gatekeeper adoption when she described CIVIC's strategy in 2008, stressing the particular value-added of associating the CIVIC cause with the organizational brands characteristic of several key issue areas. "I would aim for several organizations that really do build up our credibility, names that people who don't know CIVIC will still recognize. We want Human Rights Watch, International Crisis Group, also landmines/cluster organizations, victim's assistance groups. We aren't frankly asking for much: their name, their support, if someone says, what is this norm, do you believe in it?" Personal interview, Jessi Schimmel, September 2008.

Clinic.[31] It had become clear to CIVIC that while they continued to be success-ful at affecting state practice here and there, a different strategy was required in order to cultivate the broader norm change they desired for the "changing the rules" part of CIVIC's work.

Over the course of spring 2009, CIVIC began to implement a significant shift in its strategy. First, while it continued to work separately on promoting the practice of amends through direct advocacy with specific states, it refocused its norm-building efforts on coalition-building within global civil society, aiming to attract faith-based organizations, women's groups, and organizations head-quartered in the global South. Second, it repackaged the "changing the rules" section of the CIVIC website into a distinctive piece of the project, the Making Amends Campaign, with its own web portal. In this way, CIVIC sought to pro-tect its service-oriented "niche" while beginning to formally combine efforts with a wider coalition on the norm-building side that could eventually, poten-tially, stand on its own. Finally, the organization hired a new staff person, Scott Paul, with connections not to militaries and foreign policy experts but rather to the UN system and advocacy elites in New York. In so doing, CIVIC reconsti-tuted its relationships both with actors and issues in the wider human security network, yoking the "amends" concept successfully to the wider issue area of "protecting civilians."[32]

The most important hub for the "protection of civilians" (PoC) in the UN system is the UN Office for the Coordination of Humanitarian Affairs (OCHA), a department within the Secretariat. This international bureaucracy has three distinctive characteristics relative to other humanitarian organiza-tions. First, it is more of an advocacy hub than an operational organization: its field offices are small and unlike most humanitarian groups it does little in the way of service delivery, focusing instead on promoting the humanitarian agenda at the international level. This profile gives it particular power to con-struct and market the overall advocacy agenda for the humanitarian sector. Second, in this capacity it therefore has close ties both to the NGO commu-nity and to government ministries, so OCHA occupies a structural position of relatively high "between-ness" at the interstices of the "high politics" of

---

[31] Students in my University of Massachusetts-Amherst class on "Global Agenda-Setting" stud-ied CIVIC for a semester, wrote a strategy paper, and conducted a briefing in Washington, DC, in December 2008. See Tillmann et al. 2009. At Harvard University, Bonnie Docherty and a team of law students worked on an analysis of how the concept of "amends" might draw on humanitarian and human rights law.

[32] By the time the website was launched the following year, this "protection of civilians" trope was featured front and center in the new online description of the Making Amends Campaign: "Protection of civilians is built into the laws of war. But when these protections fail, warring parties have no for-mal responsibility to help." Web content on file with author.

governments and UN delegates and "low politics" of the NGO world. It is thus a humanitarian "hub" in every sense, yet insulated from some of the pragmatic politics of service delivery that led field-based NGOs to be particularly wary of the amends idea.[33]

Third, through its work with the Security Council, OCHA constitutes an ideational broker between two often insufficiently related issue areas: hard security and humanitarian affairs. The UN Secretary General presents a periodic report on the Protection of Civilians to the UN Security Council, a report in which the Under-Secretary General for Humanitarian Affairs plays a key role drafting. The presentation of the Report constitutes a focusing event that engages delegates to the Security Council in a diplomatic discussion about how to mitigate armed conflict and is thus an important agenda-setting exercise for the humanitarian sector, embedding human security concerns in Council discussions that otherwise tend to focus on nonproliferation, use of force, and other "hard" security issues; and legitimating them as global issues by associating them with the realm of "high politics."[34]

While the campaign focused significant attention in 2009 and 2010 in engaging state delegations directly, it was obvious to CIVIC that they needed the support of OCHA and the Secretary General's office more broadly to really engage the Security Council on amends as a "civilian protection" issue. As Cora True-Frost has shown in her study of the Security Council's approach to thematic human security resolutions, innovations in language that end up in such resolutions are generally first filtered through communities of experts in other relevant UN bureaucracies (True-Frost 2007).

Attracting formal support from OCHA was slow going at first. Although key individuals at OCHA were sympathetic to the CIVIC idea (one I spoke with had known Marla Ruzicka before she died), the organization was unprepared to easily endorse the concept. Indeed Scott Paul's phone calls went unanswered throughout much of 2009 while he shopped the amends concept around other forums at UN headquarters. However, in early 2010,

---

[33] In particular, the operational refugee and relief NGOs continued to express skepticism through this same period in the idea that there even was a gap: "We have heard this a couple of times now: that warring parties have all sort of obligations, human rights obligations, IHL obligations, refugee law obligations, IDP-related obligations, so really there is not that much of a gap . . . but from our perspective only the warring party that does damage to a civilian victim is really capable of repairing the dignity that is injured through a combat act." Scott Paul, phone interview, February 2010.

[34] See Cora True-Frost, "For example, in autumn 2010 the Security Council dealt with such topics as peacekeeping operations in Nepal, Darfur and Burundi, instability in Afghanistan, maritime piracy off Somalia, and the question of Palestine."

OCHA representatives met with Paul and invited CIVIC to provide the information needed to make the case for putting amends language in the next PoC report; facilitated a "side event" on amends during the May/June Security Council debate on protection of civilians; and introduced Paul to the incoming Section Chief for the Protection of Civilians. These efforts by OCHA helped legitimize the amends concept and heightened its salience among government delegations to the Security Council. In November 2010, the concept of amends was addressed squarely in the Secretary General's Report to the Security Council.[35] A Presidential Statement followed the presentation of the report, stating: "All civilians affected by armed conflict, including those suffering losses as a result of lawful acts under international law, deserve assistance and recognition in respect of their inherent dignity as human beings."[36]

By the end of 2010, the "making amends" concept was gaining sway among global elites, buoyed by the support of important human rights and humanitarian gatekeepers constructing "civilian protection" as a set of ideas for the global community. With OCHA incorporating amends language in public statements and reports, and with government champions increasingly supporting the idea, the issue proliferated swiftly throughout global civil society.[37] The Special Representative to the Secretary General for Children in Armed Conflict was receptive to the idea. In June 2010, Philip Alston devoted a section of his annual report to the Human Rights Council on amends for harm. The MacArthur Foundation had provided an infusion of funding. CIVIC hired Golzar Kheiltash to direct the campaign full-time as Paul returned to law school. The concept of amends was no longer a nascent idea but an issue embedded in the global agenda for protecting civilians.

---

[35] S/2010/579, "Report of the Secretary General on the Protection of Civilians," November 11, 2010. The language read: "I note the emerging practice of several States, one that other parties to armed conflict might consider, of acknowledging the harm they cause to civilians and compensating victims. The practice of making amends may range from public apologies to financial payments and livelihood assistance provided to individuals, families and communities. This practice must not be seen, however, as an alternative to prosecuting those responsible for violations of international humanitarian and human rights law and delivering justice to the victims and their families and communities."

[36] S/PRST/2010/25, "Statement by the President of the Security Council," November 22, 2010, p. 3.

[37] In September 2009, the Making Amends Campaign had included two organizations on the steering committee and ten NGO members, most of them smaller NGOs; Handicap International soon bowed out and Survivor's Network continued to stonewall. But one year later, following OCHA endorsement, the membership nearly doubled and included a more significant proportion of NGO "heavyweights": International Crisis Group, International Rescue Committee, and Physicians for Human Rights.

Constitutive Effects: Intra-Network Relations and
Gatekeeper Preferences

So far I have reiterated earlier analyses that show issue adoption by organizations with a high centrality in an issue network is causally related to the successful proliferation of new normative understandings. Norm entrepreneurs are most successful when they pitch ideas to global advocacy hubs rather than directly to states, allowing advocacy hubs a level of veto power over global discourses. But the causal impact of network structure is only part of the story, conferring greater agenda-setting influence on some nodes than others. Network structure also exerts constitutive effects on the preferences of actors in specific organizations themselves. In short, what makes an issue marketable to gatekeepers in the first place is its relational attributes, which signal to gatekeepers what their preferences are.

In the "making amends" case, the preferences of human security elites are a genuine puzzle. Why were leading human security actors initially reticent about an idea that would seem to have such humanitarian merit? In this section, I show how network relations shaped the varied support and pushback CIVIC received from advocacy hubs in the human security network. The factors that first stymied and ultimately fostered CIVIC's emerging success were related to network dynamics—perceived relationships between issues, between issue areas, between organizations, and between individuals in the broad transnational area of human security. Since this argument about advocacy elite preferences is different from the leading explanation for why some issues "take" in networks and others do not—the intrinsic attributes of issues themselves—I begin by ruling out that alternative explanation before showing how relational attributes made all the difference.

Explaining Gatekeeper Preferences: Why Issue Attributes Are Insufficient

A typical explanation for agenda-setting success or failure is the intrinsic attributes of issues, and certain attributes of the "making amends" issue did create concern for potential adopters. For example, some human security specialists cast doubt about the scope or magnitude of the problem itself. When CIVIC approached the US chapter of a leading international disability rights organization for support, senior officials there turned to the organization's counterparts in Europe before agreeing: "We wanted to know: *is* this a thematic issue that's emerging? Or is the US was the only context where such a movement has emerged strongly?"[38] Others enthusiastic about the idea of amends were

---

[38] Respondent #25, personal interview, May 2010.

also initially skeptical of a rule that seemed unduly aimed at particular states or, as one Washington-based humanitarian official put it, "victims of Western wars."[39] "Is this a global norm or an anti-US norm?" a Canadian human security expert asked skeptically when students in my class questioned him about the amends concept.

Even those who acknowledged that collateral damage was probably an issue in numerous contexts were uncertain how much importance to attach to this in the broader scheme of civilian harms. Some continued to argue that the bigger problem was intentional civilian targeting. Some argued that the key problem was simply reducing collateral damage in the first place by enforcing the proportionality rule. A staff-person from a refugee relief organization said, "Norm-building takes time and energy: why not just devote that to enforcing existing norms?"[40] CIVIC's website was full of testimonials, but in the absence of comprehensive global mechanisms for counting the civilian dead and injured in armed conflicts, it was difficult to say with certainty how serious incidental harms were as a proportion of the total.[41] Some practitioners were leery of a campaign where technical knowledge was unavailable to confirm the testimonials. This is consistent with literature suggesting *statistical measurability* is an important step in problem construction: campaigns where this is difficult or impossible have a harder job than those where the issue in question in amenable to quantification (Joachim 2007, 181–182).

Another concern related to gatekeepers' perceptions of feasibility: the ability to implement amends as a specific solution to the problem CIVIC had identified. In focus groups, human security practitioners generally demonstrated enthusiasm about the problem but skepticism about compensation as a solution. Some argued that "you'll never get governments to do that," pointing out the ways in which it would complicate counterterrorism operations. Some pointed out that many war-affected governments would be incapable of complying with such a norm: "Rwanda and Congo are in a conflict: who's going to pay compensation?"[42] Others raised concerns over the practical problems of implementing a compensation scheme: "It's an interesting campaign, but as an actual kind of

---

[39] Respondent #19, personal interview, April 2009.

[40] Respondent #22, phone interview, October 2009. However, even if existing law were enforced perfectly, incidental civilian harms would still occur.

[41] In focus groups, participants brought up the difficulty in distinguishing unintentional harms due to combat operations from secondary victimization: "For every person that gets killed on the battlefield, ten, twenty, fifty people die of disease and malnutrition. You cannot compensate those people because people also die of diarrheal disease, respiratory infections, in peacetime. So you can say there's been a 20% increase in deaths, but you can never say which are the ones that would have died or wouldn't have died otherwise."

[42] Focus group participant, December 2009.

structure, a regulation or norm, it would be extraordinarily difficult: how would you determine who the victims are, and what the compensation should be and all these other kind of questions."[43]

Ultimately, however, these issue attributes are insufficient explanations for gatekeeper reticence, since these factors remained constant while gatekeeper preferences eventually changed. Moreover, many other similar issues with the same attributes had been adopted by the same communities of practice. Few thought a ban on land mines was politically feasible when it was originally proposed (Price 1998). Far from being opposed to campaigns singling out Western states, human rights organizations in fact routinely do so (Ron, Ramos, and Rodgers 2007). Many campaigns have been launched on inadequate evidence (such as the case of sexual violence in Bosnia) or on numbers that have been made up entirely, as in the 300,000 child soldier extrapolation (Brett 2004; Oestreich 2004). And humanitarian law organizations have often sought to fill gaps in international law, promulgating new treaties and treaty language on weapons, children, and crimes such as sexual violence; but also successfully building norms through nontreaty approaches: the guiding principles on internal displacement represent an example of a successful "soft law" process (Orchard 2010).

A better question is why some human security elites initially constructed the issue in this way and came to believe that these concerns outweighed the other ways in which the issue was a plausible candidate for advocacy. Why did these issue attributes have such salience for this particular issue, pushing gatekeepers toward an initially reticent rather than receptive stance? And how did this perception change? The answer is that many of these attributes were not merely intrinsic to the issue but rather relational. What mattered was not the issue itself but how the issue was perceived to be situated within networks of issues and relevant actors. In short, *intra-network dynamics* helped constitute key actors' perceptions of the "making amends" issue and of CIVIC as a norm entrepreneur. When these factors changed, so too did humanitarian gatekeepers' willingness to adopt the amends issue.

Intra-Network Dynamics at the Agenda-Vetting Stage

An obvious and somewhat circular relational effect was precisely the absence of formal adoption by a major advocacy hub. At the start, this affected CIVIC's credibility as an entrepreneur when pitching the issues to other advocacy hubs.[44] The importance of existing network ties in early coalition-building as a

---

[43] Focus group participant, December 2009.
[44] Sarah Holewinski, personal interview, February 2008.

signal of credibility and do-ability is suggested by this quote from one early supporter: "We were attracted to it initially because we had worked with CIVIC,
worked with some of the other groups involved in the campaign, so it wasn't
that far of an extension from work that was already done, relationships that were
already developed."[45] But other specific features of CIVIC's network position—
and that of the issue it was championing—also affected the organization's initial
ability to attract supporters.

One of these features was intersectionality: "making amends" constituted
a "between the cracks" issue, falling at the interstices of a number of different
issue networks: depending on which piece of the concept one focused on, it
could be a humanitarian law issue, a human rights issue, a development issue, a
justice issue, or a protection issue. For emerging issues, this sort of liminality can
contribute to effective coalition-building, or it can incentivize "buck-passing"
within civil society. For example, as I show in my earlier work on children born
of wartime rape, the fact that the issue could be viewed through either a child
protection or a gender-based violence lens meant groups in either camp could
assume away their own responsibility to incorporate such children into their
programming (Carpenter 2010, 168–169).

In the case of "making amends," individuals I spoke with at development
and humanitarian organizations saw it as more of a post-conflict issue, whereas
the post- conflict justice community saw it as a humanitarian law/human rights
issue. In each case, the sense that the issue "belonged" elsewhere was an obstacle
to formal issue adoption.

> We understand that for a sustainable peace you need to address some
> of these issues; but our central thing is that when people are in conflict
> their basic needs are met . . . we're mostly a water and sanitation orga-
> nization . . . post-conflict amends is something we could move into but
> we're not there right now.[46]
>
> We are interested in seeing that victims of conflict are addressed—I
> think the differentiating point for us is that our work is rights-based;
> and what I think [CIVIC] has done is carve out an area where they see
> a gap, you know, where the law doesn't apply . . . they're pulling on sort
> of a humanitarian motivation, an apology for what happened but not
> saying we did something wrong . . . so we've kept in touch with them
> but we're just not part of their campaign.[47]

---

[45] Respondent #24, personal interview, June 2009.
[46] Respondent #18, personal interview, September 2009.
[47] Respondent #67, personal interview, June 2010.

According to Holewinski, this sort of buck-passing often occurred in her early efforts to pitch the issue to different sectors:

> We heard from a lot of organizations that there are already movements out there we should be joining. And whenever we looked into those movements, we realized that's not at all what we're saying. So "there are groups that are working on gender violence, why don't you do into that?" Well, a lot of war victims are men . . . so that leaves out a segment of war victims and we don't want to do that either. Or "you should link this to children and armed conflict." And yes, our issue fits into that, but not all the way. So we have to find the channel that can give us a clear path to building this norm.[48]

Intersectionality of issues across issue domains does not necessarily doom them: after all, some of the most high-profile issues in the campaigns of the 1990s were those in which entrepreneurs could mobilize broad coalitions around a master frame. The land-mines campaign was framed as a disarmament, humanitarian, and development problem (Matthew and Rutherford 2003). Conflict diamonds bridged human rights, trade, and security (Grant and Taylor 2004; Duygulu Elcim 2015). HIV-AIDS metamorphosed from a health to a human rights to a security issue (Ingenkamp 2008). But another intra-network effect initially inhibited this easy concordance across issue areas: the fact that the frame originally proposed by CIVIC was perceived to conflict with master frames associated with the relevant issue areas.

Individuals thinking through a conflict prevention or peace frame were concerned, for example, that the idea of amends constituted a legitimation of violence. By drawing attention to the notion that some deaths and maimings were in fact not against humanitarian law, some organizations worried that this would provide a legitimating discourse for armed violence. This perception of disconnect between the peace movement and the CIVIC idea dated back to Marla Ruzicka's early days lobbying on the Washington circuit: members of Code Pink were among the idea's earliest critics (Abrahamson 2006, 146). A focus group respondent at late as 2009 said: "The notion that 'that's OK, who we will, we'll fix with a little money'; it's making me uncomfortable."[49] While it was never CIVIC's actual message that a certain amount of money could adequately "compensate" civilian harms, gatekeepers' perceptions that there could be a harmful

---

[48] Sarah Holewinski, personal interview, February 2008.
[49] Focus Group Participant #1, December 2009.

side effect colored their reactions to the idea of amends during this period and overshadowed CIVIC's broader emphasis on dignifying gestures.

Within the humanitarian sector, a key concern at first was whether the "making amends" idea would compromise the well-defined distribution of labor between militaries and the civilian humanitarian sector. Humanitarian organizations operating in conflicts zones rely on a discourse of political neutrality to gain access to needy civilians: open association with weapons-bearers can compromise this image (Minear and Smillie 2004). A norm that belligerents would themselves distribute payments as compensation was seen to both compromise the association of aid with political neutrality and jeopardize "humanitarian space": some humanitarians feared a further militarization of humanitarianism that could undermine the neutrality of the entire system. In 2009, a representative from one humanitarian organization similarly told me, "We're not comfortable being inside negotiations with the military—we don't want to be there saying that we think certain levels of collateral damage are OK."[50]

According to CIVIC, there was also a sense among some humanitarian and development organizations that outsourcing victim assistance to the military would create redundancies, removing opportunities for NGO work. On a more normative level, some were concerned that such a norm would introduce inequalities among victims. Transitional justice groups were focused on reparations for war crimes: expanding the notion of compensation to those legally harmed through non-criminal military operations was viewed by some as an unhelpful dilution of their key focus. And finally humanitarian law organizations were quite skeptical of claims that the laws of war might need expanding—reflecting a general concern that if you open up the "Pandora's Box" of the Geneva Conventions existing standards might be negotiated away.[51]

So frame-shopping among these different communities of practice at first led to frustration and stalemate. At times, CIVIC staff members were offered the opportunity to gain supporters by modifying their focus, but they resisted.

> We went to one organization working on Darfur, Congo, Chad and they said, "We've been working on Responsibility to Protect, that's a natural fit, you should be coming into R2P." Well, that's about mass atrocities, not accidental deaths. By linking that with R2P, not only do we get off track of what we're trying to do, we water down R2P.[52]

---

[50] Respondent #25, personal interview, May 2010.
[51] Personal interview, ICRC staffer, April 2009.
[52] Sarah Holewinski, personal interview, February 2008.

Similarly, when CIVIC first engaged UN officials, Paul encountered resistance based on perceptions about how "amends" would be situated in the existing advocacy landscape. Some told him to delineate more clearly why amends would not simply duplicate other standards.[53] Delegates to the Security Council flagged potential competition with a related issue: those focused on the concept of reparations for war crimes were worried about watering down the message by addressing compensation for civilian victims more broadly.[54] OCHA representatives I interviewed in 2010 were also primarily concerned with what was perceived to be a zero-sum relationship between compensation for lawful civilian harms and proper legal accountability for war law violations: they worried talk of compensation might draw attention away from parallel agenda-setting efforts around reparations.[55]

These concerns about the way in which the issue was networked ideationally and socially contributed to CIVIC's initial difficulties convincing human security elites to endorse the campaign. In spring 2009, Amnesty, Survivor Corps, and Oxfam had all declined to formally come on board. Handicap International, which had previously been a member of the Steering Committee, withdrew later in the year. But in early 2010, the campaign's prospects shifted as OCHA began to engage. International Crisis Group joined the Steering Committee. The Security Council began to take an interest in the issue, and several governments had begun talk of championing it. The campaign's list of members and signatories began to grow. By 2011, it included well-known human rights and humanitarian groups such as Physicians for Human Rights, Women for Women International, and the International Rescue Committee.

How did CIVIC shift the organizations' and the issue's relationship to the broader human security network in such a way as to overcome these early obstacles and encourage engagement by humanitarian hubs? Below I argue that

[53] This issue of "duplicative-ness" was raised both with the UN High Commissioner for Human Rights (UNHCHR) and the UN High Commissioner for Refugees (UNHCR). UNHCR is the UN's key hub for work on both refugees and the internally displaced. In a July meeting, Paul learned through his contact there that the "Guiding Principles on Internal Displacement" already included the concept of compensation but not the concept of recognition for suffering. Similarly, in another meeting with a Quaker UN Office representative, Paul was reminded that the concept of liability for incidental harm was already reflected in one specific treaty: the Fifth Additional Protocol to the Geneva Conventions on Explosive Remnants of War that puts the onus on warring parties to clean up their mess when they go to war.

[54] Paul had only that fall learned how important it was to present amends as complementary or supplementary to the reparations issue, which was the key focus of the "accountability" discourse within protection of civilian's circles at this time. Doing so effectively had been a process of trial and error. By November 2009, many delegates were still unsure about this, and OCHA had not endorsed amends.

[55] Personal interview, OCHA representative, June 2010.

CIVIC was able to successfully shift key gatekeepers' perception of the organization and the issue when they reconstituted their network ties from Washington to New York; and by developing conceptual and interpersonal strategies to span the discursive empty space between advocacy "silos." In short, by shifting the issue's ideational and social ties, CIVIC was able to reconstitute gatekeeper preferences about whether to adopt.

Shifting Ties among Actors

A key decision taken in spring 2009 was to move the focus of the Making Amends Campaign from Washington to New York. This marked a significant shift from CIVIC's earlier strategy of working through Marla Ruzicka's original Washington-based networks. Those earlier connections (based on getting the United States to do something) had given CIVIC access and leverage with congressional leaders and the US Department of Defense. But it limited their reach to transnational civil society. For example, many of CIVIC's Washington-based NGO contacts worked for the US chapter of their respective organizations and so were focused on influencing US policy. Colleagues at OXFAM USA, the Friends Committee for National Legislation, and the country offices of Human Rights Watch and the ICRC were enthusiastic about CIVIC and generous with advice, but they lacked the institutional authority to formally associate their international counterparts with what the CIVIC team wanted to characterize as a global, not a US-based, norm-building process; and they lacked the connections to broker such relationships for CIVIC with their counterparts at the global level.

As CIVIC recognized at a January 2009 brainstorming meeting with its Washington-based colleagues, the appropriate gatekeepers for global agenda-setting are not national chapters but international secretariats: the NY headquarters of Human Rights Watch (rather than the Washington office), ICRC headquarters in Geneva, and UN bodies. Shifting their coalition targets from Washington to New York and Geneva was not simply about creating new connections. It was also about constituting the "amends" idea as a global thematic issue of concern to many stakeholders in many different contexts, rather than associating it primarily with US foreign policy.

Pitching to new actors meant cultivating new connections. Scott Paul's hire in March 2009 was implemented with that in mind. Paul was a first-year law student at New York University with a stipend from his university to do pro-bono work for the summer and a history coordinating advocacy campaigns through the Washington-based Center for Global Solutions (CGS). He was recruited for CIVIC by Board Member Heather Hamilton, who had worked with Paul at CGS. Hamilton described Paul as "the kind of person who can go out and just meet, meet, meet and he understands that how these things happen is you form personal relationships and just push people to get involved."[56]

Indeed, Paul spent his summer arranging coffee chats, buying drinks, attending briefings, and pitching the Making Amends Campaign over water coolers and in elevators all over New York. He fastidiously followed up on referrals, bouncing from New York–based NGOs like the International Center for Transitional Justice to the office of the "civilians" liaison to the Austrian delegate to the United Nations; to the Quaker UN Office and ICRC headquarters in Geneva and back to New York to see the civil society liaison at the UN Office of the High Commissioner for Human Rights. By summer's end, CIVIC had already achieved two of its benchmarks—to expand the campaign membership to a thematically diverse range of NGOs and to create a buzz among government representatives and UN civil servants.[57]

Shifting Ties among Issue Areas

Paul did not simply possess the ability to rapidly generate social ties to a wide range of global civil servants bustling around UN headquarters in New York. He also embodied—and knew how to cultivate—conceptual and interpersonal connections across issue areas. Coming from a sustainable development background and then moving into foreign policy and international organizations, Paul was accustomed to working across congruent circles of theory and practice. For example, at CGS he was involved in a number of campaigns, like the Law of the Sea Campaign and the Stop Bolton Campaign, that were not, in the words of Hamilton, "siloed in the human rights world . . . which is great because silos in advocacy kill your advocacy."[58]

Indeed the necessity of finding a way to exploit their ideational position at the interstices of advocacy silos—rather than seeking to situate the amends concept in one or the other—had become increasingly apparent to Holewinski and Keenan. For example, in 2008 Holewinski had expressed concern about pegging the campaign to specific issue areas like "women and children"; but by late 2009

[56] Heather Hamilton, CIVIC Board Member, May 2009.

[57] In September 2009, the campaign membership included four NGOs from the global South (Control Arms Foundation of India, Egyptian Initiative for Personal Rights, the War Legacies Project, and the National Alliance for Human Rights and Social Justice-Nepal); one faith-based group (United Methodist Church); two women's groups (Mothers Acting Up and Women for Women International); two major human rights groups (Human Rights Watch and Physicians for Human Rights), one environmental group (Global Green USA), and one multi-issue NGO (Citizens for Global Solutions).

[58] Personal interview, Heather Hamilton, May 2009.

they were rethinking this approach, wondering if the best way to build a coalition was precisely to engage small pieces of the issue in multiple sectors simultaneously to see where it might gain traction.

Through Paul, CIVIC did precisely this, building social, professional, and conceptual connections in New York and Geneva one coffee meeting at a time. In each encounter, Paul tested the resonance of amends among a variety of different advocacy communities and frames, engaging important players around transitional justice, peace-keeping and peace-building, children and armed conflict, human rights, humanitarian law, and humanitarian affairs. One of the most resonant connections, as Holewinski and Keenan had already discovered, was the nexus between humanitarian affairs and hard security issues. While victim assistance groups were increasingly skeptical of the campaign (Survivor's Network finally turned CIVIC down for the steering committee in fall 2009 and Handicapped International bowed out later), groups specializing in conflict prevention—like the International Crisis Group—were more interested. Through strategic discussions with various stakeholders, Paul honed and narrowed CIVIC's message to find the "sweet spot" that would bind together intersecting advocacy communities.

Part of this process involved dampening down aspects of CIVIC's message that attracted pushback from the wider human security network. As early as spring 2009 Holewinski and Keenan were moving away from the idea that there was a "missing law of war," looking instead for ways to "build on human rights law instead of humanitarian law" and in particular to think of amends in terms of the space between the two.[59] At the suggestion of Golzar Kheiltash, a colleague from Citizens for Global Solutions who provided legal advice to the campaign (and joined later as Campaign Director), the Making Amends Campaign began de-emphasizing terms like "norm," which carried more of a legal than moral connotation among advocacy targets, invoking images of a treaty process that CIVIC had long since decided to avoid. The campaign also began stressing that "amends" was about respect and dignity as much as about material benefits.

Although his New York University summer stipend ran out, Paul stayed on part-time in fall 2009 to push the concept of "amends." By this time, not only had CIVIC's network ties to specific communities of practice changed radically, but their sense of how to frame and pitch amends had also transformed from an emphasis on humanitarian law and human rights law to an emphasis on "protecting civilians" as an issue area. This frame shift resulted from the network

---

[59] "We can't call it a 'missing law of war' which is a shame because I really loved that phrase, but we could call it a 'gap'—not in IHL, but in international law broadly. When you put human rights law and humanitarian law together, there's a gap between the dignity and respect afforded every individual civilian and what happens to them in war." Sarah Holewinski, informal conversation, April 2009.

connections Paul forged in New York and the mentoring of advocacy gatekeepers. It also repositioned the "amends" concept conceptually in a way that created new ties to new actors and embedded the issue in a pre-existing framework bridging a number of distinct advocacy clusters.

Reconstituting Gatekeeper Preferences: "Networking"
Amends as a Civilian Protection Issue

The above analysis demonstrates how global policy networks are simultaneously networks of issues and of actors. Indeed these components of networks are mutually constitutive: marketing an issue to a specific actor can shift an issue's framing, and to some extent the frame chosen by a campaign determines who the best allies will be.

The emphasis on amends as a "protection" issue later seemed to the CIVIC team as a "natural fit," but at the time it constituted a subtle shift from CIVIC's earlier framework. In 2008, Keenan had mentioned protection as one of several advocacy discourses where the "amends" idea did not resonate. In January 2009, the "protection of civilians" concept was raised as a possible way to "hook" the Making Amends Campaign to preexisting advocacy rhetoric, but even at that time there was uncertainty whether it was the ideal frame. In part, this perception stemmed from CIVIC's sense, based on interactions with their Washington-based network, that "protection" meant too many different things to different people and was not firmly rooted under the concept of humanitarian law.[60] Another concern was the need to differentiate CIVIC's niche—redress by warring parties for incidental harms—from a protection agenda which had heretofore focused almost exclusively on preventing intentional targeting, and whose response was structured through the relief sector rather than militaries. Before Paul came onto the Making Amends Campaign, Holewinski and Keenan were leaning toward embedding it in a combination of human rights rhetoric and humanitarian law rather than engaging "protection" as a normative concept.

Turning toward New York changed this conceptual incentive structure. The concept of "protection of civilians" had much greater resonance in UN circles than in Washington; and more resonance there as a way of describing the Making Amends niche than "human rights" or "humanitarian law." In fact, although CIVIC had neither expected nor sought open support from the ICRC

---

[60] At the Interaction Protection Working Group that Keenan attended in 2008, her sense was the "protection was already a very full topic. It means so many things and varies depending on the mission of each organization. So, for example, children's organizations would use it to talk about protection of children from trafficking, which had very little connection to what we were working on." Personal interview, Marla Keenan, January 2009.

on amends through their Washington-based networks, Paul discovered on a trip to Geneva that the ICRC was in fact more receptive than they expected—so long as the frame was "protecting civilians affected by armed conflict" rather than "filling gaps in humanitarian law."

Similarly, one of the first pieces of advice Paul reported back to CIVIC headquarters when he hit New York in June 2009 came from a human rights organization: that when contacting the UN Missions, he should not ask to speak with the human rights officers because for many countries, the human rights officers would primarily be dealing with the UNGA Third Committee issues. Instead Paul was advised to ask for the officer responsible for the protection of civilians. These individuals were positioned differently, engaged not with the General Assembly committees but with the Security Council, which held thematic debates on civilian protection each summer and issued resolutions each November in response to a Secretary General's report. Such individuals therefore constituted brokers to a different configuration of social and ideational network within UN circles.[61]

The Security Council made sense as a target both institutionally and discursively. First, as a high-profile global institution involved in the "high" politics of international security, CIVIC staff at headquarters understood success there would raise the profile of the amends issue in unique ways.[62] Second was a set of practical concerns relating to the relative institutional environment of the Security Council versus the General Assembly. As Paul put it, "a ton of NGOs compete for attention in the Third Committee, while the Security Council's Protection of Civilians mandate was actively seeking input and direction from NGOs." Indeed, as Cora True-Frost (2007) has shown, the Security Council has been an active "consumer" of human security norms since 1999. Like any small NGO with limited staff and resources, CIVIC had to make strategic decisions about where to target its energy in order to garner timely and meaningful progress on the practice and principle of amends.

The CIVIC team also believed linking amends to humanitarian affairs and armed conflict made more sense conceptually than framing it as a human rights problem per se: "We weren't prepared at the start of this campaign to articulate the MAC in a rights framework." Although in some respects protection of civilians is a human rights issue, and although ultimately CIVIC's allies came to

---

[61] Generally speaking, human rights officers are tasked with covering the Third Committee of the General Assembly, and PoC experts focus on the Security Council's PoC agenda (and often Women, Peace & Security and/or Children & Armed Conflict). "The choice wasn't really just about human rights vs. protection of civilians; the choice was really about General Assembly vs. Security Council." Email correspondence, Scott Paul, December 23, 2011.

[62] For a detailed exploration of this "securitization" of global social problems, see Hudson 2009.

involve human rights and humanitarian affairs organizations, in practice the distinction was conceptually helpful given the ideational and institutional distinctions between human rights law and architecture (which typically address states' obligations to their own citizens) and humanitarian law, which governs the treatment of foreigners in conflict zones, including the protection of civilians.

All these factors shaped OCHA's gradually changing sense that the amends issue passed the test of "fit"-ness to the organization's mandate. Expressing amends as a humanitarian rather than a human rights–based concern spoke to OCHA's raison d'être; expressing it in terms of "protection" rather than "gaps in the law" dovetailed with OCHA's principles, grounded in soft law rather than treaty law. As both the campaign and its allies within global civil society began articulating the distinction between reparations and amends clearly as twin aspects of a comprehensive protection agenda, OCHA's position shifted to one of endorsement.

In short, shifting an issue's ties to networks of issues and networks of actors is an important component of its branding and a means by which to reconstitute the preferences of global elites in the organizations with the greatest influence over the advocacy agenda.

Conclusion

What does the CIVIC case tell us about networks and new norm development in global politics? First, that norm entrepreneurship while crucial is insufficient to set the global agenda, and new normative understandings do not necessarily emerge even through successful direct advocacy with governments. Instead, much depends on the dialectic between entrepreneurs and powerful players in global civil society—leading NGOs, UN agencies, and government champions. But these elite organizations make their issue adoption decisions not based on their appraisal of the entrepreneur or the issue per se but how both are positioned within networks: networks of issues, of issue areas, and of organizations all structure the way in which an issue's fit and chances of success are interpreted by agenda leaders in advocacy networks. Issue attributes clearly matter—but whether an issue is perceived to have a certain attribute—such as "magnitude," "feasibility," or "toxicity" will depend greatly on elites perception of how it is tied to other issues and to specific actors in global civil society (Carpenter et al. 2014).

Overall this case suggests that much more attention should be paid to the way in which *perceived relational ties*—between issues, between issue areas, between organizations, and between activists themselves vis-à-vis others—structure how those attributes (and thus their "fit" to specific organizational agendas) are understood. In short, network structure does not merely position some organizations as gatekeepers: it also helps to constitute gatekeepers' preferences and thus, the advocacy agenda.

Finally, attention should be given by scholars to how the politics of this process alters the course of norm development. By the time CIVIC had attracted the support of humanitarian heavyweights like OCHA, its frame had coalesced around an emphasis on the provision of "assistance" and "recognition." But by then CIVIC had also stopped talking about "changing the rules" per se, focusing on "creating an expectation" through soft law that went beyond formal rules. And it had stopped talking about a missing law of war, instead aiming to articulate a "nexus" between human rights and humanitarian law without changing the formal rules or insisting on a preexisting ethical standard.[63] The word "compensation" itself had been dropped in favor of "amends," a wider concept associated with recognition and dignity rather than primarily than material gain.[64]

So the story of global norm development is a story of the dialectic between entrepreneurs and gatekeepers. CIVIC decided against pushing for a new legal rule or binding norm, but it shifted the substance of civilian protection, working to guarantee that the harm suffered by civilians through lawful combat operations was at least acknowledged at the highest levels of the global community. And this new language, along with connections and expertise, gave CIVIC leverage and deepened credibility as it continued to work with governments and militaries on the ground to "heal the wounds."[65]

---

[63] By July 2011, the Making Amends website read: "Protection of civilians is built into the laws of war. But when these protections fail, warring parties have no formal responsibility to help. The Making Amends Campaign is a call to all warring parties to help the civilians they harm in armed conflict. It seeks to set a new standard where none currently exists." Making Amends Campaign website.

[64] In an exit interview in May 2011, Holewinski told me: "We now don't talk about compensation at all . . . compensation raises a lot of legal issues with policymakers and their lawyers, not to mention international NGOs and institutions focused on legal accountability for human rights violations . . . what we have come to mean by 'amends' is investigations, recognition of harm, public apologies and assistance." Personal interview, Sarah Holewinski, May 2011.

[65] Personal interview, Sarah Holewinski, May 2011.

4

Interpersonal Networks and International Security

US–Georgia Relations during the Bush Administration

ALEXANDER COOLEY AND DANIEL NEXON

Georgian President Mikheil Saakashvili's decision to launch, on August 7, 2008, an invasion to reclaim the breakaway region of South Ossetia met with a crushing Russian military response. For nearly three weeks, Russian forces systematically destroyed Georgian military capabilities, ousting Georgian forces from South Ossetia and pushing into undisputed Georgian territory, including the city of Gori. Some elements within the Bush administration pushed for a hardline US response. According to the late Ronald Asmus, "There were people on [Vice President Dick] Cheney's staff and [National Security Adviser Stephen] Hadley's staff who said, 'we can't let Georgia go down like this'" (Smith 2010). The conflict even briefly became a major issue in the US presidential contest. The presumptive Republican nominee, John McCain lambasted Russia for its aggression and declared, "Today we are all Georgians." In response, McCain's Democratic rival, Barack Obama, shifted from a measured position to a more overtly pro-Georgian one.[1]

Although the Bush administration ultimately decided against risking war with Russia, its degree of support for Georgia and strong impetus to defend the Georgian regime presents something of a puzzle. Both are inconsistent with Georgia's limited economic, military, and strategic importance to the United States. Indeed, the evolution of the US–Georgia relationship before, during, and immediately after the conflict presents a number of puzzles. How did Georgia achieve outsized importance in Washington's strategic thinking, especially given the risks of entrapment into a conflict with Russia? Why did then-Georgian

---

[1] Beehner (2011, 70–73) provides a good summary of the presidential politics of the conflict.

President Saakashvili and his regime overestimate the willingness of the United States to accept its offensive action to regain control over the breakaway region of South Ossetia? And why did so many US officials accept Georgia's account of events—such that Washington did take unusual steps to save the Saakashvili regime in the aftermath of the war?

We argue that the strong affective interpersonal ties that developed between US and Georgian officials, the role of elites in brokering relations between the United States and Georgia, and the knowledge developed by Georgian officials— both through education in the West and through these social ties—help explain these surprising features of US–Georgian politics. On the one hand, they facilitated Georgian officials' efforts to turn Georgia into a strategically important client for the United States. On the other hand, they created misplaced trust on both sides. We do not argue that such networks overwhelmed power-political and strategic considerations. But they did profoundly condition, and even help constitute, them.

We begin by discussing the relationship between social ties and security governance, particularly in the context of hegemonic orders and related accounts of US leadership. We then look at explanatory leverage—and limitations—of accounts that focus on the conventional security interests of the United States and Georgia. We next provide evidence in favor of our own account. We conclude with some reflections on the intrinsic and theoretical significance of the case, as well as on the direction of future research.

Networks, Hegemony, and Security Governance

By 2008, the United States and Georgia operated in a classic patron–client relationship. The United States provided various forms of economic and security assistance, and Georgia generally aligned with US foreign policy preferences. It cooperated with a number of US priorities, most notably by deploying forces to assist with Washington's efforts in Iraq. As such, Georgia operated within a much broader US-led architecture of security governance—it occupied the position of an enthusiastically subordinate state within the US international security hierarchy.

For Tbilisi, plugging into infrastructure and architecture of the US-led security system served as both means and ends. The Saakashvili regime aimed to enmesh itself into the Western order by, for example, joining the North Atlantic Treaty Organization (NATO) and the European Union (EU). These objectives played a central role in its domestic reformist political agenda. They also promised to create a powerful barrier to Russian influence and the ability of Moscow to destabilize the regime.

As we discuss later, Saakashvili's key security objectives were structured by Russian support for its two remaining breakaway regions: Abkhazia and South Ossetia. On its own, Georgia could not possibly counter Russia's superior military and economic might. It needed US assistance to develop its military capabilities and improve its economy. The more it enmeshed itself into a strategic partnership with the United States, the more chance Georgia enjoyed of securing NATO membership, and thus garnering Article V security guarantees. These, in turn, might provide a "hard" barrier to Russian attempts to restore dominance over Georgia and assist Tbilisi in recovering political control over Abkhazia and South Ossetia.

In sum, Tbilisi desperately needed US patronage in order to hedge against Russian influence, pursue an aggressive domestic agenda, and otherwise achieve objectives the regime considered critical to its success and survival. They not only wanted, as all clients do, to enhance their leverage but also to constitute Georgia as a critical client state for Washington.

At first glance, it would seem that Tbilisi faced an uphill battle in these efforts. Georgia enjoyed little in the way of material or geographic assets to render it an important US security partner. Its location endowed it with some significance as a counterterrorism partner, as well as a transit site for oil and gas from the Caspian that bypassed Russian territory on the way to Europe. But these were only modest tools for Saakashvili's grandiose plans.

This mismatch gets at the heart of the puzzling character of the US–Georgia relationship leading up to the 2008 war. In Lake's (1996, 1999) terms, Georgia lacked much in the way of important specific assets and presented an ongoing entrapment risk. Indeed, in the US–Georgia relationship, Washington held all the cards: Saakashvili needed US military, economic, and political support much more than the United States needed Georgia. As two prominent Eurasian analysts noted, while reflecting on the large support that Tbilisi still enjoyed from elites in Washington after the war:

> The centrality of Georgia to U.S. interests in the region is a oft-invoked rhetorical trope, with little evidence provided to back up the assertion besides the notion that Tbilisi is a bulwark against Moscow's influence in the region.... [T]he emphasis on engagement with this relatively poor, resource-barren (though transit-rich), deeply internally divided state on the other side of the planet seems totally disproportionate to its importance to the United States. (Charap and Peterson 2011, 10–11)

Georgia overcame these circumstances through a mutually reinforcing process of leveraging and expanding its social ties with US officials. This facilitated efforts by the Saakashvili regime to not only build trust and support from US elites, but also to engage in performances and policies that rendered it, in the eyes of the Bush administration, an increasingly important asset. Tbilisi situated itself within the Bush administration's broader "freedom agenda" as a singular success for Washington's efforts to expand the sphere of democratic and westernizing states. Its enthusiastic security cooperation, including with respect to Iraq, also rendered Georgia increasingly valuable to the United States.

In addition to providing an example of how interpersonal networks shape international relations, we submit that the Georgia case highlights the importance of understanding US hegemony—and, in particular, security governance—as operating through, and manifesting as, networks.

US Security Governance and Social Networks

Hegemonic-order theories provide one of the most venerable ways of understanding international security hierarchy (e.g., Organski 1958; Gilpin 1981). Whether under the rubric of "unipolarity," "primacy," "hegemony," or "empire," scholars operating in this broad tradition all hold that the United States plays the single most important role in structuring the international security order. It draws on its superior military capabilities and a myriad of instruments, such as alliance commitments, counterterrorism, and counter-proliferation efforts, direct military training and aid, and overseas basing and access agreements (Ferguson 2003; Posen 2003; Ikenberry 2011).

States and other actors—whether they like it or not—adjust their own security policies in light of these functions. Some actors see the US security hierarchy as generally enhancing external security, domestic stability, and their international influence. Others approach the security order with ambivalence or even actively seek to undermine it. In consequence, different actors adopt a variety of strategies including military balancing against the dominant power, leash-slipping policies designed to enhance their autonomy, and jumping on the bandwagon with the hegemon (Pape 2005; Paul 2005; Nexon 2009; Walt 2009).

Thus, hegemony structures opportunities and constraints for participants as they pursue influence, status, security, and other objectives. In standard accounts, the key elements of hegemonic orders include the distribution of power, the norms and rules established by the dominant power, the way that it allocates status and prestige, and related institutions and regimes. These pay less attention to dynamics generated by the infrastructure itself: the web of ongoing relationships that form part and parcel of that order.[2] However, we find traces of

---

[2] Contrast with Gramscian and other critical approaches to hegemony, which understand hegemony as operating at the level of classes, social groups, and even individuals (e.g., Cox 1983 and Gill 1993).

this kind of analysis in work on hegemonic socialization. Prominent accounts focus, in very general terms, on how these relations facilitate domination by superordinate states (see Wendt and Friedheim 1995). Ikenberry and Kupchan (1990, 283), for instance, contend that hegemons "assert control over other nations within the international system" via mechanisms of socialization: "elites in secondary states buy into and internalize norms that are articulated by the hegemon and therefore pursue policies consistent with the hegemon's notion of international order."

We push this insight further. We can conceptualize the infrastructure of US hegemony—including security governance—as a complex configuration of layered social networks, or what this volume terms "multiplex networks" (Avant and Westerwinter, Avant, this volume) Recent attempts to theorize security hierarchies as network structures focus on the inter-state level (e.g., Nexon and Wright 2007; Hafner-Burton et al. 2009). So too do most of the increasing number of studies that approach alliances, membership in international organizations, diplomatic connections, and trade as ties among states (e.g., Maoz et al. 2006; Kinne 2014). But if we disaggregate, for example, alliance and partnership networks, we find that they are composed of a variety of durable and fleeting interactions among individuals. Much of its "fabric" resides in interpersonal and inter-organizational relationships. These carry with them the affective characteristics of individual social relations. If we broaden our analysis to include transnational networks that shape and shove security governance, then we might include not only ties among government officials and military personnel but also those that extend into sites within civil society. Such sites include lobbyists employed by, or working on behalf of, US security partners, military contractors, and think tanks.

Indeed, a great deal of the "work" of hegemonic socialization involves the creation of cross-national ties that link individuals, officials, and organizations in the dominant power with their foreign counterparts. These take many forms, including military education and training programs, routine diplomatic meetings, and the dispatching of economic advisors. In the contemporary period, entire bureaucratic organizations exist for the purpose, in part, of routinizing interactions with officials from different countries. For example, in the creation and nurturing of US "security partnerships," the purpose of US defense diplomacy is to "maintain an extensive network of security governance that extends from inter-state cooperation to socializing foreign interlocutors into American military norms, procedure, practices, and forms of communication" (Krieger et al. 2015, 221).

We agree that the net effect of such processes favors dominant powers, but they also create opportunities for subordinate and weaker states. In brief, the "web of interactions created by participation in the hegemonic system" (Ikenberry and Kupchan 1990, 291) provides vectors of influence for actors in subordinate states as well. They potentially provide them with social capital: connections that, in principle, they can draw upon as they negotiate inter-state relationships. They allow officials to accumulate cultural capital in terms of knowledge of the workings, and prevailing cultural currency, in one another's countries and state apparatuses (Bourdieu 2008).[3] Those interpersonal ties that take on affective characteristics—that involve, for example, relations of friendship—prove particularly important for understanding aspects of the US–Georgia case. Just as routine social interactions at the micro level can contribute to the accumulation of social and cultural capital, they can also shape assessments of the reliability and commitments of participants. Moreover, constituent mechanisms and processes may bootstrap upon and reinforce one another.

Indeed, the hierarchical character of US security governance may enhance the interest and willingness of subordinate actors to take advantage of these dynamics. The often-profound asymmetry in military, economic, and diplomatic resources enjoyed by the dominant state over the weaker one places the latter at a disadvantage in negotiating the terms of the relationship. Thus, officials in client states have strong incentives to cultivate social capital, cultural ties, and positive interpersonal ties. The more they depend on the superordinate state, the more these resources emerge as the key means to shape the relationship in ways that favor their interests. The Georgian case provides a useful illustration of these dynamics precisely because of, first, the extremely unequal character of the "objective" military, economic, and political assets that Washington and Tbilisi brought to the table and, second, how the Saakashvili regime aggressively utilized social networks, and related cultural capital, to advance its interests.

Interpersonal Ties, Trust, and Credibility

One of the most interesting aspects of the US–Georgian relationship involves misplaced trust. Key decision-makers in Washington overestimated the Saakashvili regime's willingness to avoid direct confrontation with Russia. They also tended to accept Tbilisi's framing of events: in terms of interactions with Russia and breakaway regions and even with respect to what should have been clear evidence of democratic backsliding over time. In some respect, this represented their ideological priors. A number of important elites were hostile toward

---

[3] For a critique of Bourdieu's understanding of social capital—one that rightly emphasizes how the structure of social networks matters more than the number of ties, see Portes 2000. We agree with this critique, but note that we use social capital as a heuristic.

Moscow and thus predisposed toward Georgia. But their faith in the Saakashvili regime went far beyond these predispositions.

At the same time, Saakashvili overestimated the willingness of the Bush administration to risk direct confrontation with Moscow over Georgia. Some of the explanations certainly lie with Saakashvili's psychological dispositions, but these did not operate in a vacuum. They interacted with his—and the regime's—close relationship with a number of US officials and elites; the sense he developed of their strong backing for him that grew out of a combination of close personal ties and the degree that Washington enmeshed itself with Georgia through economic, military, and political support. But we should not overplay Saakashvili's miscalculations. Washington decided against direct military confrontation with Russia. But it otherwise worked hard to save the regime, including supplying significant aid to Georgia in the aftermath of the war. And it did take some risky steps to signal support for the regime. We discuss these later.

How do we make sense of this? A growing body of international-relations scholarship makes clear that affective relations play a critical role in assessments of reliability, credibility, and intentions. This work draws heavily on findings from psychology and recent neuroscience to argue that face-to-face interactions condition how individuals assess not only others' personal characteristics, but subsequent information about their behavior (Hall and Yarhi-Milo 2013; Holmes 2013). As Hall and Yarhi-Milo (2013, 560, 562) argue, leaders "can and do treat personal impressions garnered from interactions with their counterparts as credible indicators of sincerity." Interactions "serve to produce impressions based upon the appearance, expression, behavior, and tone of the interlocutor that are not simply retained as explicit assessments, but also as affective evaluations." As a result, "information about intentions that is vivid, personalized, and emotionally involving is more likely to be remembered, and hence to be disproportionately available for influencing inferences" (Hall and Yarhi-Milo 2013, 13).

This line of argument coheres with work on trust relations. Despite the social and psychological basis of trust, the majority of work on "credible commitments" in international relations stresses "objective" institutional and contractual sources of credibility. For example, scholars of international-political economy argue that certain institutional arrangements—such as the independence of Central Banks and the adoption of bilateral investment treaties—inherently enhance state credibility about commitments to policy stability and/or pursuing liberalizing reforms (Maxfield 1997; Simmons 2000; Kerner 2009). Others argue that these sources of credibility are at best orthogonal to, and at worst negatively correlated with, trust. Actors may only interpret cooperation as evidence of trustworthiness when their partners could have, but chose not to, exploit the trustor (Leach and Sabatier 2005, 491–492). This line of reasoning implies a dispositional or "moralistic" understanding of trust "based on beliefs about the honesty and integrity of potential partners" (Rathbun 2009, 351).

Here arguments about networks, social capital, and how psychological forces impact assessments of sincerity and intentions converge. Much of the existing work on the role of affective evaluations focuses on specifying the conditions under which affective evaluations guide state behavior. It pays less attention, however, to explaining variation in those affective evaluations (see Hall and Yarhi-Milo 2013, 562–563).[4] The creation of social networks and the accumulation of social capital provide one mechanism by which actors leverage transnational interpersonal relationships into positive affective evaluations. When decision-makers build close interpersonal ties—both within and outside of normal policy contexts—we should expect them to be more likely to trust one another. Indeed, "the strength of each interpersonal relationship ought to increase with the frequency of contact and the cumulative number of interactions over time" (Leach and Sabatier 2005, 492). The perception that partners share common values and beliefs is also like to increase trust.

Such increased trust, in turn, generates an enhanced "positive attitude toward the trustee's goodwill and reliability in a risky exchange situation. . . . Obviously, the more the trustor believes in the goodwill and reliability of the trustee, the more confidence in cooperation he or she will harbor" (Das and Teng 1998, 494). Research on firms indicates that "the embeddedness of firms in social network" enhances "trust between firms that can in turn mitigate the moral hazards anticipated at the outset" (Gulati et al. 2000, 209). To the extent that affective evaluations matter in international politics, these dynamics should scale to alliance and partnership politics (Lebow 2005; Eznack 2011, 244). At the same time, these dynamics may produce misplaced trust, particularly when they scale imperfectly to decision-making circles or they lead actors to incorrect perceptions of one another's sincerity.[5]

Summary

The networks that constitute the infrastructure of the US security hierarchy can give rise to interpersonal and inter-organizational relationships that, in turn, shape how participants assess one another's credibility, trustworthiness,

[4] See also Holmes (2013), who focuses on the importance of face-to-face diplomacy in establishing stable expectations about the intentions of interlocutors.

[5] Carpenter (this volume) also focuses on the importance of perception for network effects.

and intentions. These may favor of the interests of subordinate actors, including junior partners and client states.

And there are other ways in which the order provides ways for subordinates to enhance their standing. Consider Lake's discussion of symbolic obeisance, which he sees as costly acts undertaken by subordinates to affirm the authority of the dominant power. One of Lake's examples involves allied and partner participation in the 2003 US-led invasion and occupation of Iraq—Operation Iraqi Freedom. Lake argues that participation in Operation Iraqi Freedom correlated strongly with the US sphere of "security and economic hierarchy." Such evidence suggests that "subordinates may comply more generally with commands not only out of shared interests or threatened punishments but also because they respect and comply with the authority of the dominant state" (Lake 2009, 173).

However, many states joined Operation Iraqi Freedom with the aim of enhancing their position with the United States. Jose Maria Aznar, for example, sought this capital and status in the international realm despite risking significant domestic political costs within Spain itself (Cooley and Hopkin 2010, 506–508). As we argue below, an important reason that Georgia participated in Operation Iraqi Freedom was precisely to enhance its value to Washington. Indeed, their substantial contributions ensured the creation of stronger social networks among US defense officials and Georgian ones. It also allowed Georgia to perform the role of a reliable ally—a conscious strategy conditioned by the knowledge gained through preexisting social ties between US and Georgian elites.

We should stress that these dynamics are not simply a matter of interpersonal affective ties. Certainly, Tbilisi's social and, in part, bootstrapped cultural capital helped the regime to gain general information and practical knowledge that helped it to perform the role of an ideological and strategically valuable US client. But the feedback effects of greater multiplex networks played a key role in the process. As Georgia and the United States became increasingly enmeshed in mutual security, economic, and political ties, Tbilisi proved increasingly capable of leveraging each step to further its position as a trusted client. In other words, these social processes constructed Georgia as a reliable and important partner for the United States.

The important point, for our purposes, is that hegemonic socialization processes—such as routine interaction among officials, government and private educational initiatives, and so forth—operate in two directions. Not only may weaker states socialize superordinate ones but also hegemonic socialization may provide subordinate elites with an understanding of a dominant power's ideological and policy preferences (Ikenberry and Kupchan 1990).

Balancing, Hierarchy, and the US–Georgia Relationship

By 2008, the United States and Georgia had developed an extremely close political and security relationship. The seeds of this relationship extend back to Georgian independence, but witnessed significant expansion during the temporal intersection of the Saakashvili and Bush administrations. US security assistance, along with US advisors, contractors, and consultants, flooded the small country. Although it would go too far to call the security partnership an alliance, that seemed to be its trajectory.

Thus, theories on international alignment and alliance politics provide important leverage on US–Georgian relations. Indeed, balance-of-power theory, specifically in its balance-of-threat variant, explains a great deal about Georgian motivations in seeking closer ties to the United States (see Walt 1985, 1987). But it provides a less compelling account of US behavior and does little to explain the significant miscalculations made by Tbilisi and Washington. In this section, we focus on traditional power-political considerations; we suggest that they explain much about the case, but cannot make sense of the degree that the United States invested in Georgia and downplayed the risks of a patron-client relationship in the absence of significant restraints on Tbilisi.

Balance-of-threat theory accounts for much of Georgia's desire for ever-closer security ties with the United States. Georgian nationalist movements proved a potent force during the unraveling of the Soviet Union, and their demands informed Georgia's initial decision to refuse membership in the Commonwealth of Independent States (CIS). The ascent to power of a hardline nationalist, Zviad Gamsakhurdia, and ensuing conflicts with ethnic minorities in the breakaway provinces of Abkhazia and South Ossetia soon compromised Georgian statehood. In 1993, separatists drove Georgian forces and militias out of Abkhazia, along with about 200,000 Georgian residents of the region who became internally displaced persons (IDPs). The Russian Federation brokered ceasefires, earlier with South Ossetia (in June 1992) and later with Abkhazia.[6]

The price of Moscow's intervention was Georgian acquiescence to Russian regional hegemony. New premier Eduard Shevardnadze—who deposed Gamsakhurdia in a bloody coup in 1992 and would formally become president in 1995—agreed to enter the CIS and to grant indefinite basing rights to Russian forces across Georgian territory. From the ceasefire in 1993 to August 2008, Russian peacekeepers were active in both breakaway republics—under a CIS

---

[6] On the 1992-93 conflict, see De Waal 2011, ch. 5.

mandate, as well as the rubric of international monitoring missions.[7] Russia's stance certainly favored Abkhazia and South Ossetia, but Moscow maintained a public and official commitment to Georgia's territorial integrity. From 1996 to March 2008, Moscow led and enforced a CIS embargo against Abkhazia.

Russia's relations with Georgia deteriorated decisively after the so-called Rose Revolution of 2003, which swept into power Mikheil Saakashvili, a charismatic and enthusiastic pro-Western reformer and supporter of the United States. Saakashvili made building the Georgian state a public priority—including reclaiming Abkhazia and South Ossetia, rejecting Russia's regional security role, and pushing hard for Georgia's membership in NATO. As standard balancing theory would expect, Georgia sought Western security guarantees against its assertive, extremely powerful, and meddlesome neighbor (Walt 1985, 1987; Nexon 2009). Closer ties with Washington and Brussels– including the perception of building them—constituted not only a means for securing Tbilisi's interests but also an end in and of themselves (Mitchell 2009a).

Although these considerations explain why Georgia sought a close relationship with the United States and NATO, they do not account for Washington's emphasis on the strategic partnership in the period of 2004-2008—let alone during the run-up to the August war. US policymakers were under no illusions that Georgia could effectively balance against the Russian Federation. Indeed, when US officials began to privately warn Saakashvili against responding to Moscow's provocations throughout spring and summer 2008, they emphasized that Georgia could not defend itself against Russian military might (see Fried 2008).[8]

Some might argue that US policymakers viewed the Georgian relationship as a way of balancing against Russian influence in the South Caucasus. But despite extremely poor relations between Moscow and Washington during Bush's second term, the United States never demonstrated a strong desire to actively balance against the Russian Federation. It is more accurate to characterize policies such as NATO expansion, the stationing of ballistic missile defenses, support for the color revolutions, and involvement in Central Asia as indifferent to, or dismissive of, Russia's self-understanding of its geopolitical interests. Russia, in the eyes of the Bush administration, presented a threat to US interests to the extent that it undermined pro-Western governments in Moscow's "sphere of privileged interest."

---

[7] International monitoring missions were the United Nations in Abkhazia and the Organization for Security and Cooperation in Europe (OSCE) in South Ossetia.

[8] Also see Asmus (2010: ch. 5), who recounts how, during the spring of 2008, a number of high-level US officials (including Teft, Bryza, Fried, Hadley, and Rice) all delivered warnings to Tbilisi to refrain from initiating military action over Abkhazia.

But even to the degree that balancing considerations motivated the Bush administration, the exact nature of the threat posed by Russia remained far from self-evident. Rather than a consequence of putatively "objective" factors, the Bush administration's interest in balancing against Russia emerged from its Freedom Agenda and its ex ante commitment to support pro-Western regimes such as Ukraine and Georgia.[9] In fact, the US push for a NATO Membership Action Plan (MAP) for Georgia was counterproductive from a balancing perspective. As key veto players in NATO resolutely opposed a concrete pathway for Georgian membership, US efforts merely undermined NATO cohesion. Indeed, US officials, including the president himself, decided to fight for the MAP even after it became clear that they could not overcome German and French opposition (see Marquand 2008; Asmus 2010, ch. 4).

Of course, alliances are more than means of aggregating capabilities. They also are "security management institutions" (Haftendorn et al. 1999, 28). According to Snyder (1997, 33), alliances serve a variety of purposes, including providing "security against external attack," increasing a state's "internal security or domestic political stability," and providing a means to "control the ally" via threats of exit and creating "some entrée into the ally's decision making through a norm of consultation." The "alliance security dilemma," he argues, is closely related to these roles. States in alliances risk abandonment (an ally's defection from the security arrangement) and entrapment (that an ally will drag them "into a war over interests of that ally that one does not share"). Indeed, "the risks of abandonment and entrapment tend to vary inversely" as efforts to ramp up commitment increase the chances of entrapment while efforts to decrease commitment increase the chances of abandonment (Snyder 1997, 181).

As Lake (1996, 1999, 2001) argues, however, increased control—or hierarchy—presents one solution to the alliance security dilemma. And the relationship between Georgia and the United States was highly asymmetric. Tbilisi depended upon US military, economic, and political assistance. Washington's exit would almost certainly have doomed the regime to collapse and resulted in the establishment of Russian hegemony over Georgia. The relative allocation of assets, credibility of exit, and other variables central to relational-contracting theory all render the events surrounding the August war puzzling. Either the United States should have become less involved in Georgia or it should have exerted greater

[9] Upon his arrival in Bucharest for the NATO summit of April 2008, President Bush stated that: "[MAP for] Ukraine and Georgia is a very difficult issue for some nations here. It's not for me. I think these nations are qualified nations to apply for Membership Application. And I said so on Ukrainian soil. I said so in the Oval Office with the President of Georgia. And I haven't changed my mind because it's—one of the great things about NATO is that it encourages the kind of habits that are necessary for peace to exist" (Asmus 2010, 130).

control over the relationship—as the Obama administration did by imposing greater restrictions and conditions upon the terms of aid the conduct of the regime. Tbilisi, for its part, should never have come to believe that Washington would risk conflict to defend Georgia's interests.[10]

The Construction of Georgia's Strategic Importance

The rhetoric of a number of US policymakers and proponents of close US-Georgia bilateral relations during the mid-2000s painted a very different picture. According to them, Georgia held great strategic importance to the United States (Cornell 2007). But closer scrutiny reveals that none of the "objective" benefits provided by Georgia meet the criteria for high-value, specific assets—none of them provided Tbilisi with a credible threat of exit from the relationship, and therefore with much leverage over Washington.

Georgia supported key security operations led by the United States. In 2002, at the height of both the Global War on Terror and Georgian state weakness, the Shevardnadze government allowed hundreds of US military advisors—with Russian approval—to train Georgian forces to remove Chechen and Islamic insurgents from the ungoverned Pankisi Gorge (Tsygankov and Tarver-Wahlquist 2009, 310). The Georgian border guard actively combats the smuggling of nuclear materials. Georgia deployed troops to Iraq in 2003, where it kept them until the August 2008 War. And in 2009, under the Obama administration, Georgia sent nearly 1,000 troops to Afghanistan to join the International Security Assistance Force (ISAF), though the United States both trained and funded this force, and offered its assistance as a transit hub for the Afghanistan logistical effort (part of the Northern Distribution Network, south spur). Overall, however, none of Georgia's actual security contribution to US military efforts, though symbolically important, can in any way be described as "vital."

Georgia's Iraq deployments amounted to its most important material contribution to US security objectives during the Bush administration. Georgia's military presence facilitated the US "surge" by allowing US redeployments. But Georgia's outsized contribution formed part of Tbilisi's strategy to position itself as important to the United States. The Saakashvili regime, in part through its close relations with US officials, understood that such a deployment provided an opportunity to perform the role of a reliable partner. US efforts to train and equip the deployment also ensured closer security cooperation and, in turn,

[10] On asymmetric interdependence, see Keohane and Nye 1989.

both greater Georgian operational capabilities and connections into the US security architecture.

Of course, Georgia provided a relatively convivial partner in the South Caucasus. Armenia, its southern neighbor, is highly dependent on Moscow and hosts Russian military bases under the Collective Security Treaty Organization (CSTO) auspices. But because of the influence of the Armenian diaspora, Washington enjoys little room to maneuver in its relationship with Armenia and Azerbaijan. Legal and political restrictions on US assistance to Azerbaijan greatly complicate bilateral ties between Washington and Baku—despite common concerns about Russian and Iranian influence in the region. Georgia, on the other hand, was enthusiastic about building ever-closer relations with Washington.

Georgia is also, as noted earlier, a transit site for oil, and potentially for natural gas, into Europe. US and Georgian officials, and advocates of closer security ties, frequently referred to it as a critical energy transit corridor (Baran 2007; Cornell 2009; Tsereteli 2009). The Baku-Tbilisi-Ceyhan (BTC) pipeline, the first major new oil pipeline to bypass Russia in the post-Soviet era, runs as the name implies, from Azerbaijan to Turkey via Georgia. Construction of the BTC began in 2002 and it became operational in 2005. Some portray the pipeline's construction, over initial Russian objections, as a major regional triumph for US oil diplomacy, continuing to shape policymakers views on Eurasian energy geopolitics (LeVine 2007). Later officials from both countries would portray Georgia as providing a critical route through which Central Asian oil and gas, destined for Europe, could bypass Russian territory and Moscow's influence, thereby playing a pivotal role in guaranteeing Europe's energy security.[11]

The most touted of these Southern Corridor projects was the proposed Nabucco natural-gas pipeline designed to provide transit for natural gas from Azerbaijan, Turkmenistan, and/or Iraq to Europe. The project has never really gone anywhere. And it is far from clear how, even if the project were somehow realized, the Georgian link would significantly lower European vulnerability to Russian supply shocks or alter European energy firms' long-standing preferences for contracting with Gazprom (Abdelal 2013).

Notwithstanding occasional proclamations about Georgia's strategic importance, these security considerations suggest a highly asymmetric relationship favorable to the United States. On the one hand, Washington enjoys exit options and substitutes with respect to nearly every traditional power-political asset provided by Georgia. On the other hand, the Saakashvili regime itself enjoyed no real ability to withhold these assets. Subsequent deployments to ISAF and

---

[11] Authors' briefings with Georgian officials in the Ministry of Foreign Affairs, Ministry of Defense, and National Security Council, Tbilisi, June 2008. Georgian officials regularly brought up this point at briefings with foreign missions.

assistance with the Northern Distribution Network (NDN) underscore this point: when the Obama administration abandoned the close relations of the Bush administration, Saakashvili responded by continuing, and even offering to expand, cooperation. Similarly, Georgia depends on the revenues from the BTC and smaller Baku-Supsa pipelines, thus rendering these pipelines not particularly useful as a form of leverage.

All of this underscores how the causal interaction between Georgia's "relationally specific assets" and its relationship with the United States ran in the wrong direction: Georgia's putatively specific assets did not drive the US-Georgia partnership.[12] Rather, Tbilisi sought to play key roles and functions for Washington in order to maintain and deepen its existing asymmetric strategic partnership. In turn, Tbilisi's supporters in the United States invoked a variety of different strategic rationales for a strong commitment to Georgia. Georgia's behavior coheres closely with Snyder's finding that "fears of abandonment produce movement toward the ally" (Snyder 1997, 313). However, no evidence suggests that Washington feared abandonment by Georgia. And as much as Tbilisi desired such a formal security commitment, and may have come to believe that one existed de facto, the United States never extended a military defense pact to Georgia. Nevertheless, US policymakers became deeply invested in Georgia's— and the Saaksashvili regime's—success and survival.

The Role of Interpersonal and Inter-Organizational Ties

Georgia's close relations with the United States certainly did not begin in the Bush administration. US and Western officials supported Georgia since its independence, especially given the nearly legendary status of former Georgian president Edvard Shevardnadze among US foreign policymakers as a key reform figure when he was the Soviet Union's Foreign Minister during the Gorbachev era. Since Georgia's independence, US aid has been a significant crutch for the small country, especially given the central government's weakness during the 1990s, ranging between $90m and $150m between 1993 and 2003 (Mitchell and Cooley 2010, 43-45).

By 2003, the regime of President Shevardnadze proved weak, corrupt, and deeply unpopular. Some believe that Washington installed Saakashvili or even pushed for his ascension to the presidency. In fact, US officials were very cautious during the disputed 2003 Parliamentary elections and subsequent anti-government demonstration.[13] However, Washington provided substantial

[12] On specific assets and hierarchy, see Lake 1999 and 1996.
[13] The United States' initial reluctance to embrace the reform coalition is well documented in Mitchell (2009b, ch. 3).

technical assistance that indirectly contributed to the resignation of President Shevardnadze's regime—including upgrading national voters' lists and running an exit poll of the tabulation at various national precincts (Mitchell 2009b, 50-51, 59-61). These actions helped opposition leaders demonstrate electoral fraud by the Shevardnadze government. Some nongovernmental groups, media monitors, and youth groups also received funding, training, and assistance from US sources, in what some scholars refer to as a diffusion of the model of the Serbian or "Bulldozer" Revolution of 2000 (see Bunce and Wolchik 2006; Beissinger 2007).

US officials soon cast aside their reservations. The new Georgian president emerged as an energetic and charismatic leader who championed Georgia's aspirations to join transatlantic institutions and forge close relations with the West. Saakashvili quickly established a reputation as a reformer and "law and order" leader. He fired the entire Georgian police force, instituted liberalizing economic reforms, purged the bureaucracy of Soviet-era technocrats, and made the eradication of petty corruption a primary policy goal. His administration prioritized Georgia's international image. For example, it adopted policies crafted to ensure dramatic improvements in international rankings, such as the World Bank's "Ease of Doing Business Index" (see Schueth 2011).

Most of Saakashvili's reforms, however laudable, also consolidated state power. Democracy monitors and NGO watchdogs soon accused Saakashvili of failing to deliver promised political liberalization. Indeed, Saakashvili's constitutional reforms of February 2004 strengthened the presidency at the expense of the parliament. They also gave him exclusive authority to appoint regional governors and mayors.[14]

The major turning point took place in November 2007, when the Georgian government used water cannons to disperse anti-government demonstrations in Tbilisi.[15] In addition, police raided Imedi TV Georgia's most popular independent channel, destroyed its broadcasting equipment, and closed the station. President Saakashvili declared martial law. The president soon after resigned and called a snap election in January 2008, which entrenched the one-party rule of Saakashvili's United National Movement (UNM). Nevertheless, US officials rarely criticized the Georgian administration and treated it as a fully democratic

---

[14] This section draws on Cooley and Mitchell (2009) and Mitchell and Cooley (2010).

[15] In 2008, Freedom House's democracy scores for "Political Rights" in Georgia, declined from a "3" to a "4," where they have remained until 2011. Georgia is rated as "Partially Free" by the organization. According to its 2011 report, "Georgia is not an electoral democracy. OSCE monitors have identified electoral problems such as the abuse of state resources, reports of intimidation aimed at public employees and opposition activists, and apparent voter-list inaccuracies, including during the 2008 presidential and parliamentary elections."

regime. Washington scaled back its democracy assistance and eliminated its support for Georgian independent media and media reform (Mitchell 2009b, 127–137).

Of greater concern to US officials should have been Tbilisi's increasingly aggressive rhetoric concerning the breakaway territories. Prior to 2004, most Georgians treated South Ossetia and Abkhazia as, in practice, lost. But Saakashvili made the reunification of Georgia a central commitment and priority. Some initial successes included displacing the Adjarian warlord, Aslan Abishadze, in 2004 as Georgian troops re-established control of the territory; in 2007 Georgian troops mounted a successful cooperation that established control of the Upper Kodori Valley previously controlled by Abkhazia.[16]

These successes emboldened the Georgian president to make public commitments to reintegrate South Ossetia and Abkhazia. In November 2006, Tbilisi created a provisional Government in Exile for South Ossetia. During his 2008 re-election campaign, Saakashvili significantly upped the rhetorical ante on reunification. On January 3, 2008, the Georgian president "declared 2008 'the year of victory and unified Georgia,' pledging to reunify the country 'no matter what the cost'" (*Radio Free Europe/Radio Liberty* 2008).

Shevardnadze himself provides an interesting case of how connections forged over the course of inter-state interaction can influence policy. But the period following the Rose Revolution saw the development of interpersonal ties among US and Georgian officials that came to extend across multiple levels of the US decision-making hierarchy. This reflected a deliberate Georgian policy, facilitated by Georgian official's preexisting Western-oriented social and cultural capital. For example, Saakashvili, who received an LLM at Columbia University and spent time in Washington, maintained an extensive array of US contacts and understood the inner workings of US policymaking. He appointed a series of young reformers in key foreign policy positions, most of whom had spent time in the United States for studies or on academic exchanges.

The social networks built by Georgian officials involved three main trajectories. The first encompassed the many US officials and government principals who developed close personal friendships to Georgian ruling elites. The list includes David Kramer (Assistant Secretary of State for Democracy, Human Rights and Labor), Damon Wilson (Senior Director for European Affairs at the National Security Council), Joseph Wood (Deputy Assistant to the Vice President for National Security), and Matthew Bryza (Deputy Assistant Secretary of State for Europe and Eurasian affairs).[17]

---

[16] In retrospect, the lessons of Adjara were inapplicable to the breakaway territories, but they probably emboldened Tbilisi and raised public expectations. See Marten 2012.

[17] Indeed, all of these officials criticized aspects of the Obama administration's "Reset" with Moscow and its Georgia policy.

Bryza's role proved particularly important. He was the US principal responsible for dealing with the "frozen conflicts" in the South Caucasus—including
Abkhazia and South Ossetia. Throughout his tenure, Bryza regularly praised
Saakashvili and publicly identified with him. This relationship and his public
statements drew the ire of Abkhazian and South Ossetian de facto authorities.
Georgian opposition figures complained of what they saw as an excessively close
relationship between Bryza and Saakashvili (see Champion 2008). Bryza certainly provided his critics with ammunition. For example, after the July 2007
bombing by Abkhaz forces of the Upper Kodori Valley—an area recently
secured by a Georgian military operation—Bryza commented in an interview
on Georgian television that:

> It was an assault on Georgia, a US friend-country, with which we are
> connected by common interests and values. . . . We appreciate Georgia's
> reaction after the assault. On the day of the attack, *Saakashvili* proved
> himself as a true leader. I would like to point it out that the US govern-
> ment was delighted with the actions taken by Georgia. (*Regnum* 2007)

Bryza also commented on Abkhazia's rejection of negotiations with Tbilisi following Georgian military actions that "de facto the Abkhaz government has no
moral right to turn down Saakashvili's proposal."

Bryza was one of a number of brokers who not only actively supported the
Saakashvili regime but also helped it deepen and expand its ties with Western
officials. Another was Daniel Kunin, a US citizen who served as Senior Advisor
to President Saakashvili from 2003 to 2009. Kunin became the Georgian
president's most trusted confidant. He attended meetings with US principals,
including those with Secretary of State Rice and other high-level officials before
the 2008 war. Kunin claims to have organized President Bush's visit in 2005,
"tutored" the Georgian president on his press appearances, and "introduced
him [Saakashvili] to a lot of Congressmen." In an interview, Kunin described his
own role in the Georgian administration as "strengthening ties with the West,"
observing, "The first year [after the Rose Revolution] was about reforms, changing the country from a failed state to a functional state. After that it became more
about foreign [relations] and concentrating on message" (Weinberg 2008).

According to a Foreign Agents Registration Unit (FARA) disclosure of 2004,
Kunin was the foreign addressee of the "Letter of Intent" for a $163,000 contract
signed between the lobbying group Edelman and the government of Georgia.[18]

[18] Short-form FARA disclosure filed by Edelman Group, No. 3634, September 4, 2004. Available
at http://www.fara.gov.

Remarkably, until March 2009, USAID actually paid Kunin—though he reports that he was a paid "consultant" rather than a US government employee (Weinberg 2008). Later that year, after stepping down, Kunin became a paid lobbyist for the National Security Council of Georgia, securing, with his partner Greg Maniatis, a $470,000 eleven-month contract.

Third, Tbilisi worked hard to ensure its visibility on Capitol Hill and in Washington policy institutes. To that end, it employed a number of experienced Washington firms (Silverstein 2011). Georgian officials found many champions across a bipartisan spectrum including Senators Biden, Graham, McCain, and Kyle. US House and Senate staffers describe frequent visits and on-message briefings by Georgian delegations. These visits stressed the country's democratic credentials and pro-US orientation; they aimed to secure more funding and US support for Georgia's NATO aspirations.[19]

One of the most interesting lobbying firms contracted by Georgia was the politically conservative Orion Strategies, headed by Randy Scheunemann. Since the end of the Cold War, Orion had represented several Eastern European countries that sought NATO membership and generally improved ties to the United States. From 2004 to 2012, Orion represented the government of Georgia and the Georgian National Security Council, making contacts and arranging meetings with Georgian delegations and US politicians, and working hard to secure favorable press treatment for Tbilisi.[20] In return, it received an estimated $2.1 million in payments.

Scheunemann also served as a top foreign policy advisor to Senator and presumptive Republican presidential nominee John McCain. On May 15, 2008, Scheunemann resigned from Orion when the McCain campaign officially cut off ties to lobbyists. According to a *Washington Post* story, on April 17, 2008, just after he had signed a new lobbying contract for Georgia, Scheunemann arranged a call between then candidate McCain and President Saakashvili (Mosk and Bimbaum 2008). During the August conflict and its aftermath, McCain claimed to have spoken to Saakashvili "several times a day," referring to the Georgian president as a "close friend of 25 years."[21]

---

[19] Indeed, after President Obama's election, Tbilisi attempted to compensate for its loss of influence by expanding its lobbying efforts. It targeted a number of Democratic groups. From 2008 to 2010, Georgia's National Security Council signed spate of contracts with the Podesta Group, Gephardt group, Ithaca Group Glover Park Group, Public Strategies, Arete Consulting, and Orion Strategies. See Mitchell and Cooley 2010, 49, table 4.

[20] Data gathered from http://www.fara.gov. See also Silverstein 2011.

[21] Senator McCain made the comment on Fox News, August 12, 2008. How a 16-year-old Saakashvili befriended McCain remains an open question. Post on Newshounds.us, August 12, 2008. Available at: http://www.newshounds.us/2008/08/12/fox_john_mccain_has_known_georgias_president_mikheil_saakashvili_for_25_years_since_saakashvili_was_16_years_old.php.

Figure 4.1 President Bush's Tbilisi Speech, 2005.

Of course, many foreign governments employ US lobbying firms. Tbilisi's efforts are notable for their relative success. Georgian officials developed close interpersonal ties with a number of key players, both through their own efforts and with the assistance of consultants. Georgian US-oriented cultural and social capital helped, but it also mattered that Tbilisi used its networks and resources to accumulate symbolic capital as a Western-oriented, liberalizing country in tune with the Bush administration's worldview.

In the field of US foreign relations, states that persuasively claim to have a commitment to liberal-democratic principles generally derive at least some advantages from that status.[22] As Hayes (2012) demonstrates, even motivated US policymakers have difficulty securitizing relations with other democratic states (Hayes 2009). But the Bush administration made democracy and democracy-promotion a focal point of its foreign policy.

After coming to power, Saakashvili wasted little time in signaling its orientations to the Bush administration. Saakashvili requested a copy of the transcript of the State of the Union speech prior to his first meeting with President Bush in Washington in February 2004. At the meeting, Saakashvili quoted from it and paraphrased its language concerning "freedom," "liberty," and "the West."[23] Bush visited Tbilisi in May 2005, during which the Georgian government renamed the airport highway to Tbilisi in the President Bush's honor. In Tbilisi, Bush gave his now famous speech that referred to Georgia as a "beacon of liberty for this region and the world" (see figure 4.1).[24] At a joint press conference held by the two presidents, Saakashvili described Bush as a "visionary and decisive

---

[22] For a discussion of the central role of democracy in US self-understanding, see Stephanson 1995.

[23] Author's personal communication with Tedo Japaridze, former Georgian Minister of Foreign Affairs.

[24] For the full text of speech, see *BBC News* at http://news.bbc.co.uk/2/hi/europe/4534267.stm.

leader" and claimed that "no country is closer to Georgia than the US" (BBC News 2005).

At a time when the Bush administration's "freedom agenda"—of supporting the promotion of democracy and regime change abroad—was faltering (particularly in Iraq), Georgia provided an important "success story" for the US administration. Under Shevardnadze, Georgia had already joined the Iraq War, but Saakashvili significantly increased its commitment. By 2008, its more than two thousand troops represented the third largest foreign contribution to the conflict.

Indeed, it is difficult to underestimate the starting success that Tbilisi enjoyed from its utilization and pursuit of international, interpersonal, and inter-organizational ties. Over the span of a few years, Georgia became a favored US partner, securing aid packages, high visibility meetings, and ramped up military training and security cooperation. As we noted earlier, the Bush administration even mounted a quixotic effort to secure a MAP for Georgia. But even after a disastrous military defeat, the accumulated symbolic capital ensured that US Congress quickly appropriated an emergency $1 billion aid package, including $250 million in extra-budgetary support (an unprecedented commitment). This vital aid shielded Georgia from the negative economic impact of the war and, in essence, kept the Saakashvili regime in power for another four years.

In sum, extensive personal contacts between US and Georgian officials, conducted through a variety of social networks, generated surprisingly close friendships and trust relationships.[25] Georgia's importance stemmed from the widespread perception of it as westernizing, democratic, and pro-administration. Tbilisi took pains to reinforce its status as a valuable partner by providing out-sized commitments to Iraq. And despite its democratic backsliding, US officials continued to present Georgia as a model of consolidated democracy, a trusted friend and ally, and a poster-child for the president's freedom agenda. Georgia's resultant symbolic capital constituted it as a specific asset for the Bush administration.

The August War, Credibility, and the Failure of US Authority

The key dynamics of US–Georgia relations prior to August 2008 fail to conform to traditional realist and rationalist expectations. Balance-of-threat theories suggest that Tbilisi should have acquiesced to Washington's calls for restraint, as

---

[25] We cannot, unfortunately, directly measure trust in these networks. But published accounts and interviews support our claims.

any rupture in the relationship constituted a much graver threat to Tbilisi than to Washington. Similarly, a relational contracting perspective that focuses solely on the material determinants of hierarchy cannot account for the breakdown in the authority of the US–Georgia relationship, nor for why US officials, despite their asymmetric power and various instruments of influence, found themselves dealing with military hostilities between a dependent client and a nuclear-armed great power.

This outcome resulted from misplaced trust. This becomes clear when we consider the range of hierarchical contracting at stake. Georgia's asset portfolio certainly provided little incentive for Washington to impose significant levels of formal hierarchy (e.g., a protectorate or informal imperial relationship), but not from contemplating incremental differences in the form of conditions and restrictions on US assistance. Instead, US officials assumed that strong bilateral ties and interpersonal relations would suffice to restrain Georgian officials. At the same time, Tbilisi believed that those same factors would lead the United States to provide significant support for Georgian military action.[26]

The Spiral to War

The exact causes of the war and exact sequence of events that led to the Georgian assault on the South Ossetian capital of Tskhinvali remain in dispute. According to the Council of the European Union's exhaustive fact-finding investigation of the conflict, known as the "Tagliavini report," though the Georgian side launched hostilities on the night of August 7, Russia had taken a series of provocative actions in the months before.[27] Moscow was especially aggravated by the West's decision in February 2008 to recognize Kosovo's independence. The declaration of the NATO summit in Bucharest in April further antagonized Moscow. Following contentious inter-alliance debate on whether to grant Georgia and Ukraine MAPs, the organization demurred but declared that both "will [inevitably] become members of NATO."[28] The note was inserted on the final morning at the request of the US mission; many European allies agreed to it as a concession for refusing a formal MAP to Georgia.[29] But the communiqué seemed to confirm Moscow's worst fears about the Atlantic Alliance—that it intended to continue to absorb former Soviet territory without regard for Russian interests.[30]

[26] On Georgian beliefs about US support, see Bowker 2011.

[27] See the full report at http://news.bbc.co.uk/2/shared/bsp/hi/pdfs/30_09_09_iiffmgc_report.pdf.

[28] Article 23. See text at http://www.nato.int/cps/en/natolive/official_texts_8443.htm.

[29] Author's personal communications with members of European delegations at Bucharest.

[30] On NATO conditionality as a reassurance and trust-building mechanism, see Kydd 2001.

Immediately following Bucharest, Moscow escalated tensions in the breakaway territories. In April, Prime Minister Putin announced that the Russian government would establish formal relations with its ministerial counterparts in
South Ossetia and Abkhazia. The same month, Moscow sent heavy artillery and
airborne combat troops to Abkhazia and, in May, deployed construction troops
to repair an important rail link between Abkhazia and Russia.[31]

Trust and Do not Verify: Dynamics of the August War

US officials who maintained particularly close personal and ideological ties
with Georgian officials were particularly likely to accept and uncritically repeat
Georgian accounts of events, including that Georgia did not escalate hostilities on August 7, 2008. A *New York Times* analysis of the leaked US diplomatic
cables of the war concludes that US diplomats were unusually credulous of their
Georgian counterparts; they "appeared to set aside skepticism and embrace
Georgian versions of important and disputed events." They dismissed and
omitted sources that disputed the analysis of the Georgian government; they
transmitted official Georgian versions to Washington without challenge or critical reflection (Chivers 2010). In some specific examples, US officials accepted
Georgian reassurances that their forces were not deploying on the afternoon of
August 7—even though they were—and that the Georgians had responded to
an imminent invasion by Russian forces.

US Ambassador John Tefft, a strong backer of Tbilisi, proved particularly
prone to restating Georgian government communications without criticism
or question. He asserted with certainty—on the day after the beginning of
hostilities—that the Georgian leadership did not intend to become embroiled
in the war, but was only responding to South Ossetian provocations. He then
emphasized that Saakashvili's account was supported by his own country team
and their review of the evidence. Remarkably, he cited statements by Georgian
Minister for Reintegration Temuri Yakobashvili in support of this conclusion
(Chivers 2010).

Despite the fog of war, and contra Tefft's statement of certitude about the
veracity of the Georgian government, plenty of evidence was inconsistent with
Georgian accounts. Not only would the subsequent comprehensive EU investigation discredit the assertion that Georgian troops were responding to South
Ossetian shelling, but at the time observers from the Organization for Security
and Cooperation in Europe (OSCE) monitoring mission reported no signs
of South Ossetian attacks. Commenting on Georgian military actions for the

---

[31] These are detailed in Asmus (2010) and Felgenhauer (2009).

New York Times, Ryan Grist, the Senior OSCE Representative to Georgia when the war broke out, stated, "It was clear to me that the [Georgian] attack was completely indiscriminate and disproportionate to any, if indeed there had been any, [South Ossetian] provocation." His replacement subsequently confirmed this account: "If there had been heavy shelling in areas that Georgia claimed were shelled, then our people [OSCE] would have heard it, and they didn't. They heard only occasional small-arms fire" (Chivers and Barry 2008). Over the next few days, US cables would uncritically transmit other Georgian talking points— therefore exaggerating the number of Georgian casualties and insisting that Russia's ultimate goal was to enter Tbilisi and topple Saakashvili's government (see also Klußmann 2010).

Following the conflict, US officials continued to argue that Russia directly initiated the war, even as a growing number of stories in the Western media contradicted important Georgian claims (Klußmann 2009). The publication of the Tagliavini report undermined Tbilisi's credibility by challenging its account of events (Campion 2009). Georgian officials, such as Minister of Interior Vano Merabishvili, thus accused commission members of harboring pro-Russian sympathies and even accepting bribes from Moscow (Klußmann 2010).

Blame, Restraint, and US Authority

US officials insist that they repeatedly sought to dissuade Tbilisi from initiating military conflict. In his generally pro-Georgian account of the war, former US Deputy Assistant Secretary of State Ronald Asmus (2010, 48) argues that US officials clearly, and repeatedly, expressed US support for restoring Georgia's territorial integrity but opposed Georgia using military means to accomplish this. In his testimony to the congressional Helsinki Commission shortly after the war, Bryza (2008) argued that he consistently urged Tbilisi "to resist the urge of any military reactions." Bryza, along with several other US officials, also notes that US Secretary of State Rice, during her July 2008 visit to Georgia, "cautioned President Saakashvili against any temptation to use force to resolve these conflicts, *even in the face of continued provocations*" (emphasis added). In his postwar testimony before the US Congress, Assistant Secretary of State Daniel Fried (2008) similarly emphasized that: "We had warned the Georgians many times in the previous days and weeks against using force, and on August 7, we warned them repeatedly not to take such a step. We pointed out that use of military force, even in the face of provocations, would lead to a disaster. We were blunt in conveying these points, not subtle. Our message was clear."

If US principals had delivered strong and multiple messages urging restraint, why did Georgian officials fail to heed these warnings, despite the considerable asymmetry in the US–Georgia relationship? Observers advance four major explanations. The first emphasizes that though some clearly cautioned against force, other US agencies or representatives sent "mixed messages," that is, suggesting that the United States would come to Georgia's defense in the event of conflict (Boweker 2001; Cooley and Mitchell 2009).[32] The second explanation posits that the Georgian government sought to entrap the United States. The third argues that the Georgians feared a Russian invasion and convinced themselves that they needed to strike first. A fourth suggests that the US election process played a major role: that Tbilisi feared a possible Obama victory and believed that striking in August would, at worst, mean doing so with a favorable US administration and, at best, would force Obama to adopt a more pro-Georgian policy. Our sense is that all four processes played some role and probably reinforced one another. Georgian policymakers discounted private warnings, which were not backed with any threat of sanction such as US aid cutoffs, overemphasized the importance of various indications of US backing, and thus expected that Washington would provide robust support in the event of a crisis. This wager inflected their calculus concerning the downside of striking without definitive evidence of a Russian invasion. Such reasoning is consistent with the role that trust plays in leading to favorable interpretations of the likely actions of the trustee.

But regardless if the Georgians received "mixed messages" or sought to entrap the United States in its local conflict, it is clear that the personal ties and symbolic capital that the Georgians had built up undermined the credibility of US warnings and calls for restraint. Georgian planners correctly inferred that they would not pay a price with the Bush administration for defying US warnings. Indeed, rather than punish Georgia, the US Congress supported the country through an emergency appropriation.

The Obama Administration

The Obama administration partially decoupled the social and cultural aspects of US–Georgian ties from the material dimensions of Georgian dependence and US hierarchy. Washington—much to the displeasure of pro-Georgia elites— instituted safeguards designed to restrain Georgia from unsanctioned military action. They reinstated USAID funding for Georgian democracy development,

---

[32] For instance, at a joint press conference following Saakashvili's July 2008 meeting with Rice in Tbilisi, Saakashvili pleaded for US support for NATO MAP: "I understood you are going to give a tough fight for us in December." Rice responded unequivocally: "Always Mr. President. We always fight for our friends." Available at http://www.america.gov/st/texttrans-english/2008/July/20080710161637gmnanahcub0.3613092.html.

including amending the electoral law and once again promoting media independence, over the objections of Georgian elites who had sought untied aid.[33] Unexpectedly, the Obama administration also seized upon the new US–Georgia Strategic Partnership agreement, signed in January 2009 (just a few days before the end of the Bush administration), to create a set of regular institutionalized meetings and discussions covering security, democracy, and other policy issues.[34] Rather than rely on ad hoc visits by officials who were well connected to Tbilisi, the administration generally embedded US–Georgian contacts in these institutional contexts, which US principals also used to pressure Georgia on domestic political reforms.

On the security front, the Obama administration also tried to anchor its military assistance and training in the requirements of Afghanistan training and elevating Georgian forces to NATO interoperability standards. At the same time, US officials refused to grant an alliance commitment to Tbilisi, reflecting, again, the asymmetric nature of the Strategic Partnership. Resisting mounting pressure from the Georgian Minister of Defense and pro-Georgian groups in the United States, the administration also refused to sell modern air defense systems or other weapons systems that could be construed as rearming Georgia in ways that would facilitate future aggressive action.

These changes—many of which were not reflected in total aid budgets—signal the diminishing symbolic capital enjoyed by Georgia with the Obama administration and its principals. For example, US officials denied an official bilateral presidential meeting to the Georgian president. At the 2010 US-hosted nuclear summit in Washington, US officials granted bilateral meetings to twelve other heads of state, including, in the post-Soviet sphere, Presidents Sarkisian of Armenia and Yanokovych of Ukraine, but overlooked the Georgian president (Kvelashvili 2010). Coupled with the high-profile "reset" of US–Russia relations, these shifts led Georgian officials and pro-Georgian US elites to accuse the Obama administration of "abandoning Georgia" or sacrificing it to improved relations with Russia.[35] In an interview with *Newsweek* a few months after the Obama administration assumed power, the Georgian president replied to a question about possible Western abandonment, lamenting that:

> Oh, yes, I have talked to him [Obama] on the phone. The problem is not about us—the problem is about their own internal politics. *We have*

---

[33] Authors' interview with USAID officials, Tbilisi, May 2010.

[34] For the Charter's text, see http://www.state.gov/p/eur/rls/or/121029.htm. For analysis of this asymmetry, see Mitchell and Cooley 2010, 17–22; and Welt 2010.

[35] This is a common meme in the Georgian press and among Georgian political commentators. For a US argument along these lines, see Kramer 2010.

integrated into U.S. internal politics. So during the change of power, there
was some sort of vacuum in America. Nobody knew what to do with
us. Everybody, including France, was waiting for Obama's guideline on
what to do about Georgia. I admire American ideas. I used to idealize
America under Bush, when ideas were above pragmatic politics. Now it
is a new time, when pragmatic politics are in charge of ideas. That might
spoil the America I know. (Nemtsova 2009, emphasis added)

In February 2012, Obama finally met with Saakashvili at the White House.
The White House pre-meeting statement noted that the president "will underscore the importance of our defense cooperation with Georgia" including its
contributions to ISAF, but rather than effusive discussion of common values, it
concluded that the "president also looks forward to discussing upcoming elections in Georgia and the reforms that ensure Georgia's continuing transformation
into a vibrant and stable democratic state."[36] Tellingly, Obama's statements at the
meeting emphasized the importance of *future progress* on democratic reforms
and of "the formal transfer of power that will be taking place in Georgia" after
Saakashvili's term expires. Despite some Georgian claims of a major new understanding on defense, the United States did not take significant steps to upgrade
Georgia's limited defensive capabilities (see de Waal 2012).[37] In October 2012,
President Saakashvili's political party decisively lost the parliamentary elections
to an oppositional coalition headed by billionaire Bidzina Ivanishvili, rendering
Saakashvili a political lame duck until his term expired in October 2013.

Indeed, the Obama administration's policies underscore the significance of
interpersonal ties in the US–Georgia relationship. Georgia's social and cultural
capital were far from limited to the Bush administration, but it should be clear
that both centered on the neo-conservative movement. It is easy to imagine a
hypothetical McCain administration either continuing the trajectory of US–
Georgia relations prior to 2009 or even further enhancing US–Georgia ties.[38]

However, the tenor of US–Georgian relations has witnessed something of a
reversal in the wake of Russia's annexation of Crimea and the ongoing crisis in
the Ukraine. In essence, the collapse of US–Russian relations convinced many
Western officials to increase security engagement with Tbilisi. Still, prominent
member states seem unwilling to support concrete commitments to incorporate Georgia into the NATO alliance (Coalson 2015). Although changing

---

[36] Text at http://www.whitehouse.gov/the-press-office/2012/01/17/statement-press-secretary-
visit-president-saakashvili-georgia.

[37] See http://www.whitehouse.gov/photos-and-video/video/2012/01/30/president-obamas-
bilateral-meeting-president-saakashvili-georgia#transcript.

[38] For some suggestive evidence, see Rogin 2011.

geopolitical circumstances positively impacted the US–Georgia relationship, we should not commit the post hoc ergo propter hoc fallacy of using them to explain the Bush administration's relations with Georgia.

Conclusions

The saga of US–Georgian relations in the 2000s amounts to something of a foreign-policy footnote, but it illustrates a great deal about the relational dimensions of US primacy, security governance, and hegemonic orders. US security governance involves a multiplex of networks that connect individuals, government organizations, and institutions. These networks extend further, implicating a variety of individuals, firms, and organizations outside of government. The fact of US power—of its various military, economic, cultural, and symbolic capital endowments—renders those networks asymmetric. But that does not mean influence runs in a single direction.

As we have argued, interpersonal relations—and resulting social capital—may empower agents of subordinate states in their efforts to secure preferred outcomes. At the same time, the very socialization dynamics that help to stabilize the order also provide subordinate actors with knowledge that they can deploy to shape US policy.[39] In the Georgian case, the leaders of a subordinate state effectively did exactly that.[40]

These dynamics do not always produce favorable outcomes. In the US–Georgia case, they led to poor decision-making in both Washington and Tbilisi. The Russia–Georgia conflict undermined US credibility and authority as a patron in the post-Soviet space. Washington revealed itself as unwilling to confront Russian military power in the region and unable to prevent its impetuous client from initiating what turned into a humiliating defeat. Indeed, US–Georgia relations are likely far from the only example of these kinds of dynamics. Many analysts argue that the interpersonal ties and trust relations cultivated by Ahmad Chalabi and the Iraqi National Congress with US elites played a significant role in convincing the Bush administration that invading Iraq would prove relatively costless (Mayer 2004; Ricks 2006, ch. 5).

But in showing that social networks—among actual people and bureaucracies, rather than approximations measured at the inter-state level—have consequences for international relations, we hope to have demonstrated that

---

[39] Avant (this volume) provides another example how informal networks can allow otherwise weaker actors to shape US interests and policy positions.

[40] For broadly similar arguments—ones focused on the strategic use of dominant actors' rhetoric to entrap them, see Hurd 2005 and Krebs and Jackson 2007.

relational approaches can provide insights into not just the micro-dynamics of international security but also inter-state power politics. This agenda requires more systematic research into the dynamics of sub-state transnational networks, with particular attention to the conditions under which they scale-up to shape inter-state relations. Regardless, we submit that an understanding of the nexus between power politics, security, and networks must include both efforts to unpack inter-state relations into their constituent network ties and attention to social, cultural, and symbolic dimensions of those networks.

5

Netting the Empire

Relationships and US Roles Governing Small Arms and Military and Security Services

DEBORAH AVANT

At the turn of the twenty-first century efforts to regulate private military and security companies (PMSCs) were at odds. US leaders harnessed the industry for their purposes while leaders in South Africa tried to regulate the industry out of existence and the United Nations sought to outlaw it as mercenary. Some ten years later, US leaders, the United Nations, and many states (including South Africa) increasingly coordinate their efforts regarding this industry via a complex mix of national legislation, multi-stakeholder agreements and standards. The regulation of small arms, on the other hand, appeared to be gaining traction in the late 1990s among governments and civil society groups in both Europe and the United States. These efforts stalled in 2001, however, and began to recede with a set of disappointments, particularly in 2006 and 2012 (Grillot 2011, 536; Erickson 2012). The passage of the Arms Trade Treaty in 2013 may have begun to reverse the slide but the treaty and the governance of small arms more generally remains well short of what many expected in 1999.

The United States played a significant role in the trajectory of both issues. The United States set the agenda in neither, though, and US action and impact on the two paths were different. In small arms, the United States acted as an initial ally to governance efforts, then as a spoiler, then as a willing but uncommitted participant. In military and security services, the United States moved from a spoiler to a booster, bringing considerable heft behind a multi-stakeholder effort in transnational governance.

Neither realist nor liberal arguments about US hegemony can explain the juxtaposition of US behavior in these two cases. Although governance appears only when the United States participates, as would be expected by both, neither can explain why the United States participated in one and not the other or why its actions were so different. Nor did the United States play the classic Empire role (Nexon and Wright 2007). Although the United States interacted with heterogeneous intermediaries to rule indirectly as per the classic Empire role, intermediaries also interacted with one another and influenced the positions taken by the United States. I propose instead to think of the US government as a network with a variety of "multiplex" nodes that are simultaneously nodes in other networks. Which relationships "net" the United States, and whether they pursue brokerage or closure, can lead the United States to play different roles on the global political stage at the same time.

In the following section, I develop my argument and explain its advantages relative to theories of hegemony for explaining US behavior in these cases. I then examine the relational unfolding of US roles in small arms and military and security services, demonstrating how different relationships affected US behavior in these issues. US behavior, in turn, affected both the effectiveness of transnational governance and the relative breadth of the concerns it served. I end with a discussion of what the analysis of these two issues implies for thinking about the role of the United States in contemporary global governance.

Explaining the US Role(s) in Global Governance

Prominent arguments from realist and liberal perspectives see the United States as a hegemon, or one of two major powers in a world of states. Although these arguments correctly anticipate US support to be necessary for increasing governance, their logic also expects US preferences and behavior on these two issues to be similar. The United States is a major exporter of both small arms and military and security services, which in simplistic terms should lead it to prefer lax regulation on both. If one assumes that the domestic voice of established industries rather than the benefits to the United States as a whole drives support for regulation (Drezner 2007), arms and services should also show similar dynamics. Both the small arms industry and the defense giants that have acquired military services have long established voices in American politics. If one sees the degree of negative externalities the United States faces combined with the influence of exporters/consumers as driving its behavior (Efrat 2010), the United States should show even less inclination to regulate services than arms because the United States faces more negative externalities from gun violence than from misbehavior by military and security service providers. While what the United States supported carried the day in both issues, theories of US hegemony are unable to explain why the United States would support, forestall, and then more moderately engage with regulation in small arms at the same time that it moved from resisting to supporting governance in military and security services.

US action also looks pointedly different in these two issue areas. In small arms, high level representatives of the US government dealt through formal institutions with other states at the United Nations to support or stymie an international treaty. Like an ideal-typical hegemonic order, and unlike an imperial order, inter-state rather than inter-societal claims dominated. Domestic and transnational groups made claims on its behavior as either a global leader or a sovereign power protecting domestic ideals. And it used US institutional veto to block regulatory measures it did not support. In the 1990s, the United States operated as liberal/institutionalist theories of hegemony might expect, but in 2000 it switched to block governance in a way that is consistent with Drezner's (2007) more realist theory of global governance. US resistance mediated after Obama took office, but it did not resume a leadership role; rather it acquiesced to remove its opposition in 2013 and signed the Arms Trade Treaty (ATT) in 2013. Although it supported initial efforts, US behavior since 2001 is widely agreed to have diminished the effectiveness of transnational small arms governance.

In military and security services, the United States began in much the same way as in small arms—dealing directly with other states and opposing the UN's attempts to frame the PMSC industry as mercenary. After notable incidents in Iraq led Congress to call for new regulatory measures, though, the United States neither proceeded unilaterally nor engaged with other states on international regulation. Instead, US regulators at the agency level (in the Department of Defense [DoD] and Department of State [DoS]) who had connected with others through "the Swiss Initiative" worked with a mix of state and non-state actors through multi-stakeholder initiatives to develop "soft" law instruments to aid transnational coordination. While this looks more like an imperial role given the US interactions with various intermediaries, the United States did not engage with the Swiss Initiative intending to develop transnational regulations. Indeed, it was quite the reverse; the Initiative engaged the United States, and the United States only participated because it expected the Initiative to do very little; to simply take stock of existing law. US engagement with this process, however, generated creative thinking that led US representatives to conclude that US interests would be best served by transnational regulation. The demand from Congress that US regulators "do something" was surely important, but not one initiative from Congress made any mention of transnational regulation—they focused solely on changes in US law. The use of transnational initiatives to satisfy congressional demands was an idea that emerged from interaction in this transnational process. The United States not only supported the development of soft law arrangements, but wrote them into US regulations (making them enforceable) and urged others to do the same. US behavior enhanced the effectiveness of transnational governance.

Relationships and US Roles in Global Governance

Examining the US government as a network focuses attention, first, on who acts as the United States on particular issues; whether the United States is represented at the presidential level or agency level (and which agency). Any specific actor as a "node" generates distinct multiplexity as they are simultaneously nodes in a particular set of other networks. These multiplex connections can be important for how the United States approaches an issue and also for conditioning the type of claim that those acting as the United States make. Particularly important for transnational governance is whether the claim is characterized by closure (recommitting the United States to established relations and ideals) or brokerage (encouraging the creation of new connections and, potentially, new combinations of ideals).

Who acts as the United States, what networks they are connected with, and the mix of brokerage and closure logic that characterizes their interactions can lead "the United States" to play distinct roles that reveal different preferences (even at the same time). Given the centrality of the US government in many global networks as well as the military and economic resources the United States holds sway over, though, ensuring that the United States is on board with, or at least not opposed to, an effort is a necessary (if not sufficient) condition for effective transnational governance.

Who acts in the part of the United States is associated with a number of factors but prominent among them is the formality of the process. More formal treaty processes at the United Nations generally elicit attention from higher levels of government and, as Eilstrup-Sangiovanni (this volume) suggests, can be politicized by domestic interest groups. More informal intergovernmental or multi-stakeholder processes are more likely to be handled at lower levels of government and often generate less public attention. Regardless, those who act for the United States bring with them a variety of transnational, organizational, and interpersonal connections. In the course of carrying out their duties for the United States, officials also make new connections. These connections have bearing on the way officials think of the United States and its interests in policy processes.[1]

The way these connections attempt to influence the United States, through brokerage or closure, is particularly important. Put simply, brokerage draws the United States into new connections and changes information flows in ways likely to generate new ideas about roles the United States might play in global

---

[1] Indeed, it is sometimes the case that people are chosen for a particular position in government specifically because of their connection with one or another network brings a particular perspective to abide.

governance. Brokerage should lead the United States to be more open to new ways of generating collective action. Closure is more likely to limit new connections, recommit the United States to established ideas, and ensure that the United States plays prescribed roles. Closure can be invoked by a variety of actors on different bases. For instance, attempts to discipline the United States to act like a liberal global leader may lead to more effective international governance while that aimed to ensure that the United States protects its sovereign rights may lead to less. Regardless, if closure becomes tightly attached to preconceptions in ways that limit information flow the US network can rigidify, pulling some elements close, while closing off potentially productive interactions with others.[2]

The dynamics of networks connected to US officials around the governance of small arms/light weapons and military and security services look different on these dimensions. In small arms, two opposing networks both used links with US officials to pursue closure around different visions of appropriate behavior. Advocates of governance pushed for a formal process whereby the United States would act as a global leader to create small arms bans through an inter-state agreement. A change in administration, though, led opponents of governance to represent the United States and act as a sovereign state, to protect the rights of its citizens to bear arms and thus block governance measures in 2001 and 2006. With yet another new administration and different links, the United States moved to a more moderate position, engaging with and then supporting passage of a more general ATT in 2013.

In military and security services, an intentional bridging effort by the Swiss drew the United States, along with a wide variety of other government, industry, and civil society representatives, into a network through collaborative brokerage aimed at problem-solving. Beginning with a mere "taking stock" of existing agreements and their potential implications for PMSCs, the process built on small successes to develop a creative approach to transnational governance of the industry. Although the United States entered the process uninterested in transnational governance, interactions in this process led individuals to see ways that transnational governance tools could be useful for the US government. The United States used various sources of power to support governance measures. US support for the effort both generated greater interest in the process among others (states, NGOs, and companies) and worked to make it enforceable through US law. Table 5.1 summarizes these two cases.

---

[2] In the best of situations, brokerage and closure can work together allowing connections to flourish among coherent networks (Burt 2005), but this requires that closure remains open to information. A liberal hegemony argument imagines just this kind of structural arrangement.

Table 5.1 **Issue Area Summaries**

	Small Arms	Military and Security Services
Who acts as the United States?	Cabinet and agency level	Agency level
Degree of formality?	Formal	Informal
Who has multiplex connections with the US representative on the issue?	Domestic and transnational proponents of governance; domestic opponents of governance	Transnational proponents of transnational problem-solving; domestic proponents of domestic regulation
Do they connect to the United States using brokerage or closure?	Closure	Brokerage
What is the justification for US action?	Protect sovereign rights; support for governance without infringing on sovereign rights	US interests enhanced by support for transnational governance
Does the United States contribute to transnational governance effectiveness?	Varied but generally no	Yes

The United States and Governance Dynamics in Small Arms

Background

With the end of the Cold War, arms control advocates turned their attention to the small arms and light weapons that were prevalent in the intra-state conflicts of the 1990s (Boutwell and Klare 1998).[3] The supply of small arms also grew and diversified during this period. The increase in supply was due to several trends.

---

[3] Small arms generally refer to revolvers, pistols, rifles, assault rifles, and light machine-guns. Light weapons include some man-portable firearms and their ammunition, light artillery guns and rockets, some guided missiles, heavy machine-guns, hand-held and mounted grenade launchers, man-portable air defense systems (such as shoulder-fired anti-aircraft guns and missiles), anti-tank guns, portable anti-tank and rocket launcher systems, and mortars of caliber below 100 mm.

First, the demobilization of soldiers frequently led to the diversion of their weapons to black markets. Government sales and transfers also increased, in part a result of increases in production of small arms as demand for larger conventional weapons waned even as arms manufacturers grew, spread, and became more interconnected (Klare 1997; Alves and Cipollone 1998). The number of manufacturers tripled between 1980 and 2000 as the industry globalized (Bitzinger 1994; Hayward 2000; Survey 2001). Finally, in the 1990s the sale of small arms to sub-state and non-state entities increased (Laurance 1998).

Opposing Networks

The story of opposing networks focused on small arms control has been well told elsewhere (Bob 2010, 2012; Grillot 2011). Brokerage on the part of analysts and advocates with like-minded groups, governments, and the United Nations enabled sharing of ideas about both the problems created by small arms and light weapons and potential solutions to them. Crime control and disarmament networks joined forces with each other and the United Nations to create a new, somewhat unwieldy, network sharing a belief that small arms and light weapons posed a threat to global peace and security, particularly illicit manufacturing and trafficking in areas of recurrent violence (Bob 2012, 111–119). There were some closure processes surrounding the need to regulate these weapons.

Simultaneously, connections between groups that had opposed gun control measures in the United States, Australia, and other states created a network to coordinate resistance to domestic gun control. As the network to regulate small arms internationally grew, the anti-control forces turned their attention to combatting regulation on the global stage (Bob 2012, 114–117). This network developed an alternative normative perspective, claiming that arms were not the issue; people, not guns, kill (Grillot 2011). They also argued that legal restrictions would be ignored by criminals and only impact law-abiding citizens. Finally, drawing on the National Rifle Association's (NRA) use of the Second Amendment in American politics, they argued that people have a "right" to bear arms (Bob 2012, 115). Increasing closure processes and signs of echo grew as the movement took an uncompromising position to halt any regulation.

Competing US Ties

Both of these networks had ties with different parties in the US government—pro-regulators with Democrats and anti-regulators with Republicans. The growing movement to control small arms developed connections with, and endorsements from, the Clinton administration in the 1990s. President Clinton first mentioned the issue in a speech to the UN General Assembly in October

1995 (Calhoun 1998). John Holum (Director of the US Arms Control and Disarmament Agency [ACDA] and then Under Secretary of State for Arms Control and International Security once ACDA was merged with the State Department) had been long connected with the arms control/disarmament community. US representatives from ACDA served on the UN's Panel of Governmental Experts on Small Arms.[4] Secretary of State Madeline Albright made reference to the small arms problem and US efforts to support solutions to it in several speeches in 1998, in which she also voiced her hopes for a coordinated effort to be negotiated under the auspices of the United Nations.[5] She addressed the small arms issue explicitly at the UN Security Council Small Arms Ministerial in New York in 1999.

During this time, the United States supported a number of regional efforts. These included the EU's "European Programme for Preventing and Combating Illicit Trafficking on Conventional Arms" (to promote information exchange and assist developing countries in eliminating illicit trade) as well as its "EU Code of Conduct on Arms Embargo" (setting standards on arms exports). In December 1999, the United States and European Union signed a joint Statement of Common Principles on Small Arms and Light Weapons, a 10-point Plan of Action that included US support for the EU Code of Conduct on arms exports and the principles contained in its criteria. Furthermore, the United States participated in the 1997 OAS "Inter-American Convention against the Illicit Manufacturing and Trafficking in Firearms, Ammunition Explosives, and other Related Materials," aimed at combatting weapons used in the illegal drug trade.

Advocates for transnational regulation pushed for a formal international conference at the United Nations to look comprehensively at the small arms issue (Survey 2002, 205). They wanted a formal process because of its gravitas and potential for binding international commitments. Orchestrating through the United Nations was pushed by both UN bureaucrats and some states out of concern that the Ottawa Treaty (banning land mines) would set a precedent that would weaken the UN's role (Krause 2002; Bob 2010).

At the first Preparatory Committee Meeting for the 2001 UN Conference (in January 2000) the US delegation head, Lee Feinstein, State Department deputy director of policy planning, said that the United States believed the

---

    [4] Herbert Lee Calhoun, senior foreign affairs specialist from the Bureau of Multilateral Affairs of the Arms Control and Disarmament Agency. http://www.fas.org/asmp/campaigns/smallarms/Ev_ of_US_Policy.htm.

    [5] At a UN Security Council Ministerial Statement on Africa in September and then in a speech to the International Rescue Committee in November. http://www.fas.org/asmp/campaigns/smallarms/Ev_of_US_Policy.htm.

international community should pursue an integrated, comprehensive approach to the small arms issue. That sentiment was repeated as late as November 2000 when the United States "strongly supported" an Organization for Security and Cooperation in Europe (OSCE) Document on Small Arms and Light Weapons, which began with the claim that small arms "are of concern to the international community because they pose a threat and a challenge to peace, and undermine efforts to ensure an indivisible and comprehensive security."[6]

The NRA and other gun rights groups had also cultivated ties, mostly with the Republican Party. Although historically a membership organization (and one that had actually supported the Gun Control Act of 1968), the NRA set up a lobbying arm in 1975 and began to both cultivate relationships with political conservatives to protect the Second Amendment (Diaz 2013).[7] It successfully supported the Firearm Owners Protection Act of 1986 to curtail excessive federal inspections of gun dealers and forbid the creation of a national registry of gun owners (*Washington Post* 2012). The organization continued to gain power through its support for conservative politicians. Although it was unsuccessful in preventing the Assault Weapons Ban in 1994, it demonstrated its voice in US politics and its increasingly vigilant stand against regulation of any sort (Kenny et al. 2006).

The NRA's work generated strong ties in Congress in the 1990s, particularly with its large effect on Republican gains in the 1994 (Kenny et al. 2006, 3). As the United Nations began to focus on small arms the NRA used these ties to mobilize against the effort (Seelye 1997). The NRA became even closer to the Republican Party and worked with it to defeat Al Gore in 2000 (Achenbach et al. 2013). These relationships were instrumental as George W. Bush took office.

President Bush replaced officials with ties to the arms control community in key State Department positions with those whose ties were to the NRA. John Bolton, a longtime NRA supporter, was appointed Under Secretary of State for Arms Control and International Security and led the US delegation to the UN Conference in 2001. Bolton made no secret of his ties with the NRA or its influence on the administration's stance, "NRA representatives keeping close watch on international gun-ban groups sounded the alarm that brought outrageous gun ban proposals to the attention of the Bush administration" (Bob 2012, 140). The delegation also included Bob Barr, a congressman for Georgia, who had joined the NRA's Board of Directors in 2001.[8]

[6] This is excerpted from the OSCE document in a Federation of American Scientist compilation of US policy statements relevant to small arms. See http://www.fas.org/asmp/campaigns/smallarms/Ev_of_US_Policy.htm.

[7] This was simultaneous with its increasing reliance on donations from arms manufacturers.

[8] http://www.meetthenra.org/nra-member/bob-barr.

Mobilization, Closure, and Rigidity

Both networks grew as a consequence of mobilization among like-minded groups. And both exhibited signs of closure (the development of denser connections and trust) that resulted in coalescence. At least up until 2001 the network of control proponents exhibited more diversity in views and in some parts of the network, a greater openness to different approaches to the small arms problem based on information (Karp 2006). The opponents of regulation developed closure earlier and more quickly exhibited signs of resistance to new information.[9] This and the ease with which their opposition was rooted in ideas about sovereignty created a strong logic for US opposition.

The control advocates had differing opinions on how to define the issue at the outset. Activists and experts organized themselves into the International Action Network on Small Arms (IANSA) in 1998. Initially some pressed for a more measured approach focused exclusively on conflict zones in unstable states, in part to avoid a confrontation with the NRA. Others, however, pushed for a broader claim linking transnational small arms regulation to gun control in stable countries. As the organization launched those with an uncompromising stance took leadership and IANSA increasingly called for broad goals (Bob 2012, 117–123).

IANSA's connections in the US government were sympathetic to its broader claims but the Clinton administration remained open to many different ways of reaching them. Indeed, in keeping with its support for a variety of initiatives encouraging corporate social responsibility (CSR), Clinton announced an agreement with Smith & Wesson in 2000 that, according to the press release, "represents an unprecedented partnership between the government and the gun industry to bring about meaningful reforms in the way the industry does business" (White House 2000). The agreement committed the gun manufacturer to a variety of steps that would result in safer guns (such as locks and no acceptance of large capacity magazines, among others) and safer distribution (requiring its distributors to do background checks even at gun shows, to implement theft control, and cutting off distributors whose guns are disproportionately linked to crime, among others).

Clinton's Smith & Wesson agreement was consistent with the administration's pragmatic approach to small arms regulation at the transnational level. A senior foreign affairs specialist at the State Department wrote an essay in 1998 that expressed support for control measures while acknowledging that the ability to obtain arms, including small arms and light weapons, was closely connected to fundamental sovereign rights of states; that any global regime must take account

---

[9] What network scholars call "echo" (Burt 2005, 169).

of cultural, historical, and legal differences on gun ownership in different states; and that there were intricate connections between legal and illegal arms flows that would be difficult to negotiate (Calhoun 1998).

The NRA's behavior more often invoked the politics of closure, even in the 1990s. Their arguments were made in the name of using sovereignty to preserve national tradition (particularly in the United States) and gun rights. Closure around the ideas of sovereignty had strong resonance with the NRA's message against international governance. They argued about the importance of protecting the United States against foreign influences preserving American freedoms in the face of global meddling. The NRA cast the United Nations' efforts as aimed at the United States, in opposition to American tradition, and tainted by foreign guidance. For instance, in a 1995 letter to Senator Jesse Helms, the NRA's Tanya Metaksa said that a UN Disarmament Commission had adopted a working paper proposing tighter controls on the American gun trade (Seelye 1997). The organization saw the foreign tag as useful for mobilization. As the NRA's Metaksa stated in 1997: "We put it in some of our mail—that the UN has this ongoing effort, funded by the Japanese and managed by the Canadians, to regulate guns worldwide" (Seelye 1997). This kind of mobilization—linking any regulation to an attack on gun sales in the United States and focused on preconceived notions about foreigners—is characteristic of the closure dynamic associated with echo.

Ironically, this came even as the NRA was connecting with their own set of like-minded groups across national boundaries. In 1993 the NRA and its affiliated organizations around the world founded the International Conference on Firearms Legislation (ICFL) in 1993 to focus on fighting domestic gun control in the name of preserving the right to bear arms. The ICFL was then superseded by the World Forum on Sports Shooting Activities (WFSA) in 1997 so as to counter international regulatory efforts (Morton 2006; Bob 2010, 2012). The NRA generally played down its international connections.

Another sign of rigidity was the extreme language used for its opponents and the intolerance of any compromise on regulation. This was most vividly apparent in response to the 2000 Smith & Wesson deal. Action America, a group linked with the NRA, called the action a betrayal and "a deal with the devil."[10] The NRA organized a boycott of Smith & Wesson that, according to an executive at gunmaker Kimber America, sought to "make sure that no one else is going to join the surrender." Sales at Smith & Wesson plummeted. When it was acquired by new ownership, Smith & Wesson distanced itself from these policies. As the

---

[10] http://actionamerica.org/guns/swbetray.html.

new chief executive of Smith & Wesson said, "It was important that we be an active part of the industry again" (McIntire and Luo 2013).

Shifting Ties, Shifting US Positions

When President George W. Bush took office and appointed officials linked with the NRA to key administrative positions, US policy pivoted. Under Secretary Bolton's opening statement on July 9 took issue with the category of small arms and light weapons and the assumption that their proliferation necessarily led to problems. "We, therefore, do not begin with the presumption that all small arms and light weapons are the same or that they are all problematic. It is the illicit trade in military small arms and light weapons that we are gathered here to address and that should properly concern us" (Bolton 2001). He went on to outline a number of "red lines" for the United States that sharply curtailed the possibilities for agreement and carefully reflected the view of the NRA.

The result of the 2001 conference was the Program of Action (POA), a non-binding agreement that hewed to the substantive limits Bolton outlined in his opening statement. The only ground the United States gave was in agreeing to a follow-on conference in 2006. Human Rights Watch called it a "Program of Inaction."[11] Some accused the United States of "hijacking" the UN Conference (Meierding 2005).

In the wake of the 2001 conference, rancor grew on both sides. Regulation proponents were deeply disappointed with the POA. According to Aaron Karp, "the Conference brought international small-arms diplomacy to a near halt . . . repudiat[ing] the global process it was conceived to establish" (Bob 2012, 140). Some NGOs threw in the towel.[12] The United Nations established a Special Rapporteur to issue a report to demonstrate with hard evidence that human rights abuses were associated with small arms. And IANSA remobilized to push for the insertion of "teeth" in the POA at the Review Conference (RevCon) in 2006.

The NRA, on the other hand, cast the POA as a significant threat to the rights of law-abiding citizens and also geared up for the battle in 2006. Wayne LaPierre, NRA executive vice president, wrote *The Global War on Your Guns* released in 2006 before the RevCon. Its Amazon description reads:

The United Nations wants your guns. They want all of them—*now*—and they've found a way to do it. In fact, the UN is so cocksure it can

---

[11] http://www.hrw.org/news/2001/07/18/un-program-inaction-small-arms.
[12] Human Rights Watch closed its program (Bob 2012, 140).

commandeer the Second Amendment that it chose the Fourth of July, 2006, to hold its global gun ban summit in New York City. If you think there's no way an armed UN platoon of blue helmets can knock on your door to take your guns, this book just became your next must-read.

The US position at RevCon remained tied to the NRA's position. There was no agreement reached, the POA was not extended, and no additional meetings were planned.

After the disappointing outcomes in 2001 and 2006, IANSA joined with other NGOs to form the Control Arms campaign. The Control Arms campaign joined with supportive states to work toward an ATT, which broadened the focus beyond small arms to the entire range of conventional weapons (including advanced conventional weapons, tanks, armored combat vehicles, artillery systems, military aircraft, military helicopters, naval vessels, missiles, missile launchers, small arms and light weapons, and combat support equipment as well as parts, components, and/or technology to manufacture, modify, or repair the covered items). The goal, according to Control Arms, was "a bulletproof ATT"— that is "a global, legally binding agreement that will ease the suffering caused by irresponsible transfers of conventional weapons and munitions."[13] The United States distinguished itself by being the only state to vote against a resolution to pursue such a treaty in 2006.

When the Obama administration took office in 2009 it reengaged the United Nation and the proponents of regulation on the ATT. Even agreeing to take part in the process, however, caused the NRA to send out a press release telling people that the United Nations was going to regulate private gun owners in the United States. What Obama and Clinton could not get in domestic legislation, the NRA argued, they would try and bring in through the "back door" of the United Nation.[14] The Obama administration took pains to construct a measured path—bowing to the concerns of gun rights groups but arguing that the "gold standard" of US practice with respect to arms transfers should be promoted internationally (US DoS 2013). This moderate position was disappointing to regulation proponents but did little to assuage opponents. US hesitancy and Chinese resistance combined to lead the 2012 meeting to end without reaching any consensus (Gladstone 2012). Continued negotiations, however, did lead to the passage of the ATT in 2013. The NRA called it a clear violation of the Second

---

[13] http://www.controlarms.org/index_c.php.

[14] https://www.gunsamerica.com/blog/national-gun-registry-imminent-fight-the-un-small-arms-treaty-att/. In fact, the Obama administration, like the Clinton administration, pursued a cautious approach vis-à-vis UN efforts on small arms—in part because of worries about the potentially high political costs.

Amendment and vowed to work with the Senate to opposed ratification.[15] Less than a month later Fox News reported the "Good news from Washington" that the ATT was "DOA" (dead on arrival) in the Senate (Bromund 2013).

US Role and Governance Effectiveness

Support by the United States would not have guaranteed that the 2001 Conference would lead to a successful governance dynamic. China and Russia had expressed misgivings and Belarus, Iran, Syria, Egypt, and Saudi Arabia also opposed international regulation (Survey 2002; Meierding 2005; Efrat 2010; Grillot 2011). Also, a North–South split emerged on export controls with southern (non-manufacturing) states concerned that these would limit their capacity to gain access to arms for defense (Karp 2002; Survey 2002). But US opposition ensured the limits of effectiveness, preventing agreement on such things as a definition of small arms, focus on the interaction between legal and illegal arms flows, and attention to the transfer of small arms to non-state actors, among others (Krause 2002).

The ATT's passage in 2013 represents a small step forward. Although it does not focus exclusively on small arms (indeed, partly for this reason the NRA and its affiliates worried that they would be less advantaged in their opposition to it) it is, according to Small Arms Survey, "a significant addition" to global governance efforts on small arms. The ATT requires control systems for export obligations and these are legally binding. The compromise necessary to pass it, however, left provisions for importing, transporting, and brokering weaker than the non-binding commitments in the POA. Thus, some worry that it could be a step backwards in some areas (Survey 2013). Also, while the United States engaged with the process and signed the ATT, it did so while carefully avoiding its implications for small arms, and it is unlikely to ratify the treaty.

The transnational governance of small arms has been closely tied to the position taken by the United States. The US position, however, has changed depending on the connections of those in office. While the NRA and its affiliated groups have kept the pressure on, Democratic administrations with connections in the arms control community have been more supportive of governance initiatives than Republicans, with whom the NRA is closely affiliated.

The fight over small arms control has been largely fought in the formal domain. This has meant greater high-level attention from different administrations and enhanced public attention. As we might expect, this makes it easier

[15] http://www.nraila.org/news-issues/news-from-nra-ila/2013/9/obama-administration-signs-united-nations-arms-trade-treaty.aspx.

for the NRA and its allies to track the issue. Gun rights organizations, though, have been so vigilant and are so well connected to many levels of government that they are likely to have also picked up more informal measures (as the reaction to the Smith & Wesson agreement demonstrates). The formal focus, however, has given the gun rights groups' closure strategy advantage in the political debate. Arguing to preserve US sovereignty found a greater domestic constituency than urging the United States to play a global leadership role. Even the position defending the Obama administration's decision to support the ATT refers to doing so even while protecting sovereign rights.[16]

The United States and Governance Dynamics in Military and Security Services

Background

A market for military and security grew in the 1990s. PMSCs registered in many different countries began providing a wide range of military and security services to an array of global actors, including states, international organizations, nongovernmental organizations, and global corporations (Singer 2003a; Avant 2005). In the 2000s, there was a consolidation in the global suppliers of what had been domestically oriented security as companies like Group 4/Securicor began to provide security transnationally (Abrahamsen and Williams 2006, 2011). The blurring of lines between military and police and the services the private sector provides to replace both also contributed to the globalization of this market.

The US government is an important consumer in this market. The size of the US defense budget and the US government's enthusiasm for private alternatives led it to be a major purchaser in the 1990s. US dominance in the market increased after 9/11, largely the result of its use of PMSCs during the hostilities in Iraq and Afghanistan, a summary of which is provided in figures 5.1 and 5.2. Although overshadowed by Iraq and Afghanistan, there are a number of additional US initiatives, such as training foreign military forces, in which PMSCs have played a significant role.[17]

Worldwide demand outside the United States has also been important to the market's growth. A number of countries in the 1990s used PMSCs to supplement

---

[16] http://www.state.gov/t/isn/armstradetreaty/.

[17] A prominent example is the Department of State's Bureau of African Affairs' Peacekeeping Program—or AFRICAP. Four companies, PAE (owned by Lockheed), AECOM, DynCorp, and Protection Strategies Incorporated, were awarded the five-year $1.5 billion contract to support these efforts (Avant and De Nevers 2011).

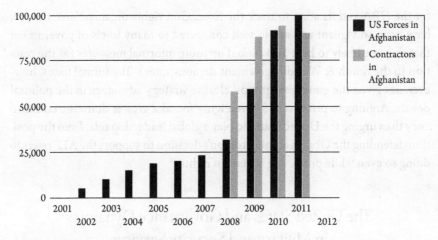

Figure 5.1 US forces and contractors in Afghanistan.

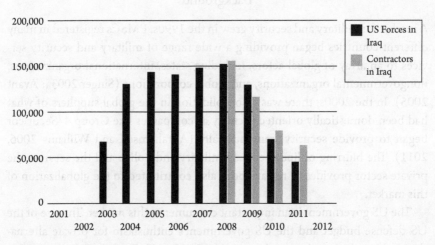

Figure 5.2 US forces and contractors in Iraq.

and upgrade the capacities of their forces including Angola, Bosnia, Croatia, Papua New Guinea, Sierra Leone, and the United Kingdom, among many others. Finally, non-state actors ranging from international organizations like the United Nations to humanitarian NGOs such as Save the Children to multinational corporations like British Petroleum have also expanded their demand for security services (Avant 2005; Stoddard, Harmer, and DiDomenico 2008; Deitelhoff and Geis 2009). More recently PMSCs have played a significant role in anti-piracy efforts.[18]

[18] See, e.g., "Protecting Ships from Somali Pirates—The Navy vs Private Security," *Forbes*, March 11, 2013. Available at: http://www.forbes.com/sites/gcaptain/2013/03/11/protecting-ships-from-somali-pirates-the-navy-vs-private-security/.

Divergent Networks

The growth of the military and security services industry in the 1990s led to divergent responses. The United Nations treated it as a potential resurgence of mercenaries (Percy 2007, 24–26). South Africa saw it as a threat to sovereignty and passed legislation aiming to put its emerging military and security services industry out of business (Herbst 1999). The United States, on the other hand, saw PMSCs as a tool to serve its foreign policy interests (Avant 2005, 146–156). The little NGO activism that there was either called the activity mercenary or called for better regulation of the emerging global industry (Shearer 1998; International Alert 1999).

The dramatic increase in the US use of PMSCs in Iraq led more attention to this issue. Congress questioned the administration and issued a succession of criticisms and requirements—all of them domestic. The administration maintained that PMSCs were an important tool for American policy. Civil society groups in and out of the United States began to mobilize around a variety of concerns (from mercenarism to profiteering). The United Nations continued its mercenary focus. South Africa protested that South African personnel were working for the United States in contravention of South African law.

The Swiss Initiative as Brokerage

In the midst of this cacophony, the Swiss government and the International Commission of the Red Cross (ICRC) launched the "Swiss Initiative" in 2006. In keeping with their more general attention to changes in the practice of conflict that have impacts on international humanitarian law (IHL), the Swiss government and the ICRC had become increasingly concerned with the problem PMSCs posed to international humanitarian law (SFC 2005). The Swiss had connections with PMSCs, civil society groups, and governments and devoted effort to pulling all who had relevant concerns into the process—pursuing an explicit brokerage strategy.

The shape of the initiative reflected attention to the various concerns of relevant parties to ensure maximum participation. Its informal quality drew in lower level representatives in seventeen governments (the United States, the United Kingdom, and South Africa as well as other important European governments and other states involved with the industry) along with representatives from industry and civil society. The first meeting took place in January 2006. Follow-up meetings were then held in November 2006 and April 2008.[19]

[19] The initial signatories are Afghanistan, Angola, Australia, Austria, Canada, China, France, Germany, Iraq, Poland, Sierra Leone, South Africa, Sweden, Switzerland, the United Kingdom, Ukraine, and the United States.

The stated purpose of the first meeting was to simply "take stock" of existing commitments and their potential relevance for PMSCs in a problem-solving mode.[20] This minimal goal drew in countries like the United States who were resistant to new transnational regulation. The premise also appealed to both those more complacent about the industry (and tired of hearing critics say there was a vacuum of law) and those more critical of how the industry was being used (and eager to bring existing obligations to light).[21] The meeting aimed to look particularly at international humanitarian and human rights law, which constitute the bulk of international commitments during conflict. This also reflected the long-standing commitments of the organizers and attracted consequential civil society organizations interested in human rights.[22]

Through three meetings, participants built on small successes, beginning with agreement on how to define PMSCs. As the logic of brokerage would suggest, relatively open interaction among previously unconnected networks resulted in new ideas. Particularly important was the idea to categorize the different relationships states had with PMSCs. Those participating also developed relations with one another and a commitment to progress on the issue through the meetings, their shared efforts to collect best practices, and their accomplishments.

The Montreux Document was issued in September 2008.[23] It created no new legal obligations and is not a legally binding document. But the document provided an entirely new frame for thinking of the industry and how to best regulate it. It defined military and security services and the companies that provide them.[24] It also categorized governments by their relations to the industry (contracting states, home states, and territorial states), catalogued the responsibilities of governments and others in keeping with obligations under existing international human rights and humanitarian law, and issued best practices for each type of state vis-à-vis PMSCs drawing on existing laws in particular states as well as from related issue areas (ICRC 2008, 9).[25]

The meetings, while contentious at times, produced more agreement than many had expected. Beyond agreement on the obligations implied by existing

[20] See "Workshop of Governmental Experts and Industry Representatives on Private Military / Security Companies 16-17 January 2006, Zurich, Switzerland," Summary of the Chair, September 1, 2006. Available at: http://psm.du.edu/media/documents/regulations/global_instruments/multi_stakeholder/montreux/montreux_document_summary_first_meeting.pdf.

[21] Singer (2003b) was one of many asserting a vacuum of law.

[22] Author interviews with civil society representatives, fall 2010.

[23] http://www.eda.admin.ch/eda/en/home/topics/intla/humlaw/pse/parsta.html.

[24] PMSCs are business entities that provide armed guarding and protection of people and objects, maintenance and operation of weapons systems, prisoner detention, and/or advice/training of local forces and security personnel.

[25] See also http://www.eda.admin.ch/psc.

commitments and opinions about best practices, participants also agreed that while international law provided useful benchmarks for states it lacked guidance on the proper behavior for PMSCs. There was particular concern with the behavior of companies providing security services (guarding of people and objects) as they were most likely to generate violations of international humanitarian law and human rights abuses. In its final meeting, then, the group also called for the launch of a related multi-stakeholder initiative to create an International Code of Conduct for private security providers (ICoC). The brokerage strategy thus yielded both new connections and new ideas, both of which generated greater progress toward coordination than many had expected.

Bridge Advantages, Information Flow, and Feedback to US Interests

The Swiss did occupy a bridge position in this nascent network, and this did advantage a focus on IHL and human rights, a concern to both the Swiss government and the ICRC. This focus had long-term impact on the agenda animating governance of PMSCs. As initiatives have unfolded, the IHL/human rights focus has continued to dominate as the governance frame for PMSCs. Ongoing efforts focused on the segment of the industry whose personnel carry arms and perform guarding or "security" tasks was a direct consequence of this focus.[26]

The brokerage strategy also promised collective benefits. Prominent among these is the sharing of information across networks that can lead to creativity and new synthesis (Burk 2005, 62–66). In the initial meetings, the United States both shared information on its practices and was able to garner new understandings from others. As one of the few countries with even skeletal regulation for military and security services in place, the United States offered one model for regulation and thus informed the development of best practices for contracting and home states. The meetings and informal communication among participants outside them, though, also allowed US agency participants to discuss and vet potential changes in response to events in Iraq and Afghanistan. As Congress increasingly called for something to be done,[27] brainstorming with

---

[26] This focus also had strategic benefits for the potential effectiveness of the effort, though. It drew in more consequential civil society groups like Amnesty International, Human Rights Watch and Human Rights First, boosting the perceived legitimacy of the effort and its potential import.

[27] Every single National Defense Authorization Act between 2005 and 2013 contained language aimed at better controlling PMSCs and other contractors. See summaries here: http://psm.du.edu/national_regulation/united_states/laws_regulations/index.html#federal_laws_and_regulations.

this larger group about the options was, according to one US official, "responsive to needs."[28]

Some of the best practices for contracting states outlined in the Montreux Document were both influenced by events in Iraq and immediately implemented by the United States in Iraq and Afghanistan. For instance, the Montreux Document calls for contracting states to keep track of the PMSCs they hire and their employees, oversee them effectively, and keep records of potential misdeeds. The need for these practices was highlighted by the US experience, and the United States has taken action to implement them.[29] The data for figures 5.1 and 5.2 are available thanks to these changes.

Synergies between the process and US agencies accelerated with the follow-on process to develop an International Code of Conduct (ICoC) and then an association to govern it in September 2009. The same DoD agency individuals participating in this process were also responsible for tracking contractors in Iraq and Afghanistan and responding to congressional requirements for further regulation. They realized that many more contractors worked for other governments, private companies, NGOs, and others than worked for the United States—and that the behavior of all contractors on the ground could affect the success of US endeavors. They thus came to see transnational coordination that promised to affect the behavior of PMSCs working for many different clients as having real benefits to the United States. By this time President Obama had also come into office and appointed Michael Posner as Assistant Secretary of State for Democracy, Human Rights and Labor. Posner came to the office from Human Rights First, with experience in multi-stakeholder initiatives and interest in solidifying the human rights focus of governance over PMSCs.[30] Although the DoD and DoS did not see eye to eye on many things, both saw benefits to US interests from transnational coordination. Furthermore, the ICoC promised benefits to agencies hiring PMSCs. By setting a floor for companies eligible to contract with the United States, it could allow agencies to pass over low bidding

[28] Interview with Chris Mayer, Washington, DC, December 2011. Members of the DoD's Office for Program Support, as well as a representative from the State Department and from the Office of Government Council participated in the process. The DoD Office for Program Support is responsible for keeping tabs on contractors working in contingency operations and has also been the primary office involved in recommending and designing implementation for specific instructions.

[29] See US DoDI 3020.41 "Operational Contract Support" (December 2011), http://psm.du.edu/media/documents/us_regulations/dod/directives_and_instructions/us_dod_3020-41.pdf, and 32 C.F.R. 159 "Private Security Contractors Operating in Contingency Operations" (August 11, 2011), http://psm.du.edu/media/documents/us_regulations/dod/directives_and_instructions/federal_register/us_dod_32_cfr_159.pdf. There are critics of the system for gathering information but most agree it is a significant step forward (HRF 2011).

[30] Interview with R. Scott Greathead, fall 2010.

but potentially risky PMSCs. All of this led US representatives to become increasingly interested in, and supportive of, the process to develop an ICoC.[31]

Shortly after the ICoC was finalized the US National Defense Authorization Act of 2011 required that the Secretary of Defense define standard practices for the performance of private security functions (USNDAA FY 2011, section 833). US officials at DoD saw this as an opportunity to marry US law and purchasing power to the ICoC, enhancing the legitimacy of US law in the eyes of the international community by linking it to the multi-stakeholder process, enhancing the power of the multi-stakeholder process by putting US purchasing power behind it, and serving US interests by improving the behavior of PMSCs.[32] They thus retained ASIS International to begin a process to develop standards for the private security industry in keeping with the principles of the Montreux Document and the ICoC.[33] US officials describe the decision to retain ASIS as an explicit attempt to link the power of the United States to the principles agreed to in the Montreux Document and ICoC to accomplish a purpose agreeable to most— encouraging private security providers to behave in a way consistent with international humanitarian and human rights obligations.[34] Compliance with the ICoC and/or PSC standard as well as membership in the ICOCA have been written into contracting requirements and are thus enforceable through US law.[35]

As this process was seen to have effect, it also generated additional connections and influence with others concerned with this industry. The UN Working Group on Mercenaries, for instance, has adopted the definition of PMSCs, the categories of states as they relate to PMSCs, and the focus on regulation of PMSCs (rather than outlawing mercenaries). While it still aims for international ("hard") regulation, individuals participating in this working group are a part of the broader network (attending similar conferences, sharing information, etc.) rather than separate from it.

---

[31] Interview with Gary Motsek and Chris Mayer, December 2011; Avant, Berlin, and Kruse 2011.

[32] Comments by Gary Motsek, January 2011; interview with Gary Motsek and Chris Mayer, Director, Contingency Contractor Standards and Compliance, December 2011.

[33] ASIS is accredited by the American National Standards Institute (ANSI) as a Standards Developing Organization. ANSI, in turn, is the US affiliate of the International Organization for Standardization (ISO). As an accredited SDO, ASIS participates actively in the ISO. See <IBT>ASIS International "Standards and Guideline: Quick Reference Guide." Available at: http://www.asisonline.org/guidelines/committees/docs/SGquickReferenceGuide.pdf</IBT>.

[34] Ibid. Thus far PSC 1 Management System for Quality of Private Security Company Operations and three complementary standards have been developed, and PSC 1 has been developed into an ISO Standard. For more see http://psm.du.edu/international_regulation/global_standards_codes_of_conduct/asis_standard.html.

[35] See, for instance, https://www.fbo.gov/index?s=opportunity&mode=form&id=6247a35a5d9816a4b5e4f067b8758ecc&tab=core&_cview=0. DoD requires compliance with the PSC standard, DoS requires membership in the ICOCA.

US Role and Governance Effectiveness

There is evidence of American power at work in support of each of these governance initiatives, but it is the power of US engagement and then the power
of binding its economic resources, regulatory frameworks, and connections to
transnational multi-stakeholder processes. Thus, it is "power over" in pursuit of
"power to." Members of the US government explicitly recognized that working
with others and through a process that was not US-led afforded more legitimacy
to their efforts than would be the case if they acted alone—and that this added
legitimacy increased the effectiveness of the initiative.[36] They were quick to
remind other stakeholders, though, that the purchasing power of the US government and its willingness to enforce global standards in its contracts and through
US law enhanced the appeal of these multi-stakeholder agreements.[37]

US efforts have contributed to a nested web of regulations developed to
govern military and security services. This web makes explicit connections
between different transnational initiatives as well as transnational initiatives and national law. The PSC standards specifically refer to the Montreux
Document and the ICoC as founding principles. The ICoC nests itself in
the UN Guiding Principles and by extension, other related initiatives such as
the Voluntary Principles on Security and Human Rights. The DoD and DoS
both have requirements linked with these standards—joining American legal
requirements to these initiatives. They have been adopted by several additional
governments, including the United Kingdom (ASIS 2012). And PSC Standards
can be written into contracts with other stakeholders, thus making adherence
enforceable through contract law.[38]

The US role has enhanced the uptake of this initiative by other governments.
As of 2015, fifty governments and three international organizations had signed
on to the Montreux Document, many more states had signified interest, and a
Montreux Document forum had been created to continue engagement among
states.[39] There are signs that the process has harmonized some law and practice
surrounding this industry in a variety of states. The ICoC and standards processes extended the Montreux principles to the PMSC industry and, potentially

---

[36] Interviews with US Department of Defense officials, January and December 2011.

[37] Remarks of a US Department of Defense official, January 2011.

[38] For the usefulness of contract law as a vehicle for regulation, see Dickinson 2007. There has
been some controversy within the governance network, particularly among some civil society
groups, about whether or not the PSC standards complement or compete with the ICoC. The PSC
standards do specifically reference the ICoC, however, and as of 2014 the two processes are working
in tandem.

[39] http://www.mdforum.ch/.

to non-state clients of PMSC who could also use ICOCA membership and standard compliance as an indicator of well-governed companies.

Similar to the logic of a regime complex, these processes have worked to harmonize not only state law and practice but also the practice of the various other powerful stakeholders whose decisions have consequence to how military and security services are provided (Keohane and Victor 2011). In the contemporary transnational governance, initiatives that draw together different powerful actors are more likely to generate effective governance (Abbott and Snidal 2009).

Network Implications for Thinking about the United States and Transnational Governance

The analysis of these two cases has important implications for thinking about the various types of US power and its role in transitional governance. As traditional theory suggests, the United States was instrumental to governance outcome in both issues. The United States has a wide array of resources and relationships that it can use to influence the course of transitional governance. As one might expect if the United States were playing an imperial role, it engages with a wide variety of state and non-state actors and pursues heterogeneous contracting (Nexon and Wright 2007).

What goals the United States pursues, though, are more easily traceable to the networks in which US policymakers operate than any structurally derived interests. The networks US policymakers are a part of can influence the network that is the US government and the trajectory of US policy. While part of this phenomenon has long been studied by domestic theories of international affairs, these cases demonstrate that networks can be transnational as well as domestic. Small arms relationships with an emerging transnational network of arms control activists were linked with the Clinton administration, while domestic (though also transnationally linked) gun rights groups had strong ties with the Bush administration. Connections with a transnational multi-stakeholder group in military and security services affected the way the United States saw its choices beginning in 2007 irrespective of whether Bush or Obama was in office.[40]

It is not only who influences US policy that matters, but how they do it. In the small arms case, connections with both Democratic and Republican administrations attempted to influence US action in a formal process through closure. Experts and activists in the 1990s aimed to get the United States on board so as

---

[40] As Cooley and Nexon (this volume) demonstrate, interpersonal ties with other government elites can also affect US goals and policy.

to push forward a formal process to curtail the flow of arms. The arms control community used their connections among Democrats (first with Clinton and then Obama) in a logic of closure, trying to get the United States to take the appropriate role of a "global leader" and lead an international agreement to stem the flow of small arms. Gun rights connections with Republicans, and particularly the George W. Bush administration, also worked under the closure logic but pushed the United States to use its sovereign power to preserve its national heritage by resisting transnational governance initiatives.

The network associated with gun rights was tighter and became rigidly attached to its aims, but the logic by which it engaged the United States was advantaged by its position and aims. As a domestic group, it had greater claims over what sovereign interests and power were than more transnationally connected governance supporters. It claimed to be pushing the United States toward its true interests rather than those espoused by foreigners. Under its influence, the United States moved boldly to stymie transnational governance in the name of protecting US sovereignty and Second Amendment rights. While many activists seeking new governance often push for more formality, closure and formal processes built on the logic of sovereignty may actually advantage domestic groups and groups that use sovereign logic to impede cooperation.

Connections with the United States in military and security services, on the other hand, operated in the logic of brokerage. The Swiss Initiative brought together multiple parties to discuss and share ideas in an informal arena. Although the Swiss and ICRC did have influence (they successfully refocused attention on IHL and human rights), their interactions did not aim to get the United States to behave according to a particular stricture but were open to exchange about what proper behavior might be. The informality of the process also allowed for the inclusion of actors from industry and civil society. The United States and others were engaged openly in ways that generated new ideas rather than committing to prescribed action.

Many who have used network analysis to understand global politics have focused on the structure of networks and thus pay attention to the position of the United States relative to others' advantages (Nexon and Wright 2007) or the advantages of particular central or bridge positions. This is warranted. Bridge and central positions in one or more networks often have great effect (Bower, Westerwinter, this volume). Indeed, the bridge position held by the Swiss and the ICRC led them to have agenda-setting power over what concerns the governance of private military and security services took up. Similarly, the central position of the US government in many global networks leads it to have pivotal power that can often stymie other governance attempts on its own.[41]

---

[41] The ability of the United States to halt governance attempts it does not like is a key feature of

The quality of interactions, however, is also key to the dynamics of networks. The logic of closure is one that scholars of global politics pay a good deal of attention to. This is the logic of claims on who "we" really are, who we trust, who is with us, and who is against us. Many discussions of national interest assume a logic of closure without talking much about it. Closure can generate important social benefits—rewarding good reputations and reinforcing norms—and pulling actors toward established and prescribed roles. It can also, however, be used strategically to foreclose new options in ways that rigidify thinking and make it hard for actors with different inclinations to understand one another.

The logic of brokerage, in which information and its exchange can have a generative logic, is worthy of more attention. Brokerage can generate connections that bring together a wider variety of actors and inspire new ways to think about global issues. Inspiring new thinking and creative collective action is associated with particular types of power. Individuals or groups that inspire innovation are often better regarded and rewarded (Burt 2005). When brokerage delivers collective benefits, as well as power to the broker, participants may be less likely to see the power in zero sum terms (Berenskoetter 2007, 4). The "power to" generate new collective action should join the "power over" others in analyses of power in global governance (Berenskoetter 2007; see also the discussion of productive power in Barnett and Duvall 2005). We should also acknowledge that the openness central to the process of brokerage can sometimes draw the United States (as well as other powerful actors) into governance schemes less by binding them and more by changing the way they think about a situation.[42]

These two logics generated quite different kinds of politics between the United States and others on these two issues. Mobilizing via closure around an established idea creates one kind of dynamic—though it was used to engage the United States as both a global leader and a sovereign power the logic held advantages for the sovereignty logic. Connecting actors with different viewpoints via brokerage creates a different dynamic. In this case, it led actors to see mutual concerns and develop some coordination around them. Scholars of global governance would be well served by paying more attention to both of these dynamics.

what some see to be US hegemony (Brooks and Wohlforth 2013).

[42] This process bears similarities to the philosophical tradition of pragmatism and new analyses using pragmatism to understand contemporary concerns (Joas 1996; Menand 2001; Kaag 2008; Avant 2016).

Conclusion

There is no doubt that the United States is an important actor in global politics. Traditional theories, though, cannot explain the variety of roles it played in these two issue areas. Examining the United States as a network yields key insights that help explain why the United States played such different roles in small arms and military and security services. Both what the United States wants and what it does are influenced by the networks US officials are a part of and the logic through which they are engaged.

PART II

NETWORKS AND GOVERNANCE OUTCOMES

6

Power and Purpose
in Transgovernmental Networks

Insights from the Global Nonproliferation Regime

METTE EILSTRUP-SANGIOVANNI

Governance networks have become the subject of a large literature in international relations (IR) and international law. Scholars have documented the proliferation of informal cross-border regulatory networks—often labeled transgovernmental networks—among central bankers, securities regulators, human rights advocates, and environmental protection agencies (e.g., Zaring 1998, 2005; Bermann, Herdegen, and Lindseth 2000; Raustiala 2002; Slaughter 2004; Baker 2006; Benvinisti 2006; Bach and Newman 2007; Eberlein and Newman 2008; Thurner and Binder 2009). Based on direct, cross-border links among national administrators and typically lacking a firm basis in international law, such networks are widely seen as offering a fast, flexible, and cheap alternative to more conventional, treaty-based forms of international cooperation (Slaughter 2004; Slaughter and Zaring 2006; Percy, this volume).

Transgovernmental networks (TGNs) are not confined to "low" political issues such as finance and banking regulation. National security and intelligence officials increasingly cooperate across borders to address problems of international terrorism, arms control, and weapons proliferation. Nonetheless, transgovernmental cooperation in the realm of security has attracted relatively little scholarly attention.[1] Extant literature broadly assumes that transgovernmentalism is confined to issue areas that are characterized by high technical complexity and low political salience. It is in such areas that national regulatory agencies or government departments are seen to have the greatest leverage by virtue of their technical/professional expertise and delegated administrative

---

[1] An exception is Lipson 2001, 2004, 2005–2006.

powers. By contrast, transgovernmental networking is expected to play a marginal role in policy areas that directly affect national security (see Russell 1973, 434; Hopkins 1976, 412; Keohane 1978, 932, 950; Raustiala 2002, 5; Slaughter 2004, 6). Transgovernmental cooperation on issues such as counterterrorism, weapons proliferation, and arms control thus presents a puzzle: What explains the reliance on loose, non-binding cooperative arrangements on issues which cut to the heart of national security?

This question is of central relevance both to the study of international security governance, which is the focus of this volume, and to the study of institutional cooperation more broadly. Since the emergence of institutionalist theory in the 1970s, a large literature has emerged exploring the causes and effects of different institutional designs. In particular, rationalist scholars have sought to explain variation in the design of international institutions as a direct function of the structure of the cooperation problems they are created to resolve. Yet, a general theory of institutional design still appears elusive. In this chapter I seek to contribute to debates on institutional design by exploring how organizational and structural network theories can enhance our understanding of institutional functionality and thereby contribute new hypotheses about variation in institutional design. Network theory, I argue, promises to advance the study of institutional design along three main lines. First, structural or social network analysis (SNA) offers an array of methodological tools that enable scholars to measure and analyze both the official institutional and informal relational structures that comprise international institutions. By providing a range of formal metrics for features such as "hierarchy," "centralization," and "density," SNA introduces more nuance and precision into analyses of institutional structures. In particular, many scholars find SNA useful for studying informal institutions (or informal aspects of formal institutions), which—due to their lack of a formal treaty-base or explicit organizational framework—can be difficult to analyze using standard institutionalist approaches (Brie and Stölting 2012, 19).

Second, much like international regime theory, both organizational and structural network theory present theoretical conjectures that relate the structural properties of institutions to policy outcomes (Hafner-Burton et al. 2009, 559). Derived mainly from sociology and economics, these models often transcend mainstream institutionalism's narrower focus on centralized versus decentralized or "soft" versus "hard" law institutions, to focus on additional properties (such as density, homophily, segmentation, and multiplexity) which may affect the functionality and boundary conditions of institutions. As such, network theory offers a rich source of new hypotheses about institutional design and functionality.

Third, network theory expands conventional conceptions of power by defining the resources and influence actors possess partly as a function of their network position. By conceptualizing power as an emergent property of networks, network theory takes us beyond a functionalist account of institutions as "efficient" solutions to cooperation problems, and invites us to examine how the different relational structures comprising international institutions empower particular actors and thereby shape preferences regarding institutional design. These insights in turn may yield new hypotheses about why states create specific institutions.[2]

The chapter is organized as follows. I begin by briefly outlining the puzzle of institutional variation in the area of international arms control/nonproliferation cooperation. How, I ask, can we explain that some arms control issues are addressed by highly formal, centralized treaty-based agreements while others are tackled through informal transgovernmental cooperation? Next I describe the institutional features and dynamics of TGNs and introduce two variants of network theory—*organizational* and *structural*—which offer supplementary tools for analyzing political networks. The following section combines rational institutionalism and network theory to derive hypotheses about the conditions in which TGNs are most likely to emerge and to be effective. This section both highlights collective benefits from networked cooperation (network-level benefits) and explores how different network structures can empower some states at the expense of others (node-specific benefits). Whereas extant literature on institutional design has focused overwhelmingly on the severity of the enforcement problem versus distributional conflict to explain institutional design variation, I use organizational network theory to identify several alternative factors that may explain variation in the choice of intergovernmental organizations (IGOs) versus TGNs as organizational tools, including "number,"[3] distribution of power, and expected frequency of enforcement actions. While networked governance entails generic functional benefits of enhanced flexibility and low sovereignty costs for all participants that allows for more effective governance, these benefits accrue disproportionately to powerful states that occupy a central network position. Moreover, an uneven distribution of power is often a functional precondition for effective networked cooperation, since concentrated power obviates

---

[2] This argument need not be limited to states. Westerwinter (this volume) examines how network structures and particularly brokerage configurations can affect the institutional design of transnational public-private governance schemes.

[3] Koremenos, Snidal, and Lipson (2001, 774–778) define "number" as the "number of actors that are potentially relevant to joint welfare because their actions affect others or others' actions affect them." Building on this understanding I conceive of "number" as the number of states/stakeholders whose cooperation is necessary in order to reap significant joint gains from cooperation on a given issue.

the need for formal centralized enforcement. The distribution of power and interests (specifically, a preference for informal over formal cooperation on the part of powerful states) is thus a crucial determinant of TGN-based cooperation. "Number" is also a determining factor. As we shall see, the unique challenges associated with networked cooperation impose size constraints on network formation. Effectively, TGNs lend themselves best to cooperation among small groups where actions can be easily coordinated, mutual behavior can be effectively monitored, and direct reciprocity can be relied on as a primary mechanism of enforcement. Thus, "number"—which I define following Koremenos et al. as the "number of actors that are directly relevant to joint welfare" (or, alternatively, as "crucial stakeholders")—is an important determining factor of TGN formation.

Although my argument has broader theoretical implications, my empirical focus is on TGNs combatting weapons proliferation. My aim is to explain why these networks arise and take the form they do. The second part of the chapter evaluates the hypotheses derived earlier against evidence from two TGNs in the realm of nonproliferation cooperation. While these cases do not constitute a full test of my hypotheses, they lend support to my conjectures and point to new avenues for further research.

The Puzzle

Rational institutionalist literature predicts little variation in the design of international arms control agreements. Indeed, most arms control issues are subject to precisely the kind of cooperation problems that rationalist scholars argue favor formal centralized and highly legalized institutions. First, most arms control agreements are subject to stark enforcement problems. This is true both for arms reduction agreements and agreements establishing universal prohibitions (such as the Chemical Weapons Convention [CWC] and the Non-Proliferation Treaty [NPT]) where the potential security gains from individual noncompliance may create incentives to cheat. It is also true for export control agreements where states may be tempted to transfer prohibited materials for financial gain (Lipson 2005–6). According to extant literature, arms control issues should therefore be prime candidates for formal "hard law" agreements, involving a high degree of obligation, centralized monitoring, and delegated dispute resolution designed to enhance the credibility of commitments (Chinkin 1989, 861; Abbott and Snidal 2000, 429, 440; Kahler 2000, 678–679; Koremenos et al. 2001; Raustiala 2005, 594; Benvenisti 2006). Second, noncompliance is often hard to detect (Abbott et al. 2006; Koremenos 2009). Again, this should create a demand for formal organizations that supply centralized monitoring and verification.

The expectation that arms control agreements tend to be highly legalized and centralized is confirmed in practice in many areas of international arms control. According to Goldstein et al. (2000, 386), "arms control agreements display increasing precision and elaboration in their commitments and in the scale of their implementing bureaucracies. The proliferation of nuclear weapons and the possession and deployment of entire classes of other weapons . . . are now subject to detailed legal conventions." Yet, the move toward stronger legalization is far from uniform. Next to a small cluster of highly legalized regimes (such as the NPT and CWC) sit a wealth of informal agreements governing arms control issues. Examples include the Cooperative Threat Reduction program, the Nuclear Supplies Group, the Proliferation Security Initiative, and various multilateral export control regimes. These agreements are informal, non-binding, and feature no centralized monitoring or enforcement. Cooperation occurs primarily between domestic agencies, away from the political limelight. In the next section I consider how network theory can help us to understand this institutional variation.

TGNs—a Network Theoretical Perspective

Despite a growing literature on "transgovernmentalism," there is so far little agreement on what specific features define TGNs or in what sense they are "networked." The term "TGN" is generally used by IR theorists to refer to multilateral arrangements for informal cooperation among representatives of different government agencies. These networks—which are typically based on memorandums of understanding (MOUs) or other non-binding instruments—bring together administrators from different countries to exchange information, collect and distill best practices, develop common regulatory standards, and enhance enforcement of national laws through voluntary international coordination (see esp. Slaughter 2004; Slaughter and Zaring 2006).

Given their non-binding status, TGNs are generally seen to combine a high degree of flexibility with low sovereignty costs (Raustiala 2002; Slaughter 2004). Thus, rational institutional theories focused on the functional benefits of "soft law" agreements provide a useful starting point for explaining transgovernmental networking. But while rational institutionalism is helpful in theorizing generic benefits from low legalization and enhanced flexibility, it pays less attention to other institutional traits—such as small membership, dispersed decision-making, and high implementation capacity—which characterize TGNs and distinguish them from the general category of informal or weakly structured international institutions.[4] These traits, I argue, can be brought into sharper focus by considering TGNs qua networks.

TGNs as Organizational Networks

A minimal definition of a network is "a set of entities (or nodes) and a set of ties that connect these entities into a system or structure." Entities could be individuals, groups, or states, and the structure of connections could be non-hierarchical, hierarchical, or heterarchical. On this view all political institutions are networks, although with different structural properties, and can be analyzed as such (see Avant and Westerwinter, this volume).

While conceiving of networks simply as "sets of interlinked nodes" has been a popular approach among sociologists and economists, most IR theorists have followed Powell (1990, 301) in conceiving networks as a distinct form of social organization that connects actors horizontally in pursuit of common goals (see Hafner-Burton et al. 2009). On this view—which is associated with what I label *Organizational Network Theory* (ONT)—a network is defined as "any collection of actors ($N > 2$) that pursue repeated, enduring exchange relations with one another and at the same time lack a legitimate organizational authority to arbitrate and resolve disputes that may arise during the exchange" (Podolny and Page 1998, 58–59). This distinguishes networks both from formal hierarchies, which involve explicit, ruled-based, top-down command, and also from markets, in which interactions are ad hoc and temporary (Powell 1990; Kahler 2009).

Several implications follow from this mode of organization. First, unlike formal hierarchies, which can rely on authoritative rules and legal arbitration to govern relations, networks are strictly self-enforcing governance structures disciplined mainly by reputation and norms of reciprocity (Powell 1990, 301–304; Podolny and Page 1998, 60–65; Thompson 2003, 43). Second, whereas organizational hierarchies are based on top-down management and a clear division of roles and responsibilities, organizational networks are generally presumed to be flat and decentralized, with decision-making and action dispersed among multiple actors that exercise significant local autonomy (Podolny and Page 1998, 59). Third, the lack of formal centralized authority implies that decision-making in networks tends to be based on deliberation and consensus seeking. This in

---

[4] I view TGNs as a subset of the wider category of informal or weakly structured international institutions. By focusing on transgovernmental versus intergovernmental cooperation rather than drawing a general distinction between more or less "structured" approaches to inter-state cooperation I seek to limit variation in the institutional design features I focus on. In comparison to the rational design framework (Koremenos et al. 2001), this allows me to isolate a smaller set of independent and dependent variables, in relation to which testable hypotheses can be formulated.

turn implies a notional "equality" among members who are considered jointly responsible for decisions and outcomes (Thompson 2003, 39–40).

How do these institutional features map onto transgovernmental cooperation? Extant literature lists several descriptive characteristics of TGNs which correspond to an organizational network form, and which distinguish TGNs from conventional treaty-based IGOs.

Non-Authoritative Rules. Most TGNs build on informal MOUs or other non-binding instruments that have no direct legal effect. Compliance thus remains inherently voluntary (Zaring 1998, 301; Slaughter 2004, 45–48).

Lack of Formal Hierarchy. While they may be initiated by heads of state or foreign ministries, day-to-day decision-making in TGNs is generally left to the discretion of specialized government agencies that interact directly on peer-to-peer basis (Raustiala 2002, 24). As Thomson notes (2003, 23–24), this contrasts with many formal IGOs where action is based on high-level "political" decisions followed up by implementation by lower administrative tiers. As we shall see, however, TGNs often entail significant elements of informal hierarchy.

Decentralization. Whereas formal IGOs may centralize tasks such as information-gathering, decision-making, implementation, and monitoring of compliance, decision-making and implementation in TGNs is generally dispersed, with each participant enacting and enforcing agreements in accordance with domestic laws (Zaring 1998, 301–304).[5]

Decision Mode. Due to their lack for formal rule-based structures, TGNs tend to rely on deliberation, with no formal voting taking place (Agranoff 2003, 21; Zaring 2005, 303; Baker 2006). To some scholars this implies a principle of "deliberative equality" (Slaughter 2004).

Before proceeding, it is important to stress that the dichotomy drawn here between treaty-based IGOs as hierarchies and TNGs as organizational networks is based on ideal types. Empirically, one can easily find examples of institutions that blur the line. Nonetheless, a cursory look at the major international institutions governing arms control/weapons proliferation suggests that we can use these ideal types to distinguish two main categories of arms control institutions. Table 6.1 provides a list of every open multilateral treaty agreement on arms control adopted since 1945 and ten informal (non-treaty based) agreements formed during the same period.[6] I have scored each institution as low/medium/

---

[5] Decentralized monitoring and enforcement is not unique to TGNs. Many ITOs rely on decentralized enforcement. However, ITOs tend to have more detailed and intrusive verification and compliance provisions than TGNs, making it politically costly to pull back from implementing agreements.

[6] I draw these from the UN Treaty Collection: https://treaties.un.org/. TGNs are harder to get a reliable count of. Here I have relied on existing scholarship in the field.

Table 6.1 **Post-1945: Open Multilateral Treaties on Arms Control and TGNs**

	Signed	Number of Members	Majority Voting
Treaty instruments			
Treaty Banning Nuclear Tests in the Atmosphere, in Outer Space and Under Water	1963	126	Yes
Treaty on Principles Governing the Activities of States in the Exploration and Use of Outer Space	1967	102	Yes
Treaty on the Non-Proliferation of Nuclear Weapons	1968	190	Yes
Treaty on the Prohibition of the Emplacement of Nuclear Weapons and Other WMD on the Seabed and Ocean Floor	1971	94	Yes
Convention on the Prohibition of the Development, Production and Stockpiling of Bacteriological and Toxin Weapons	1972	170	Yes
Convention on the Prohibition of Military or Any Other Hostile Use of Environmental Modification Techniques	1977	78	Yes
UN Conference on Disarmament	1979	65	Yes
Convention on the Physical Protection of Nuclear Material	1980	149	Yes
Convention on Prohibitions or Restrictions on the Use of Certain Conventional Weapons	1981	117	Yes
Convention on the Marking of Plastic Explosives	1991	152	Yes
Convention on the Prohibition of the Development, Production, Stockpiling and Use of Chemical Weapons . . .	1993	190	Yes
Convention on the Prohibition of the Use, Stockpiling, Production and Transfer of Anti-Personnel Mines . . .	1997	161	Yes
Convention of Cluster Munitions	2008	84	Yes

Table 6.1 **Continued**

	Signed	Number of Members	Majority Voting
Transgovernmental networks			
Zangger Committee	1971	38	No
Nuclear Suppliers Group	1975	48	No
Australia Group	1985	41	No
Missile Technology Control Regime	1987	34	No
Wassenaar Arrangement	1995	41	No
Cooperative Threat Reduction Programme	1991	n.a.	No
Materials Protection, Control and Accounting Program	1996	n.a.	No
EU Code of Conduct for Arms Transfers	1998	28	No
Hague Code of Conduct Against Ballistic Missile Proliferation	2002	134	No
Proliferation Security Initiative	2003	21	No
Global Initiative to Combat Nuclear Terrorism	2006	85	No

Note: I have excluded the Central African Convention for Control of Small Arms, signed in April 2010, since, at the time of writing, it had not received sufficient ratifications to enter into force. Number of member states as of 2015.

high with respect to standard institutional design variables such as "centralization" and "legalization". As tables 6.1 and 6.2 illustrate, there are systematic differences in the design features of international arms control institutions, which justify grouping them into separate categories. For example, in terms of membership, treaty-based arms control institutions have on average 120 members, while transgovernmental arms control initiatives average 50 members. In terms of "legalization," the vast majority of formal treaty-based agreements have a high degree of rule precision and obligation (table 6.2). In fact, more than half require members to take specific steps to implement agreements in domestic law. By contrast, in addition to lacking a formal treaty base, the majority of TGNs feature vague and imprecise rules and do not require members to take specific implementation measures.

Table 6.2 **Design Features of Arms Control/Nonproliferation Agreements**

	TGNs	IGOs
Centralization		
Centralized info-gathering, monitoring, enforcement	0% high	36% high
	7% medium	64% medium
	93% low	0% low
Legalization		
Specificity/precision	0% high	79% high
	14% medium	21% medium
	86% low	0% low
Obligation	0% high	53% high
	0% medium	47% medium
	100% low	0% low
Delegation	0% high	14% high
	0% medium	86% medium
	100% low	0% low

Note: Following Goldstein et al. (2000) a "legalized" agreement is one that scores high on two of the three dimensions (specificity, obligation, delegation).

TGNs as Structural Networks

An alternative to viewing networks as a particular form of social organization (i.e., as self-conscious collective actors) is to view them as nonspecific relational structures that link actors in different configurations. This is the approach of structural network analysis (SNA). Whereas organizational network theory (ONT) focuses on how networks make decisions and pool resources in pursuit of collective goals, the analytical focus of SNA is primarily on how different configurations of relational ties affect social outcomes by empowering or disempowering individual nodes (Emirbayer 1997, 298; Smith-Doerr and Powell 2005, 369). As Avant and Westerwinter (this volume) explain, a key insight of SNA is that the ability of a node to wield power and influence derives not only from its individual attributes but also from its network position. A node that has direct links to many other nodes (high degree centrality) is privileged because it can receive and pass information to many others and thereby play an agenda-setting role (Freeman 1979, 219–220; Carpenter 2011). Similarly, nodes that are strategically located on the direct paths linking other nodes (high betweenness centrality) can gain bargaining and brokerage power by controlling information or resources passing between other nodes (Freeman 1979, 221; Burt 1992; Hafner-Burton et al. 2009, 572). Importantly, central nodes may be able to use brokerage and "exit" power to set conditions on participation in the network (Lake and Wong 2009). As I discuss in the next section, the ability of central nodes to control access to a network is a crucial aspect of many TGNs.

The two approaches—SNA and ONT—are not mutually exclusive but offer supplementary approaches to studying governance frameworks (see Eilstrup-Sangiovanni 2014). At the macro level, ONT presents a fertile resource for deriving hypotheses about the functionality of different types of governance frameworks. Specifically, by highlighting macro-level benefits of adopting an informal, distributed structure, ONT invites us to evaluate different institutional designs as more or less efficient organizational tools for solving particular policy problems. Among business economists and economic sociologists, for example, ONT has been widely used to study the ideal organization of firms, where a horizontal networked structure has been found to enable flexible, on-demand production and prevent contractual lock-in of unproductive relationships (Williamson 1975). IR scholars have incorporated these findings into theories of transnational advocacy networks and international peace-keeping efforts, arguing that a networked organization enhances flexibility and learning capacity and strengthens local initiative (e.g., Chayes et al. 1997; Keck and Sikkink 1998; Paris 2009, 19; Percy, this volume; for a critique of IR literature on organizational networks, see Eilstrup-Sangiovanni and Jones 2008).

From an organizational analysis viewpoint, SNA complements ONT by enabling more detailed analysis of structural features of different governance networks, which may influence their functionality. For example, densely connected networks are often assumed to be more efficient at generating and distributing information than sparsely connected ones, whereas "segmentation" (fragmentation of a network into sub-clusters or "cliques") is thought to hinder exchange of information and ideas. Homophilous networks are sometimes hypothesized to be more robust but less innovative than heterophilous ones (see Eilstrup-Sangiovanni 2014).

In addition to illuminating network-level effects of different structural configurations, SNA also offers a unique toolbox for understanding how networks constrain and empower individual actors. For example, SNA enables analysts to measure how actors in a network interact, who dictates policy, and who controls the flow of information and resources around the network, thereby revealing patterns of power and subordination that may introduce elements of hierarchy into ostensibly flat governance structures. This is particularly important in the context of so-called "new governance networks," which are the subject of this volume. As Avant and Westerwinter (this volume) note, studies of organizational networks often assume that these networks are characterized by horizontal, decentralized, and egalitarian relationships of communication and exchange, without verifying this empirically. Yet structural network analysis frequently reveals a different reality. For example, recent applications of SNA to study networks in the fields of human rights and development have revealed surprising degrees of hierarchy, dependency, and political subordination within seemingly flat, egalitarian networks (Carpenter 2011, 72–73; Faul 2015).

When analyzing the TGNs in table 6.1 from a structural network perspective, we discover that Washington occupies a central position in most of these institutions and that the flow of information and resources is controlled largely by the United States. Moreover, participation in these TGNs is in many cases achieved through bilateral agreements with Washington, implying a significant degree of central control. These findings invite us to consider how extant power distributions impact on network design. If decentralization is a variable (rather than a fixture) of organizational networks, and if centrality endows individual nodes with power and influence, then this may create incentives for some actors to manipulate network structures in ways that increase their own centrality. This in turn invites us to reflect on how exogenous power distributions shape the capacity and strategic incentives for individual actors to engage in network creation and management.

Yet, when it comes to conceiving of power as an exogenous causal factor in network formation, rather than as an emergent property of networks, we encounter a blind spot in existing network theories. A frequent criticism of structural network theories is a tendency to focus exclusively on the structure of relationships while neglecting the diverse attributes of nodes, including their varied access to outside resources (see Emirbayer 1997, 298; Ansell and Weber 1999; Christopoulos 2008; Kahler 2009, 8). Structural network models also generally do not model network actors as strategic. By and large, existing SNA theories treat social networks as evolving relatively spontaneously without clear strategic purpose or central steering (see Kahler 2009). While this assumption may be plausible for large interpersonal networks (such as those connecting job seekers), it is less credible with respect to political networks, such as TGNs (Gulati 2011, 220). In the context of international politics, we can plausibly assume not only that political networks are deliberately formed but also that political actors are cognizant of the boundaries and structures of these networks and seek to influence those structures to advance their individual interests (Kahler 2009). This suggests that in order to present a useful tool for analyzing international relations, network theories need to be equipped with better micro foundations that explain the strategic behavior of individual nodes with reference to agent-specific attributes (as opposed to simply in relational terms) thereby introducing an element of strategic agency into structural network theories (Dowding 1995, 96). Such micro foundations, I suggest, can be derived in part by combining ONT, which highlights functional benefits from specific relational structures, and rational institutional theory, which stresses state power and interests as sources of diverging preferences regarding institutional design.

A Model of Transgovernmental Networking

In this section I provide a general rationale for the institutional choice of TGN-based cooperation in the realm of international arms control. As explained, my analysis focuses both on generic functional benefits arising from a networked organization, and on the incentives for individual states to embrace a dispersed, networked structure as the basis for international cooperation.

Extant literature highlights numerous benefits of transgovernmental cooperation. Like other governance networks, TGNs are said to be fast, cheap, flexible and innovative (Slaughter and Zaring 2006). For example, the horizontally dispersed yet tightly interconnected structure of governance networks omits the need for information to travel through a central processing unit, thereby facilitating dense information exchange and communication at low costs (Powell 1990, 325; Scharpf 1993, 135). Governance networks are also said to promote learning and innovation by encouraging direct exchange of ideas and knowledge and by permitting local experimentation (Podolny and Page 1998, 62–63). Moreover, the composition of governance networks is generally understood to be easier to adjust than that of formal organizations. This allows different actors to combine and recombine to solve specific problems as dictated by the nature of the problems rather than by a pre-specified division of labor or legal responsibility (Podolny and Page 1998, 64–66; Smith-Doerr and Powell 2009, 382–384). Finally, by decentralizing policy initiative and implementation, governance networks are said to promote differentiated solutions to local problems thereby enhancing efficiency and increasing responsiveness to local needs (Paris 2009, 19).

In addition to functional benefits of speed, flexibility, and expertise (which supposedly accrue to all organizational networks) a crucial advantage said to distinguish TGNs from treaty-based IGOs is reduced governance costs (i.e., costs of negotiating and implementing agreements). There are often high costs associated with negotiating and codifying international legal agreements and potentially delegating powers of dispute resolution and enforcement to IGOs. Moreover, domestic approval of international treaty agreements is often slow and costly due to complex ratification procedures (Chayes and Chayes 1993, 182–183). By contrast, transgovernmental agreements rarely require detailed negotiation or legislative authorization. Once agreed, the informal nature of TGNs ensures that agreements can be adapted without the need for costly formal renegotiation, thereby reducing overall transactions costs of cooperation (Reinicke 1998, 46; Raustiala 2002, 24; Slaughter 2004; Abbott et al. 2006).

These theoretic advantages of TGNs are easy to grasp and have been widely documented. While compelling, prevailing transaction-cost-based explanations cannot, however, serve as a general explanation for TGN-based cooperation. The reason is that they fail insofar as they fail to account for variation in the prevalence of TGNs. If TGNs are generally cheaper to initiate and maintain than IGO-based cooperation and also offer additional functional benefits such as speed, issue-specific expertise, and high capacity for innovation, why are TGNs not omnipresent? To answer this question, we must pay attention not only to the benefits of TGNs but also to potential constraints on TGN formation and functionality. Compared to treaty-based IGOs, TGNs suffer from several structural limitations—including low credibility and limited support for compliance—which may reduce their attractiveness. Simply listing generic benefits of a networked organization therefore cannot serve as a general explanation for TGN-based cooperation without careful evaluation of how these advantages stack up against alternative institutional forms in specific contexts. In the rest of this section I draw on network theory to identify a set of limiting conditions, which may constrain TGN formation and functionality. I then identify a set of facilitating factors, which may lead states to favor TGN-based cooperation in specific circumstances.

Before proceeding, two clarifications are required. First, TGNs and IGOs are cast here as functional substitutes. Some might reject this premise up front. For example, Raustiala (2002, 6) describes TGNs and international treaty regimes as "synergistic." The purpose of TGNs, he argues, is to make the system of international treaties work better by improving implementation and filling in gaps in the international legal order (see also Alvarez 2001, 212; Eberlein and Newman 2008). Others describe TGNs as precursors for formal obligatory agreements. On this view, TNGs are a means for achieving tentative and "shallow" cooperation until more binding agreements can be devised (Abbott and Snidal 2000, 423; Abbott et al. 2006; Kahler and Lake 2009). Neither view is compelling. It is certainly the case that TGNs are often "complementary" to formal treaty-based regimes in the sense that they increase the scope and depth of cooperation in specific issue areas. For example, the Australia Group (AG)—an informal chemical export control regime—reinforces compliance with the prohibition against transfers of certain chemical precursors laid down in the CWC. Yet, such complementariness does not explain why some multilateral export control regimes take the form of TGNs. After all, improving implementation or closing gaps in the international legal system can also be achieved through negotiation of supplementary formal treaties or additional protocols. Equally, TGNs cannot be plausibly viewed merely as informal "stopgaps" until more binding, treaty-based agreements can be reached. The Missile Technology Control Regime (MTCR) and the AG have been around for twenty-eight and thirty years, respectively, and show few signs of developing into formal treaty organizations. So far, Washington has vehemently resisted formalizing the Proliferation Security Initiative (PSI). This suggests that TGNs are best understood—not as temporary stopgaps or informal "add-ons" to formal treaty regimes—but as a deliberate institutional design choice.

This brings me to the second clarification. In what follows, I consider the choice of TGN formation/participation from the point of view of state executives. Transgovernmentalist literature often assumes that national regulators link across borders on their own initiative, potentially in order to promote policies that diverge from official government policy (Keohane and Nye 1974, 48; Risse 1995, 9; Colombatto and Macey 1996; Zaring 1998; Bermann et al. 2000; Newman 2008; Thurner and Binder 2009). There are, I think, several reasons to reject this "bottom-up" perspective. As Slaughter (2004, 4–7) argues, while regulatory agencies tend to enjoy a degree of independence from executive and legislative branches, TGNs in most policy areas continue to be underpinned by the power and authority of the state. Funds for operating TGNs typically must be approved by executives, and agency leaders are often politically appointed and subject to peer review.[7] Thus, although they build on agency-to-agency ties, it is reasonable to assume that executives effectively control the formation of TGNs and shape their activities. This suggests that transgovernmental cooperation is best viewed as an instance of de facto delegation whereby executives grant authority to lower level officials to pursue broad policy objectives. The question then becomes: What prompts governments to favor TGN-based cooperation on some issues and formal treaty-based agreements for others? To answer this question, I have suggested, we need to consider not just the transaction cost benefits of TGNs but also the drawbacks of and constraints on networked cooperation.

Constraints on TGN-Based Cooperation

Number

Extant literature highlights speed, flexibility, and low governance costs as crucial aspects of transgovernmental cooperation. Yet, a widely overlooked constraint on TGN-based cooperation is "number." Building on Koremenos, Lipson, and Snidal (2001, 777–778), I take "number" to refer to "the number of actors that are potentially relevant to joint welfare because their actions significantly influence outcomes in an issue area." TGNs, I conjecture, are best suited to cooperation among small numbers for two reasons. First, small groups are more likely to reap benefits of speed, flexibility, and low transaction costs associated with networked cooperation than larger collectives. As we have seen, organizational networks are postulated to collect and process information more efficiently than organizational hierarchies. Theoretically, a loose, distributed structure gives participants access to wider and more diverse sources of information without having to pass through a central authority. Yet, in practice, communication and information exchange in a horizontal network may be complicated and time-consuming. Insofar as organizational networks often lack a central point of contact tasked

---

[7] See Verdier 2008, 15. For a general discussion of regulatory independence, see Knopf 1993, 607; and Pollack 2005, 911–912.

with collecting and distributing information, information searches effectively involve each participant querying network partners until the desired information is found. As a result, each piece of information may incur higher transaction costs than in a more centralized system (Watts 2003, 157–158; McGuire and Agranoff 2007). This will be particularly true for large, distributed networks with many nodes, but less so for smaller networks of tightly connected actors.

Another alleged advantage of TGNs is flexibility. Due to their informality, TGNs are said to adapt easily to changing circumstances. Yet, flexibility may come at a price. Indeed, organizational adaptability may increase day-to-day bargaining costs, as individual nodes seek to modify agreements to serve short-term, parochial interests. Similarly, a lack of centralized leadership can undermine collective ability to decide on strategy or resource allocation (Powell 1990, 318; Thompson 2003, 46–47) or—in situations where actors' interests vary sharply—undermine a group's ability to cooperate altogether (Westerwinter, this volume). These dysfunctions may be acute among large, heterogeneous groups, but are less likely to impede cooperation among small numbers that are, *ceteris paribus*, more likely to achieve consensus in the absence of centralized leadership.[8]

A second reason TGNs are best suited to cooperation among small numbers pertains to credibility. As noted, TGNs provide no centralized monitoring and enforcement and the terms of agreement are often ambiguous, increasing the risk of self-serving interpretations of agreements or outright noncooperation. Such problems are less likely to be a liability among small numbers where effective peer-to-peer monitoring can be more easily achieved, and where direct reciprocity can support cooperation.

Power Asymmetry

A second constraint on TGN-based cooperation is the need for effective leadership. Given a lack of centralized bargaining and administrative support, networked cooperation often requires an element of leadership by a pivotal actor capable of bringing stakeholders to the table and brokering agreements. The need for leadership in governance networks is acknowledged by a large literature (see McGuire and Agranoff 2011). Leadership, I suggest, is likely to be particularly crucial in areas of "high politics," such as international arms control, where disincentives to participate are pervasive and enforcement problems rife. In such areas, effective collaboration calls for one of two solutions: either (1) a strong central organization that provides centralized monitoring and enforcement; or (2) a powerful "lead" state that is capable of providing incentives for other actors to come to the

---

[8] This expectation is consistent with Koremenos et al.'s (2001, 778) conjecture (C3) that "centralization increases with Number."

table and of inducing compliance, thereby alleviating the enforcement problem (Martin 1992, 770; Mitchell and Kielbach 2001). Generally, such a role requires a state with a relative abundance of both issue-specific and general power resources.

> *Hypothesis 1*: TGN-based cooperation is most likely to yield joint benefit when (a) smaller groups of stakeholders possess the necessary resources to effectively address a problem through joint collaboration ("number" is small); (b) a single group member is willing and able to supply an element of leadership.

Power of Networks—Power in Networks

I have identified small number and leadership (or "Asymmetric Power") as preconditions for fruitful network-based governance. These preconditions constrain TGN formation. We might assume that as long as these conditions are satisfied, TGN-based cooperation will be roundly favored on grounds of transaction cost-savings. Yet, this conclusion would ignore several potential drawbacks to a networked organization. As already noted, TGN-based agreements entail low credibility and support for compliance. To explain the choice of TGN-based cooperation we must therefore explain the conditions under which the demand for flexibility and reduced transaction costs outweighs the demand for credibility and centralized compliance. In considering this trade-off, I adopt the perspective of the most powerful state(s) in a given issue area. Functional analysis examines systemic incentives to adopt particular institutional solutions. Yet, as Stephen Krasner (1991) showed several decades ago, it is typically possible to identify more solution that meets basic functional requirements and different solutions will tend to favor different states. In order to explain institutional outcomes, we must therefore examine the *interests* of those states that are *in the strongest position to dictate* institutional design (call them regime 'Principals'). Generally, this means the most powerful states in an issue area.[9]

When considering institutional choice from the viewpoint of powerful states, SNA adds a new dimension to functional analysis. While functional institutional theories draw attention to the power that is required to establish and manage organizational networks, SNA also focuses on the power that can be acquired and exercised *through* networks—especially power that accrues from a central network

---

[9] Functionalist theories of institutional design are premised on notions of "efficiency," but to the extent that more than one solution exists to a given cooperation problem, this raises the question, efficiency for whom? While international institutions may be loosely efficient, their specific design generally embodies a compromise between different state preferences. It is therefore logical to assume that the most powerful states in an issue area have the strongest influence on institutional design.

position. As demonstrated by the chapters in this volume, different network positions can empower or disempower actors. However, a weakness of many extant
network models is that they pay inadequate attention to how exogenous or non-
relational sources of power (such as military and economic capabilities or institutional authority) interact with relational network structures. One possibility is that
network power *substitutes* for other forms of power. This view suggests that poorer
and/or militarily less powerful actors can offset their material disadvantages
through accumulation of social or network power (Hafner-Burton et al. 2009,
573–574). The Swiss Initiative's influence in the regulations of the global private
security industry is a case in point (Avant, this volume). A second possibility is that
network power reinforces existing inequalities by enabling powerful actors to engi-
neer and exploit network centrality so as to enhance their own influence. In the
remainder of this section, I draw on structural network theory to highlight ways in
which TGN-based cooperation can serve to empower already powerful states and
lower the costs of exercising leadership. On this basis I derive a set of hypotheses
about when "regime Principals" are likely to favor a TGN-based design.

Frequency of Enforcement Actions

One factor that may influence a regime Principal's preference for TGN- versus IGO-based cooperation is the expected frequency of enforcement actions.
Whereas TGNs build on non-binding guidelines and general standards, IGOs
generally feature more explicit and authoritative rules. Legal theorists often
distinguish between standards and rules based on whether the law is given
context ex post or ex ante. As Kaplow explains, "rules entail an advance deter-
mination of what conduct is permissible, leaving only factual issues for the
adjudicator, whereas standards leave both specification of what conduct is
permissible and factual issues for the adjudicator" (1992, 557–560). Indeed,
one way to conceive of the difference between a formal, legalized regime such
as the CWC, which prohibits production and stockpiling of specific chemical
substances, and an informal initiative such as the PSI which calls on members
to "act as they consider appropriate and necessary to curb proliferation" is that
the former promulgates precise rules prohibiting specific conducts, while the
latter establishes a loose standard of behavior that must be given specific content by an adjudicator[10] on an ad hoc basis.

When should we expect a regime Principal to favor loose standards over precise rules? From the viewpoint of a Principal, reliance on non-binding standards enhances flexibility and enables selective enforcement. However, reliance

---

[10] Which in the absence of delegation of authority to an independent arbitrator means state
parties themselves.

on standards may also increase the cost of individual enforcement actions by requiring ad hoc interpretation, and by making it more difficult to persuade other participants to share in the burden of enforcement.[11] Importantly, reliance on vague standards may also increase the political costs of enforcement actions due to perceived arbitrariness. This leads me to hypothesize that the flexibility afforded by non-binding standards is likely to be favored when the expected frequency of enforcement actions is low. If enforcement actions are frequent, a rule-based system which establishes clear criteria for enforcement and distributes responsibility for execution across all parties to an agreement is likely to be more cost-effective from the point of view of a regime Principal.

> *Hypothesis 2*: TGN-based cooperation is more likely when the expected frequency of enforcement action is low.

Increasing Returns to Power

IGOs are often said to constrain power. To legitimate cooperation, multilateral IGOs generally institutionalize rights for all members to propose policy and to influence decisions through majoritarian voting, thereby enabling weaker members to form blocking coalitions (Ruggie 1992; Martin 2000). Delegation of agenda-setting, information-gathering, or monitoring tasks to international secretariats, which is common practice in many IGOs, also restricts the ability of strong states to control policy agendas. In short, by instituting formal procedures for information-sharing and joint decision-making, IGOs weaken the relationship between material power and influence over collective outcomes.

TGNs do not have a similar effect. Informal transgovernmental agreements do not institutionalize expectations of co-equality in decision-making or grant formal rights of policy proposal or voting to all participants. As such, they leave powerful states relatively free to exploit their superior agenda-setting power and bargaining leverage to dictate policy. In fact, a networked organization may augment the agenda-setting power and influence of already powerful states. Consider that social networks are often found to grow through mechanisms of "preferential attachment," which implies that nodes form ties to other nodes that already have many in-links. In structural terms network expansion is thus likely to follow a "power law" whereby the "rich get richer" (Goddard 2009; Kahler 2009). If we

---

[11] According to Kaplow (1992, 562–563), rules are more costly to establish than standards because they require advance determinations of the law's content. Standards, conversely, are more costly to enforce because they demand subsequent determinations of the law's substance. Hence, he concludes, "the greater the frequency with which a legal command will apply . . . the more desirable rules tend to be relative to standards" (1992, 573).

assume that exogenous power resources are an important determinant of initial tie formation in political networks (this is a highly plausible assumption in the realm of international arms control where a preponderance of military and economic might, technological capabilities or knowledge will make a state an attractive target for cooperative "in-links"), then network dynamics will tend to reinforce an initial power advantage by increasing the centrality of powerful states. Network centrality in turn allows central nodes to control flows of information or resources, thereby permitting them to restrict agendas, or to introduce new proposals, norms, or ideas into the network (Freeman 1979; Carpenter 2011; see also Carpenter, Avant, Westerwinter, this volume). Central nodes may also be able to use brokerage and/or "exit power" to expand or restrict network participation in ways that enhance private gains (Scott 1988; Hafner-Burton et al. 2009; Lake and Wong 2009). Thus as opposed to "reducing returns to power," as IGOs are widely held to do, a networked organization may entail *increasing* returns to power.

One might object here that formal treaty organizations can also be configured in ways that grant disproportionate power to a few states. Indeed, weighted voting is common in IGOs. Still, there are limits to the contractual inequality that can be introduced in formal organizations. As Ruggie (1992, 571) argues, "formal multilateralism is widely understood to build on principles of 'non-discrimination' and roughly balanced benefits to participating states over time" (see also Mitchell and Kielbach 2001). Dominant norms of multilateralism, which stress equitable gains and formal status equality, imply that it may be difficult for states to contract into inequitable relationships. As Cooper (1975) argues, "formal arrangements induce sovereign states to insist on formal symmetry in status, partly to cater to nationalist sentiment at home" (quoted in Raustiala 2005, 598). By contrast, by masking inequalities, informal agreements entail fewer barriers to discriminatory practices or relations of subordination. Thus, when inequality of power is pronounced, dominant states may favor TGN-based cooperation as a means to preserve or augment their power advantage.

Hypothesis 3: A high degree of power asymmetry will lead regime Principals to favor TGN-based cooperation.

Reduced Cost of Regime Supply

A third reason for regime Principals to favor TGN-based cooperation is that TGNs reduce costs of supplying and maintaining regimes. As we have seen, "non-discrimination" and "diffuse reciprocity" are defining principles of formal multilateral IGOs. The former principle dictates that all parties to an agreement be treated alike; the latter implies that states eschew quid pro quo exchanges in favor of "longer-term assurances of a rough equivalence of aggregate benefits" (Ruggie 1992, 569–572). According to Ruggie, multilateralism thus contrasts sharply with bilateralism which "is premised on . . . the simultaneous balancing of specific quid-pro-quos by each party with every other" (1992, 572). As Daniel Verdier (2009, 440) has shown with reference to the NPT regime, from the perspective of a regime Principal, a multilateral approach to regime supply is both inflexible and costly, insofar as every prospective member is offered terms of cooperation equal to those required to persuade the state(s) with the highest compliance cost to enter and comply with a regime. By contrast, "bilateralism" enables Principals to offer different terms of cooperation to different partners so as to match individual compliance costs (Verdier 2009). Accepting this logic, I suggest that reliance on TGNs allows regime Principals to reduce the costs of regime supply by varying the terms of cooperation offered to individual partners. Effectively, whereas IGOs are multilateral, TGNs are pluri-lateral, insofar as they are based on multiple bilateral links (typically in the form of MOUs or joint declarations), which may differ in content. This aspect of TGN-based cooperation will be particularly attractive to a Principal that has a stronger preference for cooperation than other states, and therefore expects to bear the lion's share of the cost of regime supply.

Hypothesis 4: TGNs lower the cost of supplying and maintaining international regimes.

Co-opting Domestic Veto Players

A large scholarship focuses on how domestic preference constellations influence international institutional design. Rational institutionalist literature presents two contradictory hypotheses in this respect. The first holds that governments facing competing demands from domestic constituents will seek flexible international agreements that enable them to respond to fluctuations in domestic demands (Kahler 2000, 668; Rosendorff and Milner 2001, 831). The other predicts that governments facing competing domestic demands will favor inflexible (that is, highly precise and obligatory) agreements that lock in international bargains against domestic opposition. Typically, the first line of argument cites a desire to reduce future costs of cooperation in the event of unexpected shifts in domestic preferences, whereas the latter is premised on a desire to enhance international credibility in the face of fluctuating domestic demands. However, an equally pressing concern for many governments is domestic constraints on the ability to enter into international agreements in the first place. The negotiation of international agreements is often subject to intense domestic scrutiny which may constrain states' ability to reach and seal agreements (Chayes and Chayes 1993, 183). This is particularly true of formal treaty negotiations, which are often conducted in a highly public manner. However, TGNs can reduce domestic impediments to international cooperation in two ways:

First, TGN-based cooperation diminishes the weight of public debate. International treaties often require legislatures to vote on ratification and to implement legislation. By contrast, transgovernmental agreements require no legislative approval and limited implementing action. As such, they are less likely to become captive to domestic disputes.

Second, TGNs may reduce incentives for domestic groups to mobilize against agreements. As Goldstein and Martin (2000, 604) argue, insofar as legalization entails a process of greater rule precision, strongly legalized regimes will provide more and better information about the distributional implications of cooperation, thereby providing incentives for negatively affected groups to mobilize against agreements. By the same logic, TGN-based agreements which establish general and non-binding standards of cooperation tend to obscure distributive effects and thereby reduce incentives for domestic mobilization. These features of TGNs are particularly attractive when domestic veto players are numerous and/or strong.

Hypothesis 5: TGN-based cooperation is most likely when domestic veto players in dominant states are numerous/strong.

Privileged Clubs and Exclusion of Spoilers

A final incentive for TGN-based cooperation arises from incentives to exclude spoilers by bypassing existing institutional structures. As Avant and Westerwinter (this volume) note, political networks are not isolated entities but interact with other networks/institutions in multiple ways. Indeed, TGNs often coexist with IGOs that focus on similar or related issues and may have overlapping memberships. In this context, TGN formation may act as a form of "segmentation" designed to escape constraints imposed by existing institutions. Indeed, a key advantage of TGN-based cooperation in a context where formal treaty-based agreements are already in place is that informal networking does not have to include all parties to an existing treaty agreement. In the context of treaty-based IGOs, a broadening of institutional mandate or reform of institutional rules or procedures in response to situational exigencies typically requires agreement by all member states (or at least by a large majority). An informal transgovernmental approach, by contrast, allows a few committed parties to initiate or deepen cooperation without agreement by others. This makes it easier to get cooperation off the ground since "spoilers" (preference outliers that are likely to stall or water down agreement) and "laggards" (states that insist on a formal say but have little to contribute to cooperation in material terms) can be easily excluded.[12]

An informal approach also holds advantages when it comes to expanding cooperation. By confining cooperation to a small "coalition of the willing," "insiders" may be able to set benchmarks for cooperation that "outsiders" are subsequently compelled to observe. As Benvinisti (2006, 18) has convincingly argued, if an initial group includes powerful states in an issue area, their cooperation may create externalities, which increase the cost to other states of remaining outside a network. For example, insiders may withhold privileges (such as market access or access to information or technology) from outsiders unless they comply with their preferred cooperative solutions. In this way, initially excluded states may find that network externalities compel them to accept cooperative standards that they would not have willingly contracted into as parties to formal multilateral negotiations.[13]

Hypothesis 6: Regime Principals favor TGN-based cooperation in the presence of powerful spoilers.

Summary of Hypotheses

I have identified small, asymmetric numbers as a precondition for successful TGN-based cooperation. When this precondition is fulfilled, I have suggested that dominant states in an issue area ("regime Principals") are likely to favor a TGN design when the expected frequency of enforcement actions is low; when power is highly asymmetric; when domestic veto players are numerous and strong; and in the presence of powerful international spoilers. These hypotheses are jointly sufficient: the presence of each additional independent variable increases the probability of TGN-based cooperation. The following section probes the plausibility of these hypotheses by analyzing two cases of transgovernmental cooperation in the realm of nonproliferation—the PSI and the MTCR.

International Arms Control and Nonproliferation Cooperation

As discussed earlier, international arms control has traditionally been regarded as an area dominated by highly legalized regimes under formal executive

[12] While exclusion can also be achieved within formal regimes, through entry requirements, creating "rival" legal institutions among willing states may be controversial and potentially destabilizing for cooperation in a wider issue area.

[13] This conjecture is consistent with the idea, discussed by McLin (1979) that TGNs serve as conduits for export of regulatory standards from leading markets to followers. See also Simmons 2001, 591; Raustiala 2002; Djelic and Kleiner 2006; and Bach and Newman 2009.

control. In the aftermath of World War II, prominent formal IGOs such as the United Nations Security Council (UNSC) and the International Atomic Energy Agency (IAEA), were created to strengthen international arms control. This period also saw the conclusion of major multilateral arms control treaties, such as the Partial Test Ban Treaty (1963), the NPT (1968), and the Biological Weapons Convention (1972), many of which have near universal assent. While states continue to rely on formal treaty regimes to manage proliferation risks (witness the conclusion of the CWC, 1993), these formal regimes have been supplemented by a range of more informal, transgovernmental initiatives. Below I probe whether the hypotheses derived in the previous section can throw light on this institutional variation through analyzing two of these initiatives.

The Proliferation Security Initiative

The PSI, launched by President Bush in May 2003, is an informal, distributed network of states seeking to "stop shipments of WMD, delivery systems, and related materials flowing to and from states and non-state actors of proliferation concern." Members have adopted a joint "Statement of Interdiction Principles" urging participants to board and search vessels suspected of carrying WMD (Weapon of Mass Destruction) materiel and, if appropriate, seize their cargoes. Participants also pledge to share information and expertise, strengthen national legislation, and undertake joint training exercises. Apart from these loose principles, the PSI has few distinguishable institutional structures. The Initiative does not rest on a treaty agreement, it has no international secretariat or central coordinating body, and no dedicated funding (Nikitin 2012). No formal schedule exists for PSI meetings or training exercises, and there are no joint guidelines for when or how to undertake interdictions. Participating states have merely agreed "to share information as appropriate" and "act when they consider it necessary to thwart illicit trade" (Joseph 2004; Belcher 2009). PSI Principles also fail to specify clear operational objectives. As Joseph (2004) notes, PSI members remain vague in describing the types of shipments they are targeting, speaking only in general terms of "nuclear, chemical, or biological weapons, delivery systems and related materials." They offer no definitions of these weapons categories, nor do they reference international conventions governing the possession of WMD.

The PSI is a highly informal arrangement, but several other structural properties distinguish it as an institution. First, membership is small. Although more than one hundred countries have publicly endorsed the Statement of Principles, actual (or active) membership is quite limited. Initially, the PSI included eleven "core" states.[14] Since 2003, ten more countries have joined the core, taking current membership to twenty-one. These states comprise the Operational Experts Group (OEG) responsible for providing direction and resources to the PSI.

Second, although PSI was launched in the United States as a Presidential Initiative, day-to-day activities are decided on and coordinated by relevant government departments and functional agencies in participating countries (i.e., at transgovernmental level).[15] Meetings of the OEG typically bring together military, law enforcement, intelligence, diplomatic and legal officials, and experts (Nikitin 2012), whereas high-level political meetings are rare.

Third, implementation of the PSI Principles is highly decentralized. As a purely political agreement, the PSI does not grant states legal authority to conduct interdictions in international waters or to seize cargo. Interdiction activities must be confined to what is permissible under existing national and international laws,[16] and all prosecutions for WMD-trafficking are conducted at national level in accordance with domestic laws (Byers 2004, 529; White House 2008; Belcher 2009).

Fourth, as is the case in a number of other policy domains examined in this volume (Carpenter, Percy, Avant, Westerwinter), whereas formal centralization is low, structural analysis reveals a high degree of informal centralization of the PSI network. The Initiative was launched by John Bolton, then US Undersecretary of State for Arms Control and International Security, and Washington has closely controlled memberships by inviting individual countries to join the core group. While other OEG members are involved in hosting PSI meetings, workshops, and exercises, the United States has played a pivotal role in shaping PSI activities by leading most interdiction operations and by supplying the bulk of physical assets and intelligence. By contrast, other states primarily contribute region-specific intelligence, docking space, and/or consent for ships registered under their flags to be searched (Etzioni 2009). The United States also takes a lead in working bilaterally with specific partner states to improve their interdiction capacities (Friedman 2011; Williams 2013). For example, a 2012 report by GAO recounts that officials from the Departments of State and Defense, the CBP and FBI have extended access to PSI activities to a number of countries that are not part of the OEG. In short, whereas PSI is presented as a multilateral mechanism for

[14] The initial group consisted of the United States and ten close allies, namely Australia, France, Germany, Japan, Netherlands, Portugal, Spain, the United Kingdom, and Poland.

[15] The PSI is managed in the United States by the National Security Staff in cooperation with the Departments of State and Defense with occasional support from other functional agencies, such as the Department of Energy and the FBI. See GAO Report 2012.

[16] PSI Interdiction Principles. See also White House 2008.

coordinating the interdiction efforts of participating states, observers largely agree it is essentially a coalition-of-the-willing managed by Washington (Etzioni 2009).

Centralization is further enhanced by direct bilateral ties between the United States and individual states that maintain a large number of commercial vessels on their registries and are known to facilitate clandestine transfers of military equipment and dual-use goods transfers (so-called "flags-of-convenience states").[17] Washington has signed bilateral ship-boarding agreements with eleven of the world's largest ship registries, allowing US officials to stop and search ships displaying their flags in any location (Friedman 2011; Nikitin 2012).[18] No other PSI participant has made such agreements (Etzioni 2009). In structural terms, then, the PSI is a "scale-free" network in which a single node is connected to a large number of other nodes that are themselves thinly connected (figure 6.1).

Why A TGN

To explain the institutional design of the PSI, we must first determine what problem(s) the Initiative is a reaction to. The PSI was prompted by a series of failings of global nonproliferation policies in the early 2000s. In 2002, intelligence suggested the presence of clandestine nuclear programs in Iran and North Korea (Belcher 2009), and possibly in Libya and Iraq. Given a lack of indigenous capacity, these countries depended on imports from foreign suppliers to advance their programs, and intercepting transfers of WMD components thus became a key priority for Washington and its allies (Joseph 2004). However, current international law does not criminalize trade in WMD materiel (some of which has legitimate uses), nor does it allow states to stop and search foreign vessels in international waters simply on suspicion of transporting WMD.[19] Against this background, how could international nonproliferation efforts be strengthened?

One solution would be to seek a UNSC-sanctioned blockade of North Korea and other states of acute proliferation concern. Yet this solution was ruled out

---

[17] A 2012 study by SIPRI estimates that flag of convenience ships accounted for more than 70% of reported destabilizing military equipment and dual-use goods transfers in the past two decades. Quoted by Nikitin 2012.

[18] Washington has signed ship-boarding agreements with Antigua-Bermuda, Bahamas, Belize, Croatia, Cyprus, Liberia, Malta, the Marshall Islands, Mongolia, Panama, St. Vincent, and the Grenadines. US, DoS, "PSI Ship Boarding Agreements."

[19] Art. 110 of UNCLOS (1982) states that ships shall enjoy "innocent passage" on the high seas, meaning that they have complete immunity from the jurisdiction of any state other than the flag state. See Guilfoyle 2009; Belcher 2011.

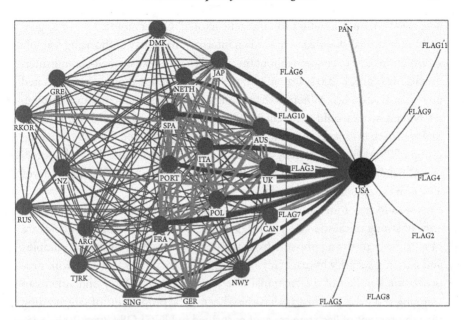

Figure 6.1 The PSI Network. *Note:* The thickness of the lines illustrate the number and strength of ties between actors. The thickest lines indicate the strongest ties, and thinner lines are progressively weaker. The data on which the diagram is based was generated by coding whether a state was party to the initial secret discussion of the PSI, whether it participating in the subsequent officials deliberations, whether it was a member of the 'core group' that launched PSI in 2003, whether it is a member of the OEG as well as the country's rate of hosting or participating in joint interdiction exercises.

by Chinese opposition.[20] Moreover, such a strategy would lack universality insofar as a formal embargo would apply only to countries specifically targeted by a UNSC resolution.

A second solution would be to seek an amendment to the UN Law of the Seas Convention (UNCLOS), which would make WMD proliferation an international criminal offence, or, alternatively, to introduce a new international treaty restricting WMD transfers. Several factors spoke against this option. As Byers (2004, 531) argues, even if a treaty were agreed, the states most prone to traffic in WMD would most likely not become parties, and their ships would thus evade interdiction. A treaty-based approach would also be liable to founder on opposition from international spoilers. Countries such as China, Russia, and India have repeatedly refused to sanction international interdiction. For example, Chinese objections led to all references to interdiction being removed from UNSC Resolution 1540, which obliges states to establish domestic controls to

---

[20] On China's insistence, UNSC Resolution 1874 (2009), which establishes a formal arms embargo against North Korea, does not authorize inspections on the high seas without flag state consent.

prevent WMD proliferation to non-state actors.[21] Observers also point to general international skepticism toward an international treaty authorizing forcible interdictions due to concerns about the potential for expansive self-serving interpretations (Joseph 2004; Datan 2005). Such international opposition dictated an informal approach. Whereas channeling cooperation on interdiction through a UN framework would have required agreement by China and Russia, an informal approach meant these countries could be easily excluded from the founding group of PSI members, thereby preventing them from watering down the agreement (Belcher 2009; Kock 2012). This supports Hypothesis 6 ("Principals favor TGNs in the presence of powerful spoilers").

A second factor militating against going down the formal route was the presence of strong domestic veto players (Hypothesis 5). Arms control policies are often subject to strong pressure from the domestic military-industrial complex and national security bureaucracy (Chayes and Chayes 1993). Faced with proposals for a policy of international interdiction, the US Navy and American shipping and fishing industries have also been vocal proponents of safeguarding the requirement of flag state consent enshrined in UNCLOS (Byers 2004, 545; Hanson 2005). As Byers (2004, 527) notes, the principle of exclusive flag state jurisdiction not only forms the legal foundation for the global mobility of US forces and military assets but also protects commercial vessels carrying goods to or from US territory. By sidestepping the requirement of flag state consent, an international agreement extending reciprocal stop-and-search powers could have unforeseen negative consequences for national security and commercial interests (Friedman 2003, 2). In this context, an informal transgovernmental agreement has allowed PSI architects to ensure that cooperation is kept sufficiently flexible to avoid constraining the legitimate activities of US military and industrial actors. Furthermore, the non-binding nature of PSI Principles combined with significant ambiguity about what specific countries or weapons are being targeted has made it difficult for domestic shipping and manufacturing companies to assess the potential commercial implications of the program. Finally, the fact that interdiction activities are kept secret and that no dedicated funding has been sought for the program has made it difficult for domestic stakeholders to monitor PSI activities or to mobilize opposition to the program (GAO 2006, 2012; Nikitin 2012).[22]

[21] Resolution 1540 was adopted under Chapter VII of the UN Charter in April 2004, but does not provide enforcement authority, nor does it mention interdiction. See Joyner 2007; Belcher 2009; Guilfoyle 2009.

[22] The GAO has complained that the departments and agencies involved in administering PSI provide insufficient funding information to ensure proper congressional oversight of the program. In 2007, Congress endorsed the recommendations of the GAO requiring the president to include funds for

So far, I have argued that the informal nature of the PSI grants flexibility to bypass domestic and international veto players. But there are also potential downsides to a TGN arrangement. As a purely political initiative, the PSI does not expand legal authority to pursue international interdictions of WMD. Also, by restricting cooperation to a small group of like-minded states, some of the world's worst proliferators have been left outside the regime. Finally, as a non-binding agreement, the PSI has relatively low credibility. What has led American proponents of an active counter-proliferation policy to favor such a "minimalist" solution? I point to four main factors.

First, a TGN-based approach to interdiction has been possible and desirable because the number of countries whose collaboration has been needed to initiate and sustain effective cooperation on interdiction is small. The United States (and to some degree Britain) dominates maritime interdiction by virtue of the global reach and strength of its navy (Etzioni 2009). By enlisting the cooperation of a small, but powerful, group of allies that agree to detain and search vessels suspected of WMD transportation, the United States has succeeded in restricting the global movement of proliferators, while at the same time escaping the limitations on cooperation that often beset larger, more heterogeneous groups (Joseph 2004). This supports Hypothesis 1 ("Small asymmetric number is a precondition for TGN-based cooperation").

Second, there is great asymmetry of power within the PSI network. As discussed, organizational networks frequently suffer from lack of strategic direction and poor compliance due to the absence of centralized enforcement. Yet, in the PSI these problems have been somewhat circumvented by the presence of a strong Principal. As discussed, the United States has given central direction to the Initiative by providing the bulk of information and resources necessary for cooperation. Most interdiction operations have been led by the United States, and the US State Department has been the main source of public information about successful interdiction missions, indicating a central US role in enforcement. The fact that the United States acts as chief organizer and enforcer in the regime ensures credibility and obviates the need for formalized central enforcement or information exchange. This again supports Hypothesis 1.

A third factor favoring a TGN is a low expected rate of enforcement. Earlier I argued (following Kaplow 1992) that flexible standards are preferable to fixed rules when the expected frequency of enforcement is low (Hypothesis 2). The operational objectives and institutional design of the PSI support this

PSI-related activities in his yearly budget request (GAO–06–937C, 2006). Congress also requested an annual report from the secretaries of Defense and State, listing all PSI-related activities and expenditures (GAO 2006, 2012). However, the scope of the Initiative has remained vague as funding for PSI activities remains in large part a component of other programs that address WMD proliferation.

hypothesis. The PSI does not seek to stop all WMD shipments but specifically targets shipments to/from countries "of proliferation concern." No list of countries of "proliferation concern" has ever been published, but most observers agree the primarily targets are North Korea and Iran. In an interview in 2003, Bolton made clear that the PSI would not target the weapons-related trade of countries such as Israel, India, and Pakistan who are seen as American allies. "There are unquestionably states that are not within existing treaty regimes that possess WMD legitimately," he explained. "We're not trying to have a policy that attempts to cover each and every one of those circumstances. What we're worried about are the rogue states and the terrorist groups that pose the most immediate threat" (quoted in Joseph 2004; see also Williams 2013). The focus on preventing proliferation to a few rogue states implies that enforcement actions are expected to be relatively infrequent. This favors a flexible standard that can be broadly interpreted and applied to different cases and settings as strategic priorities dictate.

The institutional design of the PSI responds to functional demands for flexibility and low political visibility. Yet, asymmetric power has played a fundamental role in shaping the Initiative. As we have seen, PSI's effectiveness is predicated on a disproportionate investment of American power and resources. This raises the question, why has Washington chosen to bankroll an informal regime to counter proliferation threats, as opposed to seeking a formal treaty-based agreement that might allow it to spread the cost of regime creation and management across a wider group of states? So far, I have pointed to incentives to bypass domestic and international veto players, but another important aspect of networked counter-proliferation cooperation is that it increases the returns to US power. It does so in several ways.

First, an informal transgovernmental approach has enabled the United States to sidestep constraints imposed by existing frameworks for cooperation (Hypothesis 6). NATO would seem an obvious institutional home for counter-proliferation cooperation between the United States and its close allies. Nine of the eleven PSI founding members are NATO members, and NATO's shared intelligence and surveillance capabilities have obvious applicability to forcible interdiction. Since the 1990s, talks within NATO have focused on expanding the Alliance's nonproliferation activities to include military action.[23] However, reports from officials who attended closed PSI meetings in 2003 reveals that NATO was deliberately held at arm's length by Bolton who characterized French

---

[23] In the wake of the US Counter-Proliferation Initiative in 1994, the North Atlantic Council created a series of committees and working groups to study the military aspects of counter-proliferation. See Larsen 1997.

calls for formal NATO involvement in PSI as an attempt to "dilute the Initiative."[24] Involving NATO would bring in a wider institutional membership, he objected. It would also make cooperation subject to the collective decision-making procedures of the Alliance, thereby allowing the distribution of formal institutional power within NATO to shape power distributions in the PSI. From an American perspective, this was undesirable. Since 1991, Germany and France have voiced reservations about several aspects of US counter-proliferation policy (Larsen 1997, 32; Nikitin 2012). An informal, non-institutionalized approach made it easier to bring these countries on board, as they did not have to commit to specific aspects of American interdiction policy, while at the same time avoiding granting them an institutional veto going forward. As Etzioni (2009) notes, in contrast to NATO, the PSI has no Council in which members can exercise veto power and no multistate committees that must unanimously approve targets. Whereas the Initiative allows Washington to coordinate interdiction activities with its close allies, it does not thereby allow other states to constrain American policy. This observation is consistent with the notion that an informal regime increases returns to power.

A networked approach has allowed the United States to carefully control membership. According to Kock (2012), National Security Council (NSC) staff deliberately kept the "core group" of PSI confined to close allies with a wide geographic distribution and important maritime roles. The United States first approached Britain and Australia (Belcher 2011). After gaining their support, Washington invited a small group of other states that could be expected to endorse the PSI Principles. China and Russia were both excluded from the core as their participation might "stymie agreement" (Belcher 2011; Kock 2012). Only after the founding principles were agreed did Washington invite Russia to participate (see Belcher 2011; Friedman 2011; Kock 2012). (This observation again supports Hypothesis 6.)

By closely controlling membership, the United States, as regime Principal, has also been able to vary the costs of adding new members to the network. Whereas countries such as Britain and France needed few inducements to participate, Washington has used a combination of carrots and sticks to pressure flag states to sign ship-boarding agreements. Presented as pacts for mutual benefit, these agreements often look more like instances of coercive cooperation, where the United States has used its dominant economic power to pressure

---

[24] Confidential report by a member of Airstaff, Ministry of Defense, Whitehall, October 2003. This account is corroborated by Kock (2012) who reports that Washington deliberately shunned involvement by representatives of the European Union and NATO in early meetings of the PSI Core Group on grounds that "their inclusion would have impeded progress, given the cumbersome decision processes and wide membership in each organization."

poorer flag states to grant reciprocal stop-and-search powers without gaining any of the benefits of participation in the wider network in return.[25] This flexible approach to membership has allowed the United States to keep the costs of growing the network low (Hypothesis 4: "TGNs lower the cost of regime supply"). It has also allowed Washington to exclude states with too high compliance costs, thereby preventing them from weakening the Initiative. National Security Advisor Stephen Hadley articulated this logic in his address at the fifth anniversary of the PSI: "In PSI, cops and criminals do not co-exist in the organization. PSI is a group of nations committed to be cops, a group that defines criminals clearly, and a group committed to hold themselves and each other accountable for results" (White House 2008). So far, who is cop and who is criminal has been largely defined by Washington.

In summary, in addition to standard benefits such as flexibility and low contracting costs, informal cooperation on WMD interdiction has been made desirable—and possible—by a concentration of power in the hand of the United States. In an issue context where the United States is by far the most powerful player, and has a strong interest in facilitating international cooperation, a transgovernmental approach has allowed Washington to supply and manage an effective international regime at low cost and with minimal constraints on its own freedom of action.

Missile Technology Control Regime

The MTCR was established in 1987 by the G7 countries to curb proliferation of long-range missiles and related technology. Today membership has grown to thirty-four and includes most of the world's major missile manufacturing states. The regime, which was negotiated by mid-level officials in the US State Department, is based on voluntary adherence to a set of export policy guidelines (the "Guidelines") applied to a list of controlled items (the "Equipment and Technology Annex"), which includes key equipment and technology needed for missile development, production, and operation—whether of military or dual use.

According to the US State Department, the MTCR is not an international organization that seeks to ban missiles, but rather an informal agreement aimed to deny secondary states access to missiles or missile technology (2003b; see Mistry 2003). Members agree to deny, in principle, transfers of items listed as "Category I" (complete missiles and rockets, and production facilities) and to

---

[25] Many flag states depend crucially on income from their ship registries. The main incentive to subject ships flying their flags to US inspection has been promises of financial aid or threats of economic sanction. See Vesely 2004; Parker 2007.

exercise caution in exporting Category II items, which consist mainly of dual-use items. They also agree to share technology, information, and other resources that are not available to nonmembers (Dimitrov et al. 2007).

Organizationally, the MTCR is informal and decentralized. The regime is not based on a treaty or official agreement, and has no secretariat or central administrative body that monitors exports (Lipson 2001, 2004). Decisions on what items to include in the Equipment and Technology Annex are made by consensus, but MTCR members do not make export-licensing decisions as a group. Rather individual states decide on a case-by-case basis whether to grant export licenses for specific goods. The Guidelines are highly flexible in this regard. Items listed in the Annex are not subject to an outright export ban, but may be transferred at the discretion of member states (Arms Control Association 2004).

Like the PSI, the MTCR has no central enforcement provisions; members enforce the regime exclusively through domestic legislation. There is no joint list of countries to which exports are prohibited, and no member can veto another's exports. Since export decisions are the sole responsibility of the exporting state, there are also no collective sanctions for transfers of banned items. Instead, members impose their own unilateral sanctions against transgressors. For example, US law mandates that Washington sanction actors (whether individuals, companies, or governments) that export controlled items to countries identified as "proliferators" or as potential threats to national security. It does so irrespectively of whether these actors are members of, or operate within a state that is a member of, the MTCR (Arms Control Association 2004).

Why a TGN?

The MTCR responds to a problem of growing proliferation of nuclear-capable missiles. In the 1980s, evidence surfaced about the development and sale of long-range missiles by several developing countries, prompting the G7 to seek tougher restrictions on international transfers of missile components and technology (Halevy 1993). Yet, several factors spoke against seeking an inclusive international treaty agreement that would institute a general rule against export of missile technology and hardware.

First, the military, the national security bureaucracy and domestically based manufacturers in the major missile-producing states would likely oppose a comprehensive, legally binding ban on missile exports, as such a ban would restrict legitimate trade and military cooperation with friendly countries. Like the PSI, the MTCR sidesteps domestic opposition by adopting a loose standard for cooperation that focuses on preventing proliferation only to "countries of concern" (US DoS 1993). As an informal regime, the MTCR does not establish binding rules, which draw a clear line between legitimate and illegitimate exports. Rather the Guidelines leave scope for allowing transfers of missile technology or hardware to select third states—subject to appropriate risk assessment.[26] Importantly, a transgovernmental approach also allows export-licensing decisions to be made without public debate and without political scrutiny from domestic agencies outside the national security bureaucracy. As such, the guidelines have proved agreeable to key domestic stakeholders. This confirms Hypothesis 5 ("TGN-based cooperation is likely when domestic veto players are numerous/strong").

An informal approach also facilitated exclusion of international spoilers (Hypothesis 6). The MTCR was negotiated among a small group of states that included the world's largest producers of missiles and missile technology. These countries shared an interest in preventing proliferation of hardware or technical knowledge to secondary states. Thus, when launching negotiations, the United States deliberately decided not to approach countries that were actively trying to buy or build ballistic missiles (Angelova 1999). According to Angelova (1999, 446), for example, the decision to negotiate the agreement in secret was a conscious effort by US officials to exclude China from having influence over the terms of agreement or from gaining access to sensitive missile design information.

Like the PSI, the MTCR highlights the benefits of TGN-based cooperation as a means to exclude spoilers from influence at the negotiation stage while establishing standards for cooperation that they can subsequently be coerced to accept. By restricting initial negotiations to a select group, the United States was able to prevent spoilers from watering down the agreement. Once agreement was reached, MTCR "insiders" have used their privileged access to advanced missile technology to pressure nonmembers to embrace the Guidelines (Lipson 2001; McDougall 2002). This approach has been particularly evident with respect to China. Washington has repeatedly sanctioned China (a nonmember) for breaches of the MTCR Guidelines and has denied Chinese participation in space-related research programs.[27] Such measures have increased the cost to China of remaining outside the regime. As a result, China in 1994 announced it would abide unilaterally by MTCR guidelines in return for a lifting of MTCR-related sanctions (Lipson 2001) and in 2004 Beijing sought MTCR membership. Yet the bid was rebuffed by the United States.[28] Thus, China continues to be

---

[26] The United States has supplied Tomahawk cruise missiles to the United Kingdom and Spain despite these being listed as Category 1 items and therefore subject to a "strong presumption to deny export."

[27] The United States imposed sanctions on China in 1987 (over Iran exports) and in 1991 (over missile-related exports to Pakistan and Syria) (Halevy 1993).

[28] On the Chinese membership bid, see Zaborsky 2004. As a nonmember, Russia was sanctioned in 1995 for exporting cryogenic rocket engines to India. See Pande 1999. Russia joined MTCR in 1995.

excluded from influence and access to privileged goods within the regime, while being under strong pressure to abide by its guidelines.

As with the PSI, a TGN-based approach to combatting international missile proliferation has enabled the exclusion of international spoilers and mollified domestic veto players (Hypotheses 5 and 6). Yet, as with the PSI, certain "enabling conditions" have been necessary to build effective international cooperation around an informal, TGN-based regime. First, the number of states whose cooperation has been required to restrict the proliferation of long-range nuclear-capable missiles is relatively small. Russia, the United States, China, and India are the only four countries currently known to possess land-based ICBMs, and only thirty-one countries currently possess ballistic missiles (ACA report, January 2012). Thus, effective export controls do not require a regime with universal adherence (Hypothesis 1: "Small, asymmetric number is a precondition for TGN-based cooperation"). The fact the number of states producing long-range missiles is relatively small also implies that the expected rate of enforcement actions is low, thereby favoring a flexible standard (Hypothesis 2).

Second, regime effectiveness is ensured by the presence of a strong regime Principal. As Dimitrov et al. (2007) observe, the United States dedicates more resources to export control than any other country, and other states are highly dependent on US intelligence on global proliferation activity. The United States also takes the lead in providing incentives for other states to join the MTCR by sharing technology and offering participation in civilian space-related programs (ibid.). Most important, Congress has undertaken to enforce the regime unilaterally through the Arms Export Control Act and the Export Administration Act (Angelova 1999, 437). As discussed, Washington has taken the lead in sanctioning Chinese entities for missile exports. But American sanctions also play a crucial role in eliciting cooperation from other MTCR members. While export decisions are a matter of national discretion, national legislation empowers the US president to impose sanctions against any entity or country that violates MTCR Guidelines, for example, by restricting access to trade with US manufacturers. Given US market dominance, this means that Washington's "blacklist" of countries to which missile exports should be denied is an important reference point for other MCTR members. In short, the United States plays a pivotal role in orchestrating cooperation and enforcing the regime in line with Hypothesis 1.

As in the case of the PSI, a TGN-based solution is enabled by a highly asymmetric distribution of power. Cooperation among MTCR members is sustained by a disproportionate investment of US power and resources. From a US perspective, however, reliance on an informal network holds distinct advantages. An informal approach has allowed the United States to control membership, which has in turn reinforced its central network position. An informal approach has also lowered the cost of supplying and maintaining the regime, by allowing Washington to vary the terms of participation granted to new members (Hypothesis 4). The chief aim of the MTCR is to prevent proliferation of long-range offensive missiles. Officially, the regime calls on all new entrants to renounce missiles with more than 300 km range and 500 kg payload, and most new member states have done so (MTCR Info; Mistry 2003, 127–128).[29] However, the requirement has been waived for some countries. When Ukraine joined the MTCR in 1998, for example, it was allowed to retain its Scud missiles and to continue producing offensive missiles in exchange for ending its nuclear commerce with Iran (Pande 1999). South Korea was likewise exempted from the ban on long-range missile development when joining in 2001. Such bilateral quid pro quos would likely be more politically costly and destabilizing within a formal multilateral regime.

Summary and Further Analysis

My analysis of the MTCR and PSI confirms the plausibility of my main hypotheses. In both cases, TGN-based cooperation has provided a means for a powerful regime Principal—the United States—to exclude domestic and international veto players and to assert its power with fewer institutional constraints than would have been the case within a formal, treaty-based regime. One may wonder whether the "enabling conditions" and political incentives identified in these two cases really stand out from most areas of international nonproliferation cooperation. While I cannot go into much detail here, I believe that they do. Domestic opposition to binding nonproliferation agreements is not ubiquitous. Consider as a brief illustration the CWC. The CWC was strongly endorsed by four powerful domestic constituencies in the United States; the intelligence community, the chemical industry, the general public, and the Pentagon, including the Joint Chiefs of Staff, implying an absence of strong domestic veto players (Smithson 1997, 7). "Number" also varies across different arms control issues depending on technology and the ability of countries to control weapons flows (Koremenos et al. 2001). Virtually any country with a developed chemical industry has the potential to make and deploy chemical weapons, and many non-state actors are involved in developing and proliferating chemical weapons. Thus, in contrast to long-range missile proliferation, where effective export controls can be achieved by cooperation among a relatively small group of countries, an effective regime restricting the spread and

[29] Argentina and South Africa destroyed long-range missile components and manufacturing facilities when joining MTCR in 1993 and 1995. The Czech Republic, Hungary, and Poland eliminated their Scud missiles as a condition for entry.

use of chemical weapons requires almost universal participation. Moreover the large number of chemical industries in many developing counties implies a high expected frequency of enforcement actions. Thus, no single country or handful of countries could undertake to provide effective unilateral enforcement of the regime. This may explain why cooperation on chemical weapons proliferation is governed by a strongly legalized intergovernmental regime, which features centralized monitoring and sanctioning and spreads the cost of enforcement across multiple member states (for further discussion of the institutional design of the CWC, see Eilstrup-Sangiovanni 2009).

Conclusion

In this chapter I have used a combination of organizational and structural network theory and analysis to explain why states sometimes choose to cooperate through informal TGNs while at other times they favor more formal, centralized institutions. In many ways, the nonproliferation TGNs I have analyzed here are simply a genus of the wider class of informal international institutions. Yet, I have sought to show how using network theory to analyze these institutions' structure and functionality opens up new perspectives on their institutional design.

While rational institutionalism is puzzled by informal international security cooperation, network approaches point to several features of TGNs which make them highly suitable for cooperation on arms control issues. Combining functional institutionalist theory with insights from network theory thus helps to explain variation in the design of international arms control agreements.

The application of both organizational and structural network theory to analyze the PSI and MTCR has led to three findings that either contradict or expand on received wisdom regarding TGNs:

(1) Extant transgovernmentalist literature generally describes TGNs as flat, distributed networks that bring together actors on a formally equal footing and fosters "deliberate equality" and "joint responsibility" for action. By contrast, the TGNs analyzed here take the form of scale-free networks where a small number of powerful players ("hubs") link up peripheral nodes and dominate policy-making. In short, whereas these TGNs may look flat to the naked eye, they are in fact highly centralized and entail a high degree of implicit or indirect hierarchy.

(2) Extant literature cites benefits such as enhanced speed and low contracting costs as the primary reasons why states embrace transgovernmental cooperation. Yet, transaction cost-based arguments by themselves fail to explain

variation between informal institutions, such as TGNs, and formal IGOs. By contrast, my analysis suggests that that "number," "power asymmetry," and expected frequency of enforcement are important determinants of institutional design variation.

(3) Whereas extant rationalist literature often explains high legalization and centralization as a function of severe enforcement problems, my analysis suggests that—among small numbers—decentralized or unilateral enforcement can sustain cooperation and lend credibility to informal regimes even in the presence of strong enforcement problems. The MTCR includes no formal enforcement provisions but nonetheless enjoys high compliance among members.

Whether these findings hold across the general population of informal international institutions is a topic for future research. For the purposes of this volume, informal ties in the arms control cases I have examined have generated effective governance that most often serves the interest of dominant players.

7

Networking for the Ban

Network Structure, Social Power, and the Movement to Ban Antipersonnel Mines

ADAM BOWER

The international movement to ban antipersonnel (AP) mines is often cited as among the most successful recent governance processes in global politics. This coalition of transnational civil society groups and "like-minded" states allied together to seek a legally binding prohibition, which culminated with the creation of the Mine Ban Treaty (MBT) in 1997.[1] The treaty is rightly regarded as a diplomatic and humanitarian achievement as it constitutes the first international prohibition of a weapon that was in extensive contemporary use (Goose and Williams 2008, 181). Moreover, the MBT was negotiated in a short period of time and against the wishes of the leading powers of China, Russia, and—especially—the United States of America. This outcome poses a puzzle for realist and liberal theories that would expect materially powerful states to dictate the international diplomatic agenda, especially in areas that bear upon the conduct of warfare. Advocates of the MBT were able to generate more effective governance and governance that served broader interests than these theories would expect.

Scholars have analyzed the mine ban movement and its achievements (a legally binding treaty and corresponding norm) as resulting from persuasion and social pressure (Price 1998; Herby and Lawand 2008; Rutherford 2009). These largely constructivist accounts, though, are less able to explain how a broad coalition formed around a conception of AP mines as legally and morally unacceptable in the first place. This is particularly puzzling because the United

---

[1] Convention on the Prohibition of the Use, Stockpiling, Production and Transfer of Anti-Personnel Mines and on their Destruction, Ottawa, December 3, 1997. http://www.icbl.org/index.php/icbl/Treaty/MBT/Treaty-Text-in-Many-Languages.

States framed these weapons as legitimate military technologies. Indeed, a key question in this episode is why the United States was unable to leverage its superior diplomatic and material resources to either block the emergence of a pro-ban constituency or achieve a favorable outcome in the subsequent negotiations.

Building on the framework developed in this volume, I apply insights from the literature on social networks to shed greater light on how network relations have facilitated and constrained entrepreneurial efforts in the mine ban case. My most fundamental contention, as advanced in the framework paper by Avant and Westerwinter and echoed in other empirical chapters, is that power is best conceptualized as residing in relationships not merely material resources. The position of actors within networks—as measured by the quality, density, and distribution of connections—empowers agency to reshape governance structures. Thinking in network terms thus offers a different take on power as an exercise in the management of social relationships and provides a vital insight into the puzzle that underlies the emergence of the AP mine ban.

Like other authors in this volume (e.g., Westerwinter), I show how network centrality offers a means by which otherwise weaker actors can generate effective governance and governance that serves broad interests. A constellation of less materially powerful states and transnational civil society groups were able to generate extensive ties with other actors which in turn generated informational and relational advantages that allowed them to successfully promote a new international conception of appropriate behavior despite sustained resistance from the United States and other skeptical military powers. Conversely, the United States was much less successful in building relationships among key actors as the mine ban network developed and was consequently less able to exploit these connections in conjunction with its material advantages to advance its policy goals. In this sense, social network analysis can provide insights into the structural preconditions that empowered the norm entrepreneurship so well described in previous scholarship.

I begin by introducing the mine ban network and outlining the key concepts that inform my analysis. I then turn to mapping the network's structure: while a diverse collection of actors participate in the network, relations are organized around a few hubs—composed of both state and non-state actors—that dominate policy development and execution. As anticipated in earlier accounts, the centrality of these actors is instrumental in bestowing distinctly social forms of power to shape governance outcomes by acting as norm entrepreneurs in raising the profile of an issue (agenda-setting), shaping appropriate responses (issue-framing), and promoting new norms to generate changes in actor behavior (socialization) (Price 2003, 583; Goddard 2009; Kahler 2009, 3; Carpenter 2011). Yet I also show that network position is itself generated in part by the capacity to achieve specific governance tasks and hence, that participation in networks can have recursive effects over time.

The balance of the chapter then illustrates the impact of network structure by examining forms of social power in two distinct phases in the mine ban effort, concerning the creation of the MBT and its subsequent implementation, respectively. Key actors utilized their positions within the network to reframe the debate concerning the legitimacy of AP mines and shape the content of the resulting treaty, and this influence has continued during the ongoing efforts to secure widespread adherence. Crucially, the success of these diplomatic initiatives was determined not by the raw material power of prospective entrepreneurs, or the content of their ideas in isolation, but rather by the structural conditions of the network itself, which provided certain actors with disproportionate access and brokerage opportunities in which to advance their claims. This account helps explain both the successful diplomacy of less materially powerful actors and the consequent US inability to get its way. In sum, power is understood not as an attribute or commodity, but rather a function of social relations and the resulting network position.

The AP mines case reinforces two further salient points in the study of networks that are taken up by the contributors to this volume. First, networks aim to address real-world policy issues and are often created and modified in reaction to a perceived governance need. In the case of the MBT, actor roles have evolved in response to new challenges implied by the formalization of the mine ban in a legally binding treaty: while early efforts focused on identifying the problem and advocating for a particular solution, attention has increasingly shifted to technical assistance and monitoring of state compliance with MBT commitments. Actors thus respond to their environment even as they are reshaping it, which draws attention to the importance of strategic action in network politics. Second, while structural position is critical to actor power within the network, this power is reinforced through the performance of functional roles and provision of individual or collective goods. Structure and agency are thus interactive and dynamic properties of networks (Kahler 2009, 6–11). Taken together, these insights provide further evidence that the properties of networks are of central importance in understanding norm diffusion in world politics.

Network Structure and Norm Entrepreneurship
The Antipersonnel Mine Ban Treaty

Like the other case studies presented in this volume, the ban on AP mines represents a hard case for global governance. First, the MBT prohibits the use, development, production, stockpiling, and transfer of AP mines, and thus constitutes a direct intervention in the war-fighting capacity of the state.[2] It is typically assumed that states will resist highly restrictive international obligations that implicate core matters of national security policy. Yet the MBT seeks to overturn a well-established international social standard that regarded AP landmines as unproblematic tools of war on par with other conventional military technologies like artillery shells, rockets, and personal infantry weapons (Price 1998, 617–618). This amounts to a fundamental reversal of the burden of proof that has typically privileged claims of military necessity in the first instance against concerns for humanitarian impacts (International Committee of the Red Cross 1997; Gard Jr. 1998; Morgan 2002; Jacobs 2004). In the negotiations that led to the MBT, these expansive legal obligations were rejected by key military powers, including China, the Russian Federation, and the United States (among others), who favored less stringent rules regulating but not eliminating AP mines. In this second respect, the MBT would again seem unlikely to spur significant international change, since prominent theories of international relations hold that the leadership of materially powerful states is necessary to underpin international cooperation (Mearsheimer 1994; Downs et al. 1996; Goldsmith and Posner 2005). Third and relatedly, it is expected that transnational civil society influence will be felt principally on issues that fall outside of the core security prerogatives of the state (Price 1998, 613).

For these reasons, the achievement of a legally binding global treaty was more contentious than is often realized in retrospect. Yet the mine ban movement has also been hailed as a model for a new kind of diplomacy in which like-minded governments and transnational civil society may ally together to bypass the resistance of materially powerful states in order to negotiate international rules (Axworthy 1998; Cameron 1998; Dolan and Hunt 1998; Behringer 2005; Goose and Williams 2008). Gaining greater purchase on how this outcome was achieved thus has important implications for the study of governance in the field of international security and more broadly.

Previous studies have provided important theoretical insights and empirical detail concerning the emergence of the mine ban movement and its successful negotiation of a legally binding treaty despite the opposition from leading states (Price 1998; Herby and Lawand 2008; Rutherford 2009). Price's seminal study of the issue, for example, demonstrated that transnational civil society, in concert with allies from middle power states, deployed persuasive argumentation and social pressure to promote a radically new conception of AP mines in which "their military utility is outweighed by their humanitarian costs, thus

---

[2] The MBT contains additional positive obligations to clear known mined areas and provide assistance to mine victims, though I do not address these features systematically here.

introducing a moral calculus into the definition of national interest" (Price 1998, 614). Price suggests that the impact of the socialization effort is a function of the content of the normative claim itself: emergent norms that involve "the bodily integrity of innocents," and that can be associated with existing moral taboos in related issue areas, are far more likely to generate widespread appeal (Keck and Sikkink 1998, 204; Price 1998, 639–640). Other studies have emphasized the diplomatic innovation associated with the mine ban movement and have identified the strategic use of a non-traditional negotiating forum as vital to the movement's success (Axworthy 1998; Cameron 1998; Dolan and Hunt 1998).

Yet these accounts do not address how civil society actors and less powerful states gained privileged access to the relevant international actors in order to promote their ideas in the first place. This is important, since for the view of AP mines as illegitimate weapons to gain widespread appeal, it first had to reach an audience of a critical mass that could generate a "cascade" toward widespread acceptance of the mine ban norm and its core causal claims (Finnemore and Sikkink 1998). Moreover, the norm entrepreneurship of the pro-ban coalition did not take place in a vacuum, but was in direct competition with an alternative framing—promoted by the United States and supported by other major military powers like China, India, and Russia—that regarded AP mines as militarily useful and acceptable weapons, and sought more modest legal restrictions on their continued use. What explains the substantial disparity in impact between supporters of an AP mine ban and their opponents?

Studying Social Networks: Centrality and Governance

Social network analysis provides a means of addressing this issue that locates the source of influence in the structural relations among actors, rather than the properties of the agent or issue itself (Knoke and Yang 2008, 4). A network approach seeks both to describe the actors and relationships in a defined social domain, and to provide a theoretically informed account that links network structure via mechanisms and processes to phenomena of interest. In basic terms, a network is composed of a series of actors (nodes) and connections (ties) between them through which resources flow. Ties may be represented by the exchange of material goods (e.g., trade, technology, or aid), affiliations (e.g., shared membership in intergovernmental organizations or alliances), and information and ideas (e.g., norms or values) (Hafner-Burton and Montgomery 2006, 24; Borgatti and Lopez-Kidwell 2011, 43–45). The patterns of these interactions have aggregative effects by bestowing some actors with more extensive and robust connections to other network members, making them hubs in the network (Maoz 2011, 9).

Network position, in turn, provides central actors with capabilities to influence policy choices and reshape international structures.

A key advantage of network theories, therefore, is their ability to address the interaction of structural and agentic aspects of governance. Network structures offer permissive environments for entrepreneurs to promote new norms in the international system (Avant, Carpenter, Cooley and Nexon, and Westerwinter, this volume). The interpersonal and interorganizational ties embodied in network connections facilitate the dissemination of ideas and practices via mechanisms of learning, persuasion, and social pressure, and are therefore instrumental to processes of socialization that are widely studied in international relations (Valente 2005; Dorussen and Ward 2008; Cao 2010). It is in this sense that networks enable social power, by which I mean the ability of actors to shape meanings and resulting interests and behaviors in the international system. These capacities are not inherent to the actors themselves, but are "embedded" in the network (Goddard 2009, 258). The distribution of ties, position of actors, and the quality of their connections thus mediate the agency of norm entrepreneurs, enabling action while imposing crucial constraints on which initiatives may disseminate widely (Avant and Westerwinter, this volume).

More specifically, the more connected an actor is within a network, the greater its potential to shape governance outcomes. Two conceptions of structural position encapsulate the most important forms of entrepreneurial power in the mine ban network. First, an actor may possess high *degree centrality*, meaning that it has a large number of direct ties to other nodes and is therefore well connected overall (Freeman 1979). This form of centrality is closely associated with heightened access—in both qualitative and quantitative terms—to resources flowing through the network, and hence informational advantages that can be translated into social power to influence policy. By virtue of the their location along principal lines of communication, hubs may also shape or limit the volume and destination of resources passing through the network, which provides them with an additional source of influence (Hafner-Burton et al. 2009, 570). Highly central nodes may utilize these asymmetries to identify governance challenges in need of response (agenda-setting), propose solutions in the form of new norms and legal rules (negotiating influence), and finally to assess compliance (monitoring and enforcement).

Second, well-connected actors may serve as a bridge between other nodes that lack direct ties, in which case they are said to possess high *betweenness centrality* (Freeman 1979). This measures the extent to which a given actor lies along the pathway between any two other actors and can be understood as a generic gauge of brokerage potential, meaning the extent to which a particular actor facilitates transactions between otherwise disparate members of a network (Burt 1992). The gaps that develop in network connections—known as structural holes—generate dependencies that can be exploited by hubs to increase their own influence (Goddard 2009; Hanneman and Riddle 2011b, 360–362). Betweenness thus provides a means of translating social capital into entrepreneurial power to shape collective action in two distinct ways. On the one hand, brokers can act as gatekeepers, selectively permitting or restricting the flow of resources and thereby activating or denying relationships between actors. On the other hand, hubs in brokerage positions may interpret and present information differently to various audiences, thus increasing the diversity and resonance of their entrepreneurial efforts (Goddard 2009, 265–266). Brokers are thus vital to the diffusion of ideas, norms, and even material resources, giving these actors heightened influence in promoting certain conceptions of appropriate behavior and their preferred responses.

Conceiving of international policy arenas in network terms adds further nuance to our understanding of how norm entrepreneurship operates in practice. The structural conditions of networks bestow upon some actors disproportionate capacity to introduce new ideas and direct the social and material resources necessary to steward these ideas toward widespread acceptance and adoption. These advantages have recursive effects over time, as the association with a variety of network functions generates legitimacy that allows hubs to reinforce and extend their central positions. Undoubtedly, the content of actor claims matters as well: incipient norms must appear to accord with previously endorsed standards, and certain types of norms are better suited to such grafting efforts (Keck and Sikkink 1998, 204; Price 2003, 584). Yet the ability to engage in norm advocacy, and the authority to have these entrepreneurial efforts taken seriously, is a product of the empowering effects of network relations.

Mapping the Mine Ban Network

The Scope of Inquiry

A key consideration in network analysis is choosing the relevant social setting and boundaries of study (Knoke and Yang 2008, 15–20). I focus on the international effort to eliminate AP mines that culminated in a multilateral legal prohibition in the form of the MBT.[3] Actors are included in the analysis on the basis of their participation in the policy debates surrounding this global initiative,

---

[3] The MBT does not represent the only international effort to address the humanitarian impact of AP mines, as the 1996 Amended Protocol II (APII) to the Convention on Certain Conventional Weapons places restrictions on the use of these weapons. However, APII is fundamentally aimed at regulating the weapon's use, rather than their outright elimination, and thus represents a different policy goal and regime structure.

though not all endorse the outcome of the MBT. The issue area is characterized by regularized interactions among a multiplicity of governmental and nongovernmental actors in which the MBT provides an institutional structure for
the development of network pathways. And, with few exceptions, the principal
nodes have formed associational bonds on the basis of a shared commitment to
the complete elimination (as opposed to limitation) of AP mines.[4]

Network relations are particularly relevant, since the mine ban regime
lacks the formal secretariat and enforcement structures found in many international organizations. Governance, then, remains the responsibility of the
participating actors, rather than a central authority. In this regard, the mine
ban network reflects the informality characteristic of many networks in the
security field explored in this volume (Avant and Westerwinter). Despite this,
the mine ban regime is substantially institutionalized, most notably in the
form of regular diplomatic meetings, a dedicated Implementation Support
Unit (ISU), and annual transparency reporting mechanism (Brinkert and
Hamilton 2004; Brinkert 2008). These institutions include both formal State
Parties and observer delegations from non-party states as well as extensive
participation by civil society actors. Inclusion in institutional venues creates ties and a framework for interaction through which actors may establish,
reinforce, and extend their influence within the network (Hafner-Burton and
Montgomery 2006, 4; Dorussen and Ward 2008, 192–193; Cao 2010). At
the same time, the network also exhibits considerable diversity in terms of
the types of actors, the volume and density of their connections, and hence
the relative positions they occupy. Mapping these linkages and identifying
relative power distributions is thus a valuable exercise in its own right and
provides a necessary first step to the subsequent goal of demonstrating the
effects of networks on global political outcomes (Hafner-Burton et al. 2009,
583; Hollstein 2011, 406–409).

Measuring the Network

This chapter relies on close case study analysis to ascertain the structure and
properties of the mine ban network (Hollstein 2011). The qualitative data is
derived from expert interviews, archival research, and participant observation at
diplomatic meetings of the MBT. My focus here is on characterizing and assessing

---

[4] I further restrict my analysis by focusing on the negotiation of the legal text and subsequent
compliance issues, rather than the much wider universe of humanitarian responses to mine contami-
nation, survivors, and the like. This decision is a pragmatic one designed to retain the scope of inquiry
within manageable limits and does not imply a judgement regarding the relative merits of either field
of activity.

the network at its highest level of abstraction (Knoke 2011, 210). I therefore include nodes for each UN member state, the principal civil society actors, and intergovernmental organizations focused on the creation and implementation of the MBT.[5] In order to measure the structure of the mine ban network globally, I developed a binary sociomatrix that details the presence or absence of connections between dyads of actors (Knoke and Yang 2008, 49; Carrington and Scott 2011, 4; Hanneman and Riddle 2011a, 336–339).[6] Network ties are conceptualized here as direct communication (including the transmission of ideas, values, or technical information) and material transactions (principally financial assistance) between nodes that specifically concern mine ban policy. The dyadic ties are undirected, meaning that they are treated as symmetrical and reciprocal. I model the network in two distinct phases of its evolution, representing (a) the emergence of the mine ban movement culminating in the 1997 MBT (1990–1997); and (b) the subsequent implementation phase (1998–present). This allows me to capture changes in network structure that have important consequences for governance outcomes. There are a total of 189 nodes in the first network data set, and 197 in the second; this reflects the addition of a new organization (discussed later), along with a slight increase in the total number of UN member states between 1998 and 2013.

The data reveal some important attributes of the mine ban network. First, the network is very sparsely connected overall, with only 3.4% of possible dyadic ties actually in existence.[7] The vast majority of nodes have few if any direct ties, while a very few nodes possess extensive connections to the vast majority of weakly connected others. Hence, a second key feature of the mine ban network is the extent to which it is dominated by a few centrally positioned hubs (Lake and Wong 2009; Carpenter 2011). This structural inequality has continued across time, as the introduction of new network actors has only altered these measures insignificantly at the margins. This can be further demonstrated in terms of both degree and betweenness centrality.

---

[5] Some nodes—such as those dealing principally with mine clearance and victim assistance—have little direct responsibility for the legal and policy dimensions of the AP mine ban and have been excluded here in order to simplify the network analysis. Subsequent research will aim to integrate these important actors in order to situate the currently portrayed network within the wider humanitarian space. On this, see note 4. A complete list of nodes, along with related network data, is available from the author upon request.

[6] The analysis was conducted with UCINET 6 (Borgatti et al. 2002). The software is available at: https://sites.google.com/site/ucinetsoftware/home.

[7] This is the average of the density scores for the pre-1998 network (3.3%) and 1998-2013 network (3.5%). This measure refers to the number of actual dyadic ties observed in a network divided by the total number of possible ties (if every node were directly connected to every other node). Since the numbers are so similar, I use the average of the two networks for illustrative purposes.

Table 7.1 **Top Normalized Centrality Scores for Pre-1998 Network**

	Degree	Betweenness
ICBL	1.00	32.41
ICRC	1.00	32.41
CORE GRP	1.00	32.41
USA	0.16	0.50

Note: Freeman degree centrality, with symmetrical out-degree and in-degree, calculated with UCINET. I use the normalized scores here and in table 7.2, which expresses the total direct dyadic ties for each node as a percentage of the absolute number of possible ties given the size of the network ($n - 1$). Freeman betweenness centrality, calculated with UCINET. In tables 7.1 and 7.2, I again employ the normalized scores, which account for the extent to which (as a percentage) a given node sits on the shortest pathway between two other nodes, given all of the possible shortest paths in the network.

Table 7.1 presents the most central nodes in the mine ban network during the negotiation of the MBT. Three hubs—the International Campaign to Ban Landmines (ICBL), International Committee of the Red Cross (ICRC), and Core Group of states—are directly connected to all other nodes, and lie on just under one-third of all the possible shortest pathways between any two other nodes. These three are joined by one modestly connected actor, the United States of America, which possesses direct ties to 16% of nodes and is situated along 5% of the pathways between dyads. As I discuss further below, the United States is the most connected individual state in this network analysis, but it is much less central than the Core Group states, which leveraged their collective ties to enhance their relative position and power.[8] The remaining 158 states are extremely weakly connected, with direct ties only to the ICBL, ICRC, and Core Group, and betweenness scores of 0 (they do not lie on pathways between any other actors).

The structural shift that followed the creation of the MBT is apparent in table 7.2. Particularly notable here is the emergence of a new network hub and the consequent diminishment of others. While the ICBL and Core Group remain comparably situated in absolute terms, their relative structural position is reduced by the advent of the ISU, which has become a co-equal hub both

[8] Individually, states in the Core Group are not well connected, with scores of 0.021 and 0.000 for degree and betweenness centrality, respectively, in the pre-1998 network, and the slightly higher scores of 0.026 and (again) 0.000 for the 1998-present iteration. One of the core contentions of this chapter, however, is that these states vastly increased their power within the network by pooling their resources under the auspices of the Core Group.

Table 7.2 **Top Normalized Centrality Scores**
for 1998–2013 Network

	Degree	Betweenness
ICBL	1.00	32.31
CORE GRP	1.00	32.31
ISU	1.00	32.31
ICRC	0.16	0.37
USA	0.16	0.37

with respect to degree and betweenness measures. This reorientation of network structure is even more dramatic in the case of the ICRC, as the extensive ties established with states during the negotiation of the MBT have been largely supplanted by the emergence of the ISU as a dedicated focal point for state engagement on technical matters of treaty compliance and implementation. I consider the implications of this realignment later.

Hubs in the Mine Ban Network

The International Campaign to Ban Landmines (ICBL) was founded in October 1992 by a collection of prominent international nongovernmental organizations,[9] with the aim of mounting a coordinated global campaign to achieve a legally binding prohibition of AP mines (Warmington and Tuttle 1998; White and Rutherford 1998). Today the ICBL has dedicated national campaigns in over one hundred countries, with members drawn from the disarmament, human rights, development, and refugee fields. Despite this internal diversity, the Campaign is treated as a discrete node in this analysis. This decision is justified by the role that the ICBL plays as the international face of civil society efforts on the AP mines issue. Internally, the central Campaign management— represented by a Governance Board and permanent staff in Geneva—serves as the focal point for incoming information (including updates on local advocacy and data on government policy) and material resources (including financial and technical assistance) from campaign members, and directs these resources to constituent actors within the ICBL orbit. This gives the central ICBL staff a privileged role in setting the strategic direction of civil society advocacy, while

[9] Handicap International (France), Human Rights Watch (United States), Medico International (Germany), Mines Advisory Group (United Kingdom), Physicians for Human Rights (United States), and Vietnam Veterans of America Foundation (United States) (Chabasse 1998, 60–67; Williams and Goose 1998, 22).

the execution at the domestic level is largely left to the national campaigns.[10] Externally, as the recognized international embodiment of civil society in this issue area, the ICBL acts as the chief spokesperson for the NGO movement with governments and international organizations. As will be demonstrated later, this position at the center of the network has given the ICBL important power in shaping the content of the international response to AP mines.

Much like the ICBL, the International Committee of the Red Cross's (ICRC) central position in the mine ban movement rests in its role as a source of technical expertise. As I show in the proceeding section, the ICRC's ability to marshal information concerning the humanitarian consequences of AP mines—drawn largely from its own field hospitals in conflict zones—was vital in generating early interest in a ban. This was greatly facilitated by the ICRC's existing status as the recognized "guardian" of the Geneva Conventions and broader corpus of international humanitarian law. The ICRC's international profile and scope gives it a degree of access to governments that far exceeds what is available to other civil society actors, making it a highly suitable broker.

State influence in the mine ban network centers on the so-called Core Group of states that partnered with the ICBL and ICRC in championing the cause of a legally binding prohibition on AP mines.[11] The Core Group is defined by the shared goal of a binding legal ban on AP mines—the acceptance of which is a precondition for membership—and dense intergovernmental linkages. I therefore argue that the Core Group can be conceptualized as a cohesive subgroup within the broader system of states and is recognized as a more-or-less distinctive entity by other actors within the mine ban network (Hafner-Burton, Kahler, and Montgomery 2009, 565–566; Hanneman and Riddle 2011b, 346–348). Previous research has suggested that participation in network hubs may offer less materially powerful states an important means of generating social capital and influence (Hafner-Burton and Montgomery 2006). This finding is reflected in the mine ban network, as individual state members of the Core Group are weakly connected—possessing only direct ties to other hubs—but have been able to greatly expand their connections and resulting power by virtue of their collaborative participation in, and connection to, this exclusive club.

[10] Telephone interview with senior official from the International Campaign to Ban Landmines. February 5, 2013. See also Williams and Goose 1998, 22–23; Hubert 2000, 32; Bernstein 2008, 35.

[11] This group emerged in 1996 and subsequently expanded to include twenty-eight members, notably by adding greater representation from developing and mine-affected regions. Members of the Core Group are recognized as: Austria, Belgium, Brazil, Cambodia, Canada, Colombia, Croatia, Denmark, Germany, France, Ireland, Jordan, Kenya, Malaysia, Mexico, Mozambique, the Netherlands, New Zealand, Nicaragua, Norway, the Philippines, Slovenia, South Africa, Switzerland, Thailand, the United Kingdom, and Zimbabwe (Goose et al. 2008, 3; Lawson et al. 1998, 166–168; Maslen 2005, 27–28).

A final and much more recent addition to the network architecture is the Antipersonnel Mine Ban Treaty Implementation Support Unit (Brinkert 2008, 91–93, 99–100). The MBT did not create a formal secretariat, but the challenges associated with ensuring effective implementation convinced State Parties of the need to institutionalize existing knowledge and best practices in a permanent entity. To that end, the ISU has become a central node in the distribution of technical and financial assistance from donor governments, intergovernmental organizations and civil society experts to states facing implementation challenges.

Yet in these roles the ISU is at least formally distinct from other network hubs in that it is envisioned mainly as an agent of states facilitating implementation of the MBT, rather than a principal advancing its own independent policy goals.[12] As will be suggested below, this special status poses interesting implications for theoretical expectations concerning network power.

It is also worth briefly noting the absence of some key actors as central nodes. First, major military powers like China, India, and the Russian Federation are almost entirely excluded from the network; the United States is better connected by virtue of its associations with Core Group states, but its overall centrality is modest by comparison with the principal hubs. This outcome is surprising since we might typically expect these actors to be deeply involved in governance initiatives that bear on the use of military force. The limited influence of the United States in particular deserves further explanation, which I undertake later. The United Nations also plays a more modest role in the mine ban network than might be anticipated given its prominence in the wider international system. The United Nations has virtually no presence in advocating for the specific aims of the MBT and is instead focused on the provision of technical expertise and funding for mine clearance and victim assistance projects.[13] Practitioners have suggested that these resource-based ties do translate into significant influence, particularly with respect to humanitarian mine action.[14] More broadly, though, I find that the United Nations is largely isolated from the policy debates that constitute the

---

[12] Interview with senior official from the Implementation Support Unit of the Antipersonnel Mine Ban Convention, Geneva, October 30, 2009.

[13] Brinkert (2008, 98) has suggested that this ambivalence may be due to the fact that "not all UN members are party to the treaty." Interview subjects have reported that UN field agencies were more engaged in efforts to seek a mine ban treaty than the UN Secretariat in New York. This is owing to the field agencies' more direct, first-hand experiences with the effects of AP mines, and the fact that the UN bureaucracy (Department of Disarmament Affairs most especially) was heavily invested in disarmament efforts pursued through established diplomatic processes. Telephone interview with senior official from the UN Institute for Disarmament Research (UNIDIR), January 29, 2013.

[14] Telephone interviews with UNIDIR and ICBL officials, January 29, February 5, and February 6, 2013, respectively.

mine ban network, and hence that its impact on governance is modest when compared against other actors. A final, notable aspect of the mine ban network is the absence of corporate actors, unlike other issue areas (Westerwinter, Haufler, this volume). The principal reason for this is material, as "landmines were not a highly profitable industry" (Hubert 2000, 37). Companies involved in the production of AP mines were therefore unable to build linkages to powerful actors within the network either because they remained isolated from larger corporate defense contractors (who might have served as effective advocates for the continued use of AP mines), or because they operated as state-owned entities and were therefore subject to the political decisions of their home governments.

Selling the Ban: Norm Entrepreneurship and the Creation of the Mine Ban Treaty

The literature on the emergence of the AP mine ban makes clear that the initial impetus came from transnational civil society in the form of the ICBL and the ICRC. Yet as noted already, this account fails to fully explain the conditions for entrepreneurial success, and particularly how these materially weak actors were able to counter the substantial diplomatic and coercive efforts of the United States in order to achieve a comprehensive ban. Attention to the dynamics of access and brokerage manifested in network relations can help to allay this gap. While many actors were engaged in the issue area, only a very few were sufficiently connected to the range of relevant stakeholders to be able to effectively shape global policy. The centrality of the ICBL and ICRC thus allowed them to advance a new conception of AP mines that placed the humanitarian impact on civilian populations at the center of the calculus over their legitimacy, in a process similar to the one identified by Avant (this volume) in her study of the military and security services industry. This initial agenda-setting could then be endorsed and promoted by the Core Group through its own substantial diplomatic relations.

Network structure thus facilitated two specific modes of influence. On the one hand, the ICBL and ICRC possessed direct access to the relevant stakeholders—including peace activists, military and civilian demining personnel, doctors and relief workers, aid agencies, and international lawyers—with firsthand knowledge of the impact and scale of the AP mine problem. In isolation, these various actors had limited ability to shift the international agenda because they lacked the direct ties needed to form a holistic conception of the issue area. As central hubs, however, the ICBL and ICRC could draw on technical expertise from a host of disparate sources, dramatically increasing the volume and quality of available information concerning the humanitarian impact of AP mines, their utility in contemporary military practice and the international legal context for their use and regulation (Coupland and Korver 1991; McGrath and Stover 1991; Stover and McGrath 1991; Fine 1992; International Committee of the Red Cross 1992; McGrath 1992; Africa Watch 1993; The Arms Project and Africa Watch 1993; The Arms Project and Physicians for Human Rights 1993).

Data compiled by the ICRC and distributed in conjunction with the ICBL was used to challenge the conventional wisdom concerning the role of AP mines in contemporary conflict. First, the organizations reviewed evidence on the operational deployment of AP mines in battle and concluded that their military utility was exaggerated: AP mines were less decisive than often claimed and often caused substantial "friendly" casualties to the forces that initially laid the weapons. Second, and crucially for the alternative narrative of the ban proponents, the ICRC and ICBL used extensive case studies to suggest that the horrific effects associated with AP mines were not the result of correctible mistakes—for example, human error or the irresponsible use by rebel groups—but were an inherent feature of the weapons themselves. For this reason, the humanitarian crisis of AP mines could not be addressed through a more stringent regulation on their use, as the United States and its allies suggested, but only through a comprehensive prohibition. The vast majority of states existed as isolated nodes within the wider network, meaning that they lacked access to comparable sources of empirical evidence by which to interpret or challenge these emerging claims. The ICBL and ICRC exploited these information asymmetries to recast the conception of AP mines as "a humanitarian scourge" that was fundamentally incompatible with established international legal principles relating to military necessity, proportionality, and discrimination (International Committee of the Red Cross 1997; Gard Jr. 1998; Maslen 1998; Price 1998, 623).

On the other hand, early engagement meant that the ICBL and ICRC were best equipped to act as a bridge between the wealth of state and institutional actors with potential interest in the issue. The organizations convened numerous conferences, symposia, and seminars that brought together a variety of state and non-state representatives to discuss AP mine policy on the terms set by the hosts (International Committee of the Red Cross 1993; Maslen 1998, 84–89). The dependencies that emerged from this process generated brokerage opportunities that were leveraged to promote a particular vision for the global response to AP mines. As gatekeepers, the ICBL and ICRC were able to determine what claims received the greatest attention in international fora, and to strategically target their arguments to different audiences, thereby reinforcing their centrality to subsequent discussions over the merits of a prohibition.

Both organizations were therefore principal conduits for the flow of information between the range of relevant civil society, institutional and governmental stakeholders in international disarmament, and the emerging field of human security. These relational advantages proved vital to their norm entrepreneurship. In the absence of alternative sources of information, state representatives became reliant on the information provided by civil society. Many governments were therefore persuaded by ICBL and ICRC arguments that the effects of AP mines on civilian populations rendered them illegitimate from the perspective of accepted international law, and consequently, that a prohibition was a logical response to this crisis. Just as important, actors that sought to oppose the emerging mine ban movement were impeded by their lack of access to network actors and resources, meaning that they were unable to effectively counter the arguments advanced by transnational civil society actors with their own narrative. These factors proved instrumental in shaping the domestic political conditions in favor of a prohibition in a number of states that had formerly been major producers and users of the weapons. Hubert (2000, 37) has suggested, for example, that "had comprehensive studies on the military utility of mines existed, the split between ministries of defense and foreign affairs that was critical to the success of the campaign would have been less easily achieved." As the process gathered momentum, social pressure led prominent states such as Australia, France, Japan, and the United Kingdom to endorse the mine ban in order to benefit from status considerations (being identified as among the "club of responsible states") and avoid further criticism. Hence, the early control of information was a precondition for the socialization processes noted in previous academic accounts (Price 1998; Herby and Lawand 2008; Rutherford 2009) and provides a clear demonstration of network effects in mobilizing norm entrepreneurship.

This agenda-setting power translated into substantial influence over the content of the resulting MBT. The ICBL and ICRC were given official status in the negotiations, a rarity in the usually closed world of multilateral arms control and disarmament diplomacy (Williams and Goose 1998, 34–35; Kmentt 2008, 25). The organizations made substantial contributions to strengthening the final treaty text on issues ranging from the legal definition of AP mines, the absoluteness of ban (whether to permit any exceptions or exemptions), the timelines for stockpile destruction and mine clearance, compliance provisions and state responsibility for assisting victims (Maslen 1998, 92–94; 2005, 29; Goose et al. 2008, 2). Network position thus gave the ICBL and ICRC a degree of social power in shaping the international security agenda that greatly exceeded their organizational or material capacities.[15]

---

[15] This influence was well appreciated at the time. Indeed, when "asked to identify the factors that influenced their country's decision to sign the Convention, delegates most frequently cited the pressure exercised by NGOs, particularly as a presence at the table during the treaty negotiation process" (Cameron, Lawson, and Tomlin 1998, 10; Rutherford 2009, 131).

While civil society actors were the key catalysts of the movement to ban AP mines, the impetus toward a formal diplomatic effort was greatly aided by the access and brokerage of the Core Group. First, as early advocates of a prohibition, Core Group states were well positioned to use their existing diplomatic ties to promote the aims of mine ban. Internally, its members established dense reciprocal relationships based on a shared commitment to the principle of a complete prohibition. Externally, Core Group states were well connected in regional and global fora, conducting extensive consultations to generate support for the ban policy (Lawson et al. 1998, 173–175). The Core Group thus served as a clearinghouse for state interactions and possessed a huge informational advantage vis-à-vis the majority of poorly connected states. This was most valuable in determining the current views of relevant foreign ministry, defense, and government officials and identifying actors that would be susceptible to persuasive efforts. Membership in the Core Group thus greatly magnified the diplomatic impact of any of these states acting in isolation. Second, the Core Group served as a link between states and their civil society counterparts, and consequently played a primary role in mediating the distribution of technical, financial, and informational resources. The diversity of the Core Group also allowed its members to tailor diplomatic initiatives to suit the particular perceived needs of governments. These brokerage roles were particularly valuable in drawing otherwise isolated states into pro-ban discussions and in connecting the ICBL to governments in instances where direct ties were previously underdeveloped.

This entrepreneurship was most consequential in establishing the diplomatic strategy, and in shaping content of the treaty itself. With regard to the former, the Core Group members used their central position to successfully direct political energies toward a legally binding prohibition outside of the normal diplomatic venues and to resist pressures from major international powers like the United States in order to retain a dominant influence over the process. The solution was to develop an ad hoc negotiating procedure that was not bound to the lowest-common-denominator consensus decision-making which continues to stall progress at the Conference on Disarmament and its framework treaty, the Convention on Certain Conventional Weapons (Axworthy 1998; Cameron 1998). Here the Core Group was able to use its position as a gatekeeper in discussions between states and civil society to monitor the positions of governments vis-à-vis the proposed ban, and strategically direct diplomatic resources to address concerns and shore-up support for the pro-ban position. These informational asymmetries gave the Group a distinct advantage over other states that were advocating a more gradual approach via UN diplomatic fora.

With international opinion turning in favor of a prohibition, the Core Group played an equally crucial role in determining the main features of the negotiations. First, by linking full participation in the diplomatic discussions to an acceptance of the principle of a total ban on AP mines, the Group acted as a gatekeeper in setting the basic goals of the diplomacy on its own terms. In other words, rather than considering the views of all states on equal footing, the Core Group at the outset restricted the decision-making constituency to only those states that had already accepted the outcome it was advocating. Just as important was the ability of the Core Group to use its position to shape the structure of the diplomacy, by instituting a two-thirds majority decision rule, the election of the highly supportive South African diplomat Jacob Selebi as chair of the negotiating conference, and the full inclusion of the ICBL and ICRC in the discussions (Williams and Goose 1998, 43; Hubert 2000, 37; Maslen 2005, 41–42).[16] These institutional features were widely regarded by observers as being instrumental in ensuring the pro-ban constituency could continue to dominate the diplomatic negotiations.

Finally, as the organizer of the diplomatic conference, the Core Group— in concert with the ICBL and ICRC—again leveraged its privileged access to set the terms of the final treaty. This was done by strategically positioning an Austrian draft text as the de facto language forming the basis of final negotiations, and delegating the task of resolving contentious issues in the draft treaty text to a small subset of their members, known as the "Friends of the Chair."[17] In so doing, the Core Group was able to exploit its position as the fulcrum of negotiations to anticipate diplomatic challenges from skeptical states and their allies (Lawson et al. 1998, 176–177). Hence, the Core Group's structural position provided it with the resources and political power to resist intense political challenges—most especially from the US delegation—and steward the negotiations to a favorable conclusion.

The critical development in the success of the mine ban movement was shifting global opinion of the weapons such that AP mines came to be regarded as "already" illegal, making the prospect of a ban more conceivable to policymakers (Price 1998, 622). While the initial impetus came from a small group of actors, the diplomatic process ultimately enjoyed widespread buy-in: 89 states (plus 32 observer delegations) participated in the final treaty negotiations, while 122 signed the resulting MBT. This outcome can be traced to the centrality of key hubs in the mine ban network: privileged access to weakly connected actors allowed the ICBL, ICRC, and Core Group to set the terms of the AP mine debate, and thus change state views via the mechanisms of persuasion

---

[16] Draft Rules of Procedure, Diplomatic Conference on a Convention on the Prohibition of the Use, Stockpiling, Production and Transfer of Anti-Personnel Mine and on Their Destruction, APL/CRP.2, Oslo, September 1, 1997 (Maslen 2005, 42n206).

[17] Austria, Brazil, Canada, Ireland, and Mexico (Lawson et al. 1998, 176–177; Maslen 2005, 41n205).

and social pressure highlighted in previous studies. Yet network analysis also provides vital insight into how this process was achieved in the face of countervailing pressure from materially powerful opponents of a ban. Rather than relying on traditional forms of coercive or instrumental power, transnational civil society and a collection of middle power states leveraged their superior connections to gain access to key constituencies and control the flow of information between them. This, in turn, gave these hubs a diplomatic advantage that they exploited in order to strategically promote their preferred policy outcome, and finally to maintain support among a diverse group of states during the final intense negotiations. The ability to generate governance outcomes in the face of resistance from the most materially powerful actors is the essence of the concept of social power advanced in this volume. As the earlier discussion demonstrates, it was not just the content of moral claims, but the structural conditions under which they were made, that provided the conditions for the successful advancement of the mine ban norm.

This relational view also helps explain why the United States was ultimately unable to gain widespread concessions to its demands, despite its material preponderance and active role in the diplomacy. While better connected than most states, the United States did not build the same extensive relationships with other actors within the emerging network developed by the ICBL, ICRC, and Core Group, preferring instead to deal directly with other hubs and focus on more traditional forms of bargaining and coercion. In large measure this can be explained by an assumption among US representatives that any successful diplomatic process must necessarily involve the United States as a central player—they did not appreciate the extent to which new social relationships could be built to bypass the United States' more usual predominance in international negotiations. Despite its traditional power advantages, therefore, the United States lacked the direct ties to the majority of states held by the network hubs. As a consequence, US representatives were unable to gain the depth and breadth of information concerning shifting government positions, or to effectively present their own alternative solution that emphasized the continued use of mines within legal restraints. Hence, while typically used to being able to dictate terms in multilateral negotiations, the United States was unprepared for the rapid change in international opinion concerning AP mines and the subsequent diplomatic resistance it faced during the negotiations.

This outcome points to two facets of power within networks that I return to in the final section of the chapter. First, as Avant and Westerwinter have suggested, the social forms of power manifested through network relations may in some circumstances supplant more traditional material power capacities. Ultimately, a more modest network position meant that the United States was unable to effectively challenge the agenda-setting and issue-framing by the better connected pro-ban constituencies. Recognizing that the United States may sometimes be outflanked by other, weaker actors through the deliberate construction of network pathways was identified by the editors as a key contribution of this volume. Second, the US reliance on traditional power politics appears to have been counterproductive in this case, a finding that is reflected in the framing paper and many of the substantive chapters. Considerable anecdotal evidence suggests that the aggressive bargaining by US representatives served to harden the resolve of pro-ban actors and had the unintended consequence of further reinforcing ties among civil society and Core Group hubs and the broader universe of states. Here again the relational view of power at the heart of network analyses helps account for this surprising outcome.

Implementing the Mine Ban Treaty

The successful conclusion of the MBT[18] ushered in a second phase in the development of the mine ban network. This is distinguished by the emergence of new governance tasks, which in turn generated change in the network structure and led to the further centralization of power with some hubs (the ICBL and ISU) and comparative diminishment of others (ICRC and Core Group). The evolution of the mine ban network thus provides an important example of how nodes may strategically adapt to new political conditions, reinforcing the dynamic view of networks that is at the heart of this project. I illustrate these changes through a brief discussion of governance efforts surrounding treaty universalization, monitoring, and institutional development. However, this implementation phase has received considerably less scholarly attention than the treaty-making efforts (Bower and Price 2013; Bower 2015), and so I also note some areas where further research is warranted.

The unprecedented success of the movement to ban AP mines raised questions as to the continuing relevance of the civil society campaign, as many observers felt that the most pressing challenges had been effectively addressed with the advent of the treaty (Bernstein 2008, 40; Goose et al. 2008, 3). Yet instead of disbanding as might have been anticipated, the structural position of the ICBL has been reinforced during the implementation phase, and as a consequence the organization's influence over mine ban policy has become further entrenched. The Campaign leveraged its central brokerage role to great effect in managing the distribution of technical assistance and financial resources to

---

[18] The MBT was adopted on September 18, 1997, in Oslo, and opened for signature on December 3, 1997, in Ottawa. The treaty entered into force on March 1, 1999.

facilitate state ratification of the MBT (Bernstein 2008, 34; Smith 2008, 69). The ICBL was thus able to utilize its extensive relationships with civil society campaigners, international organizations, and governments as a platform for promoting the MBT via the same social mechanisms identified earlier. The political impact of this strategy was substantial, as a cascade effect saw states rushing to be among the first to ratify the treaty. The MBT entered into force on March 1, 1999, and "thus became international law more quickly than any other major multilateral treaty in history" (Goose et al. 2008, 4). The intervening fifteen years have witnessed a rapid expansion in membership; as of June 2015, 162 states are full parties to the MBT, a figure that compares favorably with other related institutions.[19]

The ICBL's most important source of power remains its informational advantage born of its direct access to mine ban stakeholders. The inauguration of the *Landmine Monitor* in 1999 was a watershed moment in this respect, as the yearly publication presents a public accounting of global landmine policy for all states and territories (Wareham 2006, 2008).[20] Here again the ICBL's position between many diverse actors is vital to its influence, as the *Monitor* draws on the resources from its extensive web of national campaigners and its close relationships with governments. In the absence of formal verification measures, *Landmine Monitor* has become the de facto monitoring mechanism for the MBT and the authoritative resource on the international response to AP mines. By virtue of its control over information, therefore, the ICBL holds the primary, if informal, responsibility for adjudicating state compliance with the treaty (Goose et al. 2008, 8). This political power is augmented by the fact that the ICBL does not share the constraints on public advocacy faced by the ICRC and ISU.[21] There is considerable evidence that this monitoring—in conjunction with private consultations and public naming-and-shaming—has been effective in generating state change in the MBT case (Goose 2008; Herby and Lawand 2008; Bower and Price 2013; Bower 2015), but the linkages between micro-level theoretical mechanisms and specific empirical examples could be further established. Additional research in this regard would also help to connect the mine ban case with a broader literature on NGO impact in the human rights sector (Hafner-Burton 2008; Bell et al. 2012; Murdie and Davis 2012b; Hendrix and Wong 2013). At the same time, the Campaign was only able to have this impact because of its existing position at the center of the mine ban network, with control over the collection and dissemination of information. A key insight from the ICBL case is thus that the

---

[19] Most pertinently, 102 states are full parties to Amended Protocol II to the Convention on Certain Conventional Weapons. https://www.icrc.org/ihl/INTRO/575.

[20] http://www.the-monitor.org/index.php.

[21] Telephone interview with senior ICBL official, February 6, 2013.

positional advantages that made the organization so influential in mobilizing the mine ban movement have carried over into the subsequent implementation phase, suggesting that network power is a potentially fungible commodity.

The Core Group has been similarly involved in implementation, principally as a broker linking disparate state actors to governmental and nongovernmental resources. Its influence in this regard is twofold. First, the Core Group states established a Universalization Contact Group that sought to centralize information on state positions concerning MBT ratification and coordinate strategy in targeting states for diplomatic engagement (Brinkert 2008, 94; Smith 2008). Second, the MBT provided for only a general institutional architecture, so the Core Group used its extensive intergovernmental connections to promote new bureaucratic structures—such as a formal transparency reporting mechanism, informal working groups, and the ISU—to further perpetuate the diplomatic model of the mine ban movement.

In recent years, however, the Core Group has seen its position within the mine ban network wane, as a consequence of declining funding (International Campaign to Ban Landmines 2012, 49) and reduced engagement—by many members, at least—in the bureaucratic operations of the MBT regime. Interview subjects have suggested that this political withdrawal is driven by a variety of factors. On the one hand, the successful development of a series of disarmament processes beyond the MBT—including on cluster munitions, explosive remnants of war, and the trade in small arms and light weapons—dramatically increased the workload for representatives in Geneva and generated competing priorities without commensurable increase in diplomatic resources. On the other hand, shifting foreign policy priorities occasioned by changes in government and the global financial crisis have also drawn attention elsewhere.[22] This finding points to the domestic sources of international political outcomes, and the multi-level nature of network structures. Yet the Core Group retains considerable perceived influence among many network actors, and information-sharing appears to have remained relatively constant even as material transactions have declined.[23] This hints at an interesting hypothesis that different forms of ties—and the social power that flows from them—may endure or decay at different rates, a possibility that is contemplated by Avant and Westerwinter in their framework chapter and by some other contributors.

The most significant change in network structure has been the emergence of a new hub in the form of an implementation support unit. As noted briefly earlier, the ISU was created in 2001 by State Parties to the MBT, at the initiative of the

---

[22] Telephone interviews with senior UNIDIR and ICBL officials, January 29, February 5 and 6, 2013, respectively.

[23] Telephone interview with senior ICBL official, February 6, 2013.

Core Group, in order to address perceived gaps in the international community's capacity to implement the treaty.[24] As such, the ISU has established itself as a central player in the network due to its high betweenness linking the numerous actors involved in mine ban policy and humanitarian mine action more generally. The rise in prominence of the ISU is further explained by the relative decline in interest by many formerly active states in the day-to-day operations of the MBT. This has generated a partial vacuum that has been filled by the ISU in taking initiative for defining future regime goals (agenda-setting) and pursuing their operational implementation. As a conduit for the distribution of goods, the ISU has a central role in connecting states facing implementation challenges (concerning the legal process of ratification, destruction of AP mine stockpiles, clearance of deployed mines, and assistance to mine survivors) with other governments, international organizations, and civil society capable of providing material and technical assistance. In this sense, the ISU sits astride the most important lines of communication and material transactions, and acts as the central repository for information concerning state obligations and opportunities with respect to the AP mine ban.[25] Relatedly, the ISU's sponsorship program provides funds for representatives from less developed states to attend MBT meetings. These material incentives have "been key in getting and keeping numerous countries involved in the treaty's operations" (Goose, Wareham, and Williams 2008, 7–8; also Brinkert 2008, 93–96; Kmentt 2008, 26–27).

Anecdotal evidence indicates that control over the distribution of relationships and resources has given the ISU considerable power in shaping the contemporary development of AP mine policy globally (Smith 2008). Interview subjects in civil society, for example, have identified the ISU Director as a key individual player with considerable personal and institutional influence.[26] Yet the ISU is officially an agent of state interests and is not intended to conduct independent advocacy; this renders it a peculiar type of actor in the wider mine ban network. The precise linkages between ISU centrality and governance outcomes could therefore be further developed, especially by examining the potential existence, and impact, of socialization processes in this case. This offers the potential to draw causal connections between the provision of material incentives and changes in actor behavior—a key concern of rationalist approaches in international relations.

---

[24] Final Report of the Third Meeting of the States Parties to the Convention on the Prohibition of the Use, Stockpiling, Production and Transfer of Anti-Personnel Mines and on Their Destruction, APLC/MSP.3/2001/1, January 10, 2002, para. 33, at p. 7. http://www.apminebanconvention.org/meetings-of-the-states-parties/3msp/final-report/.

[25] Interviews with senior ISU official, Geneva, October 2009 and December 2010.

[26] Telephone interviews with senior ICBL officials, February 5 and 6, 2013.

Arguably the more significant consequence of the ISU's emergence, however, is its impact on the position of other network hubs (table 7.2). In relational terms, the inclusion of the ISU has resulted in the creation of new network ties, most especially with states, and thus the duplication of dyadic connections or their wholesale reorientation. It has been suggested, for instance, that the ISU has taken over many of the network roles formerly administered by members of the Core Group, with the latter consequently possessing degraded links to other states.[27] Hence, while the ICBL and Core Group remain comparably situated in absolute terms, their relative structural position is diminished by the advent of the ISU. This reorientation of network structure is most noticeable with respect to the ICRC. While the organization established extensive ties to states during the negotiation of the MBT as a focal point for the dissemination of information concerning AP mines and the legal arguments for their abolition, much of the technical and material assistance now flows via the ISU. The ICRC maintains an active role in aiding states with matters of treaty compliance and implementation, but this new actor has largely supplanted its central position within the network.

The findings with respect to structural shifts thus also speak to a concern in the literature regarding the durability of highly centralized networks. Here the view is that networks may be more prone to disruption in the event of the removal of a key hub (Knoke and Yang 2008, 49; Hafner-Burton et al. 2009, 569). Yet the case of the mine ban network suggests that the decline of particular hubs may in fact result from the emergence of others: rather than degrading communications within the network, the creation of the ISU has merely shifted ties to a different focal point, while at the same time generating a set of redundant pathways between states and the wider network. A key question for the future of the mine ban network, therefore, is whether certain pathways come to be used for the transmission of particular types of resources, and what impact such specialization might hold for the enduring power of network hubs.

Conclusion: Networks and Social Power

The international effort to ban AP mines is a prominent example of security governance through networks. The mine ban movement "showed that civil society can wield great power but, more importantly, demonstrated the power of partnerships, and of common and coordinated action by NGOs, like-minded governments, the ICRC, and UN agencies" (Goose et al. 2008, 11). This, in turn,

---

[27] Telephone interview with senior ICBL official, February 6, 2013.

speaks to the value of network analysis in making the positions of actors and their interlinkages—and the power this bestows—explicit.

In keeping with the overall theme of this volume, my most fundamental finding is that the structural features of the mine ban network conditioned the prospects for successful norm entrepreneurship and subsequent governance (Montgomery, this volume). Extensive ties to other nodes allowed a few network hubs to control access to information, actors, and resources that translated into political influence—as brokers and gatekeepers—in establishing the ban agenda, shaping diplomatic negotiations, and implementing the resulting treaty. These actors acquired their hub position, though, based in part on their promise in accomplishing particular governance tasks. These processes have feedback effects over time, wherein establishing centrality early on gave certain actors disproportionate influence over the subsequent development of policy, further reinforcing power disparities. Equally, the absence of similar centrality greatly impeded the ability of the United States to influence the trajectory and content of the mine ban. The lack of direct ties to the majority of other states meant that US positions in the negotiations could not be distributed as efficiently; as a result, US diplomacy was less persuasive when compared against the sheer density of ICBL, ICRC, and Core Group appeals. Material and social power resources are therefore not directly interchangeable. Avant and Westerwinter (this volume) have suggested that economic forms of influence such as financial transfers or other side payments may be less effective at generating new collective action than relational modes of power that emphasize social capacities like expertise and values. This assumption would seem to find strong support in the present case. Hence, it is not just the content of ideas, or the raw material power of their advocates, that determines the success of entrepreneurial efforts; rather, the structural position of actors has a key role in generating social forms of power to shape international governance outcomes (Goddard 2009, 273).

Yet while networks facilitate the accumulation and enactment of power, they are themselves the product of deliberative action, as actors deploy material and social resources to improve their positions within the network and advance their policy goals. The power manifest in networks can therefore include the capacity for established nodes to alter the network to suit changing conditions as a means through which they may further extend their power. Indeed, the notion of a "new power politics" is premised on the view that actors strategically construct and reconstruct their network position, and as such the present volume is ideally placed to contribute to an ever-growing dialogue between instrumental/rationalist and social/normative theories of action in world politics. In the present case, this form of strategic action is particularly notable in the shift from advocating for a mine ban to implementing the resulting treaty, as central actors sought to promote new role competencies and institutional structures.

In certain circumstances, therefore, the forms of power manifested in networks may be fungible across time and governance roles. However, the mine ban example also offers evidence of instances where the restructuring of network relations can lead to the diminishment of actor position, as most clearly seen with the ICRC. The specific parameters and mechanisms for translating network power into new areas remain underdeveloped, though the mine ban case suggests a few ways of conceptualizing this problem. Here I briefly offer some avenues for future research to attend to these issues.

Real world networks often overlap, and ties thus interpenetrate across a series of issue areas and personal and organizational affiliations (Avant and Westerwinter, Cooley and Nexon, Haufler, this volume). One way that network power may therefore prove fungible is through the repurposing of ideas and relationships to attend to new governance challenges. For example, a large number of the individuals and groups at the heart of the mine ban movement were subsequently involved in the successful effort to ban cluster munitions (Borrie 2009). These actors employed their established connections to generate a parallel international diplomatic initiative through the same forms of social influence. As a direct consequence, the network now encompasses cluster munitions, explosive violence, and, more recently, autonomous weapons issue areas. Carefully mapping the wider network of actors involved in disarmament and human security could uncover the extent of this "mission creep." While substantively important for capturing the totality of these overlapping networks, such research would also provide valuable evidence for refining existing theoretical insights and generating new hypotheses concerning the ways that networks preserve and extend their influence. Relatedly, Avant and Westerwinter have suggested that changes in the composition of a network will have important implications for how power is deployed since ties will be created or strengthened, while others will be severed. This study has already demonstrated that the inclusion of new network hubs inevitably alters existing structures and resulting power dynamics. Yet the specific processes of relational realignment—most especially the deliberative construction or destruction of ties—could be examined in greater detail. While the addition of new hubs may improve the efficiency of network transactions and the achievement of governance tasks, incorporating actors that do not share core expectations and diplomatic norms may equally disrupt existing procedures to the detriment of network performance.

Second, the mine ban network is conceptualized here at its highest level of aggregation, yet we know that individual nodes are composed of, and influenced by, subunits including constituent individuals and organizations (Hafner-Burton et al. 2009, 584; Kahler 2009, 6; Carpenter 2011). In effect, the mine ban community is a "nested network" (Maoz 2011, 375), raising the question of how internal dynamics at one level affect outcomes at other levels. Future research should therefore look "inside" this macro-level network, to carefully explicate processes through which network power at the micro (individual) and meso (organizational) levels is aggregated into globally relevant governance outcomes. A key question in this respect is how the inevitable change in bureaucratic actors will affect institutional memory and network dynamics. Brinkert has suggested that "individuals move on and if newcomers do not continue the unique and successful working practices there may be a return to traditional multilateralism that is flavored more by a culture of inertia than of action" (2008, 102). Examining these various hypotheses empirically would offer interesting insights into the evolution of network power over time.

Third and finally, network analysis holds important implications for debates over how to manage revisionist challenges within networks, particularly whether and how to integrate potentially ambivalent or hostile actors more deeply into network structures. The United States is the largest single donor to mine action globally, and frequently attempts to use its material resources to direct focus away from the MBT as the centerpiece of the international response to AP mines.[28] Hence, despite an implicit assumption in much of the literature that networks are rooted in shared expectations, actors may instead seek to use their network position to engage in counter-socialization. The proceeding analysis has shown that US material predominance has not translated into substantial influence within the network. As anticipated by Avant and Westerwinter (this volume), coercive power has been superseded by social forms of power in shaping global governance over AP mines. Yet it is conceivable that the United States could change its strategic approach, and instead seek to build ties as a means of gradually shifting the network focus. More attention is therefore warranted in unpacking the influence of actors that seek to challenge or undermine fundamental network goals and promote their own alternative policies. This, too, would help to reveal the sources of network durability as well as the means through which the social power manifest in networks may be augmented, translated, or resisted.

[28] Telephone interviews with senior ICBL officials, February 5 and 6, 2013.

8

Bargaining in Networks

Relationships and the Governance of Conflict Diamonds

OLIVER WESTERWINTER

In the early 2000s, the international efforts to stop "conflict diamonds"[1] from fueling civil wars in Africa underwent dramatic institutional change. After a series of ineffective UN sanctions in Angola and Sierra Leone,[2] a campaign launched by nongovernmental organizations (NGOs) triggered negotiations that started in May 2000 and ended in November 2002 with the formation of the Kimberley Process (KP) (Grant and Taylor 2004). The KP is a transnational public-private governance scheme in which states, the diamond industry, and NGOs cooperate to regulate the global diamond trade and fight conflict diamonds (Haufler 2010). Initially, KP monitoring was based on state self-reporting and had little "teeth." Soon after its launch however, negotiations started again, and within less than twelve months, KP participants established a monitoring system that combines state self-reporting with peer review inspections of national diamond control regimes.

In both negotiation episodes, states, diamond industry representatives, and NGOs shared an interest in cooperation. Yet, the monitoring mechanisms they agreed on differ markedly. First, they established a voluntary self-reporting system that reflects the interests of states and the industry. Later, they strengthened monitoring and created a peer review system in line with the changed interests of the industry, NGOs, and some states, while several powerful players were left aggrieved. Thus, in the words of the introduction to this edited volume,

---

[1] Conflict diamonds are rough diamonds used by rebel groups to finance military operations against legitimate, internationally recognized governments (United Nations General Assembly Resolution A/RES/55/56 [January 29, 2001]).

[2] Report of the Panel of Experts on Violations of Security Council Sanctions against UNITA, S/2000/203 (March 10, 2000).

governance became more effective (from self-reporting to peer review monitoring) and less subject to capture (from state and industry-controlled monitoring to a system with improved access and control of NGOs). What explains these changes?

The changes in the monitoring of conflict diamonds that occurred in the early 2000s are puzzling to rational institutionalist and realist theories of institutional design. Rational institutionalists predict that governance problems with a prisoners' dilemma-like incentive structure require centralized, independent monitoring mechanisms that provide reliable information about the compliance behavior of rule targets to deter cheating and make cooperation feasible (Snidal 1985; Abbott 1993; Dai 2002).[3] Yet, while confronted with prisoners' dilemma-like incentives, KP participants first created a self-reporting, and later, a peer review system. Rational institutionalism neither explains this transition, nor the shortcomings of both monitoring designs, in light of the prevailing incentive structure.

Realists identify the distribution of structural power as the primary determinant of institutional design (Krasner 1991; Garrett 1992; Gruber 2000). Although the distribution of material resources and relative shares in the global diamond market was stable throughout the two negotiation episodes, changes occurred in the overall effectiveness and the distribution of influence over monitoring. Even more puzzling, actors with considerable structural power could not always call the shots when negotiating monitoring provisions (e.g., Russia, Israel), and those who could, did not use their material capabilities, but used instead negotiation strategies based on relationships, information, and brokerage (e.g., De Beers). By the same token, NGOs with little structural power (e.g., Global Witness, Partnership Africa Canada) were sometimes able to induce powerful players to accept institutional provisions they initially opposed by using their relationships to change the preferences of major actors, most notably industry, and by forming coalitions in support of their objectives.

I argue that combining bargaining models of cooperation with insights from network theory helps to explain the changes in the monitoring of conflict diamonds that we observe in the early 2000s. I propose a political model that places distributional conflict and power asymmetries at the center of the study of transnational governance (Westerwinter 2014). States, businesses,

---

[3] A prisoners' dilemma-like incentive structure describes a situation in which actors have an interest to unilaterally defect from cooperation. Even if a cooperative arrangement makes everyone better off, some actors may prefer not to adhere to it because they can do better individually by cheating. In the KP, every company, for example, has an interest in tripartite regulation because it helps to protect the diamond industry from harmful consumer boycotts. At the same time, individual companies have a strong incentive to defect and save the costs of cooperation (e.g., sharing commercial information).

and NGOs bargain over the design of transnational public-private governance schemes, and which design is chosen depends on the distribution of bargaining leverage and the configuration of interests. The characteristics of transnational tripartite bargaining (i.e., unanimity decision-making in large heterogeneous groups, uncertainty about preferences and the state of the world, and integrative bargaining as mode of negotiation) place a premium on negotiation strategies based on central and broker positions in the informal communication networks that underlie the bargaining process. Actors in central and broker positions can control the flow of information among negotiators. This enables them to craft better bargaining strategies, structure the negotiation process, mediate agreement, and achieve favorable outcomes. The very same characteristics of the transnational bargaining game place constraints on the use of structural power. Thus, we should expect transnational public-private governance schemes to have organizational structures that reflect the interests of actors that occupy central and broker positions in informal negotiation networks. As a corollary, as the distribution of network positions or the preferences of the actors in these positions change, institutional structures should change. By contrast, the distribution of structural power should have no strong effect on the design of transnational public-private governance schemes.

This chapter makes two contributions to the study of transnational governance. First, building on previous work (Drezner 2007; Abbott and Snidal 2009; Buthe and Mattli 2011), I extend the bargaining model of international cooperation to negotiations among states, businesses, and NGOs. I also introduce network positions as a source of bargaining leverage and show how they can affect outcomes. As my empirical analysis illustrates, these extensions allow researchers to better understand transnational security governance outcomes that remain puzzling from the perspectives of rational institutionalism and realism. Second, I add to recent work on the network character of the KP (Bieri and Waddell 2012). While these studies focus on the trust that resides in informal relationships, I emphasize the informational capacities of transnational networks and show how changes in the allocation of network positions in combination with actors' preferences shaped the design of monitoring in the conflict diamonds regime. The data used in this chapter was collected through fifty semi-structured interviews with government officials, industry representatives, and NGO activists as well as archival sources.

The remainder of the chapter proceeds in three steps. First, I spell out my theoretical argument about transnational tripartite bargaining, network positions, and power. This discussion yields a theoretical lens which is then applied to two negotiation episodes from the KP; its initiation in 2000–2002 and the reform of its monitoring system in 2003. I conclude by discussing how my analysis adds to our understanding of transnational governance and the functioning of power in contemporary global governance.

Bargaining over Transnational Governance

Transnational public-private governance schemes are the product of distributional conflict and bargaining among states, businesses, and NGOs (Levy and Prakash 2003; Bartley 2007; Abbott and Snidal 2009). Even if states, businesses, and NGOs agree that a new institution needs to be created to address a transnational issue, they typically have conflicting interests over what rules to select because different choices vary in how they distribute the costs and benefits of cooperation (Krasner 1991; Garrett 1992; Gourevitch 1999). As a result, states, businesses, and NGOs bargain over the institutional design of transnational governance. Bargaining does not, however, end with the creation of a governance scheme. Once an initial agreement is reached, bargaining may recur as power differentials and interests change so that actors have incentives to renegotiate organizational structures (Krasner 1991; Gourevitch 1999). In short, institutional bargaining is essential to the creation and development of transnational public-private governance schemes.

Take the KP as an example.[4] In the late 1990s, states, the diamond industry, and NGOs agreed to stop the trade in diamonds to finance civil war in Africa. Apart from this general consent, they disagreed sharply on how to organize cooperation. Monitoring was a particularly contentious issue. Some states, such as Israel and Russia, rejected any attempt to establish monitoring procedures that went beyond self-reporting, based on concerns about national sovereignty and sharing confidential business information. Industry was also reluctant to include any oversight mechanism with "teeth" due to concerns about costs and intrusiveness. NGOs, by contrast, lobbied for an independent third party monitoring system, which they considered necessary for the new regime's effectiveness and credibility. These diverging interests gave rise to intense and prolonged bargaining over precisely how the monitoring system of the KP ought to be designed.

To account for the changes in the monitoring of conflict diamonds, we need to examine the characteristics of the bargaining process through which monitoring mechanisms came into being, and how they affected the power asymmetries and negotiation dynamics among the actors involved. Three dimensions of the transnational bargaining game are of particular importance: (1) unanimity

---

[4] Bartley (2007), Abbott and Snidal (2009), and Westerwinter (2014) provide additional examples of the central role of bargaining in the (re-)formation of transnational public-private governance schemes.

decision-making in large groups with heterogeneous interests; (2) uncertainty about preferences and the state of the world; and (3) integrative bargaining as the mode of negotiation.

Unanimity in Heterogeneous Groups, Uncertainty, and Integrative Bargaining

Negotiating transnational public-private governance schemes involves a large number of actors with diverging interests. For example, negotiations in the KP involve developing and developed countries, companies and business associations representing all parts of the diamond industry, civil society organizations, and various international organizations (Westerwinter 2014). These actors bring to the negotiation table a broad range of interests, beliefs, organizational cultures, and values. Compared to intergovernmental negotiations that are conducted largely by national governments, the heterogeneity of tripartite bargaining is therefore much higher (Levy and Prakash 2003, 144). This heterogeneity opens up ample space for conflicts and increases bargaining costs, which makes reaching an agreement on regime structures difficult (Levy and Prakash 2003; Abbott and Snidal 2009). Although sometimes, actors with similar preferences form coalitions, like the diamond industry in the KP, this only moderately mitigates heterogeneity because coalitions are often heterogeneous themselves and issue-specific which leaves room for inter- and intra-coalitional conflict.

Tripartite bargaining operates on the basis of unanimity in contrast to majority voting. This provides every party, even the weakest actor, with a veto and the power to block new institutional provisions (Young 1989; Steinberg 2002). As a consequence, actors that seek agreement on a particular institutional provision (as opposed to forestalling others' proposals) cannot simply impose their preferred solution because every actor that perceives their proposal as unfavorable will use its veto to block it (Young 1989). The likelihood of encountering such opposition increases with the size and heterogeneity of the group of negotiators. Thus, if bargaining occurs in large heterogeneous groups that seek consensus, those that want to produce a particular outcome have to use negotiation strategies that are conducive to garner the support of all parties for their preferred institutional arrangement (Young 1994). Those that want to forestall a proposal can simply block it by using their veto.

Uncertainty is pervasive in world politics, and negotiations over transnational public-private governance schemes are no different (Morrow 1994; Koremenos, Lipson, and Snidal 2001). It is helpful to distinguish between strategic uncertainty and "uncertainty about the state of the world" (Koremenos, Lipson, and Snidal 2001, 778). In situations of strategic uncertainty, actors have incomplete information about others' preferences (Koremenos, Lipson, and Snidal 2001). In addition, they have incentives to misrepresent their true preferences in the hope for a better deal (Morrow 1999). For individual actors, the strategic communication of preferences is rational, because it reduces the risk of being exploited and allows using pretended concessions as bargaining leverage. Yet, incomplete information yields a truncated picture of the zone of possible agreements which, in turn, makes identifying optimal bargaining strategies difficult and can lead to the breakdown of negotiations altogether (Fearon 1995). Strategic uncertainty is further exacerbated by mistrust (Kydd 2005). The relationships among states, businesses, and NGOs engaged in transnational governance are often characterized by tensions which makes the reliable communication of preferences and other information difficult.

Transnational governance is also ripe with uncertainty about the state of the world. The problems which transnational public-private governance schemes address are complex and of a transboundary nature. Examples include the prevention of human rights abuses in the global apparel industry and sustainable forest management (Bartley 2007). Creating institutions that deal with such problems is a complicated task involving technical difficulties and continuous learning (Avant, Finnemore, and Sell 2010b; Burca, Keohane, and Sabel 2013). As a result, states, businesses, and NGOs lack complete information about the problem they are dealing with, the set of available solutions, and how the outcomes associated with feasible institutional options affect their own and others' utilities. This makes influencing negotiation outcomes a difficult and information-intensive task (Morrow 1994).

Finally, negotiations over transnational public-private governance schemes are characterized by integrative bargaining. In situations of distributive bargaining, negotiators are able to identify the location and shape of the Pareto frontier (i.e., they have a clear understanding of what results a particular institutional solution is likely to produce and how this affects individual actors). Thus, their negotiation tactics naturally focus on achieving an outcome that is as close as possible to their most preferred solution (Krasner 1991). Under integrative bargaining, by contrast, negotiators lack a well-defined understanding of the Pareto frontier (Walton and McKersie 1965; Young 1989, 1994). In such situations, states, businesses, and NGOs need to explore the menu of available institutional arrangements and the effects of each alternative on the prospects for achieving their goals to identify opportunities for mutually beneficial deals. Since each party is likely to possess information about different aspects of the problem at hand, integrative bargaining is characterized by the need for the exchange of information and an ongoing restructuring of the problem (Kersten 2001). It reduces the zero-sum character of bargaining (Levy and Prakash 2003, 147). This does not, however, imply that distributive concerns play no role. In fact, actors can seek to shape the definition of the "state of the world" and the location and shape of the Pareto frontier such that it is easier for them to achieve favorable outcomes (Morrow 1994).

Network Relationships and Governance

Networks of relationships are key for understanding transnational tripartite bargaining and the changes in the monitoring of conflict diamonds. Networks are broadly defined as a set of nodes and a set of ties representing the presence or absence of relationships between nodes.[5] The nodes in the transnational networks I investigate in this chapter are states, companies, business associations, and NGOs involved in negotiating KP monitoring. In terms of ties, I focus on informal exchanges of policy-relevant information during a negotiation episode. Such informal communication networks are important for understanding tripartite institutional bargaining because access to information about, for example, problems and others' preferences, enhances an actor's ability to influence the outcomes of negotiations under unanimity decision-making in heterogeneous groups, uncertainty, and integrative bargaining.

Positions in informal communication networks constitute a source of power that can be used to resolve bargaining problems and influence governance (Hafner-Burton, Kahler, and Montgomery 2009; Kahler 2009). Actors that have a large number of direct connections occupy central network positions (Freeman 1979). Having many direct communication ties enables an actor to affect negotiations and governance because it provides it with access to strategic information (Kinne 2013). Recall that uncertainty is pervasive in tripartite bargaining. Actors with many direct ties, receive information on the problem at hand and how others perceive it, which reduces uncertainty about the state of the world. Network ties can also help mitigate strategic uncertainty when strong direct connections based on repeated interaction and trust make private information about others' preferences accessible (Jonsson et al. 1998). Such knowledge provides an actor with a more accurate picture of the zone of possible bargaining agreements which, in turn, allows it to better estimate how far it can push to obtain a better deal without risking negotiation breakdown.

The same informational benefits also enable an actor to structure the process of institutional bargaining. In situations of uncertainty and integrative bargaining, issue definition, agenda-setting, and proposal-making are information-intensive activities (Young 1994). Receiving information about problems and available

---

[5] Avant and Westerwinter (this volume) provide a more detailed discussion of network theory and how it can inform the study of transnational governance and power.

solutions early on in negotiations enables an actor to shape the agenda and draft proposals when others are still trying to find out what the problem they are dealing with is actually all about (Young 1994; Steinberg 2002). Information also facilitates experimentation and allows actors to invent new institutional options that have a chance to garner broad support, which is important for determining the outcome of integrative bargaining (Young 1989; Jonsson et al. 1998).

Actors also vary in the degree to which they connect otherwise unconnected others. Such brokers are located at critical junctures of communication flows and bridge "structural holes" that separate different parts of a network (Burt 1992; Goddard 2009). Actors on either side of a structural hole possess different information. Bridging such holes provides the broker with the opportunity to tap into this non-redundant information. Compared to actors that are part of either group, this constitutes an informational advantage (Burt 1992). This information allows brokers to arrive at more accurate estimates of key parameters of the bargaining setting which, in turn, increases their ability to forge agreement close to their preferred outcome. Further, "insofar as the brokerage role enables an actor to determine what issues are discussed and resolved, the power accorded to brokers corresponds to . . . agenda-setting power" (Gould 1989, 535). Access to diverse information also increases the broker's ability to invent innovative institutional solutions and to disseminate these innovations fast and at low cost among negotiators (Burt 2004). These new institutional solutions can then become focal points around which agreement can emerge (Young 1989).

Brokers can also control the information flow between unconnected groups and manipulate the information each side has about the other. As noted by Burt, "accurate, ambiguous, or distorted information is strategically moved between contacts by the *tertius* (i.e. the broker, the author)" (2000, 355) and can be used to manipulate their perception of the problem at hand and shape their bargaining positions. Finally, brokers can mediate between parties with opposing interests and facilitate agreement. Mediation by brokers is of particular importance for achieving cooperation in groups characterized by heterogeneity since such groups are likely to experience the structural and cultural divides that create demand for brokerage (Gould 1989). Brokers can use this mediation role to bias bargaining outcomes toward the institutional structure they prefer (Tallberg 2004).

The Limits of Structural Power

While unanimity decision-making in heterogeneous groups, uncertainty, and integrative bargaining benefit actors in central and broker positions in informal communication networks, they limit the use of structural power. Structural power is based on the possession of material resources (Keohane 1984, 32). In the context of this chapter, two prime sources of structural power are the size of an actor's share in the global diamond market and the possession of financial capabilities. Actors with vast material resources have "go-it-alone" power (Abbott and Snidal 2009, 72–73). They are able to unilaterally generate governance schemes that, at least partially, meet their interests. If exercised, such outside options impose negative externalities on other actors because the exit of a major structural power reduces the value of cooperation for others. The big African diamond producers (e.g., Botswana, South Africa, Namibia, and Zimbabwe) have "go-it-alone" power in monitoring conflict diamonds. Given their sizeable share in the global diamond production, these states can use the threat to leave the KP and establish their own governance scheme as a bargaining chip.

Structural power also enables an actor to use side payments to induce others' agreement to their preferred institutional design (Krasner 1991). Agreement on an institutional structure may depend on some form of redistribution of the costs and gains of cooperation. Actors with financial capabilities can offer their opponents side payments as compensation for their agreement to an otherwise unfavorable governance scheme (Krasner 1991; Moe 2005). Multinational corporations and industrialized states, for example, can offer financial support and technical assistance to smaller firms, developing countries, and NGOs to get their concession to a monitoring system they would otherwise not accept.

Structural power is of limited use in bargaining over the design of transnational public-private governance schemes. While the coercive force of go-it-alone power is an apt means for blocking action, it is less useful for positively producing collective action. A country that prefers no, over weak, over strong monitoring can use the threat to exit the KP to forestall monitoring provisions that it dislikes. Yet, using the same threat to organize support for a specific monitoring system is problematic. Instead, organizing such support in a large heterogeneous group where everyone has a veto requires skills in managing information flows, inventing and explaining innovative institutional solutions, and persuading skeptics (Young 1991, 1994). While these qualities are enhanced by central and broker positions in informal negotiation networks, they poorly correlate with the possession of material resources (Young 1994, 130).

Further, the tripartite bargaining game is complex and fraught with uncertainty. This complexity reduces the importance of material resources in determining the monitoring system of transnational public-private governance schemes (Levy and Prakash 2003, 146). Also, under integrative bargaining, the (re-)formation of transnational governance schemes is not a zero-sum game (Young 1989, 1994; Levy and Prakash 2003) and, as a result, the control of material resources is less important for shaping the outcome. Rather, negotiations require a great deal of information, positioning, and bargaining skill in which actors in central and broker positions in informal networks, but with little structural power, can sometimes outmaneuver stronger rivals (Levy and Prakash 2003, 147).

The discussion so far can be summarized in three observable implications. First, in a bargaining environment characterized by unanimity decision-making in a large heterogeneous group, uncertainty, and integrative bargaining, the design of transnational public-private governance schemes is likely to reflect the interests of actors that occupy central and broker positions in informal communication networks among the parties in negotiations. Second, as the distribution of network positions or the preferences of the actors in those positions change, the organizational structures of transnational public-private governance are likely to change. Third, structural power is unlikely to be a major determinant of the design of transnational public-private governance schemes. I now apply these insights to the case of the monitoring of conflict diamonds within the KP.

Governing Conflict Diamonds

In the late 1990s, a series of NGO reports demonstrated a clear association between the global diamond trade and the perpetuation of civil wars in Angola, Sierra Leone, Liberia, and the Democratic Republic of Congo (Global Witness 1998; Smillie, Gbrie, and Hazleton 2000). They showed that profits from illegally mined diamonds provided rebel groups with income to finance their fighting against legitimate governments and, therefore, fueled civil wars in the course of which thousands of Africans lost their lives and millions were forced to leave their homes. As a response to this linkage between diamonds and civil war, the United Nations imposed targeted sanctions on conflict diamonds in Angola and Sierra Leone to curb rebel funds from illegal mining activities (Wright 2004).

As the ineffectiveness of these sanctions became obvious, South Africa, Namibia, and Botswana met for consultations with the United Kingdom, the United States, and Belgium in May 2000 in Kimberley, South Africa, to discuss the issue of conflict diamonds (Grant and Taylor 2004). Representatives of the diamond industry and human rights NGOs were also present at this first of a series of meetings which later became known as the Kimberley Process. Within less than three years, states, the diamond industry, and NGOs agreed on a certification scheme for regulating the global trade in rough diamonds, the Kimberley Process Certification Scheme (KPCS), which was meant to establish a "clean diamond cartel barring conflict diamonds from entering the legal market" (Beffert and Benner 2005a, 2).

At its outset in 2000, as well as at several later stages of the KP's development, states, diamond industry representatives, and NGOs bargained over the design of institutional structures. Controversies over monitoring have been among the most fundamental ones, and at several occasions, threatened to derail the process (Wright 2012, 185). I examine two episodes in which states, the diamond industry, and NGOs negotiated over the institutional design of the monitoring of conflict diamonds; the initial negotiations over the KPCS (2000–2002) and the negotiations over the establishment of a peer review system (2003). For each negotiation episode, I analyze how informal relationships and network positions shaped the formal design of monitoring procedures and, particularly the change toward strengthened monitoring in 2003.

Monitoring without Teeth

At the outset of the negotiations in 2000, states, the diamond industry, and NGOs had several options regarding how to design the monitoring system of the KP (Beffert and Benner 2005b). Monitoring could have been delegated to the domestic authorities of participating states; actors could have delegated monitoring to the KP itself as an independent authority; transferring monitoring to independent auditors was an option; and, of course, the status quo of no systematic monitoring of conflict diamonds could have been maintained.

When on November 5, 2002, the Interlaken Declaration was adopted by thirty-six countries[6] and the European Community in the presence of the diamond industry and civil society representatives, they created a unique institution.[7] Although full membership and formal voting rights are restricted to states, the diamond industry and NGOs have observer status and can participate in all meetings and negotiations on an equal footing with governments.

At its beginning, the KP had a weak and decentralized monitoring system. States were required to provide reports to the KP annual plenary meeting (the main decision-making body of the governance scheme) about how they implement the KPCS standards within their domestic jurisdictions.[8] Further, "review missions" were envisaged as a complementary "verification measure," in case questions regarding a country's implementation efforts arise. These review missions address situations "where there are credible indications of significant non-compliance

---

[6] The countries present at the Interlaken meeting were Angola, Australia, Botswana, Brazil, Burkina Faso, Canada, Côte d'Ivoire, People's Republic of China, Cyprus, Czech Republic, Democratic Republic of Congo, Gabon, Ghana, Guinea, India, Israel, Japan, Republic of Korea, Lesotho, Malta, Mauritius, Mexico, Namibia, Norway, Philippines, Russian Federation, Sierra Leone, South Africa, Swaziland, Switzerland, Tanzania, Thailand, Ukraine, United Arab Emirates, United States of America, and Zimbabwe.

[7] Interlaken Declaration of 5 November 2002 on the Kimberley Process Certification Scheme for Rough Diamonds.

[8] Kimberley Process Certification Scheme, pp. 9–10.

with the Certification Scheme."[9] However, what precisely "credible indications of significant non-compliance" are and how to recognize them remained unspecified. This made it difficult to decide in what situations a review mission would be unleashed. In addition, launching a review mission was left to the discretion of the KP membership and required the agreement of all states (Smillie 2002b, 4). This provided potential rule violators and their allies with a veto and the ability to block review missions. Further, the case-by-case consideration of review missions made monitoring subject to political negotiations in which rule violators could bargain to secure favorable terms of being scrutinized. In short, the monitoring provisions originally enshrined in the KPCS were weak and had little "teeth."

Who Wanted What?

Although they had a shared interest in cooperation, the preferences of states, the diamond industry, and NGOs over how to design monitoring varied sharply. There were three camps: actors who pushed hard for a centralized monitoring system that provided for independent third party audits (particularly NGOs); those who were reluctant to accept any system of compliance verification (industry and states, such as Russia, Israel, China, Angola, Sierra Leone); and actors that did not take a particular position and remained passive (e.g., United Sates, European Union, Switzerland).

NGOs pushed hard for "regular, independent, expert monitoring of all national control mechanisms" (Smillie 2002a, 9). They argued that monitoring of states' national export and import control systems has to be mandatory for all KP members for the scheme to be credible and effective.[10] NGOs also wanted the institutional body responsible for monitoring to have some "teeth," which implied the specification of consequences for states and industry in case they do not live up to their commitments and, ultimately the ability to ostracize non-compliant participants (Beffert and Benner 2005b, 7). This demand for mandatory and independent verification, accompanied by the ability of the KP to expel those participants that operate in violation of its standards, was essential for NGOs: "For NGOs, this is an obvious necessity. It is not negotiable; it cannot be watered down or leavened with vague wording. We must be clear on this."[11]

By contrast, many states, notably Russia, Israel, China, Angola, Sierra Leone, as well as the industry rejected the concept of mandatory independent monitoring.[12] Instead, they argued for voluntary verification and sought to "ensure

---

[9] Kimberley Process Certification Scheme, p. 10.

[10] NGO Position Paper for the Luanda Kimberley Process Meeting, October 15, 2001.

[11] Notes for NGO Comments at World Diamond Council Meeting, Milan, March 13, 2002.

[12] NGO Report Ottawa Kimberley Process Meeting, March 20, 2002.

that the emerging scheme not be monitored by any institution outside their own national jurisdiction" (Smillie 2010, 185). Some states (e.g., Russia) even considered anything beyond voluntary self-reporting a "deal-breaker" that would have led them to walk away from the negotiation table.[13] The reluctant states were eager to make sure that the KP did not infringe on their sovereign rights and, therefore, objected to the idea of independent third party auditors monitoring their national control systems (Beffert and Benner 2005b, 7). They also warned of the costs that mandatory independent monitoring would incur and were concerned that commercial confidentiality would be undermined by an intrusive verification mechanism. Especially governments with state-run diamond sectors were not keen to have their national systems scrutinized by outside observers and exposed to state and industry competitors (Feldman 2003, 854). The industry was also strongly against monitoring. Particularly diamond dealers and their associations, such as the Israel Diamond Exchange and the World Federation of Diamond Bourses, were cautious about creating new transparency rules that deviated from the secretive trading system they had developed in the past (Beffert and Benner 2005b, 7; Spar 2006, 205). For them, a robust monitoring system based on independent auditing would have meant to grant external actors access to their trust and kinship-based business networks; a scenario which they abhorred.

Other countries, including big players in the global diamond trade, such as the United States, Canada, the European Union, and Switzerland, remained silent when it came to bargaining over monitoring provisions.[14] Notably, even though states, such as the United States, South Africa, Botswana, and the European Union, acknowledged the need for "good arrangements for compliance monitoring," they did not speak up when the issue was negotiated, but referred to the rather "soft" wording as it ultimately got incorporated in the KPCS as adequate.[15]

The monitoring mechanism which was agreed upon in November 2002 in Interlaken was no single group's ideal point. However, given the configuration of preferences, the monitoring structures which were created, closely approximate the interests of recalcitrant states and the industry (Beffert and Benner 2005b). As Feldman describes, "the business interests of De Beers . . . could be said to have overwhelmed any other values" (2003, 865). Monitoring became voluntary and primarily based on state self-reporting. Review missions could only be triggered in extraordinary circumstances and were left to the discretion of the collective of KP participants. How can this outcome be explained?

[13] NGO Memo, Gaborone Kimberley Process Meeting, November 2001.
[14] NGO Memo, Gaborone Kimberley Process Meeting, November 2001.
[15] NGO Memo, Gaborone Kimberley Process Meeting, November 2001.

What bargaining instruments did industry and their supporters use to shape the design of monitoring provisions in their favor?

Network Relationships and Bargaining over Monitoring

Due to their expertise on diamond production and trade, the representatives of the diamond industry, such as the World Diamond Council (WDC) or the market leader De Beers, were popular actors in the 2000–2002 KP network. Their expertise attracted governments that relied on the knowledge of industry for regulating the global diamond trade. This led to the formation of new communication ties between industry representatives and governments.[16]

Further, with the establishment of the WDC in July 2000, the industry created a single focal point for its interactions within the KP.[17] The representatives of the WDC had numerous relationships with diamond dealers, bourses, manufacturers, and retailers as well as ties to the United States and other governments (Feldman 2003, 849). This placed them—together with other industry actors, such as De Beers and the Belgian Diamond High Council (Hoge Raad voor Diamant [HRD])—in a broker position between states and NGOs, on the one hand, and the diamond industry, on the other hand. As brokers, they were able to provide other KP participants with scarce, otherwise inaccessible knowledge, on such crucial issues as supply chain management and techniques for the identification of rough diamonds' place of origin. This broker position provided the WDC, HRD, and De Beers with the power to influence the negotiation agenda, the definition of problems and potential solutions and, in some cases, even others' preferences. Importantly, the WDC used its brokerage role to persuade various states that state and industry self-reporting would be the only way to create an affordable and manageable monitoring system.[18]

Industry representatives could also draw on strong connections with key states. De Beers had ties based on licensing agreements and collaborative ownerships with major African diamond producers, such as South Africa, Botswana, and Namibia (Feldman 2003; Spar 2006). Further, in the early 2000s, it bought major shares in Canadian mines and expanded its activities in Russia (Spar 2006, 203). Likewise, the HRD had collaborative relationships with the Belgium government which, in turn, was closely related to the government of South Africa due to their common efforts in leading the KP negotiations (Shaxson 2001; Bieri 2010).

---

[16] Interviews with industry representatives, New York, July 28 and August 5, 2010.

[17] Interviews with industry representatives, New York, July 28 and August 11, 2010.

[18] Interviews with industry representatives, New York, August 11, 2010 and July 21, 2011.

These connections continued to exist in the KP and provided the basis for trustful interactions between the industry and several countries at a time when NGOs and other states had just started to form more collaborative relationships with one another. In short, the representatives of the diamond industry together with a few key states formed a powerful group whose members were densely connected to one another through strong collaborative ties, while outsiders—particularly NGOs—had no access. Exploiting this powerful network position based on a broker position and a large number of strong relationships, the WDC, De Beers, and the HRD were able to influence the negotiations over KP monitoring.

By contrast, NGOs were less well connected. NGOs had difficulties establishing relationships with states and the industry. Industry and many states (e.g., Russia, China, but also several African countries), on the one hand, and NGOs, on the other, had few direct relationships with one another. Major industry players, such as De Beers or the HRD, were only reluctantly willing to directly engage with NGO campaigners who had previously accused them of contributing to some of the world's most brutal civil wars. As a former NGO campaigner recalls, "[industry] was totally against us, hated the campaign, and thought we were evil, nasty, vicious, horrible terrorists who were trying to destroy the diamond industry."[19] Shaxson (2001, 218) concurs when he reports an anonymous interview with a representative of the Belgian diamond industry who describes the NGO Global Witness as a "bunch of well-intentioned hooligans." Similarly, particularly states with authoritarian political systems had a negative image of NGO groups in general and were not willing to accept them as equal partners at the negotiation table (Wright 2012, 182). Likewise, NGO activists continued to meet state and industry representatives with distrust and skepticism.[20] This lack of contact and exchange was accompanied by mistrust between the protagonists of an industry that has traditionally operated in secrecy and the activists of some of the world's biggest human rights NGOs (Bieri 2010, 70). This made the formation of ties with states and business difficult for NGOs. The few ties NGOs had to like-minded states, such as the United Kingdom (Beffert and Benner 2005a, 5), did not provide much of a strategic benefit in the negotiations because these states decided to take a backseat on the politically sensitive issue of monitoring.

As a result, NGOs had less access to the information flow within the network that evolved during the 2000–2002 negotiations. This made it difficult for them to influence the negotiations at the early stages. Neither could they acquire as

[19] Interview with Alex Yearsley, Global Witness, as quoted in Beffert and Benner (2005a, 7).

[20] Interview with industry representative, London, October 1, 2010. Telephone interview with government official, August 13, 2010.

much reliable information about others' preferences and the evolving coalitional patterns as their opponents, nor did they have the contacts necessary for disseminating their interpretation of the problem and shaping the negotiation agenda and working documents. Importantly, even though NGOs produced reports and position papers throughout the negotiations (Global Witness 2000), these reports reached only those states that were already receptive to NGO ideas (e.g., United Kingdom, Canada). The states that were skeptical about the NGO demand for mandatory and centralized monitoring, and therefore the primary targets of the information presented in these reports, had no direct communication ties with civil society. As a result, NGOs were in such a weak bargaining position that they ultimately had to back down and accept a voluntary self-reporting system.[21]

Structural Power as an Alternative Explanation?

What role, if any, did structural power play in determining the outcome of tripartite institutional bargaining? To start with, at the time of the creation of the KP monitoring system in 2000–2002, the global diamond business was centralized and dominated by a few big players. Whether it is the production, trade, manufacturing, or consumer market for rough diamonds, all were dominated by a handful of states. Take production as an example. In 1999–2000, only three countries together accounted for almost two-thirds of the global diamond production. In 1999, when the issue of conflict diamonds started to figure prominently in NGO campaigns and the media, with an annual production of $1,800 million, Botswana alone accounted for about 26% of the global production, followed by Russia, South Africa, and Angola which produced diamonds worth $1,600, $800, and $600 million, respectively. Compared to these market leaders, Western producers, such as Canada or Australia, played a minor role (table 8.1).[22]

The distribution of financial capabilities within the diamond industry was also skewed. In 2000, the market leader De Beers sold rough diamonds worth $5.9 billion, followed by the Russian monopoly ALROSA, BHP Billiton, and Rio Tinto, which registered sales of $1.7, $0.3, and $0.2 billion, respectively (Bain & Company 2011, 31). Finally, compared to the structural power

---

[21] NGO Memo, Gaborone Kimberley Process Meeting, November 2001. NGO Report Ottawa Kimberley Process Meeting, March 20, 2002. See also Smillie 2010, 191.

[22] Export was dominated by Botswana and Russia, which were responsible for about 43% of the world's diamond exports (Goreux 2001, 3); Belgium and the United Kingdom were leading the diamond import business (Shaxson 2001, 216); and the United States was the single most important consumer market (Bain & Company 2011, 49).

Table 8.1 **World Diamond Production, 1999–2000**

	1999		2000	
	Value (mi. $)	% World production	Value (mi. $)	% World production
Botswana	1,800	26.47	2,200	29.33
Russia	1,600	23.53	1,600	21.33
South Africa	800	11.76	900	12.00
Angola	600	8.82	750	10.00
Australia	400	5.88	300	4.00
Canada	400	5.88	400	5.33
Namibia	400	5.88	500	6.67
Others	800	11.76	900	12.00
World	6,800	100.00	7,500	100.00

Source: Shaxson 2001, 214.

of industry and states, the material resources of small NGOs such as Global Witness or Partnership Africa Canada, or even bigger organizations such as Amnesty International and Human Rights Watch, were miniscule.

This skewed distribution of structural power had no strong impact on the design of KP monitoring in 2000–2002. On the one hand, many actors with considerable material resources had to make important concessions with respect to monitoring. Take Russia as an example. Despite its structural power as the second largest producer and exporter of diamonds, it remained unable to fully accomplish its goals. Throughout the negotiations, Russia vehemently opposed the inclusion of any language on compliance verification into the new governance scheme. However, it did not manage to achieve this objective and ultimately agreed to the creation of a rudimentary monitoring mechanism. Thus, in instances like this, actors in possession of considerable structural power were not able to call the shots when negotiating the specificities of KP monitoring.

On the other hand, although in some cases the actors in central and broker positions also had structural power—most notably De Beers—we lack evidence that side payments and "go-it-alone" power figured prominently in their bargaining tactics. There is no recorded instance of industry representatives or states offering NGOs financial or other forms of material compensation for their agreement to a monitoring system they considered dysfunctional and inappropriate. For example, despite its structural power, De Beers did not use its material resources to exercise direct influence over the design of KP monitoring. Instead, it "sat quietly in the second row of seats and decided matters during the breaks in the negotiation" (Wright 2012, 184) by using its informal relationships to governments and exploiting the informational advantages stemming from its central position in the informal negotiation network.[23]

Growing Teeth: Peer Review Monitoring

Soon after its formation, the KP was confronted with a growing demand by some stakeholders, in particular NGOs, to strengthen its monitoring system (Beffert and Benner 2005b; Smillie 2005). While NGOs had to give in and make major concessions on monitoring in the 2000–2002 negotiations, in 2003 they launched a new attempt to bargain for a stronger verification system. This time, they were more successful.

As in 2000, states, the industry, and NGOs had several options regarding how to amend the monitoring provisions of the KP. Maintaining the status quo of self-reporting complemented by review missions was advocated by Russia, China, Israel, and a number of other countries; creating a mandatory third party auditing system was demanded by the NGOs; and expanding the review system component of the existing monitoring scheme was yet another option that was developed by the industry in cooperation with NGOs, South Africa, and Western states (e.g., Canada, European Union).[24] Ultimately, a year after the adoption of the KPCS, the KP participants created a voluntary peer review system at their October 2003 Sun City plenary meeting, to guarantee that KPCS standards are effectively implemented by all participants.[25]

This peer review system has three pillars: states' annual implementation reports, review visits, and review missions. As outlined already in the KPCS, states are obliged to provide information on an annual basis about their implementation of KPCS standards.[26] Review visits constitute the second pillar of the KP peer review system. A review visit is a mission of a small team of states, industry representatives, and NGOs to a country to assess its implementation of KPCS requirements. Review visits take place on a voluntary basis, and together with states' annual reports, form the core of the monitoring system. Finally, on recommendation of the working group on monitoring, a review mission can be sent to countries "where there are credible indications of significant

---

[23] Telephone interview with industry representative, October 22, 2010. Interview with industry representative, New York, July 20, 2011.

[24] Interview with industry representative, New York, August 11, 2010. Interviews with NGO representatives, London, September 28 and 30, 2010. Telephone interview with government official, October 8, 2010.

[25] Administrative Decision, KPCS Peer Review System, Sun City, South Africa, October 30, 2003.

[26] Administrative Decision, KPCS Peer Review System, Sun City, South Africa, October 30, 2003.

non-compliance with the Certification Scheme."[27] In contrast to review visits, the annual plenary meeting can initiate a review mission regardless of whether the country in question agrees. However, the plenary meeting decides about the launch of review missions on a case-by-case basis through negotiations and unanimity. Thus, the KP peer review system integrates elements of the previous self-reporting arrangement with voluntary peer auditing and a few mandatory elements.

Who Wanted What?

As in the first negotiation episode, states, the industry, and NGOs had a common interest in continued cooperation; no stakeholder group conceived of a termination of its engagement in the newly built KP as a viable option. Industry had an interest in the reputational benefits of participating in regulation; states needed the KP to protect their diamond industries against the threat of consumer boycotts which they could not address without the help of the industry and civil society; and NGOs wanted to remain engaged in shaping the regulation of the global diamond trade. Yet, their preferences over how to reform monitoring differed.

There were again three camps. As in 2000–2002, NGOs argued for mandatory and independent monitoring. They were confronted with a large number of states that were outspoken in their opposition to a robust monitoring system. Among others, this status quo coalition included Russia, China, India, Zimbabwe, and particularly Israel.[28] As reported by an NGO activist: "Israel saw the idea [of regular monitoring] as the thin edge of an NGO wedge which, if accepted, would result in hordes of NGOs poring over the accounts of individual Israeli diamond dealers, bringing the entire industry to a standstill" (Smillie 2005, 4). The third group consisted of the industry and a few states, such as South Africa, Canada, and the European Union, which now shared some of civil society's concerns about monitoring and the KP's credibility and reputation. As Nicky Oppenheimer, then-chairman of De Beers, said at the April 2003 KP meeting in Johannesburg:

> I believe that transparent verification of both government and industry procedures is essential to the credibility of the certification scheme in the eyes of the world. It is for this reason that the industry

[27] Administrative Decision, KPCS Peer Review System, Sun City, South Africa, October 30, 2003, p. 2.

[28] "NGOs Urge Greater Transparency of Diamond Control," United Nations Integrated Regional Information Network, October 29, 2003.

wholeheartedly supports the NGOs' objectives in securing a credible system of monitoring. (Partnership Africa Canada 2003a, 2)

As I will elaborate in greater detail in the next section, the change in the industry's position which should turn out to be critical for the negotiation dynamics was, to a good deal, a result of the NGOs' lobbying of visible retailers and producers, such as Jewelers of America and De Beers. Once NGOs had persuaded them, retailers and producers used their relationships and influence to bring the rest of the industry on board in support of a monitoring system that secures the credibility and reputation of the KP.[29] In addition, states that had remained silent on monitoring in the 2000–2002 negotiations (e.g., Canada, European Union, and Switzerland), were now more vocal and bargained for stronger monitoring. This provided NGOs with a larger and more powerful group of allies in their fight for a strengthened monitoring system. However, states and the industry still rejected mandatory monitoring—NGOs' most preferred outcome—but instead argued for a middle ground solution between the system outlined in the KPCS and a mandatory arrangement.

These differences were resolved in favor of the industry and Western states, such as Canada and the European Union. The new monitoring mechanism approximates the institutional preferences of the industry and some Western states, whereas it is at odds with the initial preferences of several big players in the diamond trade, including Israel, Australia, and Russia. NGOs ended up somewhere in the middle. While not the mandatory, independent arrangement which they preferred, the new peer review system goes well beyond the initial self-reporting framework of the KPCS.

Network Relationships and Bargaining over Monitoring

Although it initially seemed as if NGOs would have no substantive role after the adoption of the KPCS (Wright 2004), they soon became even more influential than before. Over time and repeated interactions, NGOs improved their position in the informal communication network of the KP by forming new relationships with states and the leaders of the industry.[30] For example, throughout the numerous formal and informal negotiation meetings in 2000–2002, NGOs built working relationships with many industry and state representatives (Bone 2004; Partnership Africa Canada 2001a,b). They also reduced the mistrust that

---

[29] Interviews with industry representatives, New York, August 5 and August 11, 2010, and July 21, 2011.

[30] Interview with industry representative, London, October 1, 2010. Telephone interview with industry representative, October 22, 2010.

characterized their interactions with the industry and states at the beginning of the KP. Importantly, toward the end of 2002 NGOs had obtained access to a key broker in the KP, the WDC, and established strong relationships with several important states, such as the European Union, South Africa, and the United States. These new relationships provided NGOs with the communication infrastructure needed to regularly exchange information and disseminate their ideas about strengthened monitoring among KP members. For example, once the relationships between the industry and NGOs improved, leading NGO activists, such as Ian Smillie of Partnership Africa Canada, were regularly invited to major industry meetings, such as the WDC annual meeting, to deliver presentations and participate in discussions. NGO representatives used such occasions to discuss their arguments for a strengthened monitoring system with industry members that they would otherwise not meet in the negotiation meetings of the KP.[31]

NGOs used their new relationships with key business players, such as WDC, Jewelers of America, and De Beers, to change industry's position on monitoring. In late 2002 and early 2003, NGO activists from Global Witness and Partnership Africa Canada had regular interactions with industry representatives and, particularly representatives of retailers and producers, including Jewelers of America (JA), Jewelers Vigilance Committee (JVC), and De Beers. For example, in March 2003, Global Witness together with the European Union, South Africa, Guinea, and the WDC participated in the first review mission of the KP in the Central African Republic. Among other things, the NGO used the mission to discuss its ideas about monitoring with the other members of the review team (Bieri 2010, 125). Similarly, at numerous occasions, NGOs discussed with industry and explained to them how the reputational costs associated with weak monitoring would first and foremost hit the retailers and large, publicly visible companies.[32] They also addressed industry's concerns about the intrusiveness and confidentiality implications of monitoring and explained that they do not want to establish a "carte blanche" arrangement that allows NGO activists to inspect any aspects of the diamond industry at any time and at will (Smillie 2003). Eventually, NGOs succeeded and persuaded the retailers and De Beers that a strengthened monitoring system is a means of industry self-protection and makes sense from a business point of view.[33]

[31] NGO Comments: Ian Smillie, World Diamond Council 2nd Annual Meeting, Milan, March 12-13, 2002.

[32] World Diamond Council Second Annual Meeting, Milan, March 12-13, 2002, NGO Comments.

[33] Interviews with industry representatives, New York, August 5 and 11, 2010.

Once the retailers were convinced that strengthened monitoring was important, they used their relationships and influence within the industry to bring others on board. Particularly representatives of the publicly less visible businesses (e.g., traders, manufacturers) were outright against any monitoring due to cost and confidentiality concerns. Nevertheless, using the information and arguments of the NGOs in combination with the frightening picture of the scenario of broad-range consumer boycotts, the WDC, JA, JVC, De Beers, and others ultimately garnered the support of the entire industry behind the idea of stronger KP monitoring. The leadership and personal relationships of the then-president of the WDC, Eli Izhakoff, were critical in bringing the industry in line.[34] Having spent his entire career in the diamond industry, Izhakoff knew everyone in the business and had strong relationships to all segments of the industry (Feldman 2003, 849). Everyone in the industry respected and trusted him. This allowed him to discuss with the monitoring skeptics one-by-one and explain to them how the maintenance of a weak monitoring system had the potential to destabilize the diamond market, and how little strengthened monitoring would actually cost them.[35] Importantly, as illustrated by the statement of Nicky Oppenheimer above, when after the change in the industry position, the WDC and other industry representatives articulated their support for the reform of KP monitoring, they used exactly the same wording about credibility, reputation, and effectiveness which the NGOs have been using since the early days of the KP and disseminated through their newly built network relationships in late 2002 and 2003 (Global Witness 1998, 2000; Smillie, Gbrie, and Hazleton 2000).

Backed by the industry support and their new relationships to the representatives of South Africa, which chaired the KP in 2003, NGOs became also more successful in shaping the negotiation agenda and contributing to proposal-making. Given that agenda-setting and proposal-making are not formally regulated in the KP, informal relationships are critical for knowing what issue comes up when, by whom it is supported, and in what forum.[36] While their peripheral position in the informal negotiation network in 2000–2002 made it difficult for NGOs to bring items on the agenda and shape draft documents at early stages, their increased connectedness placed them in a more favorable position in 2003. Importantly, NGOs used their informal connections to South Africa and the European Union, the chairs of the KP, and the working group on monitoring, respectively, to keep monitoring on the negotiation agenda and continue discussions (Bieri 2010, 125).

---

[34] Interview with industry representative, New York, August 11, 2010.
[35] Interview with industry representative, New York, August 11, 2010.
[36] Interview with government official, Jerusalem, November 4, 2010.

Finally, facilitated by their new relationships, NGOs became part of a coalition formed by the industry, civil society, and a few—mostly Western—states. This coalition was critical for the establishment of the KP peer review system. Its pooled social and political capital provided the group with informational and coordination advantages in the negotiations over the reform of KP monitoring that enabled it to overcome the resistance of their opponents. The WDC which was part of this coalition occupied an important broker position between the pro- and anti-monitoring camps and NGOs used their access to this broker to negotiate a mini-lateral agreement with Israel, one of the strongest monitoring opponents in the KP at that time (Bieri 2010, 125–126).

In 2003, the meaning, implications, and consequences of monitoring of conflict diamonds were unclear to many states. In particular, Israel had serious doubts about how exactly monitoring would affect its industry (Smillie 2005, 4). Among other things, they feared that monitoring would bring hundreds of independent auditors to their trading sites and force each and every diamond dealer to open his books for scrutiny. Such a monitoring procedure would be economically costly and politically intrusive. This uncertainty about the form and effects of strengthened monitoring made its potential value unclear to many states. Ascertaining the consequences of monitoring for state sovereignty and industry practices, therefore, became an essential problem particularly for Israel, but also many other countries.

Throughout 2003, the NGOs used their new relationships to the WDC to engage in mini-lateral discussions with the WDC and Israel. They provided the Israeli negotiators with detailed information about what they had in mind when they were talking about stronger monitoring and addressed their concerns about costs, intrusiveness, and commercial confidentiality. The new information and sustained dialogue induced Israel to develop a more complete understanding of the problem of monitoring, how it could be addressed, and what kind of institutional structure the NGOs were advocating. The WDC acted as mediator and mitigated the lack of trust between NGOs and the country.[37] The breakthrough came a few days before the KP plenary meeting in Sun City, when the NGOs, the WDC, and Israel hammered out a joint proposal for a system of voluntary review missions (Partnership Africa Canada 2003b, 1). In the words of an NGO activist:

What we did was we worked, we brokered a deal, really it was between Partnership Africa Canada, World Diamond Council and the government of Israel. I think it was the World Diamond Council that actually

---

did it. They were in Israel, they called and we had a three-way conversation about what we meant by monitoring. Israel was concerned that, you know, a swarm of NGOs were going to arrive and they were going to want to go through all the books of individual companies. We said no that's not what we mean by monitoring . . . When they began to understand that, they said okay we can agree to that so they did.[38]

The agreement of Israel then prepared the ground for a consensus among all KP participants.[39] Once Israel gave in, this generated momentum that cascaded through the entire KP network and allowed NGOs and the WDC to convince other reluctant states, such as China, Russia, India, Zimbabwe, and Australia (Bieri 2010, 126). By the time of the Sun City plenary meeting in October 2003, an NGO activist recalls, "it was almost impossible to object the establishment of a peer review monitoring mechanism and finally everybody agreed during that meeting."[40] Importantly, after it decided to support stronger monitoring, Israel itself joined the efforts of the NGO-WDC coalition and helped to convince others, most notably Russia (Bieri 2010, 126).

In sum, NGOs used the support of the WDC as a broker in combination with their ability to provide information to the Israeli representatives through short, trustful channels to convince Israel that a peer review monitoring system would benefit their interests (Bieri 2010, 125–126). While facilitating communication and brokering an agreement, the WDC in turn, used its influential position to shape the specificities of the new monitoring provisions and made sure that it did not incorporate items that were not in accordance with industry interests, such as an independent third party monitoring system as preferred by NGOs.

Structural Power as an Alternative Explanation?

Proponents of structural power might object that the change from a weak monitoring system based on state self-reporting to a peer review mechanism was driven by the distribution of material resources among negotiators and the changed industry position on monitoring. They might argue that once the diamond industry changed its preferences, it used its structural power to call the shots and push for strengthened monitoring by using negotiation strategies based on side payments. There is, however, no evidence to substantiate this alternative explanation. Although in some instances actors that

[38] Interview with Ian Smillie, May 4, 2005, quoted in Bieri 2010, 126.

[39] Telephone interview with industry representative, July 6, 2011. Telephone interview with NGO representative, July 22, 2010.

[40] Telephone interview with NGO representative, July 22, 2010.

occupied central and broker positions, such as the WDC, also had considerable structural power, there is no evidence in my data that they used this power to shape the outcomes of the reform of KP monitoring. Rather than using its material resources to impose its preferred outcome or offer side payments, the WDC used its broker position to persuade reluctant states (e.g., Israel) in collaboration with NGOs that a stronger monitoring system benefits their interests. This, in turn, was critical for preparing the ground for a broader agreement.

Furthermore, making the changed industry position on monitoring in combination with its structural power the primary explanation of the change in the design of conflict diamond monitoring in 2003 overlooks the critical role NGO network ties played in bringing about the change in industry preferences in the first place.[41] The informal working relationships with the WDC, HRD, De Beers, and retailer associations that NGOs established toward the end of 2002 allowed activists to provide these industry players with information and ideas about how monitoring would benefit the KP as a whole and industry in particular. They also used these communication channels to explain to industry representatives that what they thought NGOs had in mind when they were demanding stronger monitoring provisions was not what NGOs were advocating. Thus, informal relationships and network positions were not only a key element of industry's negotiation strategy, but they were also instrumental in bringing about the change in industry preferences which made them a supporter of strengthened KP monitoring.

To summarize, changes in the informal relationships and the distribution of network positions among states, the diamond industry, and NGOs in combination with changes in industry preferences led to a strengthening of the monitoring of conflict diamonds in 2003. Although weak in structural power, NGOs played a crucial role in establishing the peer review mechanism of the KP. The dominance of the industry within the KP network, which was decisive for the outcomes of the 2000–2002 negotiations, was no longer as exclusive in 2003 as it was before. Their improved network position enabled NGOs to lobby industry representatives and persuade them to adopt a more monitoring-friendly position. It also allowed them to form a coalition with the industry and like-minded states to support their reform objectives. Yet, NGOs did not accomplish their most favored outcome, a mandatory independent monitoring system. Instead, industry was able to prevent the latter using its broker position.

---

[41] Avant (this volume) and Carpenter (this volume) also highlight the importance of network relationships for the formation and change of actor preferences.

Conclusions

This chapter analyzed changes in the institutional design of the monitoring of conflict diamonds and the role informal networks among states, the diamond industry, and NGOs played in bringing about these changes. As this case suggests, in an environment characterized by unanimity decision-making in large heterogeneous groups, uncertainty about preferences and the state of the world, and integrative bargaining as negotiation mode, central and broker positions in the informal communication network that underlies tripartite negotiations are bargaining assets. They provide actors with information that can be used to define problems, identify solutions, and persuade others. Information acquired through informal communication ties also facilitates the invention of innovative institutional options that can then serve as focal points for agreement. Finally, brokers can mediate agreement among conflicting parties. Structural power, by contrast, is of limited use in transnational tripartite bargaining.

When NGOs, such as Global Witness and Partnership Africa Canada, were in a peripheral network position in the 2000–2002 negotiations, they were unable to exert influence on the design of the KP's monitoring system. Instead, industry which was a central hub and broker together with its allies from diamond producing and trading states was able to negotiate a self-reporting system that closely approximated its interests. Once NGOs improved their network position and established new relationships with the industry and several states, their bargaining leverage improved and they were able to push for a strengthened monitoring system. They used their new ties to industry representatives, such as the World Diamond Council, Jewelers of America, and De Beers, to provide them with information and engage in dialogue which triggered a change in the industry position in favor of stronger monitoring. They were also able to form a coalition with the industry which was critical to convince reluctant states, most notably Israel. In various ways, the improved network position of NGOs was crucial for strengthening the monitoring provisions of the global conflict diamonds regime of the KP.

Thus, in the case of conflict diamond monitoring, network relationships and particularly the distribution of network positions in terms of centrality and brokerage had important consequences for the effectiveness and capture of transnational security governance. While a network structure with industry as the unique network hub and broker, and NGOs at the periphery, led to weak monitoring controlled by states and industry, a more balanced configuration of positions with NGOs in more central positions set the stage for a change toward more effectiveness of governance and less capture.

This finding raises important questions about the effectiveness and legitimacy of conflict diamond governance as conducted within the KP. Previous work has emphasized the importance of the multi-stakeholder character of the KP for its effectiveness (Grant and Taylor 2004; Wright 2004; Grant 2012). According to these arguments, the involvement of states, business, and NGOs is essential for making and implementing rules that prevent profits from illegally mined diamonds from funding civil war. However, as the illustrative evidence presented in this chapter suggests, the operative work of the KP looks different. While the actors which occupy central and broker positions in the informal KP network can access the negotiations at early stages and voice their interests, those who lack such positions can only become active at later stages or are entirely excluded. As a result, not only their interests but also their expertise and knowledge is absent at the early stages of the governance process where the agenda is set, problems identified, and proposals for solutions drafted (Abbott and Snidal 2009; Avant, Finnemore, and Sell 2010b). This creates problems for the effectiveness of the KP, given that the expertise of all stakeholder groups is needed for effectively governing conflict diamonds. Such differences in access and participation also challenge the legitimacy of the KP because they run contrary to the principle of equality on which transnational public-private governance schemes are built (Wright 2004). What exactly the consequences of the variance in actors' network positions on the effectiveness and legitimacy of transnational public-private governance are, as well as what the determinants of network positions and change are, are only two of the many avenues for future research on the role of informal networks in the Kimberley Process and transnational public-private governance schemes more generally.

These results also raise important questions for future research on transnational public-private governance and network power in world politics more generally. New modes of security governance are not necessarily less hierarchical and more inclusive than traditional state-based forms of political regulation. The importance of networks as a bargaining asset does not necessarily translate into an empowerment of the weak. Networks may both compensate for the lack of structural power as well as reinforce existing inequalities. Previous work on networks in global governance has emphasized their non-hierarchical nature and their positive effects on participation (Keck and Sikkink 1998; Reinicke and Deng 2000). Yet, the empirical pattern that emerges from my analysis is mixed. At times, networks can be a channel for weak actors (e.g., NGOs) to increase their influence and punch above their weight in bargaining over the institutions of global governance. Often however, networks are just another way for the already powerful (e.g., multinational corporations) to achieve their goals. This may ultimately exacerbate rather than mitigate the inequalities between the weak and the strong, because in contrast to formal institutions, informal networks are largely unregulated so that there are no formal procedures through which access can be guaranteed for weaker stakeholders. Thus, researchers interested in better understanding the role of networks in transnational security governance should not theoretically assume network structures and effects, but empirically examine the different structural configurations networks can have and how different structures impact the effectiveness and capture of transnational security governance.

9

Corporations, Governance Networks, and Conflict in the Developing World

VIRGINIA HAUFLER

In the past two decades, we have witnessed a surprising explosion of transnational governance in which different types of actors collaborate to set standards and regulate the actions of participants. Many of these seek to regulate some aspect of security affairs. Despite the common perception of security as the sphere of "high politics" among nation-states, security issues are increasingly governed by many other actors. Contemporary security regulation in many cases operates through the market. Actors "govern" by defining what is a legitimate market and providing information about corporate behavior that might impact conflict. Corporations often play a central role in transnational governance as both the objects of regulation and participants in regulating. Looking at the growing array of transnational security governance systems, it is evident that some industry sectors, and the individual firms within them, vary in the degree and effectiveness of their governance participation. Why do companies participate in transnational governance at different rates, and why is governance more common for some industries than others? In this chapter, I explore how the relationships among firms help us understand these variations in transnational governance outcomes.

Avant and Westerwinter in the opening chapter to this volume argue that authority is deployed by a wide variety of actors who are connected to each other in governance networks. Through these relationships, different actors gain the power to influence outcomes through either their position in a network, or the quality of the ties they have to others (Avant and Westerwinter, this volume). Here, I am interested in exploring the relationships in which firms are embedded. I narrow the focus to look at the corporate participants in transnational governance systems, setting aside for now the influence of nongovernmental organizations (NGOs), governments, and intergovernmental organizations (IGOs), to which I return in the conclusion.

Companies are embedded in multiple sets of relationships that shape their preferences with regard to the social, political, and economic risks they face. They are connected through global value chains that link different firms within industries via contract, and which often confer market power to centrally positioned firms. Some firms also choose to cultivate relationships based on shared ideas and identities, through industry associations and business organizations that represent specific policy goals. In recent years, those goals have turned increasingly toward corporate social responsibility, which at least in theory should have some influence on governance outcomes. Individual firms occupy different positions within these intersecting networks. How these relationships influence transnational governance outcomes is the subject of this chapter.

I focus on so-called "conflict minerals" (i.e., minerals sourced from rebel-held territory). Many different transnational governance systems have been developed in the last fifteen years to limit the market for conflict minerals in an effort to reduce the incentives for violent rebellion. There was wide variation in the speed and timing of these developments across different minerals sectors, and the governance outcomes differed in whether they served narrow or broad interests (Mattli and Woods 2009a). This occurred despite the fact that the sectors faced very similar political dynamics—transnational activist pressure over conflicts in the Democratic Republic of Congo and neighboring states, coinciding with the rise of corporate social responsibility norms and increasing demands for business to engage in conflict prevention.

I start with the expectation that firms that join organizations that promote corporate social responsibility as a response to social and political risks will be more willing to engage in transnational governance than those that do not. Furthermore, those firms that already participate in other transnational governance initiatives will be more willing to join new ones based on their prior experience. However, the impact of these ties is mediated by the distribution of power within the global value chain of the industry. By virtue of their position within the global value chain particular firms have leverage over others and can either facilitate or obstruct the creation of effective governance networks.

The interaction of these two sets of relationships evolves over time, along with the evolution of the issue area itself—its discourse, norms, and governance. These interactions shape successive negotiations over the standards governing a particular issue, as participants gain experience with each other and with the standards, and acquire more information about regulatory alternatives. Early participants in governance may simply be trying to solve a specific narrowly defined problem, while later ones may be more concerned with diffusing norms and legitimating outcomes, which means they face a more complex governance challenge (Tolbert and Zucker 1983; Cashore, Auld, and Newsom 2004).

Clearly, these two sets of relationships cannot explain transnational governance outcomes on their own, and I do not attempt to make broad claims about them. My goal is to illuminate one corner of a wider phenomenon by assessing the plausibility of propositions concerning these two sets of relationships among firms, and how they might influence governance outcomes. In the following section, I explore the literature on corporations and networks, focusing on scholarship about inter-firm coordination, transnational governance, and supply chains. This literature establishes expectations regarding two types of inter-firm networks, how they distribute power among participant firms, and their influence on the timing and character of governance outcomes. I then explore the plausibility of these expectations through a case study of conflict minerals governance.

Preliminary evidence indicates that the structure of supply chains involved in the conflict minerals issue area has a greater influence on outcomes than other types of relationships. Ties based on ideas and identity matter only in conjunction with the structure of contractual relations. In other words, industry structure constrains the influence of social ties, but under certain conditions it is social ties that provide the substantive content and principles for collective action. In the conclusion, I discuss the limitations of the analysis and directions for future research, while considering the implications of these initial findings for corporate networks, transnational governance, and security affairs.

Corporations and Networks

In mainstream economics, firms are the quintessential alienated actor, driven by self-interested utility maximization, responding to market prices without regard for social forces. Other disciplines, from industrial organization to economic sociology, have in contrast depicted the firm as embedded within a web of relationships. Granovetter (1985) famously argued that neoclassical economic thinking is "undersocialized," and that we need to view economic action as embedded in social institutions and relationships. Decades earlier, Polanyi (1944) argued that markets are—and should be—embedded within society as a whole and not separated from and elevated above society. The discipline of sociology has done much to theorize the embeddedness of firms, though there exist significant differences in approach (Perrucci et al. 1989; Grandori and Soda 1995; Knoke 2012). For instance, White (2000) describes individual production markets as being socially constructed by relational networks that are shaped by distinctive discourse, while Fligstein (1993) looks upon these relations as structural and institutional constraints. Oliver Williamson and others argue that economic activity is organized through three different types of relationship—hierarchy, markets, and networks (Williamson 1985; Thompson 2003). These scholars all share the view that firms are not at "arm's length" from each other or from other actors within society, and their behavior can be analyzed through their relationships. A relational approach assumes that actors are above all social—they are interdependent, and behavior and preferences are mutually influenced by relationships (Easley and Kleinberg 2010; Knoke 2012).

Network approaches take the relationship between actors as the unit of analysis, and examine patterns and influences within the network. Analysts may simply identify whether or not a tie exists, or they can look at the character of the actors and their ties. These ties can represent many different relations and transactions: the exchange of information, goods, ideas, and values. The pattern of relations within the network facilitates or constrains an actor's behavior depending on its position within the network, the number and strength of its ties to others, and the character of the interaction (Scott 2013). As Avant and Westerwinter (this volume) argue, networks shape the power of particular actors, but actors can also shape the networks and thus their own power. Firms can gain power not simply through traditional material sources, such as profits and market share, but through their ties with other firms. Their position within a network may confer influence, but they can also gain power by shaping or creating networks. I examine two different types of relationships and consider how they might influence governance outcomes.

Contractual Networks: Relationships of Circumstance

In the modern economy, almost all firms are connected to other firms through relations of either trade (the traditional arm's length relations of neoclassical economics) or ownership (either direct or indirect). In the last fifty years, however, these two options—the market versus hierarchy choice—have been joined by a third, that of networks of contracts that connect firms throughout the production process, from raw materials to retail. Early analyses focused on partnerships and joint ventures between competitors, for instance, General Motors and Toyota teaming up to develop a new technology or produce in a particular developing country market. This "alliance capitalism," as Dunning (1993) calls it, represents only one form of contemporary contractual network.

The most striking development in recent years is the extensive global-spanning chains of suppliers and producers that characterize the modern economy. Labeled "commodity chains," "supply chains," and "value chains," they are based on contracts between firms at different stages of the production process, with literally hundreds of firms connected to the largest producers and buyers at either end of the chain. How these networks are governed is a question addressed from both a business operations perspective and a more political one (Gibbon, Bair, and Ponte 2008; Macdonald 2014).

Gereffi and his colleagues have provided one of the most complete accounts of power and governance within commodity chains. They argue that commodity chains are dominated either by a centrally positioned firm or sector that drives production throughout the chain of relationships or by a firm or sector that dominates through their position as major buyers. The structure of the commodity chain itself gives an advantageous position to firms that leverage their position and govern others by setting prices, standards, and other characteristics of the production process. This control is reinforced by repeated transactions, as contracts are renewed, and by reputation and social norms (Gereffi 1996; Gereffi, Humphrey, and Sturgeon 2005). Gereffi and his colleagues focus on how this governance prevents weaker firms, and the countries in which they are located, from upgrading to a higher position in the market.

Gellert (2003) brings a more political eye to commodity chain analysis by looking at how they can be manipulated and politically constructed, using the case of timber from Indonesia as an example. In his case, a coalition between leading Indonesian firms and the government manipulated the supply chain to benefit Indonesia and gain a dominant position in the timber market. Macdonald also examines the politicization of supply chains through growing activism about corporate accountability, with "open contests between rival systems of power and governance" (2014, 4).

From this emerging literature on the politics of supply chains, we can establish initial expectations about how contractual networks can influence the creation and content of transnational governance schemes. I expect that firms with central positions in a supply chain will have significant leverage over other firms, especially when an industry is highly concentrated (i.e., with several large firms and many smaller ones). If these centrally positioned firms believe that a transnational governance scheme is an effective way to counter political pressure and regulatory threat, then its preferences will prevail. Alternatively, in industries that are more diffuse and less concentrated, there will be more negotiation and coalition-building. I also expect that producer-driven commodity chains will support weaker governance systems serving narrow interests, since it is often the behavior of producer firms themselves that must change. Buyer-driven supply chains should be more likely to adopt stronger standards benefiting broad interests.

Associational Networks: Relationships of Choice

The modern corporation typically belongs to a number of associations that represent its interests and define its "social" peers. Not all firms choose to join, and there are always costs to membership. We can identify three general types of associations in which firms might choose to participate: industry associations, policy organizations, and transnational governance schemes. Industry associations represent the broad interests of a single sector, for instance, the Chemical Manufacturer's Association or the American Petroleum Institute. The main goals of these organizations are to represent the sector in political discussions, establish best practices for the industry, convey information and ideas within the industry, address challenges arising from market forces and technological innovation, and promote professional standards. They are an arena in which interests are articulated and norms can be developed. They have to be broad in their approach as they attempt to find common ground across a range of interests within often-diverse sectors. When they adopt a policy position, these associations represent fairly wide consensus within the industry or a lowest-common-denominator position. Their positions are often narrowly self-interested, but they may serve a larger public interest when there is general agreement within the sector (Mattli and Woods 2009a).

Business policy organizations are cross-industry groups that address specific issues and promote particular ideas. In recent years, many business organizations have emerged that are oriented toward global issues, such as the World Economic Forum or the Global Climate Coalition. Some of them are based on a commitment to corporate social responsibility values, such as Business for Social Responsibility or the Global Reporting Initiative. They promote a particular policy position or represent an effort to create consensus on how to address a particular issue facing business. Unlike industry associations, policy organizations clearly signal commitment to particular kinds of norms, values, and definitions of interest. They seek to create a common identity among members who want to establish a reputation on an issue. These policy organizations compete when they represent interests on opposite sides of divisive issues. For instance, both the World Business Council for Sustainable Development (WBCSD) and the Global Climate Coalition contained member firms from the oil industry, but they took opposing positions on climate change issues.[1] Other organizations overlap and reinforce common positions—the WBCSD, Business for Social Responsibility, and the Global Reporting Initiative all represent businesses that have made a commitment to sustainability. These networks provide members

[1] The Global Climate Coalition no longer exists, as support for its position weakened (Kolk and Levy 2001).

with information and knowledge to influence important debates, along with legitimacy and political access. When they are oriented toward corporate social responsibility (CSR) norms, I expect they will facilitate collective action to address social problems, and support and engage with transnational governance schemes that represent broad interests and not narrow ones.

International standard-setting organizations have become common in the last two decades. They are voluntary, multi-stakeholder standards-setting schemes in which business participation is often a key feature (Reinicke 1998; Benner, Reinicke, and Witte 2004; Avant, Finnemore, and Sell 2010b). Within these networks, members exchange ideas and information, and negotiate over values, norms, and standards. The position of corporations within these organizations varies, and they may or may not have significant power and leverage (Westerwinter, this volume). I expect that firms that participate in transnational governance schemes already will be more willing to participate in new ones due to the experience and learning they have acquired. I also expect them to support broadly targeted common-interest organizations.

To summarize, we can expect CSR policy organizations and transnational governance schemes to predispose firms to join new governance efforts that serve a broad common interest. I also expect that the longer a firm engages with other firms within CSR policy organizations and governance networks the more they will support these outcomes. An industry sector in which many members participate in CSR organizations and transnational governance should be more likely to support new common-interest governance. However, the impact of these associational networks will be mediated by the structure and character of contractual networks.

Intersections between Networks

Within a network, power derives from the position of actors, the distribution of ties, and the quality of the connections among them (Avant and Westerwinter, this volume). These connections provide actors with social capital, relevant information, or political influence (Hafner-Burton and Montgomery 2009; Kahler 2009). Actors with central positions in the network have more access to these resources and can either monopolize them or provide others with access (Carpenter 2010). Actors that do not have extensive ties and are not central to a network may still have power if they occupy a critical position linking otherwise unconnected actors, brokering relationships across network boundaries (Lake and Wong 2009).

Firms that belong to both associational and contractual networks are multiplex nodes that act as brokers between the two types of networks. When a single firm is a participant in more than one association it reinforces the values and identity that the associations represent. For instance, a firm that belongs to many different corporate social responsibility organizations will develop a strong reputation, higher legitimacy, and more influence. If this firm is also central to a particular contractual network, and acts as a broker between the meta-CSR network and the global supply chain partners, then we can expect those values to be injected into any efforts to establish transnational governance throughout the supply chain. Contractual networks provide the opportunity to create new governance schemes, but it is associational networks that provide the content, values, and design. Critical firms act as a link between them.

The intersection between associational and contractual networks generates different expectations for transnational governance outcomes. I expect that when firms belong to more than one CSR policy organization and/or transnational governance scheme, and also are central to the global supply chain, then new transnational governance is more likely to serve a broad public interest. When firms are central to the global supply chain, but do not participate in CSR organizations or other governance initiatives, then any new governance initiative is likely to serve narrowly defined self-interest. Participation in CSR networks without holding a central position in the global supply chain is likely to lead to long negotiations with weak outcomes. Without either a central position in the supply chain or membership in CSR organizations we can expect to see no transnational governance at all.

This discussion has been cast in general terms, but I am particularly interested in seeing how these expectations about corporate participation in overlapping networks play out in the security arena. Transnational governance, corporate social responsibility, and a relational analytical approach are all relatively rare in security studies. They all come together, however, in the arena of what are called "conflict minerals." In the rest of this chapter I will explore these expectations through a case study of the conflict minerals issue. This is a narrow case but rich in variation across the factors discussed above. It involves different industry sectors that vary in the organization of their global supply chains, the degree to which firms participate in CSR and networks, and transnational governance outcomes. The issue itself emerged only in the late 1990s, so it is a compact period of time to analyze. The mining sector was one of the first industries to respond collectively and globally to demands for corporate social responsibility, and some firms have been involved with CSR policy organizations and transnational governance initiatives for a long time.

Governing Conflict, Governing Minerals

"Conflict minerals" are minerals that are mined and traded by rebels in order to finance guns and soldiers.[2] Five minerals are identified as conflict-related: diamonds,

---

[2] There is a broader category of "conflict commodities," which includes timber and almost any raw material that finances violence.

tin, tungsten, tantalum, and gold (the latter four are often referred to as the 3TG minerals).[3] The conflicts at stake are in mineral-rich areas of Africa, starting with civil wars in Sierra Leone, Angola, and Liberia in the 1990s, and today focused on the eastern provinces in the Democratic Republic of the Congo, and neighboring regions in Rwanda and Uganda—loosely referred to as the "DRC region."[4] The conflicts in the DRC region are sometimes referred to as the Great War in Africa since the ongoing violence has engulfed communities across a wide swathe of the region, causing millions to lose their lives (Autessere 2010; Stearns 2012). Concern over this humanitarian disaster led to intense activist pressure to make significant and far-reaching changes in how natural resources are governed.[5]

Managing the supply chain for these critical minerals is not a simple task, since the network of transactions involved in moving stones from mines into the hands of consumers is extensive and complex. As an example, a single telecommunications company might use around 35 manufacturers for the final product, 60–80 intermediate parts suppliers, and over 1,000 commodity suppliers. Only a tiny percentage of the final product contains any of the conflict minerals—a 2 kilogram (4.5 pound) laptop contains 10 grams of tin, 0.6 grams of tantalum, 0.3 grams of gold, and 0.0009 grams of tungsten (Schuh and Strohmer 2012). The production process for each mineral alone takes many steps from mine to smelter, involving miners (often small-scale artisanal ones), consolidators, negociants, comptoirs, traders, and finally the smelters themselves (ITRI 2009).

The idea of mitigating conflict by doing something about natural resources arose within the context of the end of the Cold War and the outbreak of longrunning and brutal civil wars, particularly in the Great Lakes region of Africa. UN sanctions throughout the 1990s had done little to bring the bloodshed to an end in Angola, Sierra Leone, the DRC, and elsewhere, despite increasingly narrowly targeted sanctions policies (so-called "smart sanctions") (Cortright and Lopez 2002). Activists horrified by the ongoing bloodshed and violence began to look for new alternatives.

We can date the turn toward industry as an important target for leverage to a series of events: high-profile reports by the activist group Global Witness on Angola, which called out oil and financial firms on their contributions to the bloodshed; the activism of Ian Smillie and his NGO Global Partnership Africa

---

[3] The raw materials are cassiterite, from which tin is extracted; wolframite, which is processed into tungsten; coltan, which is an African name for the columbite-tantalite ore that tantalum comes from; and gold ore.

[4] These conflicts are winding down, raising the interesting question of what to do with conflict minerals governance when there are no longer conflicts.

[5] The main gold, tin, and tungsten producing country today is China, but the DRC is a main producer of the world's gem diamonds and tantalum (US Geological Survey 2015).

on the role of diamonds in fueling conflict in Sierra Leone; and the Fowler Report to the UN Secretary-General on sanctions-busting, which named the firms and governments involved in evading the sanctions (Global Witness 1998, 1999; Fowler 2000; Smillie, Gberie, and Hazleton 2000). This shift to target business was reinforced by a ground-breaking report, *The Business of Peace*, which made the business case for getting the private sector involved in conflict prevention and peacemaking (Nelson 2000). The role of business in conflict and conflict prevention was taken up by the newly created UN Global Compact in one of its first public policy dialogues, which further reinforced the emerging agenda on business and conflict (Haufler 2001).

The response to the outcry against the use of minerals to finance war led to the creation of a series of transnational governance initiatives. They set standards for business behavior, promote transparency and due diligence in supply chains, and establish mechanisms of assurance—certification systems, chain-of-custody management, reporting, auditing, due diligence, traceability, and general risk management. They are intended to define legitimate trade in minerals, and through this, undermine illegitimate minerals as a means to finance bloodshed.

The Kimberley Process and the Extractives Industry Transparency Initiative were the first and most prominent of these governance schemes.[6] These are both multi-stakeholder initiatives—although states are the official members, industry and civil society groups play a key role. In recent years, the tin and gold sectors established private sector governance of their supply chains, and they are also beginning to be created for coltan and tungsten. In addition, there are some international organizations involved in this arena, such as the UN Expert Group for the DRC and the OECD. Currently, both the United States and the European Union have conflict minerals legislation, although the US provisions have been challenged in court. All of these governance initiatives were debated and created between 2000 and 2015.

The first initiative that gained traction was what came to be known as the Kimberley Process, in which multiple stakeholders responded to the outcry against conflict or "blood" diamonds (Westerwinter 2014). The UN General Assembly adopted a resolution in 2000 supporting the certification of "clean" rough diamonds from conflict-free regions. By the end of the year, the first meeting of diamond producers, consumers, and activists met in Kimberley, South Africa, to discuss how to establish a certification regime. By 2003, the Kimberley Process Certification Scheme (KPCS) was implemented. It consists of an industry-led system of certification and chain of custody warranties for rough

---

[6] A related initiative is the Voluntary Principles on Human Rights, which sets standards for security forces (Avant 2005, 2007).

diamonds, implemented through the World Diamond Council; and a trade regime in which member states committed not to export or import uncertified stones. Conflict diamonds were defined as stones from rebel-held territory. The major consuming and producing states joined the KPCS; the World Diamond Council and two NGOs—Global Witness and Partnership Africa Canada (founded by Smillie)—were officially observers but participated directly in negotiating and implementing the regime. Almost the entire diamond industry participates in the Kimberley Process.

Around the same time, at the World Summit on Sustainable Development in Johannesburg in September 2002, British Prime Minister Tony Blair first proposed the Extractive Industries Transparency Initiative (EITI). Blair intended from the beginning for the EITI to be adopted widely and to evolve into a multilateral program, which it has done (see http://eiti.org). The EITI requires extractive sector companies to publish what they pay to governments, governments must publish what they receive, and the two accounts must be audited and reconciled. It was aimed primarily at reducing corruption but was also viewed as a tool to prevent violent conflict. Corporations are not official members of the EITI. It is governments that join and pass legislation to support their commitment. However, the extractive companies are obviously important players in this initiative and they can declare their support for it. Today, over forty large oil, gas, and mining companies have declared their support and work with national EITI groups. Three major industry associations have also declared their support for the EITI: the American Petroleum Institute, the International Organization of Oil and Gas Producers, and the International Council on Mining and Metals. In addition, a group of financial firms has stated their formal support for the program. About a dozen NGOs work with the EITI at the international level, while civil society groups work with it at the local level. Unlike the other initiatives, the EITI is not about governing the supply chain, but it is a prominent effort that influenced other governance schemes for conflict minerals that followed.

After this initial burst of attention to the extractives sector, the next stage focused on oversight of supply chains linking end users to the raw materials. Activist organizations such as Global Witness and the Enough Project had been pointing to these other raw materials as "conflict commodities" for a while, but initially it was the diamond campaign that gained the most attention. This second phase of activism produced a range of initiatives to establish standards of "due diligence," "responsible sourcing," and various certification, monitoring, and auditing systems.[7] Some of these were driven by major buyers, such as

---

[7] Due diligence refers to the obligation to know your business partners; responsible sourcing obligates you to trace the origins of the materials you use; and transparency requires public reporting on due diligence efforts and other information about your business.

the electronics sector, which had come under fire for obtaining critical minerals from regions where corruption and conflict dominate society—leading to a campaign against "blood coltan" in cell phones (i.e., using coltan from the DRC region). Other campaigns focused on the mineral producers, and still others focused attention on firms somewhere in the middle of the supply chain. The story is a complicated one, with different sets of actors working on governance initiatives at multiple levels.

Around the same time that the Kimberley Process was established in 2003, activists began targeting the electronics industry and minerals such as coltan (a source of tantalum) and gold. In response in 2004, the electronics industry formed the Electronic Industry Citizenship Coalition to put forth a general code of conduct to promote corporate social responsibility. It worked with the Global eSustainability Initiative (GeSI)—a partnership between industry and NGOs—to study the feasibility of supply chain transparency with regard to tantalum sourcing, later adding gold, tin, and tantalum—the 3TG minerals (Resolve 2010). They identified smelters as a chokepoint in the production process, and worked with the tin industry association ITRI to develop and implement a smelter certification program in 2009.[8] Unlike the KPCS, the main focus is a key node in the middle of the industry value chain—the smelters—instead of the producers or the end users. The tin industry itself is, through ITRI, implementing a Tin Supply Chain Initiative (iTSCI) focusing on due diligence and conformity with other governance schemes (OECD Due Diligence, Conflict Smelter Scheme, and US Dodd-Frank reporting requirements).

Negotiations over transnational governance of all conflict minerals together centered around the OECD, which initiated a multi-stakeholder discussion in 2009 on standards for "due diligence," which overlapped with the due diligence standards established by the UN Group of Experts on the DRC. Regional schemes include a tracking and certification system proposed by the International Conference on the Great Lakes Region (ICGLR) in 2006, which led to the Regional Initiative against the Illegal Exploitation of Natural Resources. This regional organization is working closely with the OECD, the UN Group of Experts, and the ITRI (discussed later). Individual governments of the ICGLR[9] also are pursuing their own national certification systems (Blore and Smillie 2011). The most significant change in conflict minerals governance, however, is the US Dodd-Frank reform legislation, which includes a provision

[8] The CFS is a voluntary audit program that verifies whether a smelter obtains 3TG minerals from the DRC region. Smelters must follow the OECD guidelines for due diligence in identifying non-conflict suppliers.

[9] Members are: Angola, Burundi, Central African Republic, Republic of Congo, Democratic Republic of Congo, Kenya, Uganda, Rwanda, Sudan, Tanzania, and Zambia.

on conflict minerals reporting. Section 1502 of the Dodd-Frank reform bill imposes reporting requirements on companies listed on US stock markets that use conflict minerals, establishing transparency and reporting requirements.[10]

In the last few years, industry-led supply chain initiatives have joined this complex of multi-stakeholder and state initiatives. Industry initiatives generally reference the OECD Due Diligence Guidelines, the EITI, and the US regulations. The tin industry association, ITRI, was the leader in addressing conflict minerals after diamonds, and it created a Supply Chain Initiative (iTSCI) to assure due diligence in the supply chain.[11] The World Gold Council lagged behind, proposing its own system of due diligence in 2013 (the OECD then added an addendum on gold to its Due Diligence Guidelines). The World Gold Council also negotiated an agreement with the London Bullion Market Association and the Responsible Jewellery Council to accept each other's third-party audits for their own individual programs.[12] As you can see, in many cases the various transnational governance initiatives are deliberately linked with each other, subjecting companies to more than one set of standards and expectations.

This is only a brief overview of the conflict minerals scene in general. It gives a sense of how complicated this one small issue area has become, and highlights the surprisingly large number of overlapping governance efforts. They vary in terms of which actors are involved, what part of the supply chain they seek to regulate, and how stringent are their conditions. This discussion is necessarily limited by its focus on industry actors alone. A complete understanding of conflict minerals would need to take account of the role of transnational and domestic activism, state interests, and the participation of intergovernmental organizations in the outcomes I explore here (Westerwinter, this volume).

All these governance systems were created within the last decade, but in two waves: the initial stage with the KPCS and EITI, both of which are comprehensive multi-stakeholder organizations; and then a variety of conflict minerals initiatives at all levels which dribbled out over the succeeding half-decade. Passage of US legislation in 2010 spurred industry to develop standards to meet the requirements of the Dodd-Frank rules, and negotiations within the European Union on similar legislation creates further pressure on industry. Even with

---

[10] If a company sources from the DRC region, it must report to the SEC and publicly disclose information about its due diligence efforts. The rule has been challenged in court and significantly weakened.

[11] The ITRI system will be in line with existing supply chain initiatives—the OECD Due Diligence Guidance, the EICC/GeSI Conflict Free Smelter program, and the US SEC reporting requirements. The iTSCI is aimed at companies up and down the supply chain. The goals of the program are to develop verifiable chain of custody/traceability information, risk assessment, and third party audits.

[12] There are other conflict minerals initiatives under consideration in Canada, in the European Union, within different minerals sectors, and by individual companies

Dodd-Frank ratcheting up the pressure, however, we do not have a repeat of the Kimberley Process model—no international conference on conflict minerals, no talk of constructing a single comprehensive governance scheme, and no commitment to certification as the primary means to govern.

Networks and Governance Outcomes

Assessment of the relationship between networks and governance schemes is complicated and rife with methodological and data challenges. This is particularly true for any examination of global supply chains, which may include literally thousands of firms around the world. However, I am simply trying to assess the plausibility of the hypotheses I established earlier concerning contractual and associational relationships. This chapter is a speculative piece, trying to draw out the implications of network participation for governance outcomes. Therefore I am only providing evidence here from a limited set of firms and their membership in a small set of relevant organizations. This very preliminary evidence indicates that centrality within contractual networks is a more important predictor of governance outcomes than associational ties, but that the associational ties are important for producing governance that serves a larger public interest.

I will focus here on the three main governance schemes in which industry was involved: the Kimberley Process for the Certification of Rough Diamonds, the Tin Supply Chain Initiative, and the Conflict-Free Gold Standard (CFGS). The Kimberley Process is industry-driven although states are the official members of the KPCS. The iTSCI and CFGS are both private governance systems in which states do not play a role. They were implemented in succession over the course of the past decade: the Kimberley Process was implemented in 2003, iTSCI was piloted in 2010, and CFGS was published in 2012.

I start by assessing the associational ties in the mining sector, looking at the top firms for each of the five conflict minerals.[13] I identify their membership in key international CSR policy organizations and governance networks in 2000, which is prior to their participation in conflict minerals governance. These include the Mining, Minerals and Sustainable Development project (MMSD), which later led to the creation of the International Council on Mining and Metals; the World Business Council for Sustainable Development; and the UN Global Compact (founded in 2000). This provides a first cut—admittedly rough—of how socially embedded and progressive each mineral sector was. The

---

[13] The exact number of top firms varied because some minerals are only produced by a few companies.

list of companies can be seen in table 9.1; companies in italics participate in two or more CSR networks.

The mining sector is particularly interesting because it was one of the first to participate in a global multi-stakeholder CSR process. The Global Mining Initiative was launched in 1998 by the CEOs of the nine largest mining companies in response to the increasing activism against the detrimental impact of mining on the environment. They agreed that "the industry needed to rethink the way in which it was arguing its case" (Littlewood 2000). They established the Mining, Minerals and Sustainable Development project, run by outside experts, to review mining practices in light of concerns about sustainable development, and to consider how to improve their practices. One outcome of the project was the establishment of a new organization, the International Council on Mining

Table 9.1 **Top Producers by Revenue in 2000 and Associational Ties**

Gold[a]	Coltan	Tungsten[b]	Tin[c]	Diamond
Barrick Gold[d]	Cabot Inc.	North American Tungsten	Yunnan Tin	DeBeers
Goldcorp	OM Group	Malaga	PT Timah	Alrosa
Yamana Gold	AVX	Pasto Bueno	Malaysia Smelting Corp	BHP Billiton
Agnico-Eagle Mines	Eagle Wings Resources	Bodo	Minsu	Rio Tinto
Eldorado Gold	Trinitech International	Cantung	Thasarco	
Freeport McMoRan	Kemet Electronics Corp	Mittersill	Guangxi China Tin	
Newmont Mining	Vishay Sprague	Panasquiera	Yunnan Chengfeng	
Newcrest Mining	HC Starck	Jangxi Rare Earth Metals	EM Vinto	
Anglogold Ashanti	EPCOS		Metallo Chimique	
Goldfields	George Forrest International		Gejiu Zi-Li	

[a] Forbes, "The Global 2000," April 1, 2012.
[b] http://www.infomine.com/commodities/tungsten.asp, 2012.
[c] ITRI, 2010.
[d] Firms with more than two associational memberships are italicized.

and Minerals (ICMM), which is the main CSR policy organization for the minerals sector. The original nine firms that began the sustainability push are: Anglo American plc, BHP-Billiton, Codelco, Newmont Corporation, Noranda Inc., Phelps Dodge Corporation, Placer Dome Inc., Rio Tinto, and WMC Limited. The founding firms in the ICMM were: Anglo American, AngloGold Ashanti, Barrick Gold, BHP Billiton, Freeport McMoRan, Newmont, JX Nippon, Rio Tinto, Codelco, Phelps Dodge, and Inco. The Global Mining Initiative and ICMM provide us with a baseline of associational ties that are CSR-related.

A second indicator of membership in CSR-related networks is the UN Global Compact, which was founded as a partnership between three UN organizations (UN Environment Programme, UN Human Rights Committee, and the ILO) and major international corporations (Kell and Ruggie 2000; Ruggie 2004; Berliner and Prakash 2012). It was launched in 2000 and one of its first policy dialogues addressed the question of how corporations should operate in zones of conflict (Haufler 2001). Among metals and mining companies, Rio Tinto was the earliest signatory, joining the Global Compact when it launched in 2000. Later participants among the major mining and metals companies included BHP Billiton (2003), AngloGold Ashanti and Newmont (2004), and DeBeers and Barrick Gold (2005). Other major players have joined over the years, with many joining very recently.

A handful of major minerals producers participated in both these CSR organizations from an early date: Rio Tinto stands out as a founding member of both the Global Mining Initiative and the UN Global Compact. BHP Billiton and AngloGold Ashanti were early members of both the ICMM and the Global Compact. Notice that DeBeers did not participate in the Global Mining Initiative or the ICMM. Rio Tinto is a diversified firm with interests in both diamonds and gold, along with interests in the smelting sector, as is BHP Billiton. If, as I speculated above, participation in CSR organizations predisposes a sector toward support for governance schemes, and early participation even more so, we would expect to see quick adoption of these schemes in gold, slower adoption in diamonds, and even slower in tin. We would also expect to find broad public interest governance for gold but more narrowly self-interested governance for tin.

What actually happened is the opposite—a very quick move to adopt a certification system for rough diamonds while a very slow process leading only recently to industry conflict minerals standards for gold. In fact, the Kimberley Process began even before the MMSD report came out, and appears to be completely unrelated to prior participation in major CSR organizations. Gold companies participate in CSR organizations at a higher rate than others, and yet this industry lagged behind the others in developing conflict minerals standards. The major tin companies hardly participated in any organizations at all aside from their sectoral industry association, the ITRI, and only in 2010 piloted their supply chain due diligence standards in the DRC. It is more difficult to evaluate which of these initiatives is more oriented toward narrow industry interest versus broad public interest. The Kimberley Process is the governance scheme that has the strictest standards and enforcement, and therefore the one most likely to reduce conflict. But it is also very clearly designed to bolster the reputation of the diamond industry and re-establish a cartel made up of the "legitimate" traders in diamonds. The conflict mineral standards for gold are much weaker, and clearly cater to the interests of the industry. The Conflict Smelter Scheme, however, has a much clearer public interest aspect to it, and applies across a number of sectors.

The Kimberley Process and the Extractive Industries Transparency Initiative (EITI) were the first transnational governance initiatives affecting the minerals producers, and therefore their participants were not influenced by prior experience in transnational governance.[14] The diamond companies participate in the Kimberley Process primarily through industry associations. Membership in the World Diamond Council, which is the industry actor in the Kimberley Process, includes the World Federation of Bourses, the International Diamond Manufacturers Association, and the Antwerp World Diamond Centre. However, individual firms have been active in the committees that carry out the work of the KPCS. The most prominent is DeBeers, but BHP Billiton and Rio Tinto also have representatives on committees. The EITI, on the other hand, is an organization whose members are states, but companies can express support and participate in deliberations. Rio Tinto has been particularly active in the EITI, partly because it has operations in so many EITI member countries. DeBeers expressed early support but has not been very active. Many firms participate through the ICMM, which channels support from the industry into the EITI process.

If we ignore diamonds and look only at gold and tin, we would expect that the experience of companies participating in the KPCS and EITI would influence their later participation in conflict minerals governance. These companies would have established ties to other firms, allowing them to exchange information, ideas, and experience relatively easily. The list of companies participating in the KPCS and EITI, however, excludes the major tin firms. The tin sector should thus be less likely to support conflict governance schemes, and would be favorable to more narrowly oriented governance schemes. Although the tin industry association ITRI began discussing the idea of a supply chain initiative

---

[14] Following Auld, Bernstein, and Cashore 2008, I distinguish between CSR initiatives that focus on learning versus those that are more about rule-setting and implementation, classifying CSR organizations as the former and transnational governance as the latter. Therefore, the Global Mining Initiative, MMSD project, ICMM, and UNGC all count as CSR organizations, while Kimberley and EITI are TGI. These are not hard and fast categories, and some would argue that all are governance schemes of different sorts.

early on, it did not implement it until 2010 and even then only in a pilot project. However, the tin industry did participate significantly in the Conflict-Free Smelter Scheme, which requires traceability from mine to smelter, certification of conflict-free sourcing and audits of each smelter facility. The CFS itself was an initiative of the electronics industry, however, and not tin.

From this initial survey and comparison across sectors and governance outcomes, it appears that association ties in the form of membership in CSR organizations and prior experience in other transnational governance initiatives have uneven effects. Contractual ties, as we are about to see, appear to be more important to governance in this area. My expectations are that firms that dominate concentrated industries will have more influence than those in less concentrated sectors, and that buyer-driven supply chains will be more likely to adopt governance that is public-interest oriented.

The diamond sector is clearly a producer-driven global supply chain, with DeBeers setting the rules of the game in the form of an international diamond cartel until recently. Diamond mining itself is dominated by a few large firms, although the rest of the supply chain is made up of many smaller enterprises. Once DeBeers decided to do something about the conflict diamonds issue, in an effort to shore up the reputation and market of the industry as a whole, the path toward creation of the Kimberley Process was quick and relatively smooth. Since it controlled so much of the supply chain itself, as a producer and through the Central Selling Organization that auctions rough stones,[15] its support for the Kimberley Process was the key to its rapid and early success. As the position of DeBeers has changed and the cartel has been dissolved, the Kimberley Process has come under increasing criticism. Members have struggled to deal with issues beyond the original conflict diamond definition, such as broader human rights issues raised by the violent takeover by Zimbabwe of the Marange diamond fields.

The tin industry is primarily driven by the buyers and not suppliers in the global supply chain. Tin was organized as a weak cartel until it fell apart in 2005.[16] The top ten firms in the tin sector are all from Asia, primarily China, with Yunnan Tin Company alone producing a large proportion of the world's tin. Although the mining side is concentrated, with relatively few firms, it is the buyers of tin who hold central positions and therefore influence the supply chain the most. These are primarily the major information and communications technology firms, which were the main movers and participants in the

---

[15] The CSO is now the Diamond Trading Company, the marketing and distribution wing for DeBeers.

[16] Trading on the London Metal Exchange was halted when the International Tin Council, made up of the major tin exporting nations, owed too much on their contracts.

Conflict Smelter Scheme. Not one of the top tin mining companies is a member of the ITRI Tin Supply Chain Initiative (iTSCI), and none participate in CSR organizations.

I would have expected to see firms in the gold industry push for a quick and comprehensive certification system. The industry is led by a number of large firms, such as Barrick Gold (the largest), Goldcorp, Newmont, AngloGold Ashanti, Goldfields, Kinross, and others (Brown 2010).[17] Barrick Gold has been a regular participant in both CSR and transnational governance networks. However, while the World Gold Council began discussing the issue in the mid-2000s, it was not until 2013 that the Conflict-Free Gold Standard was published. The standard is primarily about due diligence, traceability, and transparency, and it does not include provisions for certification or auditing. It is a weak standard, with narrow goals, and so far has had limited impact.

This preliminary overview of transnational governance of conflict minerals, and the role of contractual and associational networks in it, reveals a complicated picture. The central position of particular firms (DeBeers) or supply-chain participants (buyers versus suppliers) in contractual networks appears to have more impact on governance outcomes than associational ties. The evidence contradicted some of the initial expectations for how networks would influence governance outcomes. However, when contractual and associational ties line up, it is the CSR networks that appear to influence the interests served by conflict minerals governance efforts.

Networks, Power, and Governance: Conclusion

This chapter began by adopting a relational framework for understanding how corporations influence transnational security governance. Most scholarship in security affairs does not adopt a relational approach, nor does it look at firms as important actors in security affairs. Recent developments in transnational security governance, however, demonstrate the growing role of corporations as an instrument for reducing the incentives for violent conflict. While the traditional approach to understanding firms is not a relational one, the rise of global supply chains has stimulated recent interest in business networks. In this chapter, I speculated about the role of different types of business networks in conferring power to shape transnational security governance, looking at the issue of conflict minerals. Although the evidence I presented is extremely limited and meant

[17] These are the largest firms by market capitalization and outstrip the others by a significant margin.

only to assess the plausibility of taking this approach, it leads to some interesting conclusions.

First, and perhaps not surprisingly, firms that hold a central position in a global supply chain, especially in industries that are highly concentrated, have more power to determine governance outcomes. The character of the supply chain (i.e., whether it is supplier- or buyer-driven) influences whether the resulting governance scheme serves broad public interest or not. Second, the associations that firms join influence governance outcomes when they intersect with the structure of the global supply chain. Membership in associations that represent corporate social responsibility values matters, but only when it is the dominant firms that participate in them.

Further research would be able to explore these conclusions more effectively than I did in this somewhat speculative piece. It would require the systematic collection of data on the structure of global supply chains, and include not just the mining companies, but the entire production chain (traders, polishers, retailers, etc.) including the buyers (the electronics industry and others).[18] This research should also examine membership in a wider range of associations of all types, instead of focusing as I did on those that represent corporate social responsibility values. This would allow a more sophisticated empirical analysis of the way in which different networks influence security governance for conflict minerals.

More significantly, this research would need to include the actors that I deliberately left out of this analysis—the activist organizations, states, and intergovernmental organizations that also participate in shaping governance outcomes. I limited my discussion only to networks among firms in an effort to tease out those dynamics, and focused only on governance in which the private sector was the dominant voice. However, even when the governance is industry-led, it is often shaped by outside actors. For instance, the World Gold Council may have established a conflict-free mineral standard of its own, but it was pushed to do so by activists and influenced by the OECD and national governments. A more sophisticated analysis would include the networks formed among NGOs (for instance, see Carpenter, this volume) or the sort of multi-stakeholder network analysis conducted by Westerwinter (this volume). The timing of the Kimberley Process, and of the later conflict minerals issues, clearly can be linked to the political pressure of transnational activists. Key NGOs first pointed out the indirect complicity of firms in financing rebel violence, and key states and international organizations adopted and amplified the issue. It was the main producer states

---

[18] The data demands for this analysis are formidable, even for only four or five minerals. One of the reasons why so many firms object to traceability systems is that even they do not know all the participants in their supply chains.

that supported the Kimberley Process, and recent urgency regarding conflict minerals can be traced to action by the main consuming state, the United States.

My purpose here was to understand how the position of firms as nodes connecting multiple networks constitutes power and influences the construction of governance. I was particularly interested in understanding more about global supply chains—they are increasingly the subject of concern across a wide range of industries and issues because they obscure the accountability of firms for negative externalities associated with their global reach. Complex supply chains obscure the origins of materials and the conditions in which they are processed, raising a host of concerns. Powerful firms within those networks can impose higher standards on firms connected to them, or they can act in ways that undermine higher standards—either by setting prices and contractual standards that create incentives for socially detrimental outcomes (for instance, incentives for corruption and human rights abuses), or by politically opposing attempts to set higher standards. Therefore, I suspect that the sort of approach I adopted here, looking at the various networks in which firms are embedded, will be useful for understanding transnational governance outcomes in other issue areas (Macdonald 2014).

The multiple overlapping schemes and partial governance we see in the area of conflict minerals is representative of a transnational arena that is in the process of becoming governed. There is a growing consensus that we need transparency, traceability, and due diligence in global supply chains as tools to reduce conflict but little agreement on how these should be implemented. Firms are now embedded in a variety of relationships that support more transparency and accountability in sourcing materials—not just conflict minerals, but across a wide array of commodities they use. There are now an array of actors that support transnational governance of global supply chains, and who have institutionalized their commitments in ways that will be difficult to change.

10

Counter-Piracy in the Indian Ocean

Networks and Multinational Military Cooperation

SARAH PERCY

> Dealing with the enemy is a simple and straightforward matter when
> contrasted with securing close cooperation from an ally.
> —Major General Fox Conner on World War I (quoted in
> Bensahel 1999)

> The total power of a coalition is often less, not more, than the sum of
> its parts.
> —Nora Bensahel (1999, 227)

Attacks on international shipping by pirates operating from Somalia have captured the public imagination and international headlines since the mid-2000s.
Increased attention to the piracy problem has led to the deployment of four different types of multinational naval operation seeking to control Somali piracy: a
NATO-led force (Operation Ocean Shield); an EU force (EUNAVFOR's
Operation Atalanta);[1] a US-led force comprising twenty-four nations (CTF-
151);[2] as well as nations working independently but alongside these three missions (among others: China, India, Japan, Malaysia, and Russia). Alongside these
multilateral naval efforts are associated projects led by various UN agencies, the
African Union, and the League of Arab States, as well as NGOs. The total cost of
piracy off the Horn of Africa, including public and private counter-piracy efforts,
is estimated to be in the region of US$7bn to $12bn annually (Bowden 2010).
This network of naval counter-piracy efforts has provided effective security governance off the Somali coast and in the wider Indian Ocean.

---

[1] Officially, EU-NAVFOR-Somalia, Operation Atalanta. I will use EUNAVFOR or Operation
Atalanta for ease of reading.
[2] Part of Combined Maritime Forces (CMF).

The counter-piracy network has specifically aimed at restoring order in the Indian Ocean by reducing pirate attack. Piracy off the Horn of Africa rose sharply after 2008, with the number of attacks increasing from 24 in that year to 163 in 2009, reaching a high of 172 in 2011. In 2012, the number of attacks fell to 35 and in 2013, there were only 7. Of the 2013 attacks, none successfully resulted in taking a vessel hostage.[3] This rapid decline suggests that international naval missions have achieved effectiveness providing governance in the Indian Ocean and that counter-piracy has been a guarded success (Smith and Chonghaile 2012; Legge 2013; Rayman 2014).[4]

How is it that many disparate states—some of them hostile to one anther— have been able to cooperate to curb piracy? I argue that the counter-piracy network's combination of informal relationships and central hubs are key to its success. The anti-piracy network polices more maritime space more effectively because of its informality. It allows just enough cooperation that states can achieve their goals, without creating so much that formal multinational command is required. Its effective function is all the more remarkable considering that cooperation occurs not just among allies but also between enemies (or at least non-friends). Accordingly, counter-piracy's informal network structure allows unlikely partners to cooperate and successfully aggregate power in order to govern the Indian Ocean, enforcing the international laws and specific UN resolutions on piracy,[5] while protecting shipping.

Key hubs have been crucial for balancing the interests of a wider membership and ensuring coordination. The counter-piracy network overcomes some of the challenges of multinational military cooperation by virtue of these hubs as they perform an essential organizing role, but without creating top-down command structures. The counter-piracy network is a waystation between independent military action and shared command, and as such presents a novel form of multinational military cooperation. [6]

But these hubs have used their positions to generate coordination, not to gain advantage. Indeed the network only functions because it operates in a remarkably egalitarian fashion.[7] If those actors occupying hub positions used their position

[3] http://eunavfor.eu/key-facts-and-figures.

[4] The UN's annual report to the Security Council on Somalia points out that pirates may be turning to other land-based forms of illegal activity, but this does not detract from the maritime governance explored in this chapter. See UN Doc S/2013/412 UN Security Council, "Letter Dated 12 July 2013 from the Chair of the Security Council Committee Pursuant to Resolutions 751 (1992) and 1907 (2009) Concerning Somalia and Eritrea Addressed to the President of the Security Council."

[5] SC Resolution 1851 (2008). The relevant international law is discussed later.

[6] Counter-piracy may be part of a wider trend away from military alliances and more to ad hoc cooperation, an idea to which I will return later (Tertrais 2004, 141).

[7] Terms like "hierarchical," "formal," and "informal" might be confusing in a chapter combining network analysis with an examination of military practice. They have a specific meaning in the

strategically, it would prevent the functioning of the network. The overarching governance goal, however, and the belief that it can only be met by open collaboration has had important recursive effects on the network structure. Although often out of favor in analyses of security studies, functional governance goals play an important part in the success of the anti-piracy efforts.

The multinational naval initiatives bear some resemblance to the networks many have written about as particular organizational forms. They include "those actors working internationally on an issue, who are bound together by shared values, a common discourse, and dense exchanges of information and services" (Keck and Sikkink 1999). They are thus a "form of organization characterized by voluntary, reciprocal, and horizontal patterns of communication and exchange" (ibid., 91).

The notion that militaries accustomed to multinational cooperation requiring strictly delineated command structures and formal modes of interaction could cooperate informally in a flat network with partners who are hostile in different contexts is surprising from a traditional realist perspective. But insights from theories of governance and theories of network theory can help us understand this cooperation and its effectiveness. Functional theories of governance have long pointed to shared goals and a desire to reach them as instrumental to cooperation (Keohane and Martin 1995). Shared concerns over piracy, the existing legal structure, and a past history of cooperation among many players created the potential for broader international cooperation.

Second, the conception of interconnected or nested networks leads us to expect that features of one network can cause effects in other connected networks. The shared discourse among military (and particularly naval) organizations makes it easier for navies to cooperate, even those from very different states. Moreover, the existing networked relationship between the navies forming EUNAVFOR, NATO, and CMF-151 provided a useful cooperative basis on which to extend the network. The fact that piracy is a "Goldilocks phenomenon" magnifies the effect of the existing ease of cooperation. Piracy is serious enough that it demands resources but not so serious that national capitals seize control, and the specifics of the response have often been left to navies to devise. The counter-piracy effort thus bears some similarity to the transgovernmental networks Eilstrup-Sangiovanni (this volume) writes of in arms control.

networks literature, but in military practice "hierarchy" is likely to refer to a command hierarchy. Formal interactions are likely to occur within the command hierarchy, and informal ones outside it. As a result, this chapter will describe a centralized network of military actors where the main hubs do not exercise power over other players as "egalitarian." This captures the idea that the network is centralized but not hierarchically organized in a military sense.

Agreement on the problem, a shared discourse and "maritime code,"[8] and a shared perspective that organizational benefits could be had from coordination were the sparks that led important hubs to orchestrate an informal, flat network of navies that worked to ensure that their efforts were not in conflict. Their success was further aided by the nature of the problem; anti-piracy efforts benefited from coordination but did not require tightly linked efforts.

The counter-piracy network is voluntary, and functions only by virtue of dense and reciprocal exchanges of information and services. It uses structures outside formally articulated operating rules in order to operate. The counter-piracy network is centralized but lacks formal command authority over the whole network, in that no one navy takes priority over the others and all forms of official joint command have been resisted and successfully avoided. The most important hubs cannot dictate action to the less important hubs and nodes, and do not see a benefit in disrupting the flow of information.

Beyond an explanation for effective governance in counter-piracy, this examination of the counter-piracy network makes two important contributions. First, the informal and flat nature of counter-piracy cooperation is part of the reason for its success, and worthy of examination in its own right as a potential model for other types of multinational military cooperation. Second, the counter-piracy network provides solutions to some of the commonly asserted problems of multinational military cooperation.

This chapter proceeds in four sections. First, I outline the various multinational missions involved in counter-piracy and provide a snapshot of how they cooperate in order to provide governance in the Indian Ocean. Second, I explain why the response to Somali piracy has been not only collective but has involved so many disparate states, and why this cooperation has taken this particular networked form. Other types of problem may not have led to this type of network. Third, I consider how the counter-piracy network offers solutions to some of the problems associated with other types of multinational military cooperation. Finally, I examine how the counter-piracy network provides governance, considering whether or not its structure has implications for other types of multinational military cooperation.

The Counter-Piracy Network

This chapter is concerned with the military, specifically naval, counter-piracy network. It is however important to note that a broader network working on

---

[8] The notion of a "maritime code" and of similar naval values was brought up repeatedly by interviewees.

counter-piracy also exists. The Contact Group on Piracy off the Somali Coast (CGPCS)[9] is an umbrella organization that assists a wide variety of international agencies, including the International Maritime Organization (IMO); various UN bodies, such as the UN Office for Drugs and Crime (UNODC) and the UN Development Program (UNDP); regional organizations like the Arab League and the African Union; and multinational naval initiatives. While the wider network is also interesting and worthy of study, I am particularly interested in the part of the network that provides security governance via the exercise of military-based power, which should be a hard test for both functional and network explanations of cooperation and which challenges some existing notions of military cooperation.[10] Moreover, the poorly governed and highly problematic Somali political landscape has meant that while civil society initiatives to counter piracy exist, the bulk of the focus has been on initiatives at sea: security provided by navies and increased focus on preventive measures taken by ships.[11]

Multinational naval counter-piracy is composed of three main organized operations (CTF-151, EU-NAVFOR, and Operation Ocean Shield), accompanied by a number of other states operating outside but in cooperation with these three. This network contains nodes with a very high degree of internal organization and familiarity (NATO); nodes that are internally organized but "new," as in the EU's Atalanta, which is the EU's first ever multinational naval mission;[12] nodes that have much lesser formal organization (CTF-151,[13] which includes a disparate group of nations who have varying degrees of experience of military cooperation); and nodes that are operating independently (China, Russia). All of these nodes are cooperating on counter-piracy, and clearly there is direct

[9] The five groups are: naval and capacity-building coordination and information sharing; legal and judicial issues; shipping industry self-protection; messaging and public information; and disruption of piracy onshore. For details on the Contact Group, see Zach, Seyle, and Madsen 2013. It was created by UN Security Council Resolution (UN SC 1851, 2008) as part of efforts to authorize all reasonable means to control Somali piracy.

[10] In addition networks involving civil society groups and other actors are more common, as evidenced by Keck and Sikkink 1999, Carpenter (this volume), and processes like the Kimberley Process (Westerwinter, this volume).

[11] See the recent EUNAVFOR report on the Contact Group, "Fighting Piracy off the Coast of Somalia," ed. Thierry Tardy, European Institute for Security Studies, 2014.

[12] EUNAVFOR nations are used to operating with each other, but as part of NATO forces rather than explicitly EU forces.

[13] CTF-151 is part of the Combined Maritime Force based with the US Fifth Fleet in Bahrain. It has twenty-seven members including Australia, Bahrain, Belgium, Canada, Denmark, France, Germany, Greece, Italy, Japan, Jordan, Republic of Korea, Kuwait, Malaysia, the Netherlands, New Zealand, Pakistan, Portugal, Saudi Arabia, Seychelles, Singapore, Spain, Thailand, Turkey, UAE, the United Kingdom, and the United States.

membership overlap between the three main nodes (e.g., Canada is in CTF 151 and in NATO; the United Kingdom in Atalanta, NATO, and CTF-151).

Not every member of each group will be at sea at any one time, and smaller nations (like Canada and Australia) may not constantly have a vessel conducting counter-piracy, even though Canadian and Australian officers may be providing headquarters support. Typically vessels spend six months in the region, and during that time may be focused on other tasks as well as counter-piracy.[14]

What Is the Shape of the Network and How Do Its Participants Cooperate?

The counter-piracy network is a centralized network where the main hubs do not manipulate their position. There is no formal military hierarchy over the network.[15] Each of the navies participating in the network is a node. There are several hubs: Working Group 1 (WG1) of the CGPCS, which is closely associated with SHADE (Shared Awareness and Deconfliction, which was created by the Combined Maritime Task Force in 2008);[16] CMF itself, which coordinates CTF-151; Northwood, which is the operational headquarters for EUNAVFOR and for NATO operations; and Maritime Security Centre Horn of Africa (MSCHOA), organized by EUNAVFOR and administering the Internationally Recognized Transit Corridor (IRTC). These hubs have formal contacts, which utilize existing chains of command or modes of communication between militaries. There are also informal contacts, which occur outside official chains of command (for example in informal discussions between officers or, to a lesser extent, in meetings at SHADE).

One of the most interesting puzzles posed by the multinational naval network is how states as diverse as Russia, the United Kingdom, and China achieve successful military cooperation. There are several mechanisms through which the nodes of the network cooperate, and they do so through formal contact via the hubs but also through informal contacts at sea.

MSCHOA allows formal cooperation between nodes through its administration of the Internationally Recognized Transit Corridor (IRTC). The multinational initiatives work closely together to administer the IRTC. The IRTC provides a safe route for shipping that runs from the opening of the Suez Canal along the east coast of Africa. The goal of the IRTC is to ensure that any vessel

---

[14] Combined Maritime Forces also run two other task forces relating to different problems in the region: CTF-150 on general maritime security and CTF-152 on Gulf maritime security.

[15] This chapter will refer to military hierarchy when discussing issues of command authority. This should not be construed as hierarchy in a formal network analysis sense.

[16] SHADE is open to all nations interested in counter-piracy.

in the region is no more than about 20 minutes away from naval assistance in the event of a pirate attack. A ship wishing to transit the corridor enters it at an appointed transit time. Naval vessels are evenly spaced along the corridor. If attacked a ship can radio for help, and typically can resist for 20 minutes (even through passive measures like barbed wire) until naval assistance arrives. Up until 2011, only two ships transiting the corridor on naval instructions were attacked, forcing the pirates to conduct their attacks in more hostile waters of the Indian Ocean.[17] Ships performing this function can come from any one of the four counter-piracy groupings. The IRTC and its functions are coordinated through MSCHOA but are primarily a EUNAVFOR responsibility. Assistance is provided by CTF-151.

Each of the operational headquarters provides a hub for formal, transgovernmental cooperation using official means. NATO and EUNAVFOR headquarters are both located at Northwood, very close together but formally separate. However, it is easy for officers from these two organizations to discuss counter-piracy operations, not least because they share an Officers' Mess. The two operations frequently coordinate activities at Northwood, both inside and outside formal military channels.[18]

The Combined Maritime Force (CMF) headquarters is another important hub. CMF is based in Bahrain and its geographic proximity and multinational composition make it an obvious venue for the discussion and implementation of counter-piracy. CMF has three task forces: CTF-151, focused on piracy; CTF-150, looking at maritime security; and CMF-152, focused on Arabian Gulf cooperation and security. It has twenty-nine members, and is commanded by a US vice admiral with a Royal Navy commodore as deputy. Participation in it is voluntary and each of the navies contributes in different ways over time (such as providing staff officers, vessels, or maritime reconnaissance aircraft).[19]

Working Group 1 (WG1) of the Contact Group is another formal network hub. WG1 brings together "military, industry and government representatives, providing a forum for the exchange of views and concerns between naval forces and civilian actors" (Zach, Seyle, and Madsen 2013). However, WG1 is perhaps most important as the venue for a military organization called SHADE (Shared

<hr/>

[17] For details on the IRTC, see http://www.shipping.nato.int/operations/OS/Pages/Group Transit.aspx; Percy and Shortland 2013.

[18] Interview with Canadian NATO contingent, Northwood, June 2009.

[19] See http://combinedmaritimeforces.com/about/. Interview with Commodore Simon Ancona, May 22, 2013; interview with Captain Robert Slaven, Royal Australian Navy, May 10, 2013; interview with Captain Chris Shay, US Navy, May 10, 2013; interview with Major Andy Dow, Royal Marines, May 10, 2013. Commodore Ancona was, until November 2013, the deputy commander of CMF.

Awareness and Deconfliction) launched by Combined Maritime Forces in December 2008 (before the creation of the Contact Group).[20]

SHADE is centrally important to the operation of the counter-piracy network. It developed synergistically alongside WG1, allowing the latter to act as a forum for states to discuss their ideas, which provided the necessary trust to allow SHADE to work.[21] SHADE helped solve one of the early problems associated with so many navies interested in working on counter-piracy. As Chris Holtby, the first chair of WG1 put it, "some partners did not want to be involved in joint patrolling . . . [there was] real resistance to joint command and control."[22] SHADE is designed to allow navies to share their plans, concerns, and grievances without any attempt to create joint command. As Zach et al. explain, "it is a mechanism for shared awareness—not joint military operations" (2013, 21).

SHADE meets four times a year in Bahrain. The SHADE meetings involve navies but also other participants from WG1 and industry representatives. The meetings provide an important venue for the deconfliction in the group's title to occur but also have provided a crucial area for trust to develop among the various players. It is one of the major venues through which navies operating independently can participate in coordination activities.[23] SHADE is perhaps the most important hub in terms of keeping the three official bodies and independent navies working together.[24] For example, China initially wanted an alternative to the IRTC but was persuaded to participate in it because it saw the advantages of the SHADE mechanism (Zach, Seyle, and Madsen 2013).

There are also informal points of contact between ships at sea, which are necessary because of the significant area which counter-piracy operations must cover. For example, ships may radio or otherwise notify each other of ship movements without going through any of the hubs. The IRTC is one part of the puzzle but ships in the region can also be called upon to assist vessels under attack outside the IRTC, around the Indian Ocean; to monitor suspected pirate vessels (it is easy to confuse pirates and fishermen); and to pursue known pirates (Percy and Shortland 2013). Counter-piracy operations can occur over a vast area throughout the Indian Ocean. Pirate attacks have occurred over a region ranging

[20] Interview with Captain Robert Slaven, Royal Australian Navy, May 10, 2013; interview with Captain Chris Shay, US Navy, May 10, 2013.

[21] Interview with Captain Robert Slaven, Royal Australian Navy, May 10, 2013; interview with Captain Chris Shay, US Navy, May 10, 2013.

[22] Quoted in Zach, Seyle, and Madsen 2013, 21.

[23] Interview with Captain Robert Slaven, Royal Australian Navy, May 10, 2013; interview with Captain Chris Shay, US Navy, May 10, 2013; interview with Major Andy Dow, Royal Marines, May 10, 2013.

[24] Interview with Captain Robert Slaven, Royal Australian Navy, May 10, 2013; interview with Captain Chris Shay, US Navy, May 10, 2013.

from the Seychelles in the west, Madagascar in the south, and as far north as the Gulf of Oman on the Iranian coastline.[25]

Given that different naval vessels from different states will be available at different times and must cover a wide area, counter-piracy would not succeed without an effective communications system. Ships can, of course, use radio to communicate and relay information about suspected pirate vessels. However, this type of communication is also readily listened to by pirates. More interestingly, the UK Foreign and Commonwealth Office (FCO) helped facilitate the spread of an unclassified email system called Mercury Chat that had been used aboard British vessels[26] to all vessels engaged in counter-piracy. Mercury Chat allows a more secure method for ships to contact each other about potential pirate vessels because it does not use open radio channels. This basic mechanism overcomes one of the main challenges to counter-piracy: how vessels from hostile navies can communicate without the transfer of militarily sensitive technology but without broadcasting on the open airwaves.

The hubs of the counter-piracy network are its main information-sharing and coordination points. They are either designed to provide multinational military command (Northwood, CMF) or designed as a forum to facilitate multinational military activity (MSCHOA, SHADE, WG1). The nodes are the individual navies working on counter-piracy, connected both to the hubs but also to each other through information exchange, communication, and coordination at sea. Communication is essential to the operation of the network, and without the central hubs communication would fail.

Why Has the Counter-Piracy Response Taken This Shape?

If the development of a wide-ranging collective network designed to deter and disrupt piracy is puzzling, it is so for two reasons: first, it demonstrates the collective action of so many states, many of whom are unable to cooperate on other issue areas, particularly security issues; and second, it demonstrates cooperation outside a top-down military structure.

Piracy, the Commons, and Naval Interests

There are four reasons so many disparate states can cooperate on counter-piracy. First, piracy is obviously a sea-borne problem and specifically one that occurs

---

[25] For more information see Percy and Shortland 2013.
[26] Interview with Ancona.

on the high seas (where no state is sovereign) as well as in territorial waters. Historically, this has meant that piracy has always been a problem "of the commons" requiring a collective solution (Kraska and Brian 2009). States have had to coordinate their resources to counteract a threat that manifests itself in a space that is not under sovereign control. Furthermore, pirates (as opposed to privateers) are indiscriminate in their attacks: any vessel is usually fair game. This has meant that all states have had an interest in controlling piracy to facilitate trade, a factor which persists today. Pirates operating off the Barbary Coast (now the coast of Libya, Algeria, and Morocco) in the nineteenth century were eventually brought under control by a group of nations including the United States, the Netherlands, and Great Britain.

Second, the specific nature of Somali piracy, particularly its strategic impact and its reliance on kidnap and ransom create pressure for a collective response to solve a problem of the commons. The proximity of Somalia to the Suez Canal and the Gulf of Aden, which are maritime "choke points" for trade, has meant that the piracy problem has greater strategic impact due to potential disruption along these routes, which increases the likelihood of a state response. The fact that Somali piracy is a kidnap and ransom business, combined with the internationalized shipping industry today, usually means that at any one time a large number of states will have an interest in resolving a particular pirate hostage situation: the flag state of the ship in question; the state in which the shipping company is based; and the states from which sailors originate. This provides another pressure for a multinational response. Many states want to, need to, or both want and need to deal with piracy, but cannot do so effectively independently.

Third, the vast maritime space involved in successfully controlling piracy means it is simply impossible for a small number of vessels to provide the information exchange necessary to control piracy successfully. Even before pirates moved operations to the Indian Ocean, the area off the coasts of Somalia and Kenya and in the Gulf of Aden alone is 1.1 million square miles, or the size of the Red Sea and the Mediterranean Sea combined.[27] Some 25,000 vessels transit the Suez Canal annually. No one state, or even a small group of states, has enough ships to cover the entire area, particularly in an era of almost universal defense budget cuts. The solution has been cooperative: the implementation of the IRTC and informal links among different naval contingents to assist ships in distress.[28] The IRTC has had the unintended effect of pushing piracy

---

[27] See http://www.marinelink.com/news/article/uss-boxer-counterpiracy-in-gulf-of-aden/330 160.aspx for more details.

[28] There are legal obligations for ships on the high seas to assist each other in the event of a pirate attack.

farther out to the Indian Ocean. As the pirates realized that the IRTC was no longer a good option for attacking vessels, they sought new prey further off-shore, going as far east as the Seychelles. Covering such vast distances requires a large number of naval vessels, more than a small group of nations could provide. Coordinating between these navies over vast distances is a main reason for the networked form of the cooperation, examined in depth later.

Fourth, all of these reasons for a collective response to counter-piracy are supplemented by the fact that navies are strongly interested in counter-piracy and have advocated for a naval solution. Navies themselves have a strong interest in raising their profiles in light of defense cuts in many nations and the prominent role played by land forces in recent conflicts (Iraq and Afghanistan). The issue of "sea blindness," or of a lack of recognition of the importance of navies in a wider military service, concerns many navies (Percy and Shortland 2013). Counter-piracy is a high-profile way to demonstrate naval capacity. This may provide a partial explanation of why navies have been so keen to cooperate: successful cooperation can demonstrate their relevance.

Why the Multinational Response Has Taken an Egalitarian, Informal Form

While the pressures explain why states have collectively responded to piracy, they do not necessarily explain why states have chosen to create an ad hoc, egalitarian network to deal with piracy rather than a more formal multinational military mission. This section outlines five reasons for cooperation to take a network form.

First, the size of the maritime space, as argued earlier, requires a large number of vessels to patrol. These vessels must be able to share information swiftly and quickly to cooperate when suspected pirates are spotted. Simply having a large number of navies present without the ability to coordinate would not solve the problem. Moreover, any difficulties that resulted from an increased presence on the part of so many navies would not have a formal place for resolution.

Not only do all navies need to share information, they cannot do it only inside existing command structures, otherwise they would exclude states serving an important role in patrolling the wide area. Given that many states are unaccustomed to cooperating on security matters, or in some cases hostile, they cannot share command and they must also have a venue to share their concerns.

The network has mechanisms for information exchange, and also, crucially, a forum for members to discuss problems and "deconflict" (SHADE). SHADE, MSCHOA, and the Mercury Chat system allow the counter-piracy network to cover huge distances at low cost and without the establishment of a command hierarchy that would prevent the participation of a maximum number of states.

Although the counter-piracy network is centralized, and ties between nodes center around the main hubs, it nonetheless relies on widespread communication. Without communication between all players, the network would fail. Accordingly, the counter-piracy network functions through a "dense exchange of information and services" (Keck and Sikkink 1999). The IRTC works because of the high levels of communications between ships at sea and between the command and deconfliction hubs on land: information about commercial shipping and its location, timings through the corridor, and positions of naval vessels is essential. Ships also communicate when they see suspected pirate vessels operating in the Indian Ocean or Gulf of Aden so that these vessels can be monitored and apprehended if necessary. Without information-sharing it would be impossible to conduct counter-piracy over such massive distances.[29] The purpose of SHADE is to make sure that this dense web of communications is working without placing it under a hierarchical command structure.

Second, the presence of both the European Union and NATO, itself another curiosity of counter-piracy, has created two hubs where one might ordinarily be expected. Given that the organizations have such similar memberships, at first glance it might seem unduly costly to replicate counter-piracy missions. The NATO mission came first, but Nicolas Sarkozy, during his 2007 presidency of the European Union, spotted an opportunity to achieve one of the hitherto unachievable goals of European cooperation: defense. The year 2007 saw a sharp growth in pirate attacks, and Sarkozy quickly recognized that this was an area where the European Union could finally achieve successful military cooperation. Operation Atalanta helps demonstrate that the European Union can exercise military power independently from NATO (Germond 2013). No doubt this is in part because it is substantially out of area and is an issue on which all member states can easily agree, in addition to all the pressures to make counter-piracy collective as noted earlier.

The presence of NATO and the European Union, along with CTF-151, means that even the parts of the network that are themselves organized along traditionally hierarchical military lines are less hierarchical than they would be outside the network. At any given time British officers can be serving in CMF-151, in EUNAVFOR, and in NATO's Ocean Shield. While these officers are quick to point out that they are very aware of which "hat" they wear when they are part of different missions,[30] it breaks down the boundaries between

---

[29] I elaborate on this point later.

[30] Interviews with Captain Christopher Shay, US Navy; Major Andrew Dow, Royal Marines; Captain Robert Slaven, Royal Australian Navy, May 10, 2013.

organizations. The perspectives of, for example, a British officer working in CMF-151 will be informed by the relationships he or she has with other British officers in EUNAVFOR or in NATO. Lines of communication accordingly run through the usual command hierarchies but also between them as officers from one national navy communicate with each other across several different network hubs. Interviews with officers at CMF emphasized that CMF as an organization is very informal compared with other military organizations, and that the command hierarchy functions differently.[31] The blurring of lines between EUNAVFOR, Ocean Shield, and CMF-151, and the relatively informal nature of CMF may contribute to a higher level of comfort with operating as a network. Personnel in these groups are comfortable with each other because of a tradition of cooperating within and between all three groups.

Third, there are established international laws about piracy that provide a clear framework for international counter-piracy. The necessity of treating piracy as a collective action problem is borne out by the fact that piracy is considered to be a crime under customary international law, and pirates themselves are to be treated as "enemies of all mankind." The latter point allows the boarding of any ship suspected of pirate activity, regardless of its flag state (Roach 2010). Piracy is also subject to extensive international agreement as part of the UN Convention on the Laws of the Sea (UNCLOS), which underlines the customary international law provisions and updates them in light of modern understandings of territorial waters (including exclusive economic zones). Piracy represents an unusual point of uncontroversial and developed international legal agreement (Guilfoyle 2010), which allows a robust legal regime for the conduct of counter-piracy missions.[32] In particular, the laws of the sea allow unequivocal action by states (on the high seas, outside territorial waters) to board suspected pirate vessels, search them, and detain pirates and seize pirate vessels.[33]

The only ambiguity affecting Somali piracy was the question of whether pirates could be pursued once they entered Somali territorial waters. This ambiguity was resolved by SC resolution 1816 (2008), which "allowed states to take the same steps with respect to piracy in the Somali territorial sea as the law of piracy permits on the high seas" (Roach 2010). The nature of the operations allowed has thus been clear from early on.

[31] Interviews with Captain Christopher Shay, US Navy; Major Andrew Dow, Royal Marines; Captain Robert Slaven, Royal Australian Navy, May 10, 2013.

[32] The legal grounds on which to base counter-piracy are relatively straightforward; however, implementing them has been more difficult. Practical problems of how to arrest, try, and detain suspected pirates are legion and still not resolved (Percy and Shortland 2013).

[33] Commodore Ancona further reiterates the idea that strong legal authority facilitated counter-piracy. Interview.

The existence of clear international legal grounds for counter-piracy, combined with their universal acceptance, is an important background factor that facilitated the swift formation of a network without having to haggle about the nature of interdiction operations. While all navies have different rules of engagement regarding piracy, the clear legal framework results in fewer debates about acceptable action. In other words, there are not many "caveats" placed on participation in the network, a problem that bedevils other types of multinational military cooperation (Saideman and Auerswald 2012, 67). Moreover, broad agreement that navies can independently interdict pirates at sea means that no multinational command structures are necessary in order to do it. Unlike, for example, an operation to establish a no-fly zone, a humanitarian intervention, or a ground war, it is possible to have military actors working relatively independently at sea where on land or in the air it would cause chaos. Under multinational command, most states put their forces under "caveats," indicating the actions they will or will not undertake in pursuit of the mission. In Afghanistan, there were between fifty and eighty such caveats, and their presence "has given insurgents breathing room and forced the United States to nearly double the number of troops deployed." The absence of multinational command also means that states do not have to put as many caveats in place: they know what they are allowed to do and can decide what to do or not do independently without discussing it with a multinational command. However, operations would be less effective with no coordination, which means that the information-sharing processes are necessary to make the operation work.

Fourth, the special nature of navies provides not only an easier exchange of information and services but also the shared values and discourses Keck and Sikkink (1999) consider to be essential for informal, flat networks. It has been widely accepted that militaries are isomorphic, in that institutional constraints, such as military professionalism, create highly similar organizations across national boundaries (Ralston 1990; Thomson 1994; Finnemore 1996; Farrell 1998). Accordingly, we can think of militaries as part of a network, sharing common perceptions, values, and discourses that can lead to bonds and trust even when their national political leaderships disagree.[34] The similarities between navies are perhaps even more profound. Operating at a far remove from national capitals and facing the shared dangers of mariners, navies see themselves as very similar. Moreover, all navies operate in the same place (the ocean) rather than land forces, which may operate in vastly different spaces from each other. Navies are thus more interoperable than land forces: in other words, their modes of

---

[34] Carpenter (this volume) elaborates on the importance of common perceptions and ideas within transnational advocacy networks.

operation are more familiar to each other. This familiarity allows the development of strong interpersonal ties between navies and interlocutors at SHADE, which in turn strengthen the network.[35] As Commodore Simon Ancona puts it, in counter-piracy the "maritime has been the glue . . . before [navies] even start to talk there has been a bond that has been extraordinarily useful."[36]

Finally, many of these reasons represent the fact that piracy is a "Goldilocks" phenomenon. It is just serious enough to require international attention, but not so serious that it requires a military response closely overseen by state capitals and the involvement of different military services. While counter-piracy is multinational, it is also single-service, which makes it easier to coordinate and reduces the pressure for more formal and hierarchical organization. The relatively hands-off approach has facilitated creative solutions, such as SHADE and Mercury Chat. If the problem were more serious, this freedom would be diminished, and if it were less serious, it would not require a naval solution.

Networks, Counter-Piracy, and Other Forms of Multinational Military Cooperation

Multinational military cooperation can take many forms: alliances, alignments, coalitions, and strategic partnerships.[37] Alliances, defined by Snyder (1997) as "formal associations of states for the use (or non-use) of military force, in specified circumstances, outside their own membership," have a degree of formality and permanence not present in counter-piracy (Rice 1997; Wilkins 2012).

There is a significant literature debating the definitions and specific nature of different types of multinational military cooperation, from theories of alliances[38] to discussions of variant types of military cooperation and their future development (Wilkins 2012). Situated within this literature, the counter-piracy network as described is neither a formal nor an informal alliance (involving some type of security guarantee) (Tertrais 2004, 136). Its closest analogue is an ad hoc coalition. However, although other ad hoc coalitions are also "time limited" in that they arise in relation to a specific issue, the examples given by Tertrais (2004) and by Wilkins (2012), who also considers the variants of military cooperation, all are ad hoc only in the sense of their assembly around an issue. Once created,

---

[35] Cooley and Nexon (this volume) explore interpersonal ties.

[36] Interview with Ancona.

[37] For an extensive discussion of the various types and the relationship between them, see Wilkins 2012.

[38] The literature on alliance theory is important but not directly relevant here (Walt 1983; Snyder 1997).

these coalitions create formal command structures and usually grow out of pre-existing alliances with a history of prior military cooperation.[39]

However, the aspect of the literature on multinational military cooperation most pertinent to this article focuses on how multinational military groups, whatever their status, perform in war or perform their tasks (Rice 1997; Bensahel 1999; Weitsman 2003, 2010; Saideman and Auerswald 2012). Saideman and Auerswald (2012, 81) point out that there is still minimal scholarship on the question of how alliances function in war. The challenges of arranging the collective operation of a variety of organizations, all of which are hierarchically organized, deal with the use of lethal force, possess their own organizational traditions and histories, and all reflecting national interests which may vary even when they are united in a common cause, has proved famously problematic as the quote from the American General Fox Conner opening this article demonstrates. Problems with multinational military command are predominantly associated with developing effective command and control of multinational forces, and how to overcome problems of trust within the group.

Effective Command and Control

Establishing effective command and control in a multinational military operation is challenging, for the obvious reason that cooperative endeavors will not occur "unless participating states share an interest in a specific situation, and they cannot achieve their common goals if their members work at cross-purposes" (Bensahel 1999). Even in organizations with extensive experience of military cooperation under conditions of both peace and war, like NATO, collective operations "bear a heavily political cost, relying on procedures that require constant negotiation to reach consensus" (Tertrais 2004, 141).

The implicit and sometimes explicit assumption is that multinational military operations will struggle to achieve unity of command, and that the cost of doing so is either significant and repeated negotiation; the presence of "caveats" whereby national contingents refuse to undertake certain activities (Saideman and Auerswald 2012); and even the withdrawal of national contingents when command decisions are unpalatable (Tago 2009). Command and control problems are, under these constraints, significant and potentially unsolvable problems of multinational military cooperation (Rice 1997, 152; Bensahel 1999;

---

[39] Tertrais identifies operations in Iraq and Afghanistan, and specifically considers "why Washington finds ad hoc coalitions under US command" attractive—in other words, issue based coalitions that maintain conventional command structures (Tertrais 2004).

Weitsman 2003, 243). Bensahel (1999) argues that coalition operations should "minimize multiple or overlapping chains of command."

The counter-piracy network provides an unexpected set of solutions to the problems of multinational command and simply avoids many of the constraints of multinational command, not least because of its explicitly flat nature. The counter-piracy network has never attempted to create a single, hierarchical command. Indeed, the creation of SHADE was intended to avoid unified command and so encourage potentially reluctant partners, as discussed earlier. The use of structures like SHADE, designed to facilitate cooperation while ensuring independence, allowed national contingents to accept caveats and even withdraw without challenging the overall structure of the mission. In other words, because the counter-piracy network avoids institutionalizing a formal, hierarchical command structure it creates fewer and less specific expectations with respect to actors' behavior and leaves them freer to pursue their own agendas under the broader umbrella of the cooperative network.[40]

The network allows member states to follow their own agendas underneath an overarching umbrella that encourages but does not demand cooperation and makes repeated negotiation less important. The existence of a clear, shared goal and SHADE's facilitative role means that all efforts are directed toward the same objective and problems can be solved without resorting to traditional hierarchies. In other words, in a traditional multinational command, the force commander would direct national contingents to perform tasks required by the mission while respecting different national caveats. In counter-piracy, navies pursue their own complementary agendas while ensuring that these agendas do not create conflict (hence, SHADE is a *deconfliction* measure). States are not required to do anything by the wider network (even if they may be in their respective groupings required to do something).

The informality of the counter-piracy network also provides states, whatever their size, with an additional incentive to participate in the network. The ability to opt-in and opt-out of network activities not only means states and navies retain flexibility, but it also means that partners are not so easily criticized for failing to pull their weight in the network. Saideman and Auerswald (2012) point out that placing restrictions on activity in multinational operations can damage national reputations. Considerable restrictions in Afghanistan damaged the elite reputation of the German armed forces, and they are now viewed as "passive and unreliable." Not only does the ad hoc nature of the piracy network preserve and protect state interests, it also means that states can offer minimal

---

[40] Eilstrup-Sangiovanni (this volume) shows that in a situation of diverging interests the lack of institutionalized expectations opens up room for central hubs to bias agenda-setting and policy-making.

or highly restricted assistance without suffering such severe reputational consequences. Just being in the network assists the operation of the network.

Problems of Trust and Their Solution

Trust is of paramount importance in effective military cooperation (Bensahel
1999). States have to trust that their partners will deliver on their promises;
not renege from agreements; and that the benefits of the military arrangement
outweigh the costs (Leeds 2003). Mechanisms that build trust are thus equally
important.[41] Bensahel (1999) points out that states will be reluctant to trust
each other enough to create the sort of command and control that will effectively allocate resources and plan missions. She says that states will be reluctant
to make these arrangements when "they know that alliance commitments are
relatively easy to break, and that increased cooperation can lead to an increased
risk of entrapment."

Many of the unique structures of the counter-piracy network, either deliberately skirt the problems of creating trust between states who are adversaries in
other contexts or foster just enough trust to facilitate the operations of the network. First of all, because states are not putting their navies under a single multinational command, the need for trust is less. The NATO and EU missions use
established structures of multinational command among relatively trusted allies
and it may be that within these groups some problems of multinational command arise. However, in the wider network, the ad hoc character of the cooperation means that states need not trust each other to the same degree, as no one
state in charge of multinational command directs any other state to do anything.

The counter-piracy network is in fact built around a recognition that problems of trust could otherwise scupper the network. Mercury Chat, after all,
exists because no more secure communications could be used among all participants. Many navies are necessary in order to allow counter-piracy to function
properly, but trust prevents them from being placed under multinational command. SHADE is a mechanism that facilitates a modicum of trust but exists predominantly because the states involved in counter-piracy could not trust each
other enough to have more serious multinational command.

Finally, the counter-piracy network's focus on technical, maritime issues
lends itself both to developing trust between naval players (if not between their
states) and innovative solutions. Bensahel (1999, 238) argues that "trust and
personal relationships among commanders play an important role in binding

---

[41] The problem of "caveats" noted earlier is a classic example of why trust is an issue in military
cooperation.

multinational coalitions together" and proposes several mechanisms through which traditional coalitions or alliances can build trust. The basic similarity between navies and the notion of a maritime code, as outlined earlier, means that while states may not trust each other, individual navies start from a shared background that facilitates communication and creates a modicum of trust among diverse actors. Finally, the fact that the bulk of cooperation on counter-piracy is maritime-based and technical means that good solutions have come from the field, rather than from the command hierarchy itself. Commodore Simon Ancona points out that when the commodores have been out of the room, good solutions have occurred, and that most of the success of counter-piracy comes from solving "nitty gritty issues" and good solutions in that context must "come from the factory floor" rather than senior leadership. Once again, the fact that the senior leadership can stay out of the factory floor comes, at bottom, from the fact that piracy is not a matter for high strategy.

The Goldilocks Phenomenon

Finally, the relative success of counter-piracy operations, and its adoption of novel techniques and reliance on a non-hierarchical structure, is only possible because, as argued earlier, piracy is a problem requiring the attention but not the extensive interest of most participating states. Commodore Ancona points out that, in relation to Mercury Chat, no Western country would use this type of system against a well-matched adversary, and that the lower the threat, the easier the communication between allies. The more complex the threat, the more secure communications need to be.[42] If state interests were significantly ignited, then the sorts of problems of repeated negotiation that Bensahel identifies would be too great to be dealt with by SHADE. It is relatively easy to avoid the problem of caveats, because any navy contributing can assist even while following national orders; this would not be the case in a more severe conflict or where states were directed to perform more assertive tasks. I will return again later to a discussion of whether piracy is a *sui generis* case.

Conclusion: Counter-Piracy, Power, and Governance

This final section considers three points: first, the role of power within this centralized network; second, how effectively the network provides governance; and

---

[42] Interview with Ancona.

third, whether counter-piracy cooperation is completely *sui generis* and therefore only of limited interest for scholars of international relations.

The editors of this volume have asked us to consider how network theory can be helpful for understanding security governance. In this case, the egalitarian counter-piracy network, with hubs that ensure rather than preclude cooperation, has collaborated to provide security governance in the Indian Ocean and reduce piracy. The network's efforts, along with measures adopted by shipowners,[43] resulted in a dramatic reduction in piracy in 2013 as mentioned earlier. Navies continue to provide governance by patrolling the region, and there is relatively widespread agreement that without the naval presence piracy will again increase.[44]

Counter-piracy demonstrates that views about governance and its goals can have a recursive effect on the development of networks to provide governance. The historical international legal framework provides clear expectations that navies will act to prevent piracy and very few new policies have been required. Even the UN Security Council resolutions have been to clarify the existing rules rather than devise new ones. Collective action has been historically seen as not only possible but essential to deal with piracy as a problem "of the commons." The presence of many navies in this region and the continued desire for them to stay there—both on the part of national leadership and the organizations themselves—further encourages collective action. Moreover, counter-piracy has a relatively simple governance aim: rather than exercising governance on all issues in the Indian Ocean, it is restricted to the reduction of pirate attack. There are only a few tasks involved: protecting shipping, providing surveillance in the Indian Ocean, and intervening when an attack occurs. While coordination difficulties may occur, when they do, SHADE is designed to reduce any resulting problems.

While counter-piracy has been effectively providing governance, in the sense that pirate attacks have decreased, it is undoubtedly useful to probe the question of for whom counter-piracy has been effective. Reducing piracy, given its status as a problem of the global commons, can be perceived to have widespread benefit. Shipping can move faster, more cheaply, and more safely; seafarers are at less risk of capture. Within Somalia itself, however, the end of piracy may not be a clear-cut benefit. There are few other economic

---

[43] Other factors have also played a role, including the introduction of Best Management Practices (BMP). BMP are measures taken by shipowners to reduce the likelihood of pirate attack and increase defences against piracy. See http://eunavfor.eu/wp-content/uploads/2013/01/bmp4-low-res_ sept_5_20111.pdf. However, navies have been instrumental in devising and encouraging the use of BMP, making assessing independent impact difficult.

[44] Interview with Commodore Ancona, Captain Slaven. See also Smith and ni Chonghaile 2012.

opportunities for Somalis. Piracy had the local advantage of preying on outsiders, meaning that it provided employment without victimizing locals (Percy and Shortland 2013).[45] As piracy has become more controlled, there is evidence that the criminal networks supporting piracy are instead turning to other types of crime, including kidnapping[46] and charcoal smuggling, and some of this illegal activity is conducted jointly with the Islamist group Al-Shabaab (Coker and Paris 2013; Gettleman and Kulish 2013). This activity is bound to have greater local impact than counter-piracy. Exercising effective governance in the case of Somali piracy means focusing on where effective governance has actually been achieved, and this has been at sea rather than on land. Accordingly, crime has been pushed back into the less governed space of Somalia itself. Counter-piracy has not been successful in improving governance within Somalia.

Counter-piracy's network structure unquestionably allows it to exercise greater power than navies could individually, or even as separate multinational groupings. Moreover, navies themselves are using the network to enhance their own power in an era of "sea blindness" and military cutbacks. Avant and Westerwinter point out that network membership can be a source of power, and for individual navies, participating in the counter-piracy network increases their visibility and potentially their power in domestic discussions about military spending. Counter-piracy raises naval profiles at relatively minimal direct cost.

One unusual feature of the counter-piracy network is that hubs do not manipulate their network position in order to increase their power (Lake and Wong 2009). The network is clearly centralized but, again for functional reasons, it must remain egalitarian: those in a central position cannot be seen to be exercising any type of command authority over other actors. The exercise of command authority would cause participants to leave and the network to collapse, hence the creation of mechanisms allowing cooperation outside military command structures. In a way, central actors may sacrifice the benefits of a central position in order to allow the network to fulfill its function of providing governance. Furthermore, attempts to manipulate network centrality by having bridging or gatekeeping nodes block or charge for information would benefit no one but the pirates. The network functions because of the free flow of information about pirate vessels.

[45] There have been negative effects associated with pirate activity, such as drug use and prostitution; see Smith and ni Chonghaile 2012. However, the financial input has been very high (Shortland 2012).

[46] UN Security Council, "Letter Dated 12 July 2013 from the Chair of the Security Council Committee Pursuant to Resolutions 751 (1992) and 1907 (2009)
Concerning Somalia and Eritrea Addressed to the President of the Security Council."

However, there is no question that the actors in central positions (NATO, EUNAVFOR, and CMF) are brokering between unconnected others to allow for rapidly spreading and receiving information in ways that encourage governance that serves their goals (Avant and Westerwinter, this volume). In this case, the goal of reducing piracy is shared by all network members, regardless of centrality. If central actors achieve their goal, so too does the network, and vice versa. The counter-piracy network could not exercise the power necessary to govern without cooperative structures; this differs from a network where members may seek to affect governance processes. While the structures of the counter-piracy network may well facilitate cooperation because they do not force states to have a deeply trusting relationship, they nonetheless demonstrate that disparate states can achieve military cooperation in order to meet a specific goal.

The counter-piracy network has power for two reasons: first, its networked ability to cover and provide maritime governance over a vast area; second, and most fundamentally, drawing from the potential use of violence to coerce pirates into ceasing their activities. In other words, it is a network that has both relational power and coercive power. However, counter-piracy's unusual network attributes are responsible for its successful wielding of its coercive power thereby showing that network power interacts with other forms of power. It may well be that the fundamental problem of multinational military cooperation of all types is how coercive power can be exercised cooperatively. The counter-piracy network solves this problem through egalitarian organization, the absence of joint command, and the presence of a high degree of shared interest. Other types of multinational command have struggled to overcome this problem because of their centralized command and the strong but differing national interests of coalition partners.

The question of whether this very cooperative military network is *sui generis* is an important one. It could easily be argued that the unique antecedent conditions of counter-piracy outlined earlier are unlikely to be replicated elsewhere, and so this type of networked military cooperation is an interesting footnote in a longer and more important story about multinational operations under unified command.

However, I argue that there are perhaps other analogues worth researching. Multinational cooperation with unusual command structures appears to occur in other areas, often where militaries are attempting to deal with other unconventional threats, or with threats that straddle the border between crime and international security. For example, the military efforts to provide aid after the Asian tsunami of 2004 took a similar flat and cooperative form relying on novel uses of communication technology to overcome the difficulties of cooperation across a disparate group of states (Elleman 2007; Bradford 2013). Other complex humanitarian emergencies may prompt a similar response. International counter-narcotics operations require coordination in order to work but do not always have a unified command. One hypothesis worth pursuing is that this type of unusual networked behavior may manifest itself outside the conventional military sphere concerned with direct national defense, but in areas that are important for broader security. In other words, we may find similar types of cooperation in areas where the problems are also Goldilocks problems: just big enough to require attention but not big enough to require intense national focus and thus invigorate the national interest.

It may also be the case that ad hoc, innovative solutions that allow cooperation without formal command exist even in more conventional operations. Silkert argues that the thirty-seven members of the "coalition of the willing" that fought the first Gulf War relied on an "extraordinary" mechanism, the Coalition Coordination, Communication, and Integration Center (C^3IC) to achieve cooperation. "Command" was "conspicuously and deliberately absent from the C^3IC's title. . . . US Central Command was acutely sensitive not to appear as the outsider coming and taking over. Doing so would have been . . . simply fatal. In actual fact, the coalition had no supreme allied commander" (Silkett 1993). Counter-piracy may provide one set of solutions to the problem of how to coordinate military operations without unified command, and it would be interesting to explore others in depth.

The counter-piracy network clearly exercises security governance in the Indian Ocean. That it does so, and does so relatively effectively, demonstrates that networks can step in where more formal military cooperation might be impossible. It is interesting to note that a network was the naturally arising solution to the problems posed by piracy off the coast of Somalia. It was an improvised rather than a planned response. Given relative freedom to experiment in order to solve a complicated problem, militaries devised innovative solutions that bear little resemblance to cooperation in other areas. Given the difficulties of multinational military cooperation, it may be worth considering which features of counter-piracy could be replicated.

REFERENCES

Abbott, Kenneth W. 1993. "'Trust But Verify': The Production of Information in Arms Control Treaties and Other International Agreements." *Cornell International Law Journal* 26: 1–58.

Abbott, Kenneth W., Sandeep Gopalan, Gary E. Marchant, and Douglas J. Sylvester. 2006. "International Regulatory Regimes for Nanotechnology." Available at http://papers.ssrn.com/sol3/papers.cfm?abstract_id=907353.

Abbott, Kenneth W., Robert O. Keohane, Andrew Moravcsik, Anne-Marie Slaughter, and Duncan Snidal. 2000. "The Concept of Legalization." *International Organization* 54, no. 3: 401–419.

Abbott, Kenneth W., and Duncan Snidal. 1998. "Why States Act through Formal International Organizations." *Journal of Conflict Resolution* 42: 3–32.

Abbott, Kenneth W., and Duncan Snidal. 2000. "Hard and Soft Law in International Governance. *International Organization* 54, no. 3: 421–456.

Abbott, Kenneth W., and Duncan Snidal. 2009. "The Governance Triangle: Regulatory Standards Institutions and the Shadow of the State." In Walter Mattli and Ngaire Woods, eds., *The Politics of Global Regulation*, 44–88. Princeton, NJ: Princeton University Press.

Abdelal, Rawi, ed. 2011. *International Practices*. Cambridge: Cambridge University Press.

Abdelal, Rawi. 2013. "The Profits of Power: Commerce and Realpolitik in Eurasia." *Review of International Political Economy* 20, no. 3: 421–456.

Abrahamsen, Rita, and Michael Williams. 2006. "Privatisation, Globalization, and the Politics of Protection in South Africa." In Jef Huysmans, ed., *The Politics of Protection*, 34–47. London: Routledge.

Abrahamsen, Rita, and Michael Williams. 2011. *Security beyond the State: Private Security in International Politics*. Cambridge: Cambridge University Press.

Abrahamson, Jennifer. 2006. *Sweet Relief: The Marla Ruzicka Story*. New York: Simon Spotlight Entertainment.

Achenbach, Joel, Scott Higham, and Sari Horwitz. 2013. "How NRA's True Believers Converted a Marksmanship Group into a Mighty Gun Lobby." *Washington Post*, January 12.

Africa Watch. 1993. *Landmines in Angola*. New York: Human Rights Watch.

Agranoff, Robert. 2003. "A New Look at the Value-Adding Functions of Intergovernmental Networks." Paper presented at the 7th National Public Management Research Conference, October, Georgetown, Washington, DC.

Alvarez, Jose. 2001. "Do Liberal States Behave Better? A Critique of Slaughter's Liberal Theory." *European Journal of International Law* 12, no. 2: 183–247.

Alves, Gasparani, and Daiana Cipollone. 1998. *Curbing Illicit Trafficking in Small Arms and Sensitive Technologies: An Agenda Oriented Agenda*. Geneva: United Nations Institute for Disarmament.

Angelova, Anastasia A. 1999. "Compelling Compliance with International Regimes: China and the Missile Technology Control Regime." *Columbia Journal of Transnational Law* 38: 419–449.

Ansell, Christopher K., and Steven Weber. 1999. "Organizing International Politics: Sovereignty and Open Systems." *International Political Science Review* 20, no. 1: 73–93.

Arms Control Association (ACA). 2004. "Fact Sheet: The Missile Technology Control Regime at a Glance." Washington, DC, September. Available at http://armscontrol.org/factsheets/mtcr.asp.

Arms Project and Africa Watch. 1993. *Landmines in Mozambique*. New York: Human Rights Watch.

Arms Project and Physicians for Human Rights. 1993. *Landmines: A Deadly Legacy*. New York: Human Rights Watch.

ASIS. 2012. "ASIS Standard for Private Security Service Providers Overseas Adopted by UK." ASIS Press Release, December 20, 2012. Available at http://www.securitymanagement.com/news/asis-standard-private-security-service-providers-overseas-adopted-uk-0011403.

Asmus, Ronald. 2010. *A Little War That Shook the World: Georgia, Russia, and the Future of the West*. New York: Macmillan.

Auld, Graeme, Steven Bernstein, and Benjamin Cashore. 2008. "The New Corporate Social Responsibility." *Annual Review of Environment and Resources* 33, no. 1: 413–435.

Autessere, Séverine. 2010. *The Trouble with the Congo: Local Violence and the Failure of International Peacebuilding*. Cambridge and New York: Cambridge University Press.

Avaliani, Dmitry. 2008. "Georgia: Fears of War with Russia." Institute for War and Peace Studies.net, May 16. Available at http://iwpr.net/node/33516.

Avant, Deborah D. 2005. *The Market for Force: The Implications of Privatizing Security*. Cambridge: Cambridge University Press.

Avant, Deborah D. 2007. "NGOs, Corporations, and Security Transformation in Africa." *International Relations* 29, no. 2: 143–161.

Avant, Deborah D. 2016. "Pragmatic Networks and Transnational Governance of Private Military and Security Services." *International Studies Quarterly* 60, no. 1.

Avant, Deborah D., Mark Berlin, and Karl Kruse. 2011. "Information for Monitoring the Global Private Military and Security Industry: What Do We Know, What Do We Need To Know and How Can We Know It?" University of California Institute for Global Conflict and Cooperation (IGCC), Occasional Paper No. 4, June.

Avant, Deborah D., Martha Finnemore, and Susan K. Sell. 2010a. "Conclusions: Authority, Legitimacy, and Accountability in Global Politics." In Deborah D. Avant, Martha Finnemore, and Susan K. Sell, eds., *Who Governs the Globe?* 356–370. Cambridge: Cambridge University Press.

Avant, Deborah D., Martha Finnemore, and Susan K. Sell. 2010b. "Who Governs the Globe?" In Deborah D. Avant, Martha Finnemore, and Susan K. Sell, eds., *Who Governs the Globe?* 1–31. Cambridge: Cambridge University Press.

Avant, Deborah D., and Renee de Nevers. 2011. "Military Contractors and the American Way of War." *Daedalus* 140, no. 3: 1–12.

Axworthy, Lloyd. 1998. "Towards a New Multilateralism." In Maxwell A. Cameron, Robert J. Lawson, and Brian W. Tomlin, eds., *To Walk Without Fear: The Global Movement to Ban Landmines*, 448–469. Toronto: Oxford University Press.

Bach, David, and Abraham L. Newman. 2007. "The European Regulatory State and Global Public Policy: Micro-Institutions, Macro-Influence." *Journal of European Public Policy* 14, no. 6: 827–846.

Bach, David, and Abraham L. Newman. 2009. "Transgovernmental Cooperation and Domestic Policy Convergence: Power, Information, and the Global Quest Against Insider Trading". http://papers.ssrn.com/sol3/papers.cfm?abstract_id=1450395.

Bain & Company. 2011. "The Global Diamond Industry: Lifting the Veil of Mystery." Technical Report Bain & Company.

Baker, Andrew. 2006. *The Group of Seven: Finance Ministries, Central Banks and Global Financial Governance*. New York: Routledge.

Baldwin, David A. 1979. "Power Analysis and World Politics: New Trends versus Old Tendencies." *World Politics* 31: 161–194.

Baldwin, David A. 2002. "Power and International Relations." In Walter Carlsnaes, Thomas Risse, and Beth A. Simmons, eds., *Handbook of International Relations*, 177–191. London: SAGE Publications.

Barabási, Albert-László. 2003. *Linked: How Everything Is Connected to Everything Else and What It Means for Business, Science, and Everyday Life.* New York: Penguin Books.

Baran, Zeyno. 2007. "EU Energy Security: Time to End Russian Leverage." *Washington Quarterly* 30, no. 4: 131–144.

Barnett, Michael N., and Raymond Duvall. 2005. "Power in International Politics." *International Organization* 59, no 1: 39–75.

Bartley, Tim. 2007. "Institutional Emergence in an Era of Globalization: The Rise of Transnational Private Regulation of Labor and Environmental Conditions." *American Journal of Sociology* 113: 297–351.

BBC News. 2005. "Bush Praises Georgian Democracy." May 10. Available at http://news.bbc.co.uk/2/hi/europe/4531273.stm.

Bearce, David H., and Stacy Bondanella. 2007. "Intergovernmental Organizations, Socialization, and Member-State Interest Convergence." *International Organization* 61, no. 4: 703–733.

Beehner, Lionel. 2011. "Do Democratic Candidates Suffer 'Audience Costs'?" *Josef Korbel Journal of Advanced International Studies* 3 (Summer): 59–76.

Beffert, David, and Thorsten Benner. 2005a. "Stemming the Tide of Conflict Diamonds: The Kimberley Process. Part A." Hertie School of Governance Case Program.

Beffert, David, and Thorsten Benner. 2005b. "Stemming the Tide of Conflict Diamonds: The Kimberley Process. Part B." Hertie School of Governance Case Program.

Behringer, Ronald M. 2005. "Middle Power Leadership on the Human Security Agenda." *Cooperation and Conflict* 40, no. 3: 305–342.

Beissinger, Mark. 2007. "Structure and Example in Modular Political Phenomena: The Diffusion of the Bulldozer/Rose/Orange/Tulip Revolutions." *Perspectives on Politics* 5, no. 2 (June): 259–276.

Belcher, Emma. 2009. "A Tighter Net: Strengthening the Proliferation Security Initiative." Lowy Institute for International Policy.

Belcher, Emma. 2011. "The Proliferation Security Initiative. Lessons for Using Nonbinding Agreements." Council of Foreign Relations Working Paper, July.

Bell, Sam R., Chad K. Clay, and Amanda Murdie. 2012. "Neighborhood Watch: Spatial Effects of Human Rights INGOs." *Journal of Politics* 74, no. 2: 354–368.

Benner, Thorsten, Wolfgang H. Reinicke, and Jan Martin Witte. 2004. "Multisectoral Networks in Global Governance: Towards a Pluralistic System of Accountability." *Government and Opposition* 39, no. 2: 191–210.

Bensahel, Nora. 1999. "The Coalition Paradox: The Politics of Military Cooperation." Stanford University.

Benvenisti, Eyal. 2006. "'Coalitions of the Willing' and the Evolution of Informal International Law." Working Paper 31. Tel Aviv University Law Faculty.

Berenskoetter, Felix. 2007. "Thinking about Power." In Felix Berenskoetter and Michael J. Williams, eds., *Power in World Politics*, 1–22. London: Routledge.

Berenskoetter, Felix, and M. J. Williams, eds. 2007. *Power in World Politics.* London: Routledge.

Berliner, Daniel, and Aseem Prakash. 2012. "From Norms to Programs: The United Nations Global Compact and Global Governance." *Regulation & Governance* 6, no. 2: 149–166.

Bermann, George A., Matthias Herdegen, and Peter L. Lindseth. 2000. "Introduction." In George A. Bermann, Matthias Herdegen, and Peter L. Lindseth, eds., *Transatlantic Regulatory Cooperation: Legal Problems and Political Prospects*, 1–17. Oxford: Oxford University Press.

Bernstein, Elizabeth. 2008. "Still Alive and Kicking: The International Campaign to Ban Landmines." In Jody Williams, Stephen D. Goose, and Mary Wareham, eds., *Banning*

Landmines: Disarmament, Citizen Diplomacy, and Human Security, 31–48. Lanham, MD: Rowman & Littlefield.

Bieri, Franziska. 2010. *From Blood Diamonds to the Kimberley Process: How NGOs Cleaned up the Global Diamond Industry*. Farnham: Ashgate.

Bieri, Franziska, and Steve Waddell. 2012. "How Trust Shapes Global Action Networks: Evidence from the Kimberley Process." Paper presented at the 19th Annual Conference on Multi-Organizational Partnerships, Alliances and Networks.

Bitzinger, Richard. 1994. "The Globalization of the Arms Industry: The Next Proliferation Challenge." *International Security* 19, no. 2: 170–198.

Blore, Shawn, and Ian Smillie. 2011. *Taming the Resource Curse*. Ottawa, Canada: Partnership Africa Canada.

Bob, Clifford. 2008. *The International Struggle for Human Rights*. Philadelphia: University of Pennsylvania Press

Bob, Clifford. 2010. "Packing Heat: Pro-Gun Groups and the Governance of Small Arms." In Deborah D. Avant, Martha Finnemore, and Susan Sell, eds., *Who Governs the Globe?* 183–201. Cambridge: Cambridge University Press.

Bob, Clifford. 2012. *The Global Right Wing and the Clash of World Politics*. Cambridge: Cambridge University Press.

Boehmer, Charles, Erik Gartzke, and Tim Nordstrom. 2004. "Do Intergovernmental Organizations Promote Peace?" *World Politics* 57, no. 1: 1–38.

Böhmelt, Tobias, Vally Koubi, and Thomas Bernauer. 2014. "Civil Society Participation in Global Governance: Insights from Climate Politics." *European Journal of Political Research* 53, no. 1: 18–36.

Bolton, John. 2001. US Statement at Plenary Session, Under Secretary of State for Arms Control and International Security Affairs, UN Conference on the Illicit Trade in Small Arms and Light Weapons in All its Aspects. July 9.

Bonacich, Phillip. 1987. "Power and Centrality: A Family of Measures." *American Journal of Sociology* 92, no. 5: 1170–1182.

Bone, Andrew. 2004. "Conflict Diamonds: The De Beers Group and the Kimberley Process." In Alyson J. K. Bailes and Isabel Frommelt, eds., *Business and Security: Public–Private Sector Relationships in a New Security Environment*, 129–147. Oxford: Oxford University Press.

Borgatti, Stephen P. 2006. "Identifying Sets of Key Players in a Social Network." *Computational and Mathematical Organization Theory* 12, no. 1: 21–34.

Borgatti, Stephen P., Martin G. Everett, and Linton C. Freeman. 2002. *Ucinet for Windows: Software for Social Network Analysis*. Harvard, MA: Analytic Technologies.

Borgatti, Stephen P., Candace Jones, and Martin G. Everett. 1998. "Network Measures of Social Capital." *Connections* 21, no. 2: 27–36.

Borgatti, Stephen P., and Virginie Lopez-Kidwell. 2011. "Network Theory." In John Scott and Peter J. Carrington, eds., *The SAGE Handbook of Social Network Analysis*, 40–54. London: SAGE.

Borrie, John. 2009. *Unacceptable Harm: A History of How the Treaty to Ban Cluster Munitions Was Won*. Geneva: United Nations Institute for Disarmament Research.

Bourdieu, Pierre. 1986. "The Forms of Capital." In John G. Richardson, ed., *Handbook of Theory and Research for the Sociology of Education*, 241–258. New York: Greenwood Press.

Bourdieu, Pierre. 2008. "The Forms of Capital." In Nicole Woolsey Biggart, ed., *Readings in Economic Sociology*, 280–291. Oxford: Wiley-Blackwell.

Boutwell, Jeffrey, and Michael Klare. 1998. "Small Arms and Light Weapons: Controlling the Real Instruments of War." *Arms Control Today*, August/September.

Bower, Adam. 2015. "Norms Without the Great Powers: International Law, Nested Social Structures, and the Ban on Antipersonnel Mines." *International Studies Review* 17, no. 3: 347–373.

Bower, Adam, and Richard Price. 2013. "Moral Mission Accomplished? Assessing the Landmine Ban." In Eric A. Heinze, ed., *Justice, Sustainability, and Security: Global Ethics for the 21st Century*, 131–169. New York: Palgrave Macmillan.

References 273

Bowker, Mike. 2011. "The War in Georgia and the Western Response." *Central Asian Survey* 30, no. 2 (May): 197–211.

Bradford, John. 2013. "Waves of Change: Evolution in the US Navy's Strategic Approach to Disaster Relief Operations between the 2004 and 2011 Asian Tsunamis." *Asian Security* 9, no. 1: 19–37.

Brett, Derek. 2004. "How Many Child Soldiers: Is the 300,000 Still Valid?" Child Soldier Newsletter, May.

Brewington, David V., David R. Davis, and Amanda Murdie. 2009. The Ties that Bind: A Network Analysis of Human Rights INGOs. Paper read at 50th Annual Convention of the International Studies Association, February 15–18, at New York, NY.

Brie, Michael, and Erhard Stölting. 2012. "Formal Institutions and Informal Institutional Arrangements." In Thomas Christiansen and Christine Neuhold, eds., *International Handbook on Informal Governance*, 19–39. Cheltenham, UK and Northampton, MA: Edward Elgar.

Brinkert, Kerry. 2008. "An Emphasis on Action: The Mine Ban Treaty's Implementation Mechanism." In Jody Williams, Stephen D. Goose, and Mary Wareham, eds., *Banning Landmines: Disarmament, Citizen Diplomacy, and Human Security*, 87–104. Lanham, MD: Rowman & Littlefield.

Brinkert, Kerry, and Kevin Hamilton. 2004. "Clearing the Path to a Mine-Free World: Implementing the Ottawa Convention." In Richard A. Matthew, Bryan McDonald, and Kenneth R. Rutherford, eds., *Landmines and Human Security: International Politics and War's Hidden Legacy*, 67–80. Albany, NY: State University of New York Press.

Bromund, Theodore. 2013. "Good News from Washington—Arms Trade Treaty is DOA in US Senate." Fox News, October 18.

Brooks, Stephen G., John Ikenberry, and William C. Wohlforth. 2013. "Don't Come Home America: The Case against Retrenchment." *International Security* 37, no. 3: 7–51.

Brooks, Stephen G., and William C. Wohlforth. 2008. *World out of Balance: International Relations and the Challenge of American Primacy.* Princeton, NJ: Princeton University Press.

Brown, Dave. 2010. "Top 10 Gold Producers." *Gold Investing News.* November 15.

Bryza, Matthew. 2008. "Russia, Georgia, and the Return of Power Politics." Testimony prepared for the Commission on Security and Cooperation in Europe. September 10.

Bunce, Valerie J., and Sharon L. Wolchik. 2006. "International Diffusion and Postcommunist Electoral Revolutions." *Communist and Post-Communist Studies* 39, no. 3 (September): 283–304.

Burca, Grainne de, Robert O. Keohane, and Charles Sabel. 2013. "New Modes of Pluralist Global Governance." *International Law and Politics* 45: 723–786.

Burris, Scott, Peter Drahos, and Clifford Shearing. 2005. "Nodal Governance." *Australian Journal of Legal Philosophy* 30: 30–58.

Burt, Ronald S. 1992. *Structural Holes: The Social Structure of Competition.* Cambridge: Cambridge University Press.

Burt, Ronald S. 2000. "The Network Structure of Social Capital." *Research in Organizational Behavior* 22: 345–423.

Burt, Ronald S. 2004. "Structural Holes and Good Ideas." *American Journal of Sociology* 110: 349–399.

Burt, Ronald S. 2005. *Brokerage and Closure: An Introduction to Social Capital.* Oxford: Oxford University Press.

Buthe, Tim, and Walter Mattli. 2011. *The New Global Rulers: The Privatization of Regulation in the World Economy.* Princeton, NJ: Princeton University Press.

Butts, Carter T. 2009. "Social Network Analysis: A Methodological Introduction." *Asian Journal of Social Psychology* 11: 13–41.

Butts, Carter T. 2013. sna: Tools for Social Network Analysis R package version 2.3-1.

Buzan, Barry. 1991. "New Patterns of Global Security in the Twenty First Century." *International Affairs* 67: 431–451.

Byers, Michael. 1999. Custom, Power and the Power of Rules: International Relations and Customary Law. Cambridge: Cambridge University Press.

Byers, Michael. 2004. "Policing the High Seas: The Proliferation Security Initiative." *American Journal of International Law* 98, no. 3: 526–545.

Byers, Michael. 2005. *War Law*. New York: Grove Press.

Calhoun, Herbert L. 1998. "Small Arms and Light Weapons: Can They Be Controlled?" *World Military Expenditures and Arms Transfers*. Washington, DC: Government Printing Office.

Cameron, Maxwell A. 1998. "Democratization of Foreign Policy: The Ottawa Process as a Model." In Maxwell A. Cameron, Robert J. Lawson, and Brian W. Tomlin, eds., *To Walk Without Fear: The Global Movement to Ban Landmines*, 424–447. Toronto: Oxford University Press.

Cameron, Maxwell A., Robert J. Lawson, and Brian W. Tomlin. 1998. "To Walk Without Fear" In Maxwell A. Cameron, Robert J. Lawson, and Brian W. Tomlin, eds., *To Walk Without Fear: The Global Movement to Ban Landmines*, 1–19. Toronto: Oxford University Press.

Cao, Xun. 2010. "Networks as Channels of Policy Diffusion: Explaining Worldwide Changes in Capital Taxation, 1998–2006." *International Studies Quarterly* 54, no. 3: 823–854.

Carpenter, Charli R. 2010. "Governing the Global Agenda: 'Gate-keepers' and 'Issue Adoption' in Transnational Advocacy Networks." In Deborah D. Avant, Martha Finnemore, and Susan K. Sell, eds., *Who Governs the Globe?* 202–237. Cambridge: Cambridge University Press.

Carpenter, Charli R. 2011. "Vetting the Advocacy Agenda: Network Centrality and the Paradox of Weapons Norms." *International Organization* 65, no. 1: 69–102.

Carpenter, Charli R. 2014. ""Lost" Causes: Agenda Vetting in Global Issue Networks and the Shaping of Human Security." 1st ed. Ithaca, NY: Cornell University Press.

Carpenter, Charli R., Sirin Duygulu, Alexander H. Montgomery, and Anna Rapp. 2014. "Explaining the Advocacy Agenda: Insights from the Human Security Network." *International Organization* 68, no. 2: 449–470.

Carrington, Peter J., and John Scott. 2011. *The SAGE Handbook of Social Network Analysis*. London: SAGE.

Carrington, Peter J., John Scott, and Stanley Wasserman. 2005. *Models and Methods in Social Network Analysis*. Structural Analysis in the Social Sciences. Cambridge: Cambridge University Press.

Cashore, Benjamin, Graeme Auld, and Deanna Newsom. 2004. *Governing through Markets: Forest Certification and the Emergence of Non-State Authority*. New Haven, CT: Yale University Press.

Chabasse, Phillippe. 1998. "The French Campaign." In Maxwell A. Cameron, Robert J. Lawson, and Brian W. Tomlin, eds., *To Walk Without Fear: The Global Movement to Ban Landmines*, 60–67. Toronto: Oxford University Press.

Champion, Marc. 2008. "U.S. Diplomat, Close to Saakashvili, Plays Key Role in Conflict." *Wall Street Journal*, August 16. Available at http://www.wsj.com/articles/SB121885135947146439.

Champion, Marc. 2009. "Tbilisi Started '08 War, but Moscow also at Fault, EU Finds." *Wall Street Journal*, October 1. Available at http://www.wsj.com/articles/SB125431087432152321.

Charap, Samuel, and Alexandros Peterson. 2011. "Reimagining US Interests and Priorities in Post-Soviet Eurasia." In Paul J. Saunders, ed., *Enduring Rivalry: American and Russian Perspectives on Post-Soviet Space*, 5–20. Washington, DC: Center for the National Interest.

Chaulia, Sreeram. 2011. *International Organizations and Civilian Protection*. I.B. Tauris.

Chayes, Abraham, and Antonia H. Chayes. 1993. "On Compliance." *International Organization* 47, no. 2: 175–205.

Chayes, Antonia Handler, Abram Chayes, and George Raach. 1997. "Beyond Reform: Restructuring for More Effective Conflict Intervention." *Global Governance* 3, no. 2: 117–146.

Chinkin, Christine M. 1989. "The Challenge of Soft Law: Development and Change in International Law." *International and Comparative Law Quarterly* 38: 850–866.

Chivers, C. J. 2010. "Embracing Georgia, U.S. Misread Signs of Rifts." *New York Times*, December 2. Available at http://www.nytimes.com/2010/12/02/world/europe/02wikileaks-georgia.html.

Chivers, Christopher J., and Ellen Barry. 2008. "Georgia Claims on Russia War Called into Question." *New York Times*, November 7. Available at http://www.nytimes.com/2008/11/07/world/europe/07georgia.html?pagewanted=all.

Christopoulos, Dimitrios C. 2008. "The Governance of Networks: Heuristic or Formal Analysis? A Reply to Rachel Parker." *Political Studies* 56, no. 2: 475–481.

Chuter, David. 2003. *War Crimes: Confronting Atrocity in the Modern World*. Boulder, CO: Lynne Reinner.

Coalson, Robert. 2015. "After 10 Years and 30 Deaths, Georgians Question Their NATO Ambitions." *Radio Free Europe/Radio Liberty*, June 11. Available at http://www.rferl.org/content/nato-georgia-afghanistan-mission/27066471.html.

Coker, Margaret, and Costas Paris. 2013. "Somali Pirates Shift Course to Other Criminal Pursuits." *Wall Street Journal*, November 1.

Colombatto, Enrico, and Jonathan Macey. 1996. "A Public Choice Model of International Economic Cooperation and the Decline of the Nation State." *Cardozo Law Review* 18, no. 3: 925–956.

Commission on Global Governance. 1995. *Our Global Neighborhood*. New York: Oxford University Press.

Cook, Karen S., and Toshio Yamagishi. 1992. "Power in Exchange Networks: A Power-Dependence Formulation." *Social Networks* 14, nos. 3–4: 245–265.

Cooley, Alexander, and Jonathan Hopkin. 2010. "Base Closings: The Rise and Decline of the US Military Base Issue in Spain, 1975–2005." *International Political Science Review* 30, no. 4: 494–513.

Cooley, Alexander, and Lincoln Mitchell. 2009. "No Way to Treat Our Friends: Recasting Recent U.S.–Georgian Relations." *Washington Quarterly* 32, no. 1 (January): 27–41.

Cooley, Alexander, and Daniel Nexon. 2013. "The Empire Will Compensate You: The Structural Dynamics of the U.S. Overseas Basing Network." *Perspectives on Politics* 11, no. 4: 1034–1050.

Cooley, Alexander, and James Ron. 2002. "The NGO Scramble: Organizational Insecurity and the Political Economy of Transnational Action." *International Security* 27, no. 1: 5–39.

Cooley, Alexander, and Hendrik Spruyt. 2009. *Contracting States: Sovereign Transfers in International Relations*. Princeton, NJ: Princeton University Press.

Cooper, Richard N. 1975. "Prolegomena to the Choice of an International Monetary System." *International Organization* 29, no. 1: 63–97.

Corbetta, Renato. 2010. "Determinants of Third Parties' Intervention and Alignment Choices in Ongoing Conflicts, 1946–2001." *Foreign Policy Analysis* 6, no. 1: 61–85.

Cornell, Svante. 2007. "Georgia after the Rose Revolution: Geopolitical Predicament and Implications for U.S. Policy." Report prepared for the Strategic Studies Institute, US Army War College.

Cornell, Svante. 2009. "Pipeline Power: The War in Georgia and the Future of the Caucasian Energy Corridor." *Georgetown Journal of International Affairs* 10, no. 1: 131–139.

Cornell, Svante, and Fredrik Starr, eds. 2009. *The Guns of August 2008: Russia's War in Georgia*. Armonk, NY: M. E. Sharpe.

Cortright, David, and George A. Lopez. 2002. *Smart Sanctions: Targeting Economic Statecraft*. Lanham, MD: Rowman & Littlefield.

Coupland, Robin M., and Korver Adriaan. 1991. "Injuries from Antipersonnel Mines: The Experience of the International Committee of the Red Cross." *British Medical Journal* 303, no. 6816: 1509–1512.

Cox, Robert W. 1983. "Gramsci, Hegemony and International Relations: An Essay in Method." *Millennium—Journal of International Studies* 12, no. 2: 162–175.

Cranmer, Skyler J., and Bruce A. Desmarais. 2011. "Inferential Network Analysis with Exponential Random Graph Models." *Political Analysis* 19, no. 1: 66–86.

Cranmer, Skyler J., Bruce A. Desmarais, and Elizabeth J. Menninga. 2012. "Complex Dependencies in the Alliance Network." *Conflict Management and Peace Science* 29, no. 3: 279–313.

Cranmer, Skyler J., Tobias Heinrich, and Bruce A. Desmarais. 2014. "Reciprocity and the Structural Determinants of the International Sanctions Network." *Social Networks* 36: 5–22.

Dahl, Robert A. 1957. "The Concept of Power." *Behavioral Science* 2: 201–215.

Dai, Xinyuan. 2002. "Information Systems in Treaty Regimes." *World Politics* 54: 405–436.

Das, T. K., and Bing-Sheng Teng. 1998. "Between Trust and Control: Developing Confidence in Partner Cooperation in Alliances." *Academy of Management Review* 23: 491–512.

Datan, Merav. 2005. Security Council Resolution 1540. WMD and Non-state Trafficking. Disarmament Diplomacy 79 (April/May). Available at http://www.acronym.org.uk/dd/dd79/79md.htm.

Deitelhoff, Nicole, and Anna Geis. 2009. "Securing the State, Undermining Democracy: Internationalization and Privatization of Western Militaries." TranState Working Paper No. 92. University of Bremen.

de Waal, Thomas. 2011. *The Caucasus: An Introduction*. New York: Oxford University Press.

de Waal, Thomas. 2012. "More than Georgia on Obama's Mind." *The National Interest*, February 23. Available at http://nationalinterest.org/commentary/georgia-obamas-mind-6557.

Diaz, Tom. 2013. *The Last Gun: How Changes in the Gun Industry Are Killing Americans and What It Will Take to Stop It*. New York: New Press.

Dickenson, Laura. 2007. "Contracts as a Tool for Regulating Private Military Companies." In Simon Chesterman and Chia Lehnardt, eds., *From Mercenaries to Market: The Rise and Regulation of Private Military Companies*, 217–239. New York: Oxford University Press.

Dimitrov, Radoslav, Detlef F. Sprinz, Gerald M. DiGiusto, and Alexander Kelle. 2007. "International Non-Regimes: A Research Agenda." *International Studies Review* 9, no. 2: 230–258.

Djelic, Marie-Laure, and Thibaut Kleiner. 2006. "The International Competition Network: Moving towards Transnational Governance." In Marie-Laure Djelic and Kerstin Sahlin-Andersson, eds., *Transnational Governance: Institutional Dynamics of Regulation*, 287–308. Cambridge: Cambridge University Press.

Dolan, Michael, and Chris Hunt. 1998. "Negotiating in the Ottawa Process: The New Multilateralism." In Maxwell A. Cameron, Robert J. Lawson, and Brian W. Tomlin, eds., *To Walk Without Fear: The Global Movement to Ban Landmines*, 392–423. Toronto: Oxford University Press.

Dorussen, Han, and Hugh Ward. 2008. "Intergovernmental Organizations and the Kantian Peace: A Network Perspective." *Journal of Conflict Resolution* 52, no. 2: 189–212.

Dowding, Keith. 1995. "Model or Metaphor? A Critical Review of the Policy Network Approach." *Political Studies* 43, no. 1: 136–158.

Downs, George W., David M. Rocke, and Peter N. Barsoom. 1996. "Is the Good News about Compliance Good News about Cooperation?" *International Organization* 50, no. 3: 379–406.

Drezner, Daniel. 2007. *All Politics Is Global: Explaining International Regulatory Regimes*. Princeton, NJ: Princeton University Press.

Duffield, Mark. 2002. *Global Governance and the New Wars: The Merging of Security and Development*. New York: Zed.

Dunning, John. 1993. *The Globalization of Business*. New York: Routledge.

Duygulu Elcim, Sirin. 2015. "The Effects of Using Security Frames on Global Agenda-Setting and Policy Making." Doctoral Dissertation, University of Massachusetts.

Easley, David, and Jon Kleinberg. 2010. *Networks, Crowds, and Markets: Reasoning about a Highly Connected World*. Cambridge: Cambridge University Press.

Eberlein, Burkard, and Abraham L. Newman. 2008. "Escaping the International Governance Dilemma? Incorporated Transgovernmental Networks in the European Union." *Governance* 21, no. 1: 25–52.

Efrat, Asif. 2010. "Toward Internationally Regulated Goods: Controlling the Trade in Small Arms and Light Weapons." *International Organization* 64, no. 1: 97–132.

Eilstrup-Sangiovanni, Mette. 2009. "Varieties of Cooperation: Government Networks in International Security." In Miles Kahler, ed., *Networked Politics: Agency, Power, and Governance*, 194–227. Ithaca, NY: Cornell University Press.

Eilstrup-Sangiovanni, Mette. 2014. "Network Theory and Security Governance." In James Sperling, ed., *Handbook of Governance and Security*, 41–63. Cheltenham, UK and Northampton, MA: Edward Elgar.

Eilstrup-Sangiovanni, Mette, and Calvert Jones. 2008. "Assessing the Dangers of Illicit Networks: Why Al-Qaeda may be Less Dangerous than Many Think." *International Security* 33, no. 2: 7–44.

Elkins, Zachary. 2009. "Constitutional Networks." In Miles Kahler, ed., *Networked Politics: Agency, Power, and Governance*, 43–63. Ithaca, NY: Cornell University Press.

Elleman, Bruce A. 2007. "Waves of Hope: The US Navy's Response to the Tsunami in Northern Indonesia." Newport, RI: Naval War College.

Emerson, Richard M. 1962. "Power-Dependence Relations." *American Sociological Review* 27, no. 1: 31–41.

Emirbayer, Mustafa. 1997. "Manifesto for a Relational Sociology." *American Journal of Sociology* 103, no. 2: 281–317.

Emirbayer, Mustafa, and Ann Mische. 1998. "What Is Agency?" *American Journal of Sociology* 103: 962–1023.

Erickson, Jennifer L. 2012. "Social Incentives for Policy Commitment: International Reputation and 'Responsible' Arms Export Controls." Paper presented at the annual meeting of the International Studies Association Meeting, San Diego, CA, April 1–4.

Etzioni, Amitai. 2009. "Tomorrow's Institution Today: The Promise of the Proliferation Security Initiative." *Foreign Affairs* 88, no. 3: 7–11.

Eznack, Lucile. 2011. "Crises as Signals of Strength: The Significance of Affect in Close Allies, Relationships." *Security Studies* 20, no. 2: 238–265.

Farrell, Theo. 1998. "Culture and Military Power." *Review of International Studies* 24, no. 3: 407–416.

Faul, Moira V. 2015. "Networks and Power: Why Networks Are Hierarchical not Flat, and What to Do about It." *Global Policy Journal*.

Fearon, James D. 1995. "Rationalist Explanations for War." *International Organization* 49: 379–414.

Feldman, Daniel L. 2003. "Conflict Diamonds, International Trade Regulation, and the Nature of Law." *University of Pennsylvania Journal of International Law* 24: 835–874.

Felgenhauer, Pavel. 2009. "After August 7: The Escalation of the Russia–Georgia War." In Svante Cornell and Frederick Starr, eds., *The Guns of August: Russia's War in Georgia*, 162–180. Armonk, NY: M. E. Sharpe.

Ferguson, Niall. 2003. "Hegemony or Empire?" *Foreign Affairs* 82: 154–161.

Fine, Jonathan E. 1992. *Hidden Enemies: Land Mines in Northern Somalia*. Boston, MA: Physicians for Human Rights.

Finnemore, Martha. 1996a. *National Interests in International Society*. Cornell Studies in Political Economy. Ithaca, NY: Cornell University Press.

Finnemore, Martha. 1996b. "Norms, Culture and World Politics: Insights from Sociology's Institutionalism." *International Organization* 50, no. 2 (Spring): 325–347.

Finnemore, Martha, and Kathryn Sikkink. 1998. "International Norm Dynamics and Political Change." *International Organization* 52, no. 4: 887–917.

Fligstein, Neil. 1993. *The Transformation of Corporate Control*. Cambridge, MA: Harvard University Press.

Forbes. 2012. "The Global 2000." April 1. Available at http://forbes.com/.

Fowler, Robert R. 2000. "Report of the Panel of Experts on Violations of Security Council Sanctions against UNITA." New York: United Nations Security Council.

Freeman, Linton C. 1979. "Centrality in Social Networks: Conceptual Clarification." *Social Networks* 1: 215–239.

Freeman, Linton C. 2004. *The Development of Social Network Analysis: A Study in the Sociology of Science*. Vancouver, BC: Empirical Press.

Freeman, Linton C., Stephen P. Borgatti, and Douglas R. White. 1991. "Centrality in Valued Graphs: A Measure of Betweenness Based on Network Flow." *Social Networks* 13, no. 2: 141–154.

Fried, Daniel. 2008. Prepared Statement for the Hearing "U.S.–Russia Relations in the Aftermath of the Georgia Crisis." US House of Representatives, Committee on Foreign Affairs, September 8.

Friedkin, Noah E. 1991. "Theoretical Foundations for Centrality Measures." *American Journal of Sociology* 96, no. 6: 1478–1504.

Friedman, Jonah. 2011. "The Proliferation Security Initiative: A Model for Future Nonproliferation Efforts?" Centre for Strategic and International Studies, August 1 (http://csis.org/blog/proliferation-security-initiative-model-future-nonproliferation-efforts).

Friedman, Benjamin. 2003. The PSI. The Legal Challenge. Bipartisan Security Group Policy Brief, 1–11. Washington, DC, September.

Fuller, Ted, and Yumiao Tian. 2006. "Social and Symbolic Capital and Responsible Entrepreneurship: An Empirical Investigation of SME Narratives." *Journal of Business Ethics* 67: 287–304.

Gard, Robert, Jr. 1998. "The Military Utility of Anti-Personnel Landmines." In Maxwell A. Cameron, Robert J. Lawson, and Brian W. Tomlin, eds., *To Walk Without Fear: The Global Movement to Ban Landmines*, 136–157. Toronto: Oxford University Press.

Garrett, Geoffrey. 1992. "International Cooperation and Institutional Choice: The European Community's Internal Market." *International Organization* 46: 533–560.

Gellert, Paul K. 2003. "Renegotiating a Timber Commodity Chain: Lessons from Indonesia on the Political Construction of Global Commodity Chains." *Sociological Forum* 18, no. 1: 53–75.

Gereffi, Gary. 1996. "Global Commodity Chains: New Forms of Coordination and Control among Nations and Firms." *Competition & Change* 1, no. 4: 427–439.

Gereffi, Gary, John Humphrey, and Timothy Sturgeon. 2005. "The Governance of Global Value Chains." *Review of International Political Economy* 12, no. 1: 78–104.

Germond, Basil. 2013. "The European Union at the Horn of Africa: The Contribution of Critical Geopolitics to Piracy Studies." *Global Policy* 4, no. 1: 80–85.

Gettleman, Jeffrey, and Nicholas Kulish. 2013. "Somali Militants Mixing Business and Terror." *New York Times*, September 30.

Gheciu, Alexandra. 2005. "Security Institutions as Agents of Socialization? NATO and the 'New Europe.'" *International Organization* 59, no. 4: 973–1012.

Gibbon, Peter, Jennifer Bair, and Stefano Ponte. 2008. "Governing Global Value Chains: An Introduction." *Economy and Society* 37, no. 3: 315–338.

Gill, Stephen, ed., 1993. *Gramsci, Historical Materialism and International Relations*. Cambridge: Cambridge University Press.

Gilpin, Robert. 1981. *War and Change in World Politics*. New York: Cambridge University Press.

Gladstone, Rick. 2012. "UN Misses Its Deadline for Arms Pact." *New York Times*, July 27.

Global Witness. 1998. *A Rough Trade: The Role of Companies and Governments in the Angolan Conflict*. London: Global Witness.

Global Witness. 1999. *A Crude Awakening: The Role of Oil and Banking Industries in Angolan Civil War and the Plunder of State Assets*. London: Global Witness.

Global Witness. 2000. *Conflict Diamonds. Possibilities for the Identification, Certification and Control of Conflict Diamonds*. London: Global Witness.

Goddard, Stacie E. 2009a. "Brokering Change: Networks and Entrepreneurs in International Politics." *International Theory* 1, no. 2: 249–281.

Goddard, Stacie. 2009b. *Indivisible Territory and the Politics of Legitimacy: Jerusalem and Northern Ireland*. New York: Cambridge University Press.

Goddard, Stacie E. 2012. "Brokering Peace: Networks, Legitimacy, and the Northern Ireland Peace Process." *International Studies Quarterly* 56: 501–515.

Goddard, Stacie E., and Daniel H. Nexon. 2005. "Paradigm Lost? Reassessing Theory of International Politics." *European Journal of International Relations* 11, no. 1: 9–61.

Goddard, Stacie, and Daniel Nexon. 2016. "The Dynamics of Global Power Politics." *Journal of Global Security Studies* 1, no. 1.

Goldsmith, Jack L., and Eric A. Posner. 2005. *The Limits of International Law*. New York: Oxford University Press.

Goldstein, Judith, Miles Kahler, Robert O. Keohane, and Anne-Marie Slaughter. 2000. "Introduction: Legalization and World Politics." *International Organization* 54, no. 3: 385–399.

Goldstein, Judith, and Lisa Martin. 2000. "Legalization, Trade Liberalization, and Domestic Politics: A Cautionary Note." *International Organization* 54, no. 3: 603–632.

Goose, Stephen D. 2008. "Goodwill Yields Good Results: Cooperative Compliance and the Mine Ban Treaty." In Jody Williams, Stephen D. Goose, and Mary Wareham, eds., *Banning Landmines: Disarmament, Citizen Diplomacy, and Human Security*, 105–126. Lanham, MD: Rowman & Littlefield.

Goose, Stephen D., Mary Wareham, and Jody Williams. 2008. "Banning Landmines and Beyond." In Jody Williams, Stephen D. Goose, and Mary Wareham, eds., *Banning Landmines: Disarmament, Citizen Diplomacy, and Human Security*, 1–14. Lanham, MD: Rowman & Littlefield.

Goose, Stephen D., and Jody Williams. 2008. "Citizen Diplomacy and the Ottawa Process: A Lasting Model?" In Jody Williams, Stephen D. Goose, and Mary Wareham, eds., *Banning Landmines: Disarmament, Citizen Diplomacy, and Human Security*, 181–198. Lanham, MD: Rowman & Littlefield.

Goreux, Louis. 2001. "Conflict Diamonds." African Region Working Paper Series No. 13. World Bank.

Gould, Roger V. 1989. "Power and Social Structure in Community Elites." *Social Forces* 68: 531–552.

Gourevitch, Peter Alexis. 1999. "The Governance Problem in International Relations." In David A. Lake and Robert Powell, eds., *Strategic Choice and International Relations*, 137–164. Princeton, NJ: Princeton University Press.

Gourevitch, Peter, and James Shinn. *Political Power and Corporate Control: The New Global Politics of Corporate Governance*. Princeton, NJ: Princeton University Press.

Grandori, Anna, and Giuseppi Soda. 1995. "Inter-Firm Networks: Antecedents, Mechanisms and Forms." *Organization Studies* 16, no. 2: 183–214.

Granovetter, Mark S. 1973. "The Strength of Weak Ties." *American Journal of Sociology* 78: 1360–1380.

Granovetter, Mark S. 1985. "Economic Action and Social Structure: The Problem of Embeddedness." *American Journal of Sociology* 91, no. 3: 481–510.

Grant, Andrew J. 2012. "The Kimberley Process at Ten: Reflections on a Decade of Efforts to End the Trade in Conflict Diamonds." In Päivi Lujala and Siri Aas Rustad, eds., *High-Value Natural Resources and Peacebuilding*, 159–179. London: Earthscan.

Grant, Andrew J., and Ian Taylor. 2004. "Global Governance and Conflict Diamonds: The Kimberley Process and the Quest for Clean Gems." *The Round Table* 93: 385–401.

Grant, Ruth W., and Robert O. Keohane. 2005. "Accountability and Abuses in World Politics." *American Political Science Review* 99: 29–43.

Grillot, Suzette R. 2011. "Global Gun Control: Examining the Consequences of Competing International Norms." *Global Governance* 17: 529–555.

Grimsley, Marc, and Clifford Rogers, eds. 2008. *Civilians in the Path of War*. Lincoln: University of Nebraska Press.

Gross, Michael. 2010. *Moral Dilemmas of Modern War*. Cambridge: Cambridge University Press.

Gruber, Lloyd. 2000. *Ruling the World: Power Politics and the Rise of Supranational Institutions*. Princeton, NJ: Princeton University Press.

Guilfoyle, Douglas. 2007. "Maritime Interdiction of Weapons of Mass Destruction." *Journal of Conflict and Security Law* 12, no. 1: 1–36.

Guilfoyle, Douglas. 2009. *Shipping Interdiction and the Law of the Sea*. Cambridge: Cambridge University Press.

Guilfoyle, Douglas. 2010. "The Laws of War and the Fight against Somali Piracy: Combatants or Criminals." *Melbourne Journal of International Law* 11: 141–153.

Gulati, Ranjay, D. Lavie, and Ravi Madhavin. 2011. "How Do Networks Matter? The Performance Effects of Interorganizational Networks." *Research in Organizational Behavior* 31: 207–224.

Gulati, Ranjay, Nitin Nohria, and Akbar Zaheer. 2000. "Strategic Networks." *Strategic Management Journal* 21: 203–215.

Hafner-Burton, Emilie M. 2008. "Sticks and Stones: Naming and Shaming the Human Rights Enforcement Problem." *International Organization* 62, no. 4: 689–716.

Hafner-Burton, Emilie M., Miles Kahler, and Alexander H. Montgomery. 2009. "Network Analysis for International Relations." *International Organization* 63, no. 3: 559–592.

Hafner-Burton, Emilie M., and Alexander H. Montgomery. 2006. "Power Positions: International Organizations, Social Networks, and Conflict." *Journal of Conflict Resolution* 50, no. 1: 3–27.

Hafner-Burton, Emilie M., and Alexander H. Montgomery. 2008. "Power or Plenty: How Do International Trade Institutions Affect Economic Sanctions?" *Journal of Conflict Resolution* 52, no. 2: 213–242.

Hafner-Burton, Emilie M., and Alexander H. Montgomery. 2009. "Globalization and the Social Power Politics of International Economic Networks." In Miles Kahler, ed., *Networked Politics: Agency, Power, and Governance*, 23–42. Ithaca, NY: Cornell University Press.

Hafner-Burton, Emilie M., and Alexander H. Montgomery. 2012. "War, Trade, and Distrust: Why Trade Agreements Don't Always Keep the Peace." *Conflict Management and Peace Science* 29, no. 3: 257–278.

Haftendorn, Helga, Robert O. Keohane, and Celeste Wallander, eds. 1999. *Imperfect Unions: Security Institutions over Time and Space*. New York: Oxford University Press.

Halevy, Tammy. 1993. "Chinese Compliance with the Missile Technology Control Regime: A Case Study." *National Security Quarterly* 3: 14–23.

Hall, Todd, and Karen Yarhi-Milo. 2013. "The Personal Touch: Leaders' Impressions, Costly Signaling, and Assessments of Sincerity in International Affairs." *International Studies Quarterly* 56: 560–573.

Handcock, Mark S., David R. Hunter, Carter T. Butts, Steven M. Goodreau, and Martina Morris. 2008. "statnet: Software Tools for the Representation, Visualization, Analysis and Simulation of Network Data." *Journal of Statistical Software* 24, no. 1: 1–11.

Hanneman, Robert A., and Mark Riddle. 2005. "Introduction to Social Network Methods." Riverside, CA: University of California, Riverside. Available at http://faculty.ucr.edu/~hanneman/.

Hanneman, Robert A., and Mark Riddle. 2011a. "A Brief Introduction to Analyzing Social Network Data." In John Scott and Peter J. Carrington, eds., *The SAGE Handbook of Social Network Analysis*, 331–339. London: SAGE.

Hanneman, Robert A., and Mark Riddle. 2011b. "Concepts and Measures for Basic Network Analysis." In John Scott and Peter J. Carrington, eds., *The SAGE Handbook of Social Network Analysis*, 340–369. London: SAGE.

Hanson, Marshall. 2005. "LOST at Siege? Renewed Debate over Long-Stalled Treaty." *Naval Services* 81, no. 2: 33–34.

Haufler, Virginia. 2001. "Business in Zones of Conflict: Rapporteur's Report." New York City: United Nations Global Compact.

Haufler, Virginia. 2010. "The Kimberley Process Certification Scheme: An Innovation in Global Governance and Conflict Prevention." *Journal of Business Ethics* 89: 403–416.

Hayes, Jarrod. 2009. "Identity and Securitization in the Democratic Peace: The United States and the Divergence of Response to India and Iran's Nuclear Programs." *International Studies Quarterly* 53, no. 4: 977–999.

Hayward, Keith. 2000. "The Globalisation of Defence Industries." *Survival* 42, no. 3: 115–132.

Held, David, Anthony McGrew, David Goldblatt, and Jonathan Perraton. 1999. *Global Transformations: Politics, Economics and Culture*. Stanford, CA: Stanford University Press.

Hendrix, Cullen S., and Wendy H. Wong. 2013. "When Is the Pen Truly Mighty? Regime Type and the Efficacy of Naming and Shaming in Curbing Human Rights Abuses." *British Journal of Political Science* 43, no. 3: 651–672.

Herbst, Jeffrey. 1999. "The Regulation of Private Security Forces." In Greg Mills and John Stremlau, eds., *The Privatization of Security in Africa*, 107–127. Johannesburg: SAIIA Press.

Herby, Peter, and Kathleen Lawand. 2008. "Unacceptable Behavior: How Norms Are Established." In Jody Williams, Stephen D. Goose, and Mary Wareham, eds., *Banning Landmines: Disarmament, Citizen Diplomacy, and Human Security*, 199–216. Lanham, MD: Rowman & Littlefield.

Hollstein, Betina. 2011. "Qualitative Approaches." In John Scott and Peter J. Carrington, eds., *The SAGE Handbook of Social Network Analysis*, 404–416. London: SAGE.

Holmes, Marcus. 2013. "The Force of Face-to-Face Diplomacy: Mirror Neurons and the Problem of Intentions." *International Organization* 67: 829–861.

Hopkins, Raymond F. 1976. "The International Role of 'Domestic' Bureaucracy." *International Organization* 30, no. 3: 405–432.

HRF (Human Rights First). 2011. "State of Affairs Four Years after Nisoor Square: Accountability and Oversight of US Private Security and other Contractors." Washington, DC: Human Rights First, September.

Hubert, Don. 2000. "The Landmine Ban: A Case Study in Humanitarian Advocacy." Thomas J. Watson Jr. Institute for International Studies Occasional Paper. Working Paper. Boston: Tufts University.

Hudson, Natalie Florea. 2009. "Securitizing Women's Human Rights and Gender Equality." *Journal of Human Rights* 8, no. 1: 53–70.

Hurd, Ian. 2005. "The Strategic Use of Liberal Internationalism: Libya and the UN Sanctions, 1992–2003." *International Organization* 59: 495–526.

ICRC, see International Committee of the Red Cross.

Ingenkamp, Nina. 2008. *How HIV-AIDS Has Made It: An Analysis of Global HIV-AIDS Agenda-Setting Between 1981 and 2002*. VDM Verlag Dr. Muller.

Ikenberry, G. John. 2001. *After Victory: Institutions, Strategic Restraint, and the Rebuilding of Order after Major War*. Princeton, NJ: Princeton University Press.

Ikenberry, G. John. 2004. "Liberalism and Empire: Logics of Order in the American Unipolar Age." *Review of International Studies* 30: 609–630.

Ikenberry, G. John. 2011. *Liberal Leviathan: The Origins, Crisis, and Transformation of the American World Order*. Princeton, NJ: Princeton University Press.

Ikenberry, G. John, and Charles Kupchan. 1990. "Socialization and Hegemonic Power." *International Organization* 44: 283–315.

Infomine—Mining and Intelligence. 2012. "Tungsten." http://www.infomine.com.

International Alert. 1999. "An Assessment of the Mercenary Issue at the Fifty-fifth Session of the UN Commission on Human Rights." London: International Alert (May).

International Campaign to Ban Landmines. 2012. *Landmine Monitor 2012*. Geneva: ICBL. Available at http://www.the-monitor.org/lm/2012/resources/Landmine_Monitor_2012.pdf.

International Committee of the Red Cross. 1992. *Mines: A Perverse Use of Technology*. Geneva: ICRC.

International Committee of the Red Cross. 1993. *Report of the Montreaux Symposium on Anti-Personnel Mines*. Geneva: ICRC.

International Committee of the Red Cross. 1997. *Anti-personnel Landmines: Friend or Foe?* Geneva: ICRC.

International Committee of the Red Cross. 2008. *The Montreux Document: On Pertinent International Legal Obligations and Good Practices for States related to Operations of Private Military and Security Companies during Armed Conflict*. Geneva: ICRC and Swiss FDFA.

ITRI. 2009. ITRI Tin Supply Chain Initiative: Discussion Paper version 2. UK: ITRI Ltd.

Jacobs, Christopher W. 2004. "Taking the Next Step: An Analysis of the Effects the Ottawa Convention May Have on the Interoperability of United States Forces with the Armed Forces of Australia, Great Britain, and Canada." *Military Law Review* 180: 49–114.

Jervis, Robert. 1976. *Perception and Misperception in International Politics*. Princeton, NJ: Princeton University Press.

Joachim, Jutta. 2007. *Agenda Setting, the UN, and NGOs: Gender Violence and Reproductive Rights*. Washington, DC: Georgetown University Press.

Joas, Hans. 1996. *The Creativity of Action*. Chicago: University of Chicago Press.

Jonsson, Christer, Bo Bjurulf, Ole Elgstrom, Anders Sannerstedt, and Maria Stromvik. 1998. "Negotiations in Networks in the European Union." *International Negotiation* 3: 319–344.

Joseph, Jofi. 2004. "The Proliferation Security Initiative: Can Interdiction Stop Proliferation?" *Arms Control Today*, June.

Joyner, Daniel H. 2007. "Non-proliferation Law and the United Nations System: Resolution 1540 and the Limits of the Power of the Security Council." *Leiden Journal of International Law* 20: 489–518.

Kaag, John Jacob. 2008. "We Are *Who*? A Pragmatic Reframing of Immigration and National Identity." *The Pluralist* 3, no. 3: 111–131.

Kahler, Miles. 2000. "Conclusion: The Causes and Consequences of Legalization." *International Organization* 54, no. 3: 661–683.

Kahler, Miles. 2009. "Networked Politics: Agency, Power and Governance." In Miles Kahler, ed., *Networked Politics: Agency, Power and Governance*, 1–22. Ithaca, NY: Cornell University Press.

Kahler, Miles, and David A. Lake. 2003. "Globalization and Governance." In Miles Kahler and David A. Lake, eds., *Governance in a Global Economy: Political Authority in Transition*, 1–30. Princeton, NJ: Princeton University.

Kahler, Miles, and David A. Lake. 2009. "Economic Integration and Global Governance: Why So Little Supranationalism?" In Walter Mattli and Ngaire Woods, eds., *Explaining Regulatory Change in the Global Economy*, 242–276. Princeton, NJ: Princeton University Press.

Kaplow, Louis. 1992. "Rules versus Standards: AN Economic Analysis." *Duke Law Journal* 42, no. 3: 557–629.

Karp, Aaron. 2002. "Laudible Failure." *SAIS Review* 22, no. 1: 177–193.

Karp, Aaron. 2006. "Escaping Reutersward's Shadow." *Contemporary Security Policy* 27, no. 1: 12–28.

Keck, Margaret E., and Kathryn Sikkink. 1998. *Activists beyond Borders: Advocacy Networks in International Politics*. Ithaca, NY: Cornell University Press.

Keck, Margeret E., and Kathryn Sikkink. 1999. "Transnational Advocacy Networks in International and Regional Politics." *International Social Science Journal* 51, no. 1: 89–101.

Kell, Georg, and John Gerard Ruggie. 2000. "Reconciling Economic Imperatives with Social Priorities: The Global Compact." Paper read at Carnegie Council on Ethics and International Affairs, New York, February 25.

Kenny, Christopher B., Michael McBurnett, and David J. Bordua. 2006. "Does the NRA Affect Federal Elections?" The Independence Institute, IP-8-2006, Golden, CO. Available at http://www.davekopel.org/2A/OthWr/Does-the-NRA-Influence-Federal-Elections.pdf.

Keohane, Robert O. 1978. "The International Energy Agency: State Influence and Transgovernmental Politics." *International Organization* 32, no. 4: 929–951.

Keohane, Robert O. 1984. *After Hegemony: Cooperation and Discord in the World Political Economy*. Princeton, NJ: Princeton University Press.

Keohane, Robert O., and Lisa L. Martin. 1995. "The Promise of Institutionalist Theory." *International Security* 20, no. 1: 39–51.

Keohane, Robert O., and Joseph S. Nye. 1974. "Transgovernmental Relations and International Organizations." *World Politics* 27, no. 1: 39–62.

Keohane, Robert O., and Joseph S. Nye. 1977. *Power and Interdependence*. New York: Little, Brown.

Keohane, Robert O., and Joseph S. Nye. 1989. *Power and Interdependence*. 2nd ed. New York: HarperCollins.

Keohane, Robert O., and Joseph S. Nye. 2000. "Introduction." In Joseph S. Nye and John D. Donahue, eds., *Governance in a Globalizing World*, 1–41. Washington, DC: Brookings.

Keohane, Robert O., and David G. Victor. 2011. "The Regime Complex for Climate Change." *Perspectives on Politics* 9, no. 1: 7–23.

Kerner, Andrew. 2009. "Why Should I Believe You? The Costs and Consequences of Bilateral Investment Treaties." *International Studies Quarterly* 53, no. 1: 73–102.

Kersten, Gregory E. 2001. "Modeling Distributive and Integrative Negotiations: Review and Revised Characterization." *Group Decision and Negotiation* 10: 493–514.

Kim, Hyung Min. 2010. "Comparing Measures of National Power." *International Political Science Review* 31, no. 4: 405–427.

Kinne, Brandon J. 2012. "Multilateral Trade and Militarized Conflict: Centrality, Openness, and Asymmetry in the Global Trade Network." *Journal of Politics* 74, no. 1: 308–322.

Kinne, Brandon J. 2013. "Network Dynamics and the Evolution of International Cooperation." *American Political Science Review* 107, no. 4: 766–785.

Kinne, Brandon J. 2014. "Dependent Diplomacy: Signaling, Strategy, and Prestige in the Diplomatic Network." *International Studies Quarterly* 58, no. 2: 247–259.

Klare, Michael. 1997. "East Asia's Militaries Muscle Up." *Bulletin of the Atomic Scientists* 53, no. 1: 56–61.

Klußmann, Uwe. 2009. "A Shattered Dream in Georgia: EU Probe Creates Burden for Saakashvili." *Spiegel Online*, June 16. Available at http://www.spiegel.de/international/world/a-shattered-dream-in-georgia-eu-probe-creates-burden-for-saakashvili-a-630543.html.

Klußmann, Uwe. 2010. "'Terrible Losses Overnight': Cables Track US Diplomatic Efforts to Avert Russian-Georgian Conflict." *Spiegel Online*, December 1. Available at http://www.spiegel.de/international/world/terrible-losses-overnight-cables-track-us-diplomatic-efforts-to-avert-russian-georgian-conflict-a-732294.html.

Kmentt, Alexander. 2008. "A Beacon of Light: The Mine Ban Treaty since 1997." In Jody Williams, Stephen D. Goose, and Mary Wareham, eds., *Banning Landmines: Disarmament, Citizen Diplomacy, and Human Security*, 17–30. Lanham, MD: Rowman & Littlefield.

Knoke, David. 1990. *Political Networks: The Structural Perspective, Structural Analysis in the Social Sciences*. Cambridge: Cambridge University Press.

Knoke, David. 2011. "Policy Networks." In John Scott and Peter J. Carrington, eds., *The SAGE Handbook of Social Network Analysis*, 210–222. London: SAGE.

Knoke, David. 2012. *Economic Networks*. Cambridge: Polity.

Knoke, David, and Song Yang. 2008. *Social Network Analysis*. Los Angeles: SAGE.

Knopf, Jeffrey W. 1993. "Beyond Two-Level Games: Domestic-International Interaction in the Intermediate-Range Nuclear Forces Negotiations." *International Organization* 47, no. 4: 599–628.

Kock, Susan H. 2012. "PSI: Origins and Evolution." Occasional Paper #9. Centre for the Study of WMD. Washington, DC: National Defense University Press.

Kolk, Ans, and David Levy. 2001. "Winds of Change: Corporate Strategy, Climate Change and Oil Multinationals." *European Management Journal* 19, no. 5: 501–509.

Koremenos, Barbara. 2005. "Contracting around International Uncertainty." *American Political Science Review* 99, no. 4: 549–565.

Koremenos, Barbara. 2009. "An Economic Analysis of International Rulemaking." Unpublished manuscript.

Koremenos, Barbara, Charles Lipson, and Duncan Snidal. 2001. "The Rational Design of International Institutions." *International Organization* 55: 761–799.

Kramer, David J. 2010. "U.S. Abandoning Russia's Neighbors." *Washington Post*, May 15. Available at http://www.washingtonpost.com/wp-dyn/content/article/2010/05/14/AR2010051404496.html.

Kraska, James, and Brian Wilson. 2009. "The Pirates of the Gulf of Aden: The Coalition Is the Strategy." *Stanford Journal of International Law* 45: 243–249.

Krasner, Stephen D. 1983. "Structural Causes and Regime Consequences: Regimes as Intervening Variables." In Stephen D. Krasner, ed., *International Regimes*, 1–22. Ithaca, NY: Cornell University Press.

Krasner, Stephen D. 1991. "Global Communications and National Power: Life at the Pareto Frontier." *World Politics* 43: 336–366.

Krause, Keith. 2002. "Multilateral Diplomacy, Norm Building, and the UN Conferences: The Case of Small Arms and Light Weapons." *Global Governance* 8: 247–263.

Krebs, Ronald R., and Patrick Thaddeus Jackson. 2007. "Twisting Tongues and Twisting Arms: The Power of Political Rhetoric." *European Journal of International Relations* 13: 35–66.

Kreiger, Miriam, Shannon L. C. Souma, and Daniel Nexon. 2015. "US Military Diplomacy in Practice." In Ole Jacob Sending, Vincent Pouliot, and Iver B. Neumann, eds., *Diplomacy and the Making of World Politics*, 220–255. Cambridge: Cambridge University Press.

Kushner, David. 2014. "The Masked Avengers." *New Yorker*, September 1.

Kvelashvili, Giorgi. 2010. "Obama Snubs Saakashvili: What Does It Mean?" *New Atlanticist*, April 13.

Kydd, Andrew H. 2001. "Trust-Building, Trust-Breaking: The Dilemma of NATO Enlargement." *International Organization* 55, no. 4: 801–825.

Kydd, Andrew H. 2005. *Trust and Mistrust in International Relations*. Princeton, NJ: Princeton University Press.

Lake, David A. 1996. "Anarchy, Hierarchy and the Variety of International Relations." *International Organization* 50: 1–33.

Lake, David A. 1999. *Entangling Relations: American Foreign Policy in Its Century*. Princeton, NJ: Princeton University Press.

Lake, David A. 2001. "Beyond Anarchy: The Importance of Security Institutions." *International Security* 26: 129–160.

Lake, David A. 2007. "Escape from the State of Nature: Authority and Hierarchy in World Politics." *International Security* 32, no. 1: 47–79.

Lake, David A. 2009. *Hierarchy in International Relations*. Ithaca, NY: Cornell University Press.

Lake, David A. 2010. "Rightful Rules: Authority, Order, and the Foundations of Global Governance." *International Studies Quarterly* 54: 587–613.

Lake, David A., and Wendy H. Wong. 2009. "The Politics of Networks: Interests, Power and Human Rights Norms." In Miles Kahler, ed., *Networked Politics: Agency, Power and Governance*, 127–150. Ithaca, NY: Cornell University Press.

Larsen, Jeffrey A. 1997. "The Development of an Agreed NATO Policy on Nonproliferation." USAF Institute for National Security Studies.

Laurance, Edward. 1998. "Small Arms, Light Weapons, and Conflict Prevention: The New Post–Cold War Logic of Disarmament." In Barnett R. Rubin, ed., *Cases and Strategies for Preventive Action*, 135–168. New York: Century Foundation Press.

Lawson, Robert J., Mark Gwozdecky, Jill Sinclair, and Ralph Lysyshyn. 1998. "The Ottawa Process and the International Movement to Ban Anti-Personnel Mines." In Maxwell A. Cameron, Robert J. Lawson, and Brian W. Tomlin, eds., *To Walk Without Fear: The Global Movement to Ban Landmines*, 160–184. Toronto: Oxford University Press.

Leach, William D., and Paul A. Sabatier. 2005. "To Trust an Adversary: Integrating Rational and Psychological Models of Collaborative Policymaking." *American Political Science Review* 99: 491–503.

Lebow, Richard Ned. 2005. "Reason, Emotion and Cooperation." *International Politics* 42, no. 3: 283–313.

Leeds, Brett Ashley. 2003. "Alliance Reliability in Times of War: Explaining State Decisions to Violate Treaties." *International Organization* 57, no. 4: 801–828.

Legge, James. 2013. "Huge Decline in Hijackings by Somali Pirates." *The Independent*, May 3.

Le Vine, Steve. 2007. *The Oil and the Glory: The Pursuit of Empire and Fortune on the Caspian Sea*. New York: Random House.

Levy, David L., and Aseem Prakash. 2003. "Bargains Old and New: Multinational Corporations in Global Governance." *Business and Politics* 5: 131–150.

Lewis, Jeffrey. 2005. "The Janus Face of Brussels: Socialization and Everyday Decision Making in the European Union." *International Organization* 59, no. 4: 937–971.

Lin, Nan. 2001. "Building a Network Theory of Social Capital." In Nan Lin, Karen Cook, and Ronald S. Burt, eds., *Social Capital: Theory and Research*, 3–29. New York: Aldine Transaction.

Lin, Nan, Karen S. Cook, and Ronald S. Burt, eds. 2001. *Social Capital: Theory and Research*. New York: Aldine de Gruyter.

Lipson, Michael. 2001. "Organizational Fields and International Regimes." Working Paper 01–03. Harrisburg, Penn.: Christopher H. Browne Center for International Politics University of Pennsylvania.

Lipson, Michael. 2004. "Transaction Cost Estimation and International Regimes: Of Crystal Balls and Sheriff's Posses." *International Studies Review*, 1–20.

Lipson, Michael. 2005–2006. "Transgovernmental Networks and Nonproliferation: International Security and the Future of Global Governance." *International Journal* 61, no. 1: 179–198.

Littlewood, George. 2000. "The Global Mining Initiative: Address to Mining 2000." Melbourne.

Macdonald, Kate. 2014. *The Politics of Global Supply Chains*. Cambridge: Polity Press.

MacDonald, Paul K. 2014. *Networks of Domination: The Social Foundations of Peripheral Conquest in International Politics*. Oxford: Oxford University Press.

Manger, Mark S., Mark A. Pickup, and Tom A. B. Snijders. 2012. "A Hierarchy of Preferences: A Longitudinal Network Analysis Approach to PTA Formation." *Journal of Conflict Resolution* 56: 1–26.

Maoz, Zeev. 2010. *Networks of Nations: The Formation, Evolution, and Effect of International Networks, 1816–2001*. New York: Cambridge University Press.

Maoz, Zeev, Ranan D. Kuperman, Lesley Terris, and Ilan Talmud. 2006. "Structural Equivalence and International Conflict: A Social Networks Analysis." *Journal of Conflict Resolution* 50, no. 5: 664–689.

Maoz, Zeev, Ranan D. Kuperman, Lesley G. Terris, and Ilan Talmud. 2006. "Network Centrality and International Conflict, 1816–2001: Does It Pay to be Important?" In Thomas N. Friemel, ed., *Applications of Social Network Analysis: Proceedings of the 3rd Conference on Applications of Social Network Analysis*, 121–152. Konstanz: Universitat Verlag Konstanz.

March, James G., and Johan P. Olsen. 1998. "The Institutional Dynamics of International Political Orders." *International Organization* 52: 943–969.

Marquand, Robert. 2008. "NATO Divided over Ukraine, Georgia Membership Bids." *Christian Science Monitor*, March 28. Available at http://www.csmonitor.com/World/Europe/2008/0328/p01s01-woeu.html.

Marten, Kimberely. 2012. *Warlords: Strong-Arm Brokers in Weak States*. Ithaca, NY: Cornell University Press.

Martin, Lisa L. 1992. "Interests, Power, and Multilateralism." *International Organization* 46, no. 4: 765–792.

Martin, Lisa L. 2000. *Democratic Commitments: Legislatures and International Cooperation*. Princeton, NJ: Princeton University Press.

Martin, Lisa L., and Beth A. Simmons. 1998. "Theories and Empirical Studies of International Institutions." *International Organization* 52, no. 4: 729–757.

Maslen, Stuart. 1998. "The Role of the International Committee of the Red Cross." In Maxwell A. Cameron, Robert J. Lawson, and Brian W. Tomlin, eds., *To Walk Without Fear: The Global Movement to Ban Landmines*, 80–98. Toronto: Oxford University Press.

Maslen, Stuart. 2005. *Commentaries on Arms Control Treaties: The Convention on the Prohibition of the Use, Stockpiling, Production, and Transfer of Anti-Personnel Mines and on Their Destruction*. 2nd ed. Oxford: Oxford University Press.

Matthew, Richard, and Kenneth Rutherford. 2003. "The Evolutionary Dynamics of the Movement to Ban Landmines." *Alternatives* 28: 29–56.

Mattli, Walter, and Ngaire Woods. 2009a. "In Whose Benefit? Explaining Regulatory Change in Global Politics." In Walter Mattli and Ngaire Woods, eds., *The Politics of Global Regulation*, 1–43. Princeton, NJ: Princeton University Press.

Mattli, Walter, and Ngaire Woods. 2009b. *The Politics of Global Regulation*. Princeton, NJ: Princeton University Press.

Maxfield, Sylvia. 1997. *Gatekeepers of Growth: The International Political Economy of Central Banking in Developing Countries*. Princeton, NJ: Princeton University Press.

Mayer, Jane. 2004. "The Manipulator: Ahmad Chalabi Pushed a Tainted Case for War. Can He Survive the Occupation?" *The New Yorker*, June 7.

McDougall, Robert. 2002. Remarks to the Canada-Japan Seminar, Department of Foreign Affairs and International Trade of the Government of Canada.

McGrath, Rae. 1992. *Hidden Death: Land Mines and Civilian Casualties in Iraqi Kurdistan.* New York: Middle East Watch/Human Rights Watch.

McGrath, Rae, and Eric Stover. 1991. "Injuries from Land Mines." *British Medical Journal* 303, no. 6816: 1492.

McGuire, Michael, and Robert Agranoff. 2007. "Answering the Big Questions, Asking the Bigger Questions: Expanding the Public Network Management Empirical Research Agenda". Paper prepared for the 9th Public Management Research Conference, Tucson, Arizona, October 25–27.

McGuire, Michael, and Robert Agranoff. 2011. "The Limitations of Public Management Networks." *Public Administration* 89, no. 2: 265–284.

McIntire, Mike, and Michael Luo. 2013. "Gun Makers Saw No Role in Curbing Improper Sales." *New York Times*, May 27.

McLin, Jon. 1979. "Surrogate International Organization and the Case of World Food Security, 1949–1969." *International Organization* 33, no. 1: 35–55.

Mearsheimer, John J. 1994. "The False Promise of International Institutions." *International Security* 19, no. 3: 5–49.

Mearsheimer, John J. 2001. *The Tragedy of Great Power Politics.* New York: Norton.

Meierding, Emily. 2005. "Missing the Target: Light Weapons and the Limits of Global Governance." Paper prepared for the annual International Studies Association Conference, March.

Menand, Louis. 2001. *The Metaphysical Club: A Story of Ideas in America.* New York: Farrar, Straus, and Giroux.

Meyer, John W., John Boli, George M. Thomas, and Francisco O. Ramirez. 1997. "World Society and the Nation-State." *American Journal of Sociology* 103, no. 1: 144–181.

Minear, Larry, and Ian Smillie. 2004. *The Charity of Nations: Humanitarian Action in a Calculating World.* Boulder, CO: Kumarian Press.

Mistry, Dinshaw. 2003. "Beyond the MTCR: Building a Comprehensive Regime to Contain Ballistic Missile Proliferation." *International Security* 27, no. 4: 119–149.

Mitchell, Lincoln. 2009a. *Uncertain Democracy: U.S. Foreign Policy and Georgia's Rose Revolution.* Philadelphia: University of Pennsylvania Press.

Mitchell, Lincoln. 2009b. "Georgia's Story: Competing Narratives Since the War." *Survival* 51, no. 4: 81–100.

Mitchell, Lincoln, and Alexander Cooley. 2010. *After the August War: A New Strategy for U.S. Engagement with Georgia.* New York: Harriman Institute.

Mitchell, Ronald B., and Patricia M. Keilbach. 2001. "Situation Structure and Institutional Design: Reciprocity, Coercion, and Exchange." *International Organization* 55, no. 4: 891–917.

Moe, Terry M. 2005. "Power and Political Institutions." *Perspectives on Politics* 3: 215–233.

Moore, Spencer, Eugenia Eng, and Mark Daniel. 2003. "International NGOs and the Role of Network Centrality in Humanitarian Aid Operations: A Case Study of Coordination during the 2000 Mozambique Floods." *Disasters* 27, no. 4: 305–318.

Morgan, Matthew J. 2002. "A New Kellogg-Briand Mentality? The Anti-Personnel Landmine Ban." *Small Wars and Insurgencies* 13, no. 3: 97–110.

Morrow, James D. 1994. "Modeling the Forms of International Cooperation: Distribution versus Information." *International Organization* 48: 387–423.

Morrow, James D. 1999. "The Strategic Setting of Choices: Signaling, Commitment, and Negotiation in International Politics." In David A. Lake and Robert Powell, eds., *Strategic Choice and International Relations*, 77–114. Princeton, NJ: Princeton University Press.

Morton, David. 2006. "Gunning for the World." *Foreign Policy*, January.

Mosk, Matthew, and Jeffrey H. Bimbaum. "While Aide Advised McCain, His Firm Lobbied for Georgia." *Washington Post*, August 13.

MTCR. n.d. "Objectives of the Missile Technology Control Regime." Available at http://www.mtcr.info/english/objectives.html.

Murdie, Amanda M. 2014. "The Ties that Bind: A Network Analysis of Human Rights International Nongovernmental Organizations." *British Journal of Political Science* 44, no. 1: 1–27.

Murdie, Amanda M., and David R. Davis. 2012a. "Looking in the Mirror: Comparing INGO Networks across Issue Areas." *Review of International Organizations* 7, no. 2: 177–202.

Murdie, Amanda M., and David R. Davis. 2012b. "Shaming and Blaming: Using Events Data to Assess the Impact of Human Rights INGOs." *International Studies Quarterly* 56, no. 1: 1–16.

Murdie, Amanda M., Maya Wilson, and David R. Davis. 2016. "The View from the Bottom: Networks of Conflict Resolution Organizations and International Peace." *Journal of Peace Research.*

Nagel, Jack H. 1968. "Some Questions about the Concept of Power." *Behavioral Science* 13: 129–137.

Nelson, Jane. 2000. *The Business of Peace: The Private Sector as a Partner in Conflict Prevention and Resolution.* London: Prince of Wales Business Leaders Forum.

Nemtsova, Anna. 2009. "Mikheil Saakashvili Says He's Been Abandoned." *Newsweek,* April 10. Available at http://www.newsweek.com/mikheil-saakashvili-says-hes-been-abandoned-77451.

Newman, Abraham L. 2008. "Building Transnational Civil Liberties: Transgovernmental Entrepreneurs and the European Data Privacy Directive." *International Organization* 62: 103–130.

Nexon, Daniel H. 2009a. "The Balance of Power in the Balance." *World Politics* 61: 330–359.

Nexon, Daniel H. 2009b. *The Struggle for Power in Early Modern Europe: Religious Conflict, Dynastic Empires, and International Change.* Princeton, NJ: Princeton University Press.

Nexon, Daniel H., and Thomas Wright. 2007. "What's at Stake in the American Empire Debate." *American Political Science Review* 101, no. 2: 253–271.

Nikitin, Mary Beth. 2012. "Proliferation Security Initiative." Report, Congressional Research Service. June 15. Washington, DC: CRS.

Nye, Joseph S. 1990. "Soft Power." *Foreign Policy* 80: 153–171.

Oatley, Thomas, William Winecoff, Andrew Pennock, and Sarah Bauerle Danzman. 2013. "The Political Economy of Global Finance: A Network Model." *Perspectives on Politics* 11, no. 1: 133–153.

Obstfeld, David. 2005. "Social Networks, the *Tertius Iungens* Orientation and Involvement in Innovation." *Administrative Science Quarterly* 50: 100–130.

Obstfeld, David, Stephen P. Borgatti, and Jason Davis. 2014. "Brokerage as a Process: Decoupling Third Party Action from Social Network Structure." *Research in the Sociology of Organizations* 40: 135–159.

Oestreich, Joel. 2004. "The Impact of War on Children: What Can We Know and How Can We Know It?" Working Paper, Prepared for Presentation at the Children and War: Impact Conference. April. Edmonton, Canada.

Oneal, John R., and Bruce M. Russett. 1999. "The Kantian Peace: The Pacific Benefits of Democracy, Interdependence, and International Organizations, 1885–1992." *World Politics* 52, no. 1: 1–37.

Oneal, John R., Bruce Russett, and Michael L. Berbaum. 2003. "Causes of Peace: Democracy, Interdependence, and International Organizations, 1885–1992." *International Studies Quarterly* 47: 371–393.

Orchard, Phil. 2010. "The Guiding Principles on Internal Displacement: Soft Law as a Norm-Generating Mechanism." *Review of International Studies* 36: 281–303.

Organski, Abramo F. K. 1958. *World Politics.* New York: Alfred A. Knopf.

Orsini, Amandine, Jean-Frédéric Morin, and Oran Young. 2013. "Regime Complexes: A Buzz, a Boom, or a Boost for Global Governance." *Global Governance* 19: 27–39.

Padgett, John F., and Christopher K. Ansell. 1993. "Robust Action and the Rise of the Medici, 1400–1434." *American Journal of Sociology* 98, no. 6: 1259–1319.

Padgett, John F., and Walter W. Powell. 2012. *The Emergence of Organizations and Markets.* Princeton, NJ: Princeton University Press.

Pande, Savita. 1999. "Missile Technology Control Regime: Impact Assessment." *Strategic Analysis* 23, no. 6: 923–945.

Pape, Robert A. 2005. "Soft Balancing against the United States." *International Security* 30: 7–45.

Paris, Roland. 2009. "Understanding the 'Coordination Problem' in Postwar Statebuilding." In Roland Paris and Timothy D. Sisk, eds., *The Dilemmas of Statebuilding: Confronting the Contradictions of Postwar Peace Operations,* 53–78. London: Routledge.

Parker, Quincy. 2007. "US Pushes Bahamas to Sign Maritime Initiative." *The Bahamas Journal,* January 2.

Parkinson, Sarah. 2013. "Organizing Rebellion: Re-thinking High Risk Mobilization and Social Networks in War." *American Political Science Review* 107, no. 3: 418–432.

Partnership Africa Canada. 2001a. "Other Facets." Number 1.

Partnership Africa Canada. 2001b. "Other Facets." Number 3.

Partnership Africa Canada. 2003a. "Other Facets." Number 11.

Partnership Africa Canada. 2003b. "Other Facets." Number 12.

Paul, Thazha V. 2005. "Soft Balancing in the Age of U.S. Primacy." *International Security* 30: 46–71.

Percy, Sarah. 2007. "Morality and Regulation." In Simon Chesterman and Chia Lehnardt, eds., *From Mercenaries to Market: The Rise and Regulation of Private Military Companies,* 11–28. Oxford: Oxford University Press.

Percy, Sarah, and Anja Shortland. 2013. "The Business of Piracy in Somalia." *Journal of Strategic Studies* 36, no. 4: 1–38.

Perrucci, Robert, and Harry R. Potter. 1989. *Networks of Power: Organizational Actors at the National, Corporate, and Community Levels.* New York: Aldine de Gruyter.

Pevehouse, Jon C., and Bruce M. Russett. 2006. "Democratic International Governmental Organizations Promote Peace." *International Organization* 60, no. 4: 969–1000.

Podolny, Joel M., and Karen L. Page. 1998. "Network Forms of Organization." *Annual Review of Sociology* 24: 57–76.

Polanyi, Karl. 1944. *The Great Transformation: The Political and Economic Origins of Our Time.* Boston: Beacon Press.

Pollack, Mark. 2005. "The New Transatlantic Agenda at Ten: Reflections on an Experiment in International Governance." *Journal of Common Market Studies* 43, no. 5: 899–919.

Portes, Alejandro. 2000. "Social Capital: Its Origins and Applications in Modern Sociology." In Eric L. Lesser, ed., *Knowledge and Social Capital: Foundations and Applications,* 43–67. Boston: Butterworth-Heinemann.

Posen, Barry. 2003. "Command of the Commons." *International Security* 28: 5–46.

Powell, Walter W. 1990. "Neither Market nor Hierarchy: Network Forms of Organization." *Research in Organizational Behavior* 12: 295–336.

Powell, Walter W., and Paul DiMaggio. 1991. *The New Institutionalism in Organizational Analysis.* Chicago: University of Chicago Press.

Praelle, Sarah. 2003. "Venue Shopping, Political Strategy, and Policy Change: The Internationalization of Canadian Forest Advocacy." *Journal of Public Policy* 23, no. 3: 233–260.

Price, Richard. 1998. "Reversing the Gun Sights: Transnational Civil Society Targets Land Mines." *International Organization* 52, no. 3: 613–644.

Price, Richard. 2003. "Transnational Civil Society and Advocacy in World Politics." *World Politics* 55, no. 4: 579–606.

Radio Free Europe/Radio Liberty. 2008. "Newsline—January 4, 2008." Available at http://www.rferl.org/content/article/1144024.html.

Ralston, David B. 1990. *Importing the European Army: The Introduction of European Military Techniques and Institutions in the Extra-European World, 1600–1914.* Chicago: University of Chicago Press.

Rathbun, Brian C. 2009. "It Takes all Types: Social Psychology, Trust, and the International Relations Paradigm in our Minds." *International Theory* 1, no. 3 (November): 345–380.

Rathbun, Brian C. 2010. "Before Hegemony: Generalized Trust and the Creation and Design of International Security Organizations." *International Organization* 65, no. 2: 243–273.

Rathbun, Brian C. 2011. "From Vicious to Virtuous Circle: Moralistic Trust, Diffuse Reciprocity, and the American Security Commitment to Europe." *European Journal of International Relations* 18, no. 2: 323–344.

Raustiala, Kal. 2002. "The Architecture of International Cooperation: Transgovernmental Networks and the Future of International Law." *Virginia Journal of International Law* 43, no. 1: 1–92.

Raustiala, Kal. 2005. "Form and Substance in International Agreements." *American Journal of International Law* 99 (July): 581–614.

Raustiala, Kal, and David G. Victor. 2004. "The Regime Complex for Plant Genetic Resources." *International Organization* 55: 277–309.

Rayman, Noah. 2014. "Did 2013 Mark the End of Somali Piracy?" *Time*, January 6.

Regnum. 2007. "Matthew Bryza: Abkhaz Leadership has no Moral Right to Turn Down Saakashvili's Proposal." July 18.

Reinicke, Wolfgang H. 1998. *Global Public Policy: Governing Without Government?* Washington, DC: Brookings Institute Press.

Reinicke, Wolfgang H., and Francis Deng. 2000. *Critical Choices: The United Nations, Networks, and the Future of Global Governance.* Ottawa: International Development Research Centre.

Republic of South Africa. 1998. "Regulation of Foreign Military Assistance Act," No. 18912. May 20. Available at http://www.gov.za/acts/98index.html.

Resolve. 2010. "Tracing a Path Forward: A Study of the Challenges of the Supply Chain for Target Minerals Used in Electronics." Resolve, Inc., April.

Rice, Anthony J. 1997. "Command and Control: The Essence of Coalition Warfare." *Parameters* 27: 152–167.

Ricks, Thomas. 2006. *Fiasco: The American Military Adventure in Iraq.* New York: Penguin.

Risse-Kappen, Thomas. 1995. *Cooperation among Democracies: The European Influence on U.S. Foreign Policy.* Princeton, NJ: Princeton University Press.

Roach, J. Ashley. 2010. "Countering Piracy Off Somalia: International Law and International Institutions." *American Journal of International Law* 104, no. 3: 397–416.

Robins, Garry. 2015. *Doing Social Network Research: Network-Based Research Design for Social Scientists.* London: Sage.

Rogin, Josh. 2011. "Saakashvili Honors Liberman for Bringing 'Joe-Mentum' to Georgia's Cause," *Foreign Policy*, January 14. Available at http://thecable.foreignpolicy.com/posts/2011/01/14/saakashvili_honors_lieberman_for_bringing_joe_mentum_to_georgias_cause.

Ron, James, Howard Ramos, and Kathleen Rogers. 2005. "Transnational Information Politics: NGO Human Rights Reporting, 1986–2000." *International Studies Quarterly* 49, no. 3: 557–588.

Ronen, Yael. 2008. "Avoid or Compensate? Liability for Incidental Injury to Civilians During Armed Conflict." Research Paper No. 04-08, International Law Forum of the Hebrew University of Jerusalem Law Faculty.

Rosenau, James N. 1992. "Governance, Order and Change in World Politics." In James N. Rosenau and Ernst-Otto Czempiel, eds., *Governance Without Government: Order and Change in World Politics*, 1–29. Cambridge: Cambridge University Press.

Rosendorff, Peter, and Helen V. Milner. 2001. "The Optimal Design of International Trade Institutions: Uncertainty and Escape." *International Organization* 55, no. 4: 829–857.

Ruggie, John Gerard. 1992. "Multilateralism: The Anatomy of an Institution." *International Organization* 46, no. 3: 561–598.

Ruggie, John Gerard. 2004. "Reconstituting the Global Public Domain: Issues, Actors, and Practices." *European Journal of International Affairs* 10, no. 4: 499–531.

Russell, Robert W. 1973. "Transgovernmental Interaction in the International Monetary System, 1960–1972." *International Organization* 27: 431–464.

Russett, Bruce M. 1971. "An Empirical Typology of International Military Alliances." *Midwest Journal of Political Science* 15, no. 2: 262–289.

Russett, Bruce M., and John R. Oneal. 2001. *Triangulating Peace: Democracy, Interdependence, and International Organizations*. New York: Norton.

Russett, Bruce M., John R. Oneal, and David R. Davis. 1998. "The Third Leg of the Kantian Tripod for Peace: International Organizations and Militarized Disputes, 1950–85." *International Organization* 52, no. 3: 441–467.

Rutherford, Kenneth R. 2009. "The Anti-Personnel Landmine Ban Convention: A Non-Hegemonic Regime." In Stefan Brem and Kendall Stiles, eds., *Cooperating Without America: Theories and Case Studies of Non-Hegemonic Regimes*, 123–146. New York: Routledge.

Saideman, Stephen M., and David P. Auerswald. 2012. "Comparing Caveats: Understanding the Sources of National Restrictions upon NATO's Mission in Afghanistan." *International Studies Quarterly* 56: 67–84.

Scharpf, Fritz W. 1993. "Coordination in Hierarchies and Networks." In Fritz W. Scharpf, ed., *Games in Hierarchies and Networks: Analytical and Empirical Approaches to the Study of Governance Institutions*, 125–165. Boulder, CO: Westview.

Schimmelfennig, Frank. 2000. "International Socialization in the New Europe: Rational Action in an Institutional Environment." *European Journal of International Relations* 6, no. 1: 109–139.

Schimmelfennig, Frank. 2005. "Strategic Calculation and International Socialization: Membership Incentives, Party Constellations, and Sustained Compliance in Central and Eastern Europe." *International Organization* 59, no. 4: 827–860.

Schueth, Sam. 2011. "Assembling International Competitiveness: The Republic of Georgia, USAID, and the Doing Business Project." *Economic Geography* 87, no. 1: 51–77.

Schuh, Christian and Michael Strohmer. 2012. "Conflict Minerals: Yet Another Supply Chain Challenge." ATKearney, June, p. 4.

Scott, John. 1988. "Social Network Analysis." *Sociology* 22, no. 1: 109–127.

Scott, John. 2001. *Power*. Cambridge: Polity Press.

Scott, John. 2008. "Modes of Power and the Re-Conceptualization of Elites." *Sociological Review* 56: 25–43.

Scott, John. 2013. *Social Network Analysis*. 3rd ed. London: Sage.

Seelye, Katharine Q. 1997. "National Rifle Association Is Turning to World Stage to Fight Gun Control." *New York Times*, April 2.

SFC (Swiss Federal Council). 2005. "Report by the Swiss Federal Council on Private Security and Military Companies." June 1. Available at http://www.eda.admin.ch/etc/medialib/downloads/edazen/topics/intla/humlaw.Par.0021.File.tmp/PMSCs%20Bericht%20Bundesrat%20en.pdf.

Shaxson, Nicholas. 2001. "Transparency in the International Diamond Trade." Technical Report, Transparency International.

Shearer, David. 1998. *Private Armies and Military Intervention*. Adelphi Paper 316. Oxford: Oxford University Press.

Shortland, Anja. 2012. "Treasure Mapped: Using Satellite Imagery to Track the Development Impact of Piracy." In Africa Programme Paper. London: Chatham House.

Silkett, Wayne A. 1993. "Alliance and Coalition Warfare." *Parameters* 23, no. 2: 74–85.

Silverstein, Ken. 2011. "Neoconservatives Hype a New Cold War." October 5. Available at http://politics.salon.com/2011/10/05/neoconservatives_hype_a_new_cold_war/.

Simon, Herbert. 1953. "Notes on the Observation and Measurement of Political Power." *Journal of Politics* 15: 500–516.

Simmons, Beth A. 2000. "International Law and State Behavior: Commitment and Compliance in International Monetary Affairs." *American Political Science Review* 94, no. 4: 819–835.

Simmons, Beth A. 2001. "The International Politics of Harmonization: The Case of Capital Market Regulation." *International Organization* 55, no. 3: 589–620.

Simmons, Beth A., and Allison Danner. 2010. "Credible Commitments and the International Criminal Court." *International Organization* 64, no. 2 (April): 225–256.

Singer, Peter. 2003a. *Corporate Warriors: The Rise of the Privatized Military Industry*. Ithaca, NY: Cornell University Press.

Singer, Peter. 2003b. "War, Profits, and the Vacuum of Law: Privatized Military Firms and International Law." *Columbia Journal of International Law* 42: 521.

Slaughter, Anne-Marie. 2004. *A New World Order*. Princeton, NJ: Princeton University Press.

Slaughter, Anne-Marie, and David Zaring. 2006. "Networking Goes International: An Update." *Annual Review of Law and Social Science* 2: 211–229.

Slim, Hugo. 2010. *Killing Civilians: Methods, Madness and Morality in War*. New York: Columbia University Press.

Smillie, Ian. 2002a. "Dirty Diamonds: Armed Conflict and the Trade in Rough Diamonds." Fafo Institute for Applied Social Sciences.

Smillie, Ian. 2002b. "The Kimberley Process: The Case for Proper Monitoring." Occasional Paper 5. Diamond and Human Security Protect.

Smillie, Ian. 2003. "Motherhood, Apple Pie and False Teeth: Corporate Social Responsibility in the Diamond Industry." Occasional Paper Number 10. Diamonds and Human Security Project.

Smillie, Ian. 2005. "The Kimberley Process Certification Scheme for Rough Diamonds." Verifor Case Studies.

Smillie, Ian. 2010. *Blood on the Stone: Greed, Corruption and War in the Global Diamond Trade*. London: Anthem Press.

Smillie, Ian, Lansana Gberie, and Ralph Hazleton. 2000. *The Heart of the Matter: Sierra Leone, Diamonds, and Human Security*. Ottawa: Partnership Africa Canada.

Smith, Ben. 2010. "U.S. Pondered Military Use in Georgia." *Politico*, February 3.

Smith, David, and Clar ni Chonghaile. 2012. "Somali Pirates Hijacking Fewer Merchant Ships." *The Guardian*, October 23.

Smith, Shannon. 2008. "Surround the City with Villages: Universalization of the Mine Ban Treaty." In Jody Williams, Stephen D. Goose, and Mary Wareham, eds., *Banning Landmines: Disarmament, Citizen Diplomacy, and Human Security*, 69–86. Lanham, MD: Rowman & Littlefield.

Smith-Doerr, Laurel, and Walter W. Powell. 2005. "Networks and Economic Life." In Neil J. Smelser and Richard Swedberg, eds., *The Handbook of Economic Sociology*, 379–401. Princeton, NJ: Princeton University Press.

Smithson, Amy. 1997. "Separating Fact from Fiction: The Australia Group and the Chemical Weapons Convention." Occasional Paper, No. 43.Washington, DC: Henry L. Stimson Center.

Snidal, Duncan. 1985. "Coordination versus Prisoners' Dilemma: Implications for International Cooperation and Regimes." *American Political Science Review* 74: 923–942.

Snijders, Tom A. B., Gerhard G. van de Bunt, and Christian E. G. Steglich. 2010. "Introduction to Stochastic Actor-Based Models for Network Dynamics." *Social Networks* 32, no. 1: 44–60.

Snyder, Glenn Herald. 1997. *Alliance Politics*. Ithaca, NY: Cornell University Press.

Sørensen, Eva, and Jacob Torfing, eds. 2007. *Theories of Democratic Network Governance*. Houndmills: Palgrave Macmillan.

Spar, Debora L. 2006. "Continuity and Change in the International Diamond Market." *Journal of Economic Perspectives* 20: 195–208.

Stearns, Jason. 2012. "Dancing in the Glory of Monsters: The Collapse of the Congo and the Great War of Africa." Public Affairs reprint.

Stein, Arthur A. 1982. "Coordination and Collaboration: Regimes in an Anarchic World." *International Organization* 36: 299–324.

Steinberg, Richard H. 2002. "In the Shadow of Law or Power? Consensus-Based Bargaining and Outcomes in the GATT/WTO." *International Organization* 56: 339–374.

Stephanson, Anders. 1995. *Manifest Destiny: American Expansionism and the Empire of Right*. New York: Hill & Wang.

Stoddard, Abby, Adele Harmer, and Victoria DiDomenico. 2008. "The Use of Private Security Providers and Services in Humanitarian Operations." London: Humanitarian Policy Group, Overseas Development Institute.

Stoll, Richard, and Michael D. Ward. 1989. *Power in World Politics*. Boulder, CO: Lynne Rienner Publishers.

Stover, Eric, and McGrath Rae. 1991. *The Coward's War: Landmines in Cambodia*. New York: Human Rights Watch and Physicians for Human Rights.

Survey (Small Arms Survey). 2001. *Profiling the Problem*. Cambridge: Cambridge University Press.

Survey (Small Arms Survey). 2002. *Counting the Human Cost*. Cambridge: Cambridge University Press.

Survey (Small Arms Survey) 2010. *Gangs, Groups and Guns*. Cambridge: Cambridge University Press.

Survey (Small Arms Survey) 2012. *Small Arms Transfer Control Measures and the Arms Trade Treaty: A Small Arms Survey Review (2007–2010)*. Cambridge: Cambridge University Press.

Survey (Small Arms Survey) 2013. "The Arms Trade Treaty: A Step Forward in Small Arms Control?" *Research Notes*, no. 30 (June): 1–4.

Tago, Atsushi. 2009. "When Are Democratic Friends Unreliable? The Unilateral Withdrawal of Troops from the 'Coalition of the Willing.'" *Journal of Peace Research* 46, no. 2: 219–234.

Tallberg, Jonas. 2004. "The Power of the Presidency: Brokerage, Efficiency and Distribution in EU Negotiations." *Journal of Common Market Studies* 42: 999–1022.

Tallberg, Jonas. 2010. "The Power of the Chair: Formal Leadership in International Cooperation." *International Studies Quarterly* 54: 241–265.

Tannenwald, Nina. 2007. *The Nuclear Taboo: The United States and the Non-Use of Nuclear Weapons since 1945*. Cambridge: Cambridge University Press.

Tertrais, Bruno. 2004. "The Changing Nature of Military Alliances." *Washington Quarterly* 27, no. 2: 133–150.

Thompson, Grahame. 2003. *Between Hierarchies and Markets: The Logic and Limit of Network Forms of Organization*. New York: Oxford University Press.

Thomson, Janice E. 1994. *Mercenaries, Pirates, and Sovereigns: State-Building and Extraterritorial Violence in Early Modern Europe*. Princeton, NJ: Princeton University Press.

Thurner, Paul W., and Martin Binder. 2009. "EU Transgovernmental Networks: The Emergence of a New Political Space beyond the Nation State?" *European Journal of Political Research* 48, no. 1: 80–106.

Tolbert, Pamela S., and Lynne G. Zucker. 1983. "Institutional Sources of Change in the Formal Structure of Organizations: The Diffusion of Civil Service Reform, 1880–1935." *Administrative Science Quarterly* 28, no. 1: 22–39.

Tracy, Jonathan. 2007. "Responsibility to Pay: Compensating the Civilian Casualties of War." *Human Rights Brief* 15, no. 1: 16–19.

True-Frost, C. Cora. 2007. "The Security Council and Norm Consumption." *International Law and Politics* 40: 115–217.

Tsereteli, Mamuka. 2009. "The Impact of the Russia–Georgia War on the South Caucasus Energy Corridor." Washington, DC: Jamestown Foundation.

Tsygankov, Andrei P., and Matthew Tarver-Wahlquist. 2009. "Dueling Honors: Power, Identity and the Russia–Georgia Divide." *Foreign Policy Analysis* 5: 307–326.

US Geological Survey. 2015. "Mineral Commodity Summaries." Washington, DC: US Geological Survey.

UN Security Council. 2013. "Letter Dated 12 July 2013 from the Chair of the Security Council Committee Pursuant to Resolutions 751 (1992) and 1907 (2009) Concerning Somalia and Eritrea Addressed to the President of the Security Council."

United States, Department of Defense. 2009. Instruction: Private Security Contractors (PSCs) Operating in Contingency Operations, Number 3020.50, July 22.

United States, Department of Defense. 2010. Third Party Certification of Private Security Contractors: Report to Congressional Defense Committees. Washington, DC: Pentagon.

United States, Department of Defense. 2011a. Instruction 3020.41 "Operational Contract Support," December. Available at http://psm.du.edu/media/documents/us_regulations/dod/directives_and_instructions/us_dod_3020-41.pdf.

United States, Department of Defense. 2011b. 32 C.F.R. 159 "Private Security Contractors Operating in Contingency Operations," August 11. Available at http://psm.du.edu/media/documents/us_regulations/dod/directives_and_instructions/federal_register/us_dod_32_cfr_159.pdf.

United States, Department of State. 2003. Proliferation Security Initiative: Statement of Interdiction Principles. Fact sheet. September 4. Washington, DC. Available at http://www.state.gov/t/isn/c27726.htm.

United States, Department of State. 2013. "US Support of the Arms Trade Treaty." Available at http://www.state.gov/t/isn/armstradetreaty/.

United States, Department of State, Bureau of Nonproliferation. 1993. Missile Technology Control Regime. January 7. Washington, DC.

United States, Department of State, Bureau of Nonproliferation. 2003. Fact Sheet. Missile Technology Control Regime (MTCR). December 23.Washington, DC.

United States, Government Accountability Office. 2012. Report GAO-12-441. Proliferation Security Initiative, March.

United States, Government Accountability Office. 2006. "Better Controls Needed to Plan and Manage Proliferation Security Initiative Activities." GAO-06-937C. Washington, DC.

USNDAA (United States National Defense Authorization Act). 2011. Washington, DC.

Valente, Thomas W. 2005. "Network Models and Methods for Studying the Diffusion of Innovations." In Peter J. Carrington, John Scott, Stanley Wasserman, eds., *Models and Methods in Social Network Analysis*, 98–116. New York: Cambridge University Press.

Verdier, Daniel. 2009. "Multilateralism, Bilateralism, and Exclusion in the Nuclear Proliferation Regime." *International Organization* 62: 439–476.

Verdier, Pierre-Hugues. 2008. "Regulatory Networks and Their Limits." Discussion Paper 22. September. John M. Olin Center, Harvard University.

Vesely, Milan. 2004. "Liberia's Flag of 'Inconvenience.'" *African Business*, April 24.

Walt, Stephen M. 1985. "Alliance Formation and the Balance of Power." *International Security* 9: 2–43.

Walt, Stephen M. 1987. *The Origins of Alliances*. Ithaca, NY: Cornell University Press.

Walt, Stephen M. 1991. "The Renaissance of Security Studies." *International Studies Quarterly* 35: 211–239.

Walt, Stephen M. 2009. "Alliances in a Unipolar World." *World Politics* 61: 86–120.

Walton, Richard E., and Robert B. McKersie. 1965. *A Behavioral Theory of Labor Negotiations*. New York: McGraw-Hill.

Waltz, Kenneth N. 1979. *Theory of International Politics*. 1st ed. New York: McGraw-Hill.

Walzer, Michael. 2006. *Just and Unjust Wars*. 2nd ed. New York: Basic Books.

Ward, Hugh. 2006. "International Linkages and Environmental Sustainability: The Effectiveness of the Regime Network." *Journal of Peace Research* 43, no. 2: 149–166.

Ward, Michael D., John S. Ahlquist, and Arturas Rozenas. 2013. "Gravity's Rainbow: A Dynamic Latent Space Model for the World Trade Network." *Network Science* 1, no. 1: 95–118.

Ward, Michael D., and Lewis L. House. 1988. "A Theory of the Behavioral Power of Nations." *Journal of Conflict Resolution* 32, no. 1: 3–36.

Ward, Michael D., Randolph M. Siverson, and Xun Cao. 2007. "Disputes, Democracies, and Dependencies: A Reexamination of the Kantian Peace." *American Journal of Political Science* 51, no. 3: 583–601.

Wareham, Mary. 2006. "The Role of Landmine Monitor in Promoting and Monitoring Compliance with the 1997 Anti-Personnel Mine Ban Convention." In John Borrie and Vanessa Martin Randin, eds., *Disarmament as Humanitarian Action: From Perspective to Practice*, 79–108. Geneva: United Nations.

Wareham, Mary. 2008. "Evidence-Based Advocacy: Civil Society Monitoring of the Mine Ban Treaty." In Jody Williams, Stephen D. Goose, and Mary Wareham, eds., *Banning Landmines: Disarmament, Citizen Diplomacy, and Human Security*, 49–67. Lanham, MD: Rowman & Littlefield.

Warmington, Valerie, and Tuttle Celina. 1998. "The Canadian Campaign." In Maxwell A. Cameron, Robert J. Lawson, and Brian W. Tomlin, eds., *To Walk Without Fear: The Global Movement to Ban Landmines*, 48–59. Toronto: Oxford University Press.

Washington Post. 2012. "History of Gun Control Legislation." December 22.

Wasserman, Stanley, and Katherine Faust. 1994. *Social Network Analysis: Methods and Applications*. Cambridge: Cambridge University Press.

Watts, Duncan J. 2003. *Six Degrees: The Science of a Connected Age*. London: William Heinemann.

Weber, Katja. 2000. *Hierarchy Amidst Anarchy: Transaction Costs and Institutional Choice*. Albany, NY: State University Press of New York.

Weinberg, Kate. 2008. "Daniel Kunin Interview: Georgia's Alistair Campbell." *The Telegraph*, August 23. Available at http://www.telegraph.co.uk/news/worldnews/europe/georgia/2608953/Daniel-Kunin-interview-Georgias-Alistair-Campbell.html.

Weiss, Thomas, and Cindy Collins. 2000. *Humanitarian Challenges and Intervention*. 2nd ed. Boulder, CO: Westview Press.

Weitsman, Patricia A. 2003. "Alliance Cohesion and Coalition Warfare: The Central Powers and Triple Entente." *Security Studies* 12, no. 3: 79–113.

Weitsman, Patricia A. 2010. "Wartime Alliances versus Coalition Warfare: How Institutional Structure Matters in the Multilateral Prosecution of Wars." *Strategic Studies Quarterly* 4, Summer: 113–136.

Welt, Cory. 2010. "How Strategic is the US–Georgia Strategic Partnership?" Unpublished paper part of the series of seminars on Limited Sovereignty and Soft Borders in Southeastern Europe and the Former Soviet States: The Challenges and Political Consequences of Future Changes in Legal Status. New York: Harriman Institute.

Wendt, Alexander, and Daniel Friedheim. 1995. "Hierarchy under Anarchy: Informal Empire and the East German State." *International Organization* 49: 689–721.

Westerwinter, Oliver. 2012. "Networks, Power Politics, and the Design of Public–Private Security Governance". Paper presented at the annual meeting of the International Studies Association, San Diego, CA, April 1–4.

Westerwinter, Oliver. 2013. "Formal and Informal Governance in the United Nations Peacebuilding Commission." In Anja P. Jakobi and Klaus Dieter Wolf, eds., *The Transnational Governance of Violence and Crime: Non-State Actors in Security*, 61–83. Houndmills: Palgrave.

Westerwinter, Oliver. 2014. "The Politics of Transnational Institutions: Power, Bargaining, and Institutional Choice." Ph.D. dissertation, European University Institute.

White House. 2000. "Clinton Administration Reaches Historic Agreement with Smith and Wesson." Press Release, March 17. Available at http://clinton4.nara.gov/WH/New/html/20000317_2.html.

White House. 2008. "Remarks by National Security Advisor Stephen J. Hadley at the PSI Fifth Anniversary Senior Level Meeting." May. Washington, DC. Available at http://merln.ndu.edu/archivepdf/wmd/WH/20080528-3.pdf.

White, Harrison C. 1995. "Network Switchings and Bayesian Forks: Reconstructing the Social and Behavioral Sciences." *Social Research* 62 (Winter): 1035–1063.

White, Harrison C. 1997. "Can Mathematics Be Social? Flexible Representation for Interaction Process in its Socio-Cultural Constructions." *Sociological Forum* 12: 53–71.

White, Harrison C. 2000. "Modeling Discourse in and around Markets." *Poetics* 27, nos. 2–3: 117–133.

White, Jerry, and Rutherford R. Kenneth. 1998. "The Role of the Landmine Survivors Network." In Maxwell A. Cameron, Robert J. Lawson, and Brian W. Tomlin, eds., *To Walk Without Fear: The Global Movement to Ban Landmines*, 99–117. Toronto: Oxford University Press.

Wilkins, Thomas S. 2012. "*Alignment* Not *Alliance*: The Shifting Paradigm of International Security Cooperation: Towards a Conceptual Taxonomy of Alignment." *Review of International Studies* 38, no. 1: 53–76.

Williams, Ian. June 2013. "The Proliferation Security Initiative (PSI) at a Glance." Available at http://www.armscontrol.org/factsheets/PSI.

Williams, Jody, and Stephen D. Goose. 1998. "The International Campaign to Ban Landmines." In Maxwell A. Cameron, Robert J. Lawson, and Brian W. Tomlin, eds., *To Walk Without Fear: The Global Movement to Ban Landmines*, 20–47. Toronto: Oxford University Press.

Williamson, Oliver E. 1975. *Markets and Hierarchies: Analysis and Antitrust Implications: A Study in the Economics of Internal Organization.* New York: Free Press.

Williamson, Oliver E. 1985. *The Economic Institutions of Capitalism.* New York: Free Press.

Wong, Wendy. 2008. "Centralizing Principles: How Amnesty International Shaped Human Rights Politics Through its Transnational Network." Doctoral Dissertation, UCSD.

Wright, Clive. 2004. "Tackling Conflict Diamonds: The Kimberley Process Certification Scheme." *International Peacekeeping* 11: 697–708.

Wright, Clive. 2012. "The Kimberley Process Certification Scheme: A Model Negotiation?" In Päivi Lujala and Siri Aas Rustal, eds., *High-Value National Resources and Peacebuilding*, 181–187. London: Earthscan.

Yarhi-Milo, Karen. 2013. "In the Eye of the Beholder: How Leaders and Intelligence Organizations Assess Intentions." *International Security* 38: 7–51.

Young, Oran R. 1980. "International Regimes: Problems of Concept Formation." *World Politics* 32: 331–356.

Young, Oran R. 1989. "The Politics of International Regime Formation: Managing Natural Resources and the Environment." *International Organization* 43: 349–375.

Young, Oran R. 1991. "Political Leadership and Regime Formation: On the Development of Institutions in International Society." *International Organization* 45: 281–308.

Young, Oran R. 1994. *International Governance: Protecting the Environment in a Stateless Society.* Ithaca, NY: Cornell University Press.

Young, Oran R. 1999. *Governance in World Affairs.* Ithaca, NY: Cornell University Press.

Zaborsky, Victor. 2004. "China's Bid to Join the MTCR: Cost and Benefits." *Asian Export Control Observer* 2 (June): 12–14.

Zach, Danielle A., D. Conor Seyle, and Jens Vestergaard Madsen. 2013. "Burden-Sharing Multi-Level Governance: A Study of the Contact Group on Piracy off the Coast of Somalia." Broomfield, CO: One Earth Future and Oceans beyond Piracy.

Zaring, David. 1998. "International Law by Other Means: The Twilight Existence of International Financial Regulatory Organizations." *Texas International Law Journal* 33: 281–330.

Zaring David. 2005. "Informal Procedure, Hard and Soft, in International Administration." *Chicago Journal of International Law* 5: 547.

INDEX